SWEDISH STUDIES IN EUROPEAN LAW

The Swedish Network for European Legal Studies is happy to announce the launch of a new annual publication which will act as a forum for the publication of studies on European law by Swedish scholars, entitled Swedish Studies in European Law. This will be a hardback of some 300 pages annually, containing peer-reviewed articles aimed at disseminating Swedish legal research on European law to a wide international audience. The editors of the yearbook are Professor Nils Wahl, chairman of the board of the Swedish Network, and Professor Per Cramér. The articles in the volume are concerned with European law, its development, impact and reform; furthermore they are original, analytical contributions to doctrinal debates and questions, by legal researchers mainly, but not exclusively, connected with the Swedish universities.

Swedish Studies in European Law

Volume 1, 2006

Edited by

Professor Nils Wahl and Professor Per Cramér

•HART•
PUBLISHING

OXFORD AND PORTLAND, OREGON
2006

Published in North America (US and Canada) by
Hart Publishing
c/o International Specialized Book Services
920 NE 58th Avenue, Suite 300
Portland, OR 97213–3786
USA
Tel: +1 503 287 3093 or toll-free: (1) 800 944 6190
Fax: +1 503 280 8832
E-mail: orders@isbs.com
Website: www.isbs.com

Hart Publishing, 16C Worcester Place, Oxford, OX1 2JW
Telephone: +44 (0)1865 517530 Fax: +44 (0) 1865 510710
E-mail: mail@hartpub.co.uk
Website: http://www.hartpub.co.uk

British Library Cataloguing in Publication Data
Data Available

ISBN–13: 978–1–84113–655–4 (hardback)
ISBN–10: 1–84113–655–7 (hardback)

Typeset by Hope Services, Abingdon
Printed and bound in Great Britain by
TJ International Ltd, Padstow, Cornwall

Preface

European law is constantly developing as a result of case law emanating from the Court of Justice and the Court of First Instance, but also as a result of the writings of learned scholars from all over the European Union and other countries.

For this first edition of *Swedish Studies in European Law* the Swedish Network for European Legal Studies has invited contributions from some of Sweden's many prominent scholars who specialise in European law. The authors have written on subjects of their own choosing, thus making the book an interesting collection of topics currently being discussed in Sweden and the rest of the Union.

The aim of the Network is to publish a new edition annually, each with new contributors and new topics, and in this manner to promote Swedish studies in European law.

Nils Wahl
Professor, Dr Jur of European law
Stockholm University

Per Cramér
Professor, Dr Jur of International law
Göteborg University

Contents

Table of Cases

European Court of First Instance

European Court of Justice

EFTA

European Court of Human Rights

Table of Legislation

Regulations

Finland

Germany

Hungary

Italy

Latvia

Lithuania

Norway

Poland

Romania

Slovakia

Slovenia

Sweden

Abbreviations

AMO	Antimonopoly Office
CEE	Central and Eastern Europe
CFI	Court of First Instance
CICPP	Consumer Institutions and Consumer Policy Programme
CILFIT	a case before the ECJ, Judgment of 06/10/1982 , CILFIT / Ministero della Sanità
CMPA	Act on Counteracting
COMECON	The Council for Mutual Economic Assistance
CPA	Competition Protection Act
CPC	Commission for the Protection of Competition
CPRTA	Act on Consumer Protection and the Rules on Trade
CTCP	Commission for Trade and Consumer Protection
ECHR	European Convention on Human Rights
ECJ	European Court of Justice
ECtHR	European Court of Human Rights
EEA	European Economic Area
EEC	European Economic Community
EHLASS	Community system of information on home and leisure accidents
EP	European Parliament
ESDP	European Security and Defence Policy
EU	European Union
FTZ	Federal Trade Commission
GPA	Government Procurement Agreement
ICISS	International Commission on Intervention and State Sovereignty
HCO	Hungarian Competition Office
JK	Justitiekanslern (Chancellor of Justice, Sweden)
LAS	Lagen om Anställningsskydd, Employment protection Act (Sweden)
LO	Swedish Confederation of Trade Unions
MBL	Medbestämmandelagen (Sweden's 1976 Co-Determination Act)
NATO	North Atlantic Treaty Organization
OEC	Office for Economic Competition
OECD	Organisation for Economic Cooperation and Development
OPCC	Office for Protection of Competition and Consumers

PHARE	Poland and Hungary: Aid for Restructuring of the Economies, programme financed by the European Union to assist the applicant countries of Central and Eastern Europe in their preparations for joining the European Union
TACIS	Technical Aid to the Commonwealth of Independent States, restructuring programme implemented by the European Commission to help those members of the Commonwealth of Independent States that once comprised the USSR, (and in addition Ukraine and Mongolia), in their transition to democratic market-oriented economies
PPMs	Production processes and methods
PUCA	Act for Prevention of unfair Competition
RB	Rättegångsbalken (Code of Procedure, Sweden)
RF	Regeringsformen (Sweden)
SANCO	European Commission Health and Consumer Protection Directorate General
SAF	Confederation of Swedish Enterprise
SkL	Tort Liability Act (Sweden)
SIDE	a case before the CFI, cited in note 16 in Simonsson's article, Case T–49/93 SIDE v Commission [1995] ECR II-02501
SOU	Statens Offentligen Utredningar (Sweden)
TCE	Treaty on a Constitution for Europe
TEU	Treaty on European Union
URMPA	Act on Unfair and Restrictive Market Practices
UWG	Gesetz gegen den unlauteren Wettbewerb
WEU	Western European Union

1

Grey Zones, Legitimacy Deficits and Boomerang Effects: On the Implications of Extending the Acquis *to Central and Eastern Europe*

ANTONINA BAKARDJIEVA ENGELBREKT*

ABSTRACT

THIS ARTICLE TAKES a critical look at the mechanisms of formal and informal influence exerted over law—and institution-building in the Central and East European (CEE) countries in the process of their accession to the European Union (EU). The focus is on the impact of the Community *acquis* on the institutional framework of core areas of economic law (competition law, market conduct rules and consumer protection) in Hungary, Poland and Bulgaria. Translated in the terms of the Commission's White paper of 1995, these areas largely coincide with chapters 6 and 23 of the Community *acquis*. The article provides a glimpse into the dynamics of the institutional 'taming' of emerging markets, identifying the influence of Community institutions at several junctures where crucial issues of institutional choice and of institutional design were decided. The mechanisms behind, and consequences flowing from this influence are critically reviewed, identifying *grey zones* and *legitimacy concerns*. As a whole, the process of accession is seen to have tilted institutional design in a direction towards greater reliance on public agencies and to have occasionally frustrated promising endogenously generated institutional solutions. In a concluding section, some instances of

* Antonina Bakardjieva Engelbrekt holds a degree in law from Sofia University 'St. Kliment Ohridski', a LL.M. degree from the European University Institute, Florence and a doctoral degree in law from Stockholm University. She is Associate Professor at Örebro University and Stockholm University and is currently a Jean Monnet Fellow at the European University Institute (EUI), Florence. Financial support from *Institutet för Rättsvetenskaplig Forskning and Justitierådets Edvard Cassels stiftelse* is gratefully acknowledged. The author wishes to thank the participants in the staff seminar of the Law Department, EUI Florence (8 November 2005) for valuable comments.

repercussion of Community legal advice from the CEE back to the Community level are analysed, in particular the recent Regulation 2006/2004 on consumer protection cooperation (*boomerang effects*).

1 INTRODUCTION

The eastward enlargement of the EU is in many respects already acknowledged as a success. The eight Central and East European (CEE) states that formally joined the Union on 1 May 2004 have demonstrated impressive zeal and effectiveness in the implementation of the Community *acquis*.[1] In less than a decade multiple volumes of EC rules and regulations were engrafted onto the legal systems of these states, apparently meeting the requirements of a fairly vigilant Commission. After the limelight has faded, however, the more mundane task of making sense of the new legal acquisitions comes to the fore. Indeed, this part of the accession process requires sober analysis. In contrast to legal integration in established market democracies, we know that the implementation of the *acqui*s in CEE countries is not just about adaptation of pre-existing national standards to Community requirements. The European integration of post-communist CEE is notably parallel to a complex, simultaneous process of market, nation, and civil-society-building.[2]

In this process the *acquis* has often been assigned the uncharacteristic task of serving as model legislation for the conception of whole new branches of national law and regulation. Moreover, as early as in 1993 the Community recognized the importance of enforcement and stressed the applicant states' administrative capacity to implement the *acquis* as a condition for accession. Following the Copenhagen European Council the Community and in particular the European Commission saw itself involved in a multi-faceted mission of organizing not only legislative transfer but also institutional assistance and civil society building.

This mission is not unproblematic. It tends to frequently stumble on limitations flowing from the very essence of Community law. Underpinned by constitutional principles of enumerated powers and subsidiarity, Community law is by necessity fragmented and pointillist. It eschews coherence and leaves the crucial questions of implementation and enforcement deliberately open. As is well known, in an attempt to bridge the gap between normative realities and practical needs the Community institutions set in motion a mass-scale project of legal and institutional advice for the Candidate countries of CEE, thus entering a

[1] F Schimmelfennig and U Sedelmeier 'Governance by Conditionality: EU Rule Transfer to the Candidate Countries of Central and Eastern Europe' (2004) *Journal of European Public Policy*; see also F Schimmelfennig and U Sedelmeier (eds) 'The Europeanization of Central and Eastern Europe' (Imprint Ithaca, NY, Cornell University Press, 2005).

[2] J Elster, C Offe and U Preuss *Institutional Design in Post-Communist Europe. Repairing the Ship at Sea* (Cambridge, CUP, 1998).

'*grey zone*' between implementation of formally binding Community acts and informal legal policy assistance. While implementation of the legal *acquis* rests on (more or less) well defined obligations, advice aimed at creating coherent and comprehensive regulation or designing national institutional frameworks is based on shaky ground, inevitably giving rise to *legitimacy* concerns.

This article takes a critical look at the mechanisms of formal and informal influence exerted by Community institutions on the law and institutions of CEE countries in the process of accession. The focus is on the impact of the *acquis* on the institutional framework of core areas of economic law (competition law, market conduct rules and consumer protection) in the acceding states. Translated in the terms of the Commission's White paper of 1995, these areas largely coincide with chapters 6 and 23 of the Community *acquis*. Given the limited scope of the present paper no systematic comparison is attempted. Instead, a number of examples are taken from recent legislative and institutional developments in Hungary, Poland and Bulgaria that may be seen as variations on a theme. The paper provides a glimpse into the dynamics of the institutional 'taming' of emerging markets, identifying the influence of Community institutions at several junctures where crucial issues of institutional choice and of institutional design were decided. The mechanisms behind, and consequences flowing from this influence are critically reviewed, as are issues related to legitimacy. As a whole, the process of accession is seen to have tilted institutional design in a direction towards greater reliance on public agencies and to have occasionally frustrated institutional solutions that may be imperfect from a Community point of view, but that have evolved as a result of incremental trial-and-error practices and are thus better anchored with local institutional actors and organizations.

Finally, specific instances of *boomerang effects*, ie secondary repercussions of Community legal advice given to CEE countries, finding its way back to the Community level, are discussed. A particularly interesting case is the recent Regulation 2006/2004 on consumer protection cooperation and on a more general level the expansion of the Community in the sphere of enforcement.

There are several reasons why economic law is chosen as the focus of this article. Firstly, economic law is a field of law and regulation where a clear break with the legacies of the old system had to be carried through in CEE. The work on implementing the respective chapters from the *acquis* has therefore not been confined to scrupulous transposition of the numerous relevant Treaty provisions, directives and regulations. Community law was rather used as a springboard for launching ambitious legislative programmes, for introducing novel substantive, procedural and participatory rights and for setting up new regulative authorities with broad range of competences. Second, economic law notoriously challenges established distinctions between public and private law and involves important institutional choices between market, regulation and judicial enforcement. One objective of the article is to explore how accession influences these choices. Third, the areas enumerated above vary in terms of their history and status in Community law and policy. While competition law is well anchored in the Treaty and one of the cornerstones of European integration, consumer law is a relative new-comer in Community law and unfair competition law is fairly sporadically treated.[3] Also in the course of accession competition law has been defined as an area of high priority, whereas consumer law has been among the medium-term priority chapters. The repercussions of this differential treatment on the candidate countries represent another theme deserving further exploration. Finally, whereas extending the *acquis* in the area of constitutional law has attracted massive attention in particular in the context of the European Constitution project,[4] the same process in the field of economic law has been explored to a lesser extent, probably because it is treated as a technical field to be left to experts.[5]

2 STUDYING ENLARGEMENT: MAPPING THE THEORETICAL BACKDROP

The process of enlargement has been at the centre of intensive debate involving scholars from many disciplines. The massive transfer of rules, regulations, institutions and modes of governance from the EU to the accession states as well as the seemingly easy acceptance under the hallmark of conditionality, have presented a challenge to established conceptualisations in both law and political science.

The main research questions for students of international relations seem to have been: what are the conditions for an effective accession process and why do actors comply in international relations? Answers to these questions have been generated through a plethora of theoretical approaches and perspectives: from studies on international organisations and norm emulation, to studies based on rational and institutional choice theories. Schimmelfenning and Sedelmeier have grouped these approaches into two main genres: rationalist bargaining models, weighing the benefits of accession against domestic adoption costs[6] and social learning models, stressing the importance of persuasion in the appropriateness of EU rules and evaluating factors such as legitimacy,

[3] On the competition/unfair competition conundrum see H Ullrich 'Anti-Unfair Competition Law and Anti-Trust Law. A Continental Conundrum' (2005) *EUI Working Papers Law* no 2005/01.

[4] W Sadurski 'Accession's Democracy Dividend: From Conditionality to Post-Accession' (2004) (10(4)) *European Law Journal*; C Dupré 'Anticipating EU Membership: Importing the Law of the West', *Paper at the Workshop: Implications of Enlargement for the Rule of Law and Constitutionalism in Post-Communist Legal Orders*, EUI, 28–29 November 2003 and other papers presented at the EUI Workshop November 2003.

[5] See, however, H-W Micklitz (ed) Rechtseinheit oder Rechtsvielfalt in Europa? Zur Rolle und Funktion des Verbraucherrechts in den MOE-Staaten und in der EG (Baden-Baden, Nomos, VIEW Band 1, 1996); H-W Micklitz 'Verbraucherschutz West versus Ost–Kompatibilizierungsmöglichkeiten in der Europäischen Gemeinschaft–Einige Vorüberlegungen' in: H Heiss (ed) Brückenschlag zwischen den Rechtskulturen des Ostseeraums (Tübingen, Mohr Siebeck, 2001).

[6] This cost-benefit assessment then depends on five factors: determinacy of conditions, size and speed of reward, credibility of conditionality, veto players and adoption costs, Schimmelfennig and Sedelmeier, 2004, above.

identity and resonance.[7] Irrespective of the differences in approach, the perspective has predominantly been that of the EU as an exporter of norms, practices and governance modes; hence the term 'external governance'.[8]

While these studies are attractive with the clarity of the framework providing the urgently needed possibility of analytically grasping a highly complex project of prohibitive dimension, they are marked by the fallacy of inevitable simplifications inherent in reductionist 'if—then' type of reasoning. The quest is after more efficient mechanisms of norm compliance and transfer. The perspective is apparently that of the EU and not of the individual acceding states. Moreover, the specific context of the simultaneous transition process in CEE, which precedes and also shapes this particular accession process, seems to play only a limited role.[9]

Legal scholars have also been eager to make their contribution to the theory and practice of enlargement. The transposition of the Community *acquis* in candidate states legislation provided formidable material for dogmatic legal analysis of the accurateness of implementation of Community law into national law. An impressive amount of legal studies, many commissioned or supported by the Commission, have been devoted to juxtaposing rules of Community law in particular areas with the respective national laws in the applicant states, trying to identify similarities and differences and to outline the gaps to be filled in order to achieve full compliance.[10]

A rarer genre is legal studies trying to place the accession process in context, namely employing perspectives gained from legal and constitutional theory, comparative law, and theories of legal transplants. The focus here has, however, largely been on constitutional law.[11] The effects of enlargement in the area of economic law have certainly also attracted attention but have been subject to less detailed scrutiny.[12]

[7] J Checkel 'Sanctions, Social Learning and Institutions' (1999) *Arena Working Papers* no 11.

[8] Schimmelfennig and Sedelmeier, 2004, n 1 above.

[9] See however, K Engelbrekt 'Installing the *acquis* in Central and Eastern Europe' (2004) available at: http://www.epsnet.org/2004/pps/Engelbrekt.pdf. See also A Dimitrova 'Enlargement, Institution-Building and the EU's Administrative Capacity Requirement' (2002) (25(4)) *West European Politics*; A Dimitrova *Driven to Change. The European Union's Enlargement Viewed From the East* (Manchester and New York, MUP, 2004).

[10] For the area of competition law see the OECD Reports on the Role of Competition Policy in Regulatory Reform, available at: http://www.oecd.org; see also M Ojala *The Competition Law of Central and Eastern Europe* (London, Sweet & Maxwell, Ltd, 1999). For the area of consumer law see Th Bourgoignie and JP Pritchard (eds) *Consumer Protection Policy in Central and Eastern Europe: Achievements and Prospects for Future Action* (1996), CICPP no 5 and the other monographs in the CICPP series of Centre de droit de la consummation, Louvain-la-Neuve.

[11] Sadurski above n 4; D Smilov 'EU Enlargement and Judicial Independence in Candidate States', Paper at the Workshop: Implications of Enlargement for the Rule of Law and Constitutionalism in Post-Communist Legal Orders, EUI, 28–29 November 2003; C Dupré *Importing the Law in Post-Communist Transitions* (Oxford, Hart Publishing, 2003).

[12] For consumer law and policy see, however, the thought-provoking contributions of Micklitz, 1996, n 5 above; Micklitz 2001, above, n 5.

In this limited analysis the (formal) effectiveness of conditionality is not contested. Nor do I doubt that rules and norms transfer in certain areas has taken place in the form of social learning rather than due to external incentives. My overall questions are, however, what is being transferred and why? The focus is on the process of transforming the *acquis* from a loose set of Community Directives, Regulations and policy documents into seemingly coherent guides for legal and institutional change in the many areas where no clear European rules can be elicited. Who are the actors involved in this process, what is the logic of preferring certain rules, institutional options and models to others? In what way is this transformation justified and what are the mechanisms for its legitimation?

The objective is further to provide a glimpse into the effects of the allegedly 'successful' transfer of the *acquis* on the legal and institutional system of the recipient states. While acknowledging the overall positive impact of enlargement for stabilising democracy and market economy in the CEE, I wish to direct the search light at the micro level and ask whether the techniques used by the Community institutions withstand a rigorous test of legitimacy and efficiency and are there some lessons to be learned for future enlargements and for the integration process as a whole.

The perspective is obviously that of the recipient states. In this the study is more in line with the 'import of law' approach suggested by Dupré.[13] However, my attempt is also to merge the perspectives and try and contribute to improved communication between exporters and importers, where facing of and learning about each other appears imperative.

3 THE EVOLUTION OF ECONOMIC LAW IN CENTRAL AND EASTERN EUROPE: A BRIEF OVERVIEW

To grasp the influence of the *acquis* and of the requirement for their efficient implementation on the economic law of the accession states a brief outline of the legacies from the past and the early evolution of economic law in CEE is in order.

3.1 The legacy of economic law in the command economy

An obvious point of departure is the almost complete absence of competition and consumer law in these countries during the years of planned economy. This is not to say that economic law did not exist. Quite to the contrary. With the forced conversion of CEE to centrally-planned economy, bureaucratic regulation substituted market coordination. If economic law is about regulation, then

[13] C Dupré *Importing the Law in Post-Communist Transitions*, n 11 above.

in a socialist economy economic law was omnipresent. Yet the concerns of economic law were radically different from those in a (social) market economy. Rather than setting the framework conditions for free economic activity, economic law was about giving detailed instructions about production and economic exchange, including basic parameters of quality, quantity, forms and conditions of distribution.[14]

3.1.1 Competition law without competition?

Clearly, antitrust law with its main objective of protecting competition would make little or no sense in an economic system based on state property of means of production and governed by the plan. Most of the CEE countries consequently did not have competition legislation and pre-World War II competition laws were repealed. In Bulgaria, for instance, the first domestic statute assuring protection against unfair competition from 1940 was abolished through the remarkable 1951 Law on the abolishment of all laws enacted before 1944. Other states had competition law 'in a state of hibernation'.[15] In Hungary the Act Against Unfair Competition of 1923 (Act No V/1923) was declared by the Supreme Court to have lost its substance. However, major parts of the act remained in force by virtue of the Introductory part of the 1959 Civil Code. Formally in force was also the Act on Agreements Regulating Economic Competition of 1931 (Act No XX/1931). In Poland the Act on Cartels of 1933 was not expressly repealed but had no influence on doctrine or practice whatsoever. The 1926 Act on the Combat of Unfair Competition stirred some discussion in the 1960s and 1970s. In its civil law part the Act was never formally abolished during the times of command economy.[16]

In the 1980s, attempts at introducing some market elements in the economy were undertaken in some of the The Council for Mutual Economic Assistance (COMECON) countries. This led in Hungary to the adoption of the Act on Prohibition of Unfair Economic Activity, Act IV of 31 October 1984. The act was mainly devoted to unfair trade practices, but contained provisions also on cartels and abuse of dominance.[17] In Poland an Act on Countering Monopolistic Practices in the National Economy was adopted in 1987. Unlike the Hungarian act this was a purely anti-monopoly piece of legislation that did

[14] Of course one can raise the question of whether it is law we are talking about in the case of such regulation. This touches upon the fundamental issue about the blurred distinctions between law and politics in an authoritarian society and command economy.

[15] T Várady 'The Emergenece of Competition Law in (Former) Socialist Countries' (1999) (47) *American Journal of Comparative Law*.

[16] See decision of the Constitutional Court of 1991, *GRUR Int*. 1991, p 654. *Cf* I Wiszniewska 'Recht der Werbung in Polen' in Schricker (ed) *Recht der Werbung in Europa* (Baden-Baden, Nomos Verlagsgesellschaft, 1999) No 26.

[17] Várady, n 15 above; K Cseres 'The Hungarian Cocktail of Competition Law and Consumer Protection: Should it be Dissolved?' (2004) (27) *Journal of Consumer Policy*.

not tackle unfair trade practices. Apart from governing monopolistic practices and monopolistic agreements, the act was the first to—at least on paper—control mergers. Importantly, a special agency for the enforcement of competition law and policy was set up—the Antimonopoly Office.

Predictably, these Acts remained with no, or very limited, practical application. With the benefit of hindsight, however, we may now say that their main importance was that they introduced the concepts of competition law in legal discourse, a fact that facilitated the diffusion of competition law and policy culture in the beginning of the 1990s.[18]

3.1.2 Consumer law without consumerism?

The situation with consumer law was slightly more ambiguous. The rise of the consumer movement in the 1960s and 1970s and the following consumer law activism in the West did not leave legal doctrine in the CEE untouched. Scholars from CEE were invited to make their contribution to the debate and brought the consumerist concerns back home.[19] Yet, they experienced serious justification problems. Consumer law and policy as they evolved in the West responded to the grievances of a highly developed 'affluent society'.[20] In contrast, the socialist economy has been pertinently characterized as economy of shortage.[21] The focus of the debate was consequently markedly different on the two sides of the Iron Curtain. Whereas the Western consumer was to be protected from the susceptive marketing efforts of traders working under conditions of competition and oversupply of goods and services, the socialist consumer's main problems were the constant deficit of consumer products and bad quality of the available alternatives. Consequently, some problems which were at the centre of attention of Western legal scholars, like misleading marketing techniques, unfair terms in consumer contracts, aggressive practices, concluding contracts at unusual places, appeared 'exotic, distant and almost imaginary' when seen from the East.[22] Scholars in an economy where demand surpassed supply were understandably more interested in the 'subtleties of warranties and guarantees'. As Łêtowska observes, 'the perspective of withdrawal from the contract (that is, refund of money) was by no means satisfying, because it meant being "thrown back on the market" and again joining those who still were seeking goods and services'.[23]

[18] Cseres 'The Hungarian Cocktail of Competition Law and Consumer Protection: Should it be Dissolved?' (2004) (27) *Journal of Consumer Policy*; Várady *ibid*.

[19] J Stalev 'Verbraucherschutz in Bulgarien' (1976) *RabelsZeitschrift*; J Łętowski 'Verbraucherschutz in Polen, Rechtslage, Wirklichkeit und Zukunft' (1976) *RabelsZeitschrift;* E Łętowska 'Consumer Protection as Public Interest Law' (1999) (1–4) *Droit polonais contemporain*.

[20] J Galbraith *The Affluent Society* (London, Hamish Hamilton, 1968).

[21] Kornai (1980) referred in A Kozminski, 'Consumers in Transition from a Centrally Planned to a Market Economy' (1991) (14(4)) *Journal of Consumer Policy*.

[22] Łętowska, 1999, n 19 above.

[23] *Ibid* at p 55.

The more important differences lied, however, at the level of ideology and institutional 'mentality' in the two societies. The whole theory of consumer protection, developed in the West, was built on the premises of free market economy. It addressed situations of market failures and proposed different instruments to compensate for such failures. The socialist economy was per definition not a market economy and could not be admitted to have failed in any way. Since under planned economy the performance of the state-run enterprises was a matter for the state, any critique against this performance could easily be perceived as political. The dominance of public ownership in the planned economy brought about the mistaken identification of the interest of state enterprises with the interest of the public at large. This attitude prevailed in administrative institutions and in the courts. In this light, individual consumer claims were not welcome, but were critically scrutinized as against the public interest.[24]

In none of the CEE did the scholarly discussion flow over into major legislative and institutional initiatives.

3.2 Experiments in the free-fall stage

With the collapse of state socialism at the end of the 1980s the CEE countries embarked on a difficult process of transition to democracy and market economy. The need for taming the freshly unleashed forces of free markets was invariably experienced by all CEE countries. Although ties with the European Community (now Union) were rapidly established and institutionalised through assistance programmes (notably Poland and Hungary: Aid for Restructuring of the Economies, programme financed by the European Union to assist the applicant countries of Central and Eastern Europe in their preparations for joining the European Union (PHARE)) and Association (Europe) Agreements, the prospect of EU membership seemed at this stage rather distant even for the most convinced pan-Europeans. The pressing need for 'furnishing capitalism'[25] was therefore pursued through a process of seemingly free and even random search among alternative legislative and institutional models, in which European but also American and other foreign prototypes were considered and combined with local solutions.[26]

3.2.1 Competition vs. unfair competition law

A first generation of economic legislation in CEE came into being already at the beginning of the 1990s. It was made of acts on competition and fair trade practices and revealed a surprisingly rich array of regulative solutions, particularly

[24] *Ibid* at p 54.

[25] Elster, Offe and Preuss above.

[26] G Adjani 'By Chance and Prestige. Legal Transplants in Russia and Eastern Europe' (1995) (43) *American Journal of Comparative Law*.

when it comes to systemic arrangements and enforcement techniques. At the cost of some simplification, the alternative solutions can be ordered into two main groups:

(i) In a first group can be classified the countries that followed traditional continental models and treated antitrust law and unfair competition law separately. Thus Poland and Romania were obviously inspired by the German Gesetz gegen den unlauteren Wettbewerb (UWG) approach.[27] Both countries opted for a separate piece of legislation for the area of unfair competition, where the interests of competitors, but also of consumers and the general public, are represented and where the protection of these interests is mainly enforced by private law means (eg injunction and claims for damages) on the initiative of individual competitors, trade and consumer associations. Also in this group but offering a slightly different systematic solution one can classify the Czech and the Slovak approach, where rules on unfair competition were incorporated in the Commercial Code along with other matters of company law, bankruptcy, etc.[28] Antitrust was invariably subject to separate legislation and was enforced by special government enforcement agencies.[29]

(ii) A more unusual approach in the Continental context was taken by a group of CEE countries that opted for an integrated regulation of the areas of antitrust law and unfair trade practices law. This model, the precursor of which is probably to be found in the Federal Trade Commission (FTC) Act in the USA, was first introduced in Hungary, which built on the experience with the 1984 Unfair Economic Activity Act. Bulgaria, Estonia, Latvia, Lithuania, and Slovenia followed suit.[30] Characteristic for this approach are comprehensive Competition Acts regulating both freedom and fairness of competition. Also under this systemic arrangement the interests of competitors, consumers and the general public are taken into consideration. Yet the approach reveals on the whole more administrative law flavour, involving a public agency with strong investigatory and/or jurisdictional powers and placing emphasis on administrative law remedies.

[27] **Poland**: Act on Combating Unfair Competition of 1993; **Romania**: Act on the Combat of Unfair Competition of 1991.

[28] **Czech Republic**: First Part of the Commercial Code of 5. 11. 1991.

[29] **Poland**: Act Counteracting Monopolistic Practices of 1990: **Czech Republic**: Act on the Protection of Economic Competition of 1991; **Romania**: Competition Act of 1992.

[30] *Cf* **Bulgaria**: Act on Protection of Competition of 1991; **Estonia**: Competition Act of 9 July 1993; **Hungary**: Act on the Prohibition of Unfair Trade Conduct of 20 November 1990; **Latvia**: Competition Act of 2 December 1991; **Lithuania**: Competition Act of 15 September 1992; **Slovenia**: Act on Protection of Competition of 1993; **Slovakia**: First Part of the Commercial Code of 5 November 1991. For an overview see A Dietz 'Die Einführung von Gesetzen gegen den unlauteren Wettbewerb in ehemals sozialistischen Staaten Mittel- und Osteuropas' (1994)(8–9) *GRUR Int*.

3.2.2 Competition law as consumer protection law

A common characteristic of these initial efforts to institutionally furnish a free market economy is the almost complete absence of direct rules of consumer protection.[31] As Łętowska explains, one reason for this may be the rapid supplanting of the central-plan paradigm with the 'invisible-hand' paradigm. Consumer law has for a second time proved to be politically incorrect.[32]

At the expense of missing tools for direct consumer protection, however, the competition acts in the countries taking an integrated approach have been unusually receptive to consumer interests. Apart from the ideologically underpinned idea of 'competition as consumers' best friend', and the technical advantage of using institutional synergies, one factor for this integrative approach might have been what Micklitz describes as the cooperative spirit associated with the specific sort of transition to democracy and free market in CEE. The building of the market economy is not only a matter of the entrepreneurs but is intimately related to the parallel running processes of nation and civil-society building, which requires solidarity by consumers as market participants and citizens.[33]

3.3 Experiencing the gravity force of European integration

A second wave of legislative activity took place during the second half of the 1990s and brought about wide-ranging reforms and restructuring of economic law in CEE. The pressure for change came mainly under EU influence. Formal ground for approximation of legislation with Community law was first provided by the Europe Agreements entered into by all candidate States from CEE during the first half of 1990s. Complying with EU Competition law was an explicit obligation set up in the Agreements, but also consumer protection was mentioned there as one area where approximation of legislation should be achieved (*cf* Article 68 Europe Agreement with Hungary, Article 69 Europe Agreement with Poland). Moreover, in special chapters on economic cooperation detailed steps for the approximation of consumer law and policy were outlined, including technical assistance for establishing the necessary institutional infrastructure (*cf* Article 92 of Europe Agreement with the Czech Republic, Article 95 Europe Agreement with Estonia).

In 1995 the Commission White Paper on the Preparation of the Associated Countries of CEE for Integration into the Internal Market of the Union exerted a catalysing effect on the harmonisation process by providing it with a concrete plan of action and order of priorities. The *acquis* in the area of competition law

[31] See, however, the early CPAs in Romania (1992) and the Czech Republic (1992).
[32] Łętowska, 1999, n 19 above.
[33] Micklitz, 2001, n 5 above.

and policy were summarized in chapter 6 and compliance was set as a high priority. Other rules on market conduct such as rules on advertising and fair trading practices fell under chapter 23, together with the rich and somewhat disparate variety of Community 'Consumer protection' *acquis*, subdivided in turn into Key Stage I and Stage II measures.[34]

Importantly, the White Paper also defined the institutional conditions that had to be met in order to make consumer legislation operative. Among these conditions the setting up of an adequate institutional structure in charge of consumer affairs was emphasized, as well as setting up of consultative procedures which should represent the consumer interest and ensure consumer participation in the decision making process, granting consumers efficient redress mechanisms and helping to ensure the development of non-governmental organisations.[35]

Starting from 1997, the perspective for membership was made ever more palpable. Powerful pressure on institutional and law reform was exerted through the Regular Reports from the Commission on the Candidate Countries' Progress toward Accession. In their brief statements the Regular Reports synthesised a multitude of less visible and more detailed sets of recommendations contained in other official and semi-official documents produced by experts, partners in twinning projects, PHARE/TACIS assignees, and the like. Whereas the normative value of these documents is formally weak, they often have been accepted with intense attention by the acceding states and occasionally perceived as outright instructions.

Broadly speaking EU leverage was exerted into two directions:

(i) There has been an attempt to refine antitrust legislation and bring it closer to Community requirements. The enforcement powers of the responsible agencies were strengthened and more severe sanctions for violations of the law were introduced.[36] Indirectly this has affected the regulation of fair trading and consumer protection. In some CEE countries Competition Acts

[34] According to the Commission:

> the *acquis* for the chapter on consumers and health protection is composed of the following areas: misleading advertising, product liability, doorstep sales, consumer credit, dangerous imitations, package travel and holiday tours, product safety, unfair terms in consumer contracts, time-share, distance selling, comparative advertising, prices on foodstuffs, guarantees for sale of consumer goods and injunctions. It also contains a Council Decision establishing a Community system of information on home and leisure accidents (Community system of information on home and leisure accidents (EHLASS)) and three Commission decisions on a consumer committee and scientific committees. Two further Commission decisions adopted in February 2000 concerning on-the-spot checks in the veterinary field carried out by Commission experts in the member states and in third countries complete the *acquis* for the chapter'.

See web-page of the Commission, Enlargement Directorate General.

[35] J-P Pritchard (ed) (2000a) *Consumer Protection in Poland*, CICPP no 23.

[36] *Cf* **Bulgaria**: Act on Protection of Competition of 1998; **Estonia**: Competition Act of 1998; **Hungary**: Act LVII of 1996 on The Prohibition of Unfair And Restrictive Market Practices; **Lithuania**: Competition Act of 1999; **Poland,** Act on Competition and Consumer Protection of 15 December 2000 replacing the Act on Counteracting Monopolistic Practices and Protection of Consumer Interests of 24 February 1990.

were purged of consumer protection objectives while fair trading concerns were downgraded in the priority order of enforcement agencies.

(ii) In a massive effort to raise consumer protection standards in the CEE to the level of those in the Community, ambitious comprehensive consumer protection acts were introduced in many of the applicant states.[37] Sometimes these acts were complemented by legislation ensuring the transposition of particular directives from the consumer *acquis* such as the Misleading and Comparative Advertising Directive, the Television Directive, the Electronic Commerce Directive, to name but a few.

4 THREE TALES OF INSTITUTIONAL CHOICE AND DESIGN IN THE SHADOW OF ACCESSION

The above sketched review of institutional evolution was admittedly cursory. To be able to penetrate in the logic and legitimacy of Community advice under the prospect of accession, a closer look in individual countries' institutional choices is warranted. In the following, three tales of institutional choice and institutional change will be told trying to identify the role of accession and of the Community *acquis*. The Commission's Regular Reports on Progress toward Accession build a natural starting point for analysing the process of accession and the Community strategy in this process. For a more complete picture of the advice flowing from the Community institutions to the candidate states, however, a look into the underlying expert opinions and reports is indispensable. In the case of competition law these are chiefly the Organization for Economic Cooperation and Development (OECD) Competition reports and in the area of consumer protection, these are the reports prepared by the Centre de droit de la consommation, Louvain-la-Neuve under the Consumer Institutions and Consumer Policy Programme (CICPP) funded by the PHARE/TACIS programmes of the European Commission and comprising 26 volumes of analyses and recommendations.

4.1 Hungary: the difficult balance between a consolidated approach and a comprehensive consumer policy

As already mentioned, Hungary was the major exponent of an integrated approach to regulating the marketplace. Drawing on the expertise gained from

[37] **Bulgaria**: Act on Protection of Consumers and on the Rules of Commerce of 18 March 1999; **Czech Republic**: CPA of 16 December 1992; **Estonia**: CPA of 1994, amended 15 December 1999; **Hungary**: Act CLV of 1997 on Consumer Protection; **Latvia**: CPA of 29 October 1992, New Act on Protection of Consumer Rights of 18 March 1999; **Lithuania**: Law on Consumer Protection of 10 November 1994, Law on Amendment of the Law on Consumer Protection of 19 September 2000; **Poland**: Act on Competition and Consumer Protection of 15 December 2000; Act on Certain Rights of Consumers of 2 March 2000.

the 1984 Act on Prohibition of Unfair Economic Activity, in 1990 Hungary adopted a new Act on the Prohibition of Unfair Trade Practices, Act No LXXXVI/1990 (1990 UTPA). The Act set out to control antitrust, unfair competition and consumer deception in a consolidated manner, thus laying down the main rules of conduct in the market economy. Echoing German Ordo-Liberal thought the Hungarian Prime Minister at the time called the Act 'the constitution of economic life'.[38]

The integrated approach was embodied in a remarkably comprehensive general clause (Article 3 1990 UTPA) which obliged entrepreneurs to respect freedom and fairness of economic competition and prohibited unfair economic activities offending or jeopardising the legitimate interests of rivals and consumers or contrary to the requirements of fair business practices. Within the consolidated approach, the substantive rules were divided into three rather distinct parts, namely unfair trade practices (chapter I), consumer deception, including a rule allowing correct comparative advertising (chapter II) and antitrust law (chapter III and IV 1990 UTPA).

Having drawn these relatively clear lines in the substantive provisions, it has been easier for the Hungarian legislator to define the jurisdiction of the competent public agency in a balanced manner. The Office for Economic Competition (OEC) was granted jurisdiction to rule on the merits in antitrust cases and in cases of consumer fraud. By contrast, actions of unfair competition under chapter I were in principle to be brought before the general courts by the interested parties at their own expenses.[39] During the first years of its activity the OEC proved to be a very committed advocate of consumer interests. Although it was agreed that the emphasis should in principle be on the antitrust provisions, in practice equal, if not greater, part of the decisions of the OEC were devoted to consumer deception.[40] Yet, analyses of the practice of the OEC in consumer deception cases indicate that the Hungarian approach has been carefully based on findings in modern economic theory, including information economics. The selection of deception cases has generally followed sound economic reasoning on the importance of consumer information in sectors of complex goods and services (eg financial and telecommunication services) and in monopolistic markets, where competition is distorted.[41]

The institutional design of the OEC demonstrated already at the early stage of its existence a fine understanding about the delicate balance between independence, accountability and efficiency. The Office is conceived as a high-ranking, independent and competent public authority. The President and Vice President of the OEC are appointed by the President of the Republic and the

[38] Cseres, n 18 above; OECD Report, The Role of Competition Policy in Regulatory Reform, Hungary (2000).

[39] In cases falling under the general clause of Art. 3, ch II (Prohibition of deceiving consumers), the interested party could choose between the general courts or the OEC (Art. 28 1990 UTPA).

[40] OECD Report, Hungary (2000).

[41] Cseres, n 18 above, p 62.

Office reports directly to the Parliament.[42] In this way the integrity of the Office against pressure by the government was secured at the same time as the activity of the Office was subject to parliamentary control.

An important factor for strengthening independence, but also for ensuring efficiency and safeguard of individual rights has been the internal structure and division of competences within the OEC. Investigations are launched either by the competition authority *ex officio*, or at the request of the interested party and are carried out by relatively well-insulated investigators. Decisions are taken by a separate body, the so-called Council, hearing cases in 3-member panels in formal and public trial-type proceedings.[43] The decisions of the agency are subject to judicial review within 30 days following rules of administrative proceedings, with the final instance being the Supreme Court.

4.1.1 Adjusting the scope of the Competition Act

In 1996 a new and refined Act on Prohibition of Unfair and Restrictive Market Practices (URMPA) was adopted.[44] The title of the Act demonstrates an increased awareness of the priority of antitrust rules, whereby the prohibition of anticompetitive practices had been expressly extended to vertical agreements. However, the strong emphasis on consumer fraud remained unchanged. The 1996 URMPA even complemented the consumer protection rules with a provision on protecting freedom of consumer choice against aggressive business practices.[45] The URMPA further clarified the competencies of the OEC, whereby the parallel competence of civil courts in consumer fraud cases was abolished.

Judging from the Regular Reports on Hungary's progress towards EU accession the Commission generally praised the country for its adequate legislation, to a large extent satisfying Community requirements.[46] Yet the Commission systematically took issue with the integrated approach of the URMPA. Already from the first report of 1998 the focus on consumer deception in the enforcement of the OEC is mentioned with some disapproval. The fact that 40 per cent of the decisions were related to misleading consumers (while 30 per cent were related to abuse of dominant position) is particularly mentioned.[47] In 1999 the number of cases decided was 180, of them violation was established in 39 cases, of which 38 were consumer fraud cases.[48] In the 2000 Regular Report the fact that 40 per cent of cases were still devoted to consumer fraud was openly given a negative evaluation.[49] Recommendation was directed to the Office to give priority to cases that concern the most serious distortions of competition. Apparently,

[42] Várady, n 15 above; OECD Report, Hungary (2000).
[43] OECD Report, Hungary (2000).
[44] Act No VII of 1996, still in force with many amendments.
[45] Art 10 URMPA; *cf* Cseres, n 18 above.
[46] Regular Report Hungary 1998 p 23.
[47] *Ibid* p 42.
[48] Regular Report Hungary 1999 p 65.
[49] Regular Report Hungary 2000 p 41.

partly as a result of this palpable pressure, the 2001 Regular Report reports on a changed balance of 144 competition decisions, of which 71 mergers, 55 abuse cases and 11 on horizontal agreements and seven on vertical agreements.

4.1.2 Strengthening the powers of the OEC

The OEC enjoyed considerable powers already under the first Act of 1990. These powers were additionally strengthened and consolidated by the 1996 URMPA. The OEC can issue 'cease and desist orders' (injunctions) under threat of penalty upon further violation, award damages or impose fines in line with European competition law. The design of the OEC was largely preserved under the 1996 URMPA.

Institutionally the Hungarian Competition Office (HCO) is acknowledged by the European Commission as a competent authority, qualified to enforce the URMPA. The staffing with 115 employees, its budgetary support (€2.1 million) and the powers of the Office (including seizure of documents, prohibitions of certain types of practices and the possibility of imposing fines, including consumer fraud cases) are seen as satisfactory. Likewise, the structure of the office and the organisation of the decision-making process receive approval. The Competition Council within the Office is seen as a body working with full autonomy.[50] The legal and financial independence of the Office receives positive assessment.[51]

4.1.3 Expanding consumer protection

In the area of consumer law, the CICPP experts identified considerable weaknesses in Hungary.[52] Apparently to meet the requirements of Community institutions and despite certain resistance against a system of rules running parallel to established civil law, Hungary adopted a framework Consumer Protection Law (Act No CLV of 1997, Consumer Protection Act (CPA)).[53] The Act proclaimed some basic consumer rights in the area of consumer safety, protection of consumer economic interests and set out the institutional framework of consumer protection. This move received the acclamation of the Commission.[54] Nevertheless, alignment in a number of areas was viewed as deficient, eg product liability, consumer credit, distance contracts, time share, etc.[55]

Interestingly, despite the well elaborated provisions on consumer fraud and comparative advertising in the URMPA, a new Law on Advertising was intro-

[50] Regular Report Hungary 1999 p 64.

[51] Regular Report Hungary 2000 p 41.

[52] See Alexiev *et al*, *Consumer Protection in Bulgaria, Czech Republic, Estonia, Hungary, Latvia, Lithuania and Romania. National Reports and Comparative Analysis* (1996) CICPP no 4, p 107.

[53] Cseres above.

[54] Regular Report Hungary 1998, p 35; Regular Report Hungary 1999, p 50.

[55] Regular Report Hungary 2000, p 68.

duced in 1997 in order to better (and more visibly) implement the Community *acquis* in the area of advertising. Nevertheless, the Commission concluded that the laws on commercial advertising and on the prohibition of unfair and restrictive market practices did not fully comply with the *acquis*.[56] These conclusions seemed in turn to be based on the rather strict recommendations of the CICPP experts, especially having in mind the minimum harmonisation character of the Misleading Advertising Directive.[57]

Institutionally, the CPA is within the competence of the so called Bureau of Consumer Affairs. The Commission notes that with entry into force of the CPA the authority of this body has been extended. This Bureau is entitled to launch investigations into any complaint and to impose unlimited consumer protection fines. The Bureau and civil organisations would be able to apply to the courts to protect consumers in cases when damage does not affect a particular person. The Bureau was in 1999 transformed into a General Inspectorate on Consumer Affairs responsible also for comprehensive market surveillance and having an autonomous budgetary chapter in the Ministry of Economic Affairs. Building the administrative capacity for the implementation of the consumer protection *acquis* is further associated with a number of other new agencies and bodies. In 2001 both a Food Safety Agency and a Market Surveillance Council are set up. The CPA also prescribes the instituting of conciliatory bodies (Arbitration boards) connected to regional economic chambers designed as independent mediating institutions for out-of-court dispute settlement.[58]

The status of consumer organisations is mentioned in the 2001 Report for the first time, commending the Government of providing financial support to the ten consumer organisations (€285,000) and of the creation of the National Federation of Associations for Consumer Protection in Hungary with the aim of developing a common position in relation to consumer policy.[59]

In a 2000 OECD Report there is explicit recommendation for Hungary to consider relocating the competences of the OEC in the consumer deception field to the consumer protection agency.[60] Obviously this opinion is shared by the Commission, which builds its assessment largely on the OECD competition reports on the basis of formalised cooperation. As convincingly argued by Cseres, this advice, though seemingly sound, may involve a number of institutional and efficiency drawbacks, which have to be seriously considered. The

[56] Regular Report Hungary 1998, 35; Regular Report Hungary 1999, p 50; Regular Report Hungary 2000 p 68.

[57] The latter advised 'to define misleading advertising and to develop the features to evaluate the misleading character of the advertising; to extend the powers of the authorities to include imminent publication of advertising; to introduce the possibility of a reversal of the burden of proof', see V Cambier *Comparative and Misleading Advertising Legislation in Central and Eastern Europe: Approximation, Harmonisation and Compatibility with European Union Law* (1999) CICPP no 12, p 45).

[58] Regular Report Hungary 1998, p 44; critically Cseres above.

[59] Regular Report Hungary 2002, p 109.

[60] OECD Report, Hungary (2000).

high level of independence of the OEC and the competence of its staff render legitimacy and efficiency to the enforcement by this agency. Moreover, the agency has demonstrated a sophisticated understanding about the interconnections between competition, consumer protection and fair trade. In contrast, newly built consumer protection authorities are often the successors of control agencies in a planned economy, which carry the institutional legacies of rigid enforcement and confrontational attitude towards business actors, something hardly beneficial for the success of consumer policy.[61]

4.2 Poland: the Office for Competition and Consumers as main avenger of consumer interests and resistance to a Consumer Protection Act

Poland took a different turn from Hungary. It opted for a dualist approach with a clear dividing line between antitrust law and unfair competition law, while consumer protection was not given special legislative attention. The Act on Counteracting Monopolistic Practices of 1990 (1990 CMPA) was among the first statutes seeking to provide the legal and institutional framework of a market economy. In contrast to the Hungarian approach, the Polish CMPA was a purely antitrust statute with provisions on anticompetitive agreements, monopolistic practices and mergers. Enforcement of antitrust law was vested in an Antimonopoly Office (AMO), with a number of regional branch offices. The AMO was designed as a separate agency not pertaining to any Ministry but still within the government, unlike the Hungarian OEC. The powers were vested in the President of the Office as a central organ of state administration subordinate to the Council of Ministers (Article 17 AMC). The President of AMO was appointed and could be dismissed by the Prime Minister so the position of the Office was far from the independent and autonomous status of the Hungarian OEC.[62] The decisions of the President of the Office were subject to appeal before a specialized Antimonopoly Court.

On a parallel track, an Act for Prevention of Unfair Competition (PUCA) entered into force on 9 December 1993.[63] Although the PUCA was inspired by its historical predecessor of 1926, its drafters showed sensitivity to consumer interests in both the substantive and the procedural rules. Thus, in its portal paragraph the Act declares that 'fair competition should be promoted in the interests of the public at large, of competitors and of the clients and among them most of all the consumers'. Consumer deception is prohibited in a separate section, with detailed exemplification of possible deceptive practices (Article 10 PUCA). Moreover, the Act lays down in a very radical manner standards on

[61] *Cf* Cseres n 5; Micklitz, 2001, n 18 above.

[62] See OECD Report, The Role of Competition Policy in Regulatory Reform, Poland (2002).

[63] R Skubisz 'Das Recht des unlauteren Wettbewerbs in Polen' (1994) (8–9) *GRUR Int.*, 681; Wiszniewska, n 16 above.

fairness in advertising that relate to human dignity, discrimination, protection of the private sphere, etc (Article 16 PUCA).

The procedural and institutional instruments for breathing life into the substantive rules were initially of the traditional type, ie relying chiefly on competitors and their associations. Following the German UWG, the main agents for protecting the consumer interest were consumer organizations. Article 19 PUCA explicitly recognized them as plaintiffs in proceedings on grounds of the general clause, and the provisions on misleading and unfair advertising.[64] Essentially, the Unfair Competition Act was conceived as a private law statute.

4.2.1 Redesigning the Antimonopoly Office

In the course of accession a serious critique was levelled at the Polish government for its insufficient commitment to consumer protection.[65] The most immediate (and probably institutionally most feasible) response to this critique was to reform the AMO into a combined Antitrust and Consumer Protection Agency. In 1996 the Antimonopoly Act was amended and renamed as to Act for Protection of Competition and Consumers (PCCA). The AMO was correspondingly transformed into Office for Protection of Competition and Consumers (OPCC) (Urząd Ohrony Konkurencij i Konsumentow).

According to commentators, the emergence of this mega-Office constituted in effect a rather 'cosmetic' change, because it basically carried through a merger between the AMO and the former Department of Consumer Protection of the Ministry of Trade and Industry, without adding any substantial new competences. The functions of the OPCC in the field of consumer policy were mainly monitoring and consultative.[66] The OPCC was entitled to institute administrative proceedings only upon the existence of a monopoly or of a dominant position, which precluded intervention in many cases of serious consumer detriment.

The existence of the OPCC exerted, however, its impact on the enforcement options under the 1993 Unfair Competition Act. Originally as already mentioned, *locus standi* under the PUCA was only granted to individual competitors, as well as to business or consumer associations. With time, the capacity of consumer organizations to represent the interests of consumers and of the general public before the courts was considered insufficient. Therefore with the 1996 amendment, the President of OPCC was granted standing to sue in certain matters of unfair competition where consumer interests are seriously impaired (Article 19(2) PUCA).

A more unexpected and unfortunate result of this institutional reshuffling was the legislative change in 2002. In an attempt to satisfy the requirements of

[64] Skubisz *ibid.*; Wiszniewska *ibid.*

[65] D Meuwly 'Consumer Policy in Poland: Institutional and Legal Features' (1998) (1) *Review of Central and East European Law*; J P Pritchard (2000a) n 35 above.

[66] Meuwley *ibid.* at p 12.

the Injunctions Directive and to extend collective action beyond the scope of the Unfair Competition Act, the direct right of action of consumer associations under the PUCA was repealed (*cf* Article 19 PUCA). Instead, consumer associations, together with the so called local consumer ombudsmen, the Ombudsman for citizens' rights and the ombudsmen of the rights of the insured were furnished with right to institute proceedings before the OPCC for protection of collective consumer interests, including certain factual situations under the PUCA.[67] Mańko calls this the clearest example of 'publicization of private law' as a result of enlargement.[68] The example may also be symptomatic of the proclivity of newly built agencies to expand their competencies at the expense of private initiatives. The negative impact could be to insulate ordinary courts from the most important problems of economic life and to rely heavily on bureaucratic institutions. The reform is all the more surprising given the relatively strong position of consumer associations in Poland with one of the oldest associations in CEE founded in the early 1980s and with a number of other active organizations.[69]

4.2.2 *The quest for systemic coherence*

In 1998 the Commission opined that Poland had made little progress in the adoption and application of the *acquis* in the field of consumer and health protection since 1997. Delays in transposing the General Product Safety *acquis* continued to have a negative impact on the fulfilment of Poland's consumer protection policy. Surprisingly, although the PUCA contained elaborate standards for consumer deception, the existing legislation on misleading advertising and price indications was found to require further alignment.[70] Consumer protection offices at regional level, consumer organizations and consumers' education still needed to be further developed according to the Commission.[71] In view of the fact that consumer protection was a medium term priority in the Accession Partnership, Poland was advised to make substantial efforts in this field.

Given this negative assessment, a number of advisors stressed the desirability that Poland follow the example of other CEE countries in adopting a comprehensive consumer protection act, thus 'reflecting the recognition of the need for a policy specifically directed to consumers'.[72] Despite some discussions on the possible introduction of a comprehensive CPA outside and parallel to the Civil

[67] See pt V, Proceedings before the President of OPCC, ch 4 Proceedings concerning practices infringing on collective consumer interests, Art. 100a *ff*. PCCA.

[68] R Mańko 'The Culture of Private Law in Central and Eastern Europe After Enlargement: A Polish Perspective' (2005) (11) *European Law Journal*.

[69] Pritchard, 2000a, n 35 above, p 51.

[70] Also for this candidate country the recommendations of the CICPP experts have proved influential, see Pritchard, 2000a, n 35 above.

[71] Regular Report Poland 1998, p 35.

[72] D Meuwly, n 65 above, p 38.

Code,[73] this alternative was eventually rejected. The main arguments against such a move apparently related to the risk of disrupting the coherence of civil law. The remaining obligations flowing from the consumer protection *acquis* have been incorporated in the Act on Certain Rights of Consumers of 2000, representing an attempt to integrate consumer protection in the fabric of the Civil Code, and partly in other sectoral or specific legislation.

4.3 Bulgaria: partly surrendering the consolidated approach and a windfall of consumer rights and institutions

In its first Competition Protection Act (1991 CPA) Bulgaria followed the Hungarian example and adopted a consolidated approach to freedom and fairness of competition, and consumer protection (*cf* Article 1 1991 CPA). This triad of objectives and their mutual interrelation was moreover constitutionally recognized in Article 19(2) of the Bulgarian Constitution of 1991.[74] The 1991 CPA contained separate chapters on monopolistic practices, anticompetitive agreements and unfair competition, whereby the interests of consumers were taken into account.

The Commission for the Protection of Competition (CPC) was set up as an independent public authority, whose chairman and members were elected by the National Assembly. The CPC was charged with broad competences to monitor the market and to ensure compliance with the law. Proceedings before the CPC could be instituted by the Commission *ex officio* or upon the complaint of interested parties, both in situations of anti-competitive practices and of acts of unfair competition. In addition, competitors and other private parties had the parallel opportunity to institute proceedings directly before the ordinary courts.

Yet, in its detail and institutional design the approach was far less consistent and less elaborate than its Hungarian counterpart. The Hungarian URMPA employed clear and economically sound (or at least defensible) criteria for public intervention in relevant cases of consumer detriment. The Bulgarian Act, by contrast, channelled all disputes on fair trading grounds—even those between private parties—to the competent public agency, CPC. The possibility for private lawsuit was scarcely used by traders because of the low-cost and fast-track avenue provided by the CPC. This solution was unreasonable from many vantage points. Moreover, the CPC was not designed as a decision-making and dispute-solving body, but as a sort of intermediary agency. The decisions of the CPA were not directly enforceable. The Agency had to lodge a petition for final decision with the ordinary civil courts. The procedure proved unduly heavy and

[73] E Łętowska, 1999, n 19 above; S Heidenhain *Das Verbraucherschutzrecht in Polen und in der Europäischen Union* (Berlin, Springer, 2000).

[74] Art 19(2) 'The state shall establish and guarantee equal legal conditions for economic activity to all citizens and corporate entities by preventing any abuse of a monopoly status and unfair competition, and by protecting the consumer'.

cumbersome and the efficiency of the CPA's enforcement was rightly called into question. On the positive side, with time, the CPC improved its capacity to select cases of genuine consumer detriment and of public interest for *ex officio* action. Furthermore, civil courts were slowly accumulating competence in matters of competition law and unfair trade practices.

4.3.1 Adjusting the scope of the Competition Protection Act

As in the case of Hungary, the Bulgarian Competition Act also attracted criticism of unclear priorities. Recommendations were made for emphasis on relevant cases of antitrust violations and for strengthening the powers of the CPA. In the mid 1990s suggestions for amendment of the CPA were submitted based on the accumulated experience with the Act.[75] Such proposals were, however, not radical enough to respond to the requirements set in the process of accession. Therefore, in response to the criticism a new Competition Act was adopted in 1998 (1998 CPA) set out to better define the objectives and scope of the Act and to streamline the activity of the CPC.[76]

Surprisingly, however, instead of shifting the competence in the area of unfair trade practices to the civil courts, the major move has been to strike down the explicit task of consumer protection from the programmatic Article 1 CPA. The purpose of this symbolic amendment appears to have been to signal a change in orientation and priorities. Indeed a survey of cases before the new Commission demonstrates a starkly diminished action in the interest of consumers on the own initiative of the Commission.[77] At the same time the provisions on unfair competition remained as a whole preserved and even complemented with explicit prohibitions on special and combined offers (Article 34 1998 CPA). The wisdom of this change can be questioned. It is difficult to justify the retreat of the CPC from a field where there has been a visible public interest (consumer protection) while retaining competences on matters of individual competitor's interests.

4.3.2 Streamlining the powers of the reformed Competition Authority

The 1998 CPA purported to strengthen the powers of the CPC and to improve enforcement. Changing radically the 1991 institutional design, the CPC was transformed into a decision-making body of first instance for all competition and unfair trading practices cases. The decisions of the CPC can now be appealed before the Supreme Administrative Court. The previously existing

[75] On these proposals see A Bakardjieva 'Das neue Wettbewerbsgesetz in Bulgarien' (1998) *GRURInt*.

[76] *Cf* the discussions in Parliament on the Government Bill to the Competition Act where accession and the ensuing need for alignment was the leading argument often precluding debate on important substantive and procedural issues. *Cf* Bakardjieva, 1998 ibid.

[77] *Cf* Annual Reports, Bulgarian Commission for Protection of Competition, Sofia, 2001–2003.

possibility to file parallel lawsuits before civil courts was abolished, also in respect to disputes between individual competitors, with the only exception of claims for damage compensation. It is noteworthy, that the Act even purported to impose an obligation on the civil courts in damage compensation cases to accept the decisions of the CPC in the part concerning establishing infringement of the CPA. However, this provision was challenged and repealed as violating the basic principles of division of powers between the judiciary and the executive in the Bulgarian Constitution.[78]

With the 1998 amendment the CPA was equipped with broad powers to require information, to summon evidence, and to impose severe sanctions. With the emphasis on independence and powers the law-maker sought to grant the Competition Agency a position equivalent to those of its counterparts in the EU Member States. However, independence and powers have their necessary counterpart in accountability, transparency, democratic control and effective guarantees for individual rights and due process. In a well-functioning democracy many of these principles do not have to be repeated in each and every legislative act but flow from established constitutional principles of government or are incorporated in general statutes on public administration. In a transition economy however these principles need to be carefully anchored in statutory provisions. So, for instance, the Bulgarian CPA does not envisage formal procedure for reporting to Parliament, which leaves the issue of accountability and democratic control open. There are also deficiencies in the guarantees for the procedural rights of the respondents in CPA proceedings.[79]

4.3.3 Windfall of consumer rights and institutions

An even stronger reason for the reduced activity of the CPC in the consumer protection domain was most likely the enactment of a new and comprehensive Act on Consumer Protection and the Rules on Trade (CPRTA) in 1999.[80] The legislative work on such an Act advanced rapidly in an effort to satisfy the requirements for implementation of chapter 23 on consumer protection in the Community *acquis* (see Governmental Bill to CPRTA of 25 March 1999).[81] To ensure some coordination with the area of unfair competition and antitrust

[78] Judgment of the Bulgarian Constitutional Court No 22 of 24 September 1998 in Case No 18/98, State Gazette, No 112, 29 September 1998, p 1–8; Bakardjieva, 1998, n 75 above.

[79] Bakardjieva, 1998 *ibid.*

[80] Act on Consumer Protection and the Rules of Trade (ACPRT) of 2 April 1999, State Gazette No 30/1999.

[81] See Regular Report Bulgaria 1998 above:

> Bulgaria has made limited progress in the sector [consumer protection]. If Bulgaria is to comply with Community legislation the protection of consumers, which is a medium priority in the Accession Partnership, it needs to accelerate its preparation of Consumer Protection legislation. The main principles of the *acquis* have still to be transposed into Bulgarian law. There is also a need for efficient institutional structures to ensure the application of legislation. The consumer movement will only develop if it gets increased resources and support.

law, the decision was apparently taken to relocate consumer concerns from the Competition Act to the CPRTA.

The CPRTA goes far beyond any firm obligations set out in the Community *acquis* and in this respect Bulgaria clearly stands out when compared with Hungary, and in particular with Poland. The Act incorporates into Bulgarian law the catalogue of consumer rights as formulated in the Preliminary Programmes on European Economic Community (EEC) Consumer Protection and Information Policy of 1975 and 1981, and (weakly) restated in Article 153 EC Treaty, ie the right to protection of health and safety, the right of protection of economic interests, the right of access, right of association and right to information (Article 2 CPRTA). These rights are then fleshed out through detailed and comprehensive provisions. To take just one example, Article 34 CPRTA prohibits unfair advertising and defines as unfair 'any advertising which contains elements of discrimination in respect of gender, race, nationality, political conviction, age, physical or intellectual capacities or which is against human dignity'.

By introducing specific provisions on misleading and unfair advertising largely overlapping with the unfair trading rules of the Competition Act but with special emphasis on the consumer interest, the CPRTA enhanced the feeling of division of competencies. The impression has been created that the consumer interest receives its own, particular treatment. Similarly, the competent agency under the CPRTA is the Commission for Trade and Consumer Protection (CTCP).

In its structure and main functions the CTCP is designed as a public agency of the traditional type, the emphasis being on repressive action and direct sanctioning.[82] The CTCP is an organ of the Ministry of Trade and Tourism and is respectively supervised by the Ministry. The Agency inherited much of the staff (and the premises) of the previous Commission for Control of Prices which raises questions of institutional legacy.

The CPRTA introduces a range of procedural rights and opportunities—from right of injunctive action on the part of any individual whose rights under the CPRTA have been infringed, in his own name or in the name of the collective of consumers, to the right of *actio popularis* to be brought by the CTCP before the competent courts (Article 51–53 CPRTA). It should be noted that the representative action has no traditions in Bulgaria. The first market law statutes like the Competition Acts of 1991 and of 1998 did not break new ground in this respect and shied away from explicitly granting such standing to business or consumer associations. Consequently the CPRTA was the first statute providing more detailed regulation of collective interest representation.

The practical use of these new procedural and remedial devices stumbles however on not insignificant impediments. Important procedural details do not find their answer in the CPRTA and the Code of Civil Procedure has not been

[82] Generally for the administrative reform see Dimitrova, 2002, n 9 above.

amended accordingly. Likewise rules on cost of litigation remain unchanged and are largely tailored to regular adversarial proceedings. The links with general tort law are not clarified. Although the CPRTA opens the way for *actio popularis* for the Agency (Article 51–53 CPRTA) it can be questioned whether the CTCP would give priority to this type of action in view of the broad scope of its responsibilities. So far the Agency scores highly in monitoring the market for price information and labelling. When it comes to more sophisticated cases of marketing practices the Agency has initiated only a limited number of proceedings.[83] The multiple institutional and procedural devices are not carefully designed to fit the overall legal framework of Bulgarian civil and procedural law and leave the impression of a somewhat hastily prepared hotchpotch of 'showcase' legislative measures.

The biggest obstacle on the way to intense use of the new procedural avenues is however the factual situation of consumer associations in Bulgaria. Similarly to other CEE countries, few organisations have experience in the field of consumer protection. Some have emerged first after the enactment of the new CPRTA and largely on governmental initiative (and financed by Community funds). The two more active associations have only assembled with difficulty the necessary statutory number of 300 members for registration and financial support. The relations between the various associations are characterised by rivalry for scarce resources rather than by cooperation.

In the area of consumer protection the Regular reports of the Commission are mostly focused on the CTCP. What is mentioned in the Regular Reports is the number of checks carried out by the CTCP and the number of penalty acts issued following such checks. No wonder that the number of these checks raises from 7063 in 2000[84] to 20,984 between September 2002 and the end of April 2003.[85] What remains untold is the number of penalty acts that enter into force after being challenged in judicial proceedings. The quality of the checks and the penalty acts is likewise an aspect that does not yield to easy verification and reporting.

4.4 Tentative summary

If we try to find a common denominator for the sporadic and sometimes enigmatic formal and informal interventions on the part of Community institutions and their (perceived) representatives, it appears that they have pushed institutional design towards separate treatment of competition law, unfair competition law and consumer protection. This may not have been a directly expressed requirement or even an intention. However, it is the result of the combination of emphasising the need for strong competition authorities with focus on antitrust

[83] See, however, the cases described by E Millan and R Elliott 'Offensive Advertising, Public Policy, and the Law: The Rulings on the Zagorka Case' (2004) (27(4)) *Journal of Consumer Policy*.

[84] Regular Report Bulgaria 2001, p 78.

[85] Regular Report Bulgaria 2003, p 97.

enforcement, on the one hand, and the insistence on comprehensive consumer protection legislation and a corresponding central enforcement body, on the other. The institutional division of competencies at the level of the Commission has certainly also contributed to this development.

In contrast to competition law, where having legislation in place was a well-identified priority already at the pre-accession stage, the implementation of a fully-fledged consumer law and policy has been essentially a bi-product of European integration. It would not be exaggerated to state that even today, consumer protection is not perceived as an important, let alone priority, area of government. Therefore the area has largely evolved under 'pure' conditionality. In this context the sometimes surprising ease of alignment, like in the case of Bulgaria, could probably more easily be explained through a wide-spread perception of consumer protection measures as symbolic and by the strategy of 'picking your fights' in the process of negotiations.

The ambitious legislative and institutional reforms aimed at promotion of the consumer interest appear to have produced mixed results. The new CPAs and Consumer Agencies have undoubtedly raised the awareness for consumer interests among politicians, lawyers and citizens. Important procedural channels for voicing consumer concerns have been opened for individual consumers, for consumer organisations or for public authorities. Consumer associations have received increased funding and institutional assistance.

On the negative side, the hectic legislative activity has brought an overlapping between substantive provisions of the Competition Act, general civil law and sector-specific legislation together with competencies between various public agencies.[86] Such overlapping of powers and competencies is often described as a typical source of regulatory failure or at least regulatory inefficiency.[87] The Consumer Protection agencies that have emerged in one form or another in the countries under analysis are all firmly anchored in the executive branch of government and work with traditional methods of control and sanctions. Introducing elements of deliberative democracy, transparency and accountability has certainly been attempted, but is only weakly present in the institutional design of these agencies.[88] The reforms may have occasionally even been counterproductive in that emerging consumer-friendly attitudes of Competition

[86] In 2000 after eight years of advice and reforms, Pritchard identifies a multitude of common problems for consumer protection in CEE, among them 'lack of staff, insufficient financial respires, lack of awareness of consumer laws by judges and municipal representations, lack of awareness of consumers of their rights, lack of developed consumer protection jurisprudence, little practical experience with enforcing the newly adopted laws, confusion caused by differing definitions in different laws, confusion concerning the powers of enforcement bodies resulting in conflicts of competence between different institutions'. J-P Pritchard (ed) (2000a) above; J-P Pritchard (ed) (2000b) *Consumer Protection in Bulgaria* CICPP n 17.

[87] C Sunstein, *After the Rights Revolution: Reconceiving the Regulatory State* (Cambridge, Mass., Harvard Univ. Press, 1990).

[88] For analysis of the difficult process of building deliberative democracy and accountable government in Hungary and Poland see S Rose-Ackerman *From Elections to Democracy, Building Accountable Government in Hungary and Poland* (Cambridge, CUP, 2005).

Agencies or courts have been perturbed and that voluntary consumer protection associations have been rapidly made dependent on public authorities, thus experiencing loss on credibility.

5 EXTENDING THE COMMUNITY *ACQUIS*: GREY ZONES AND LEGITIMACY DEFICITS

A logical question to be approached after this overview is the question about the character of the Community *acquis* and its binding force for the Candidate countries. Clearly, from the premises of public international law accession to the EU is a voluntary act on the part of these states, enjoying moreover broad popular support. All obligations and commitments conditioning membership are willingly entered into on the part of the Candidate States.[89] Yet, even voluntary commitments have to be clear and transparent. A problem with the Community *acquis* has been their vague and ever changing contours and ambiguous status forming grey zones and giving rise to legitimacy concerns:[90]

(i) Naturally, different hierarchical status and form of the legal *acquis* result in their differential quality as a manual for law-makers. Requirements set in the Treaty text (eg the main rules on competition) represent obviously clear and unambiguous imperatives for implementation. Conversely, minimum harmonisation instruments (typically Directives) have as many faces as there are Member States of the Union. Whereas concepts and rules in such Directive are subject to binding interpretation by the European Court of Justice (ECJ), there is a considerable variety in the detail and respectively in the raw material for advice. At least, until recently, harmonisation in the field of consumer law has been a typical example of an area with mostly minimum requirements leaving ample room for adaptation by the Member States.[91]

(ii) Irrespective from their legal status, the parallel between competition and consumer law demonstrates that there is a varying degree of comprehensiveness and exactness of Community standards in different legal policy areas. Thus, while competition law has evolved into a discipline with well-defined guiding principles and rich interpretation practice, Community consumer law can be characterised as fragmentary and pointillist.[92] The prohibitive number of Community acts in the area has prompted even the

[89] Sadurski, n 4 above.

[90] I am here not dealing with the more fundamental problem of conditionality and power asymmetry in the process of accession. For a provocative analysis see K Engelbrekt 'Multiple Asymmetries: The European Union's Neo-Byzantine Approach to Eastern Enlargement' (2002)(39) *International Politics*, 37–52.

[91] For a change in this philosophy see Green Paper on Consumer Protection in the Internal Market COM (2001) 531 final, 21 October 2001 and the recent Unfair Commercial Practices Directive (Dir 2005/29/EC of the European Parliament and of the Council of 11 May 2005).

[92] Micklitz, 1996; 2001, n 5 above.

Community legislator to embark on initiatives of simplification and streamlining.[93]

(iii) Another grey zone ensues from the general lack of well-elaborated *acquis* in the area of enforcement. Neither Community competition law, nor Community consumer law offers clear guidance for institutional choice and design. There is no common Community institutional model of consumer protection. And even in competition law, Member States have divergent institutional legacies and enforcement procedures. It is not by chance that the Copenhagen European Council had to resort to political, rather than to legal means for setting requirements in the area of administrative capacity and enforcement. Interestingly, the Regular Reports until 1999 are subdivided into a part called 'Ability to assume the obligations of membership' devoted chiefly on incorporation of the *acquis* into national legislation, and a part called 'Administrative capacity to apply the *acquis*' discussing institutional issues. Since 2000 the Regular Reports follow a unified structure where the implementation of the *acquis* and the analysis of enforcement and institutional issues are merged in one section.

(iv) Connected to the previous two points is the question concerning the bodies and institutional actors providing authoritative interpretation of the *acquis* in the accession process and fleshing out open standards with the crucial details of implementation. These are typically Commission officials, but may likewise be public officials or academics from Member States as partners and experts in PHARE or 'twinning projects', other organisations being commissioned to supervise a particular area, etc. The *acquis* thus changes shape, content and strictness partly as a result of arbitrary factors.

(v) More specifically, it appears that division of competencies at Community level may flow over and contaminate institutional advice offered to the Candidate states. The sharp dividing lines between Community Directorates (Competition, Internal Market, European Commission Health and Consumer Protection Directorate General (SANCO)) may contribute to furthering a water-tight division of competition, unfair competition and consumer protection regulative areas respectively, also in the legal and institutional framework of acceding states. The unfortunate effect of such unintended institutional biases may be to prevent valuable cross-fertilization between these fields of regulation and communication between the respective circles of affected interests.[94]

[93] Commission Green Paper on Consumer Protection in the Internal Market COM (2001) 531 final 2002. Some indication of this dispersed and non-systematic character and the lack of clear conception about the place and role of consumer policy in the Community can be found in the uncertain systematic place of consumer protection in the Regular Reports. Consumer protection 'migrates' from the ch on Free Market to Life Quality, Health Protection, Agriculture, Food Safety, until it finally finds peace within a separate ch 23.

[94] On the effect of institutional biases for the harmonization of unfair competition law at Community level see A Bakardjieva Engelbrekt *Fair Trading Law in Flux? National Legacies, Institutional Choice and the Process of Europeanisation*, Stockholm, 2003.

Given the existing grey zones, the mixed nature of the *acquis* as harmonisation standard, model legislation and bargaining chip raises *legitimacy* concerns. Political scientists measure legitimacy by the quality of the EU rules, the rule-making process, and the process of rule transfer.[95] These criteria may also be helpful in our analysis. The quality of EU rules can be evaluated by the already mentioned coherence and straight-forwardness of the policy pursued with respective rules. In this respect competition law with its lucid, straightforward and comprehensive rules well anchored in the EC Treaty, powerful policy message and elaborate court practice demonstrates high quality and represents a convincing role model. It is not by chance that a number of old Member States have shaped their competition law legislation after that of the Community. By contrast, consumer law is fragmentary, opaque and carries a mixed policy message. Social policy, protection of the weak, correction of market failures and as a vehicle of European integration are only some of the manifold reincarnations of Community consumer policy.

Another factor for judging the quality of the rules and hence the legitimacy of rule-transfer under conditionality is the bindingness in respect to the Member States, or 'the seriousness and determination with which the EU has held its own member states to those standards'.[96] In this respect as well competition law ranks high as an area with high prestige and arguably among the most diligently litigated in Community law. Conversely, most instruments of Community consumer law have been adopted in the form of minimum standards. To take just one example, when the Misleading Advertising Directive had to be implemented in the old Member States in the mid 1980s a great number of countries declared that their legislation was in line with the Directive and did not need special legislative measures for transposition. It is therefore strange when the same Directive is used as a basis for drafting separate Advertising Acts in countries with reasonable standards of consumer deception, for instance Hungary.

Related to the quality of the rules is the quality of the rule transfer. The requirement of approximating and gradually adopting the Community rules on competition has been firmly stated already in the first Association Agreements of the early 1990s. Consumer law was certainly also mentioned but without specification. Moreover the description of the consumer *acquis* in the Commission White Paper of 1995 has followed the fragmentary character of this legal area and has, moreover, openly been defined as of secondary importance.[97] Against this backdrop, the requirements for wide-ranging reforms in consumer

[95] Checkel, n 7 above.

[96] Sadurski, n 4 above.

[97] Still institution building in the consumer protection domain has received the most limited financial support when compared with other areas of the *acquis*. The Phare program spent some 12,9 mln. Euro on consumer protection in 1998, €12,63m in 1999; €12,28m in 2000 and was thus the most modest item on the PHARE budget. No data are available on 2001, only that the so called TAIEX (Technical Assistance Information Exchange Office) offers events in consumer protection (medium term twinning—twinning light).

law coming from the Community have had to cope with serious justification problems.

The actors involved in the transfer operation have clearly not only been Community officials. The Commission obviously lacks the resources to manage such a colossal task. So, often national experts travelled and diffused under the guise of Community *acquis* their own model and vision of consumer protection. Comprehensive consumer protection codes have obviously been a preferred model for the adviser team in Louvain-la-Neuve. Such consolidated solutions are not necessarily expression of hidden biases, but probably also a more feasible way for foreign experts to reduce and cope with the complexity of an unfamiliar legal system. In addition, the interpretation of the binding standards in Community Directives in the consumer protection field by CICPP experts has often been over-extensive, if not outright wrong.[98]

A more serious legitimacy concern is related to the impoverishing effect that 'external governance'[99] may occasionally have on the domestic rule-making process. Predictably, this effect has manifested itself differentially in different areas of Community law and policy. In areas such as constitutional law local interest groups have had well-articulated interests and were keen to participate in the transposition process and to counterbalance occasionally poorly motivated advice and demands for change. In areas like consumer law, however (but even in competition law) no potent local groups were mobilized—neither on the consumer, nor on the business side. This has typically led to legislation without participation, contributing to the continuous vindication of the 'black letter' approach to law characteristic of the time of state socialism.[100]

Interestingly, the greater the success of rule-transfer on the surface, the greater the suspicion of rubber-stamp law making with limited participation of and influence by domestic groups. As the Bulgarian consumer protection legislation demonstrates, the formidable success with establishing comprehensive consumer protection legislation has been in reverse proportion to the actual involvement of consumer groups and other interested actors in the law making process.

Of course I am not the first to note that the rapid transposition of the *acquis* may exacerbate the already existing proclivity in CEE of adopting formal laws, poorly consulted with the polity and affected interest groups and hardly representative of popular concerns.[101] This is a legitimate critique that could be levelled not only at EU enlargement policy but also at other massive and scantily reflected legal aid programs of foreign aid agencies and consultants.[102]

[98] Concerning the Misleading Advertising Directive see Pritchard, 2000a, n 35 above, p 119.

[99] Schimmelfennig and Sedelmeier, 2004, n 1 above.

[100] Micklitz, 2001; E Łętowska 'Bariery naszego myślenia o prawie w perspektyvie integracji z Europa' (1996) (4–5) *Państwo i Prawo*.

[101] Micklitz, 2001 *ibid.*; see however Sadurski n 4 above.

[102] S Holmes 'Can Foreign Aid Promote the Rule of Law?' (1999)(8(4)) *East European Constitutional Review*.

My main concern is, however, that in the zeal of reform efforts and sometimes fascinated by the ease of acceptance, Community institutions may not be sufficiently attentive to those rare and precious moments of law making from within, of promising institutional innovations that are (on the verge of becoming) internalized by local actors and institutions. With a glance too steadily fixed on the success of rule transfer, the actors involved in the accession process may contribute to suffocating spontaneous institutional responses to truly perceived social challenges.

6 EXTENDING THE COMMUNITY *ACQUIS*: BOOMERANG EFFECTS

In a number of analyses enlargement is described as a one-way street of 'exporting' or 'transferring' norms, values and rules from Member States and Union to applicant countries.[103] Given the scale of the operation and its duration, however, it is more plausible to view enlargement as an inevitably two-way avenue, where part of the experience and insights gained from the process of accession flow back to the Union and transform into new strategies, policies and priorities. The logic of such 'boomerang effects' is twofold. On the one hand, it is a result of what Sadurski calls the 'dominant liberal legalism paradigm' in Western societies, meaning that legal standards apply to all.[104] Consequently, the standards elaborated and held as benchmark against CEE states in the process of enlargement gradually convert into universal standards for the whole Union. On the other hand, from a public choice perspective it is plausible that the conceptualizations and systematizations elaborated in the process of legal and institutional advice turn readily into programmes for future action strengthening the positions of certain institutional actors at the EU level (notably the Commission).

What are the specific boomerang effects of the extension of the economic law *acquis* to the CEE on the EU?

Arguably one important consequence of the accession strategy has been the insight in (or rather the pertinent reminder of) the intricacy and importance of enforcement for the actual working of legal rules and for Community law as a whole. One can see this in the field of competition policy[105] and consumer policy, but also in other fields of community law such as intellectual property law.[106] Whereas until recently, problems of enforcement and institutional structures

[103] See eg Schimmelfennig and Sedelmeier, 2004, n 1 above.

[104] Sadurski, n 4 above.

[105] See Council Reg (EC) No 1/2003 of 16 December 2002 on the implementation of the rules on competition laid down in Arts 81 and 82 of the Treaty, O.J. L 1/1, 4 January 2003: Preamble (1) . . . In the light of experience, however, that Regulation [Council Reg 17/1962, First regulation implementing Arts 81 and 82] should now be replaced by legislation designed to meet the challenges of an integrated market and a future *enlargement* of the Community. (emphasis added).

[106] See Dir 2004/48/EC of the European Parliament and of the Council on the enforcement of intellectual property rights, L 195/16, 2 June 2004.

were seen as sensitive issues of sovereignty indisputably within the sacred sphere of competence of the Member States, this is no longer the case. Accession has pushed open the discourse on enforcement and the efforts at harmonization and equalization of standards are in full motion. This has arguably followed the dual logic just described.

(i) Partly, it has been important to set European standards about enforcement before letting the new candidate States in as a kind of 'defence strategy', thus ensuring a relatively adequate implementation of the *acquis*, ie not law in the books but in legal practice.
(ii) Partly, drawing the guidelines for the new Member States has simultaneously been a process of rethinking and comparing national experiences and has provided a rich database material for drafting new European Directives on enforcement.

A noteworthy example of the importance of enlargement for the Community's *demarche* in the area of enforcement provides Regulation on consumer protection cooperation (Regulation 2006/2005).[107] In the Explanatory Memorandum to the Commission Proposal[108] enlargement is emphatically referred to both in the opening and the closing section:

> 1. The effective functioning of the internal market calls for a significant improvement in the way laws that protect consumers economic interests are enforced in cross-border cases. . . . *Enlargement* further reinforces the need for action.
>
> 54. The Commission considers that adoption of the proposed regulation by Council and Parliament should be undertaken as quickly as possible, in particular, given the imminent *enlargement* of the EU. (emphasis added)

Another boomerang effect can be discerned in the fact that the Regulation is exclusively devoted to public law enforcement of consumer protection laws. It purports to establish a network of public consumer protection authorities in the Community Member States. These authorities are to be identified, clearly listed and obliged to offer information and mutual assistance. It is interesting to note the language in the Explanatory Memorandum. The thesis of the indispensability of public authorities for the proper enforcement of consumer protection laws is advanced with remarkable vigour. The advantages of public intervention are seen to lie in: reliable investigation powers; guarantee for confidentiality and privacy; effectiveness and efficiency; accountability and impartiality. Although the Commission underlines the 'valuable role' to be played by consumer organizations in the process of enforcement, it does not appear ready to sustain the 'privileged position' provided to these organizations by Community law and especially by the Injunctions Directive.

[107] Reg (EC) No 2006/2004 of the European Parliament and of the Council of 27 October 2004 on cooperation between national authorities responsible for the enforcement of consumer protection laws (the Regulation on consumer protection cooperation), O.J. L 364/1, 9 December 2004.
[108] COM (2003) 443 final.

The Commission makes explicit recourse to enlargement to draw additional support for its preferred emphasis on enforcement by public authorities. The availability of public authorities for the enforcement of consumer protection in CEE is used to bolster the potential of the advanced Regulation to achieve a uniform and adequate enforcement across a wider Community. According to the Commission:

> 32. . . . A large majority of Member States and *acceding countries* nevertheless have public authorities with specific consumer protection enforcement responsibilities.

And further:

> 34. *in fine* The prospect of *enlargement* demands action to safeguard consumer interests in an *enlarged* internal market. Most of the new Member States do not have a long tradition of consumer protection enforcement, although they *have established public authorities*. The proposed regulation is therefore an opportunity to ensure that effective enforcement is in place throughout the new internal market. (emphasis added)

Finally, when reassuring Member States that the institutional changes advanced with the Draft Regulation are not necessarily as great as they appear, the Commission opens for assigning the consumer protection tasks required in the Regulation to a competition authority.

> 36. . . . For example, in several Member States and third countries, enforcement responsibilities for consumer protection are carried out by the agency responsible for the enforcement of competition law matters. *Positive synergies exist between the consumer protection and competition dimensions of market surveillance and enforcement.*

It appears that the experience gained in the process of enlargement can be instructive also for the Community institutions. Although combining functions of antitrust and consumer protection is not unfamiliar in the old Member States, this model is particularly influential in the CEE and has arguably attracted interest in the course of accession. So if there indeed is a process of social learning, then it may, at least occasionally, be one of mutual learning as well.

5 CONCLUSION

In their analysis of conditionality and the transfer of EU rules by external governance, Schimmelfennig and Sedelmeier give a rather murky forecast on the future of compliance with the obligations of membership in the new Member States once the sword of conditionality is removed.[109] They predict instances of non-compliance and attempts at renegotiation of imposed commitments perceived as unjust. On a more general level, they see a negative impact of external

[109] Schimmelfennig and Sedelmeier, 2004, n 1 above.

governance in compromising the beneficial effects of democratic conditionality by weakening the democratic process in the CEECs.

The above overview of institutional change under accession suggests that part of these concerns may be justified. Accession has indeed resulted in a mushrooming of regulatory agencies in the candidate countries and has in many cases contributed to the continuous vindication of the 'black letter', or 'textocentrist', approach to law.[110] Designing enforcement and procedure has often been highly imperfect and fraught with credibility and efficiency problems. This is crucial from the perspective of the accession states, because enforcement determines whether the institutions built in the pre-accession stage will manage to live a life of their own and be put to the services of the legitimate interests of citizens and market participants, for whom they were created, in the first place.

Despite the rather pessimistic assessment of the outcome of the legislative reforms, there is, however, evidence of unexpected openings and innovations that have managed to involve local actors and resulted in solid, accountable and transparent institutions. Such innovative practices shall be nurtured and given attention also on the part of the old Member States. Although legacies from past experience and engrained habits are always an important factor in reform efforts, under a time of upheaval we observe a shift of layers in the legal system and opportunities for new creative institution-building.

The lesson for future enlargements seems to be one of moderation and sensitivity. Moderation would imply a critical review of the *acquis* and less insistence on its zealous and comprehensive transposition.[111] Sensitivity would entail greater respect for imperfect but endogenously produced normative and institutional solutions. More than pursuing doctrinal ideals of systemic coherence and exhaustiveness, the task should be to open avenues for channelling private, collective and public interests into a continuous process of shaping 'sustainable' laws and institutions.

BIBLIOGRAPHY

Adjani, G, 'By Chance and Prestige. Legal Transplants in Russia and Eastern Europe' (1995) (43) *American Journal of Comparative Law*, pp 93–117.

Alexiev *et al*, *Consumer Protection in Bulgaria, Czech Republic, Estonia, Hungary, Latvia, Lithuania and Romania. National Reports and Comparative Analysis* (1996) CICPP no 4.

Bakardjieva, A, 'Das neue Wettbewerbsgesetz in Bulgarien' (1998) *GRURInt*, pp 671–6.

Bakardjieva Engelbrekt, A, *Fair Trading Law in Flux? National Legacies, Institutional Choice and the Process of Europeanisation*, Stockholm, 2003.

Bourgoignie, Th and Pritchard, J-P (eds) *Consumer Protection Policy in Central and Eastern Europe: Achievements and Prospects for Future Action* (1996) CICPP no 5.

110 Łętowska, 1999, n 19 above.

111 *Cf* 'prioritisation', Pritchard, 2000a, n 35 above, p 230.

Cambier, V, *Comparative and Misleading Advertising Legislation in Central and Eastern Europe: Approximation, Harmonisation and Compatibility with European Union Law* (1999) CICPP no 12.

Checkel, J, 'Sanctions, Social Learning and Institutions' (1999) *Arena Working Papers* no 11.

Cseres, K, 'The Hungarian Cocktail of Competition Law and Consumer Protection: Should it be Dissolved?' (2004) (27(1)) *Journal of Consumer Policy*, pp 43–74.

Dietz, A, 'Die Einführung von Gesetzen gegen den unlauteren Wettbewerb in ehemals sozialistischen Staaten Mittel- und Osteuropas' (1994) *GRUR Int.*, pp 649–70.

Dimitrova, A, 'Enlargement, Institution-Building and the EU's Administrative Capacity Requirement' (2002) (25(4)) *West European Politics*, pp 171–90.

—— *Driven to Change. The European Union's Enlargement Viewed From the East* (Manchester and New York, MUP, 2004).

Dupré, C, *Importing the Law in Post-Communist Transitions* (Oxford, Hart Publishing, 2003).

—— 'Anticipating EU Membership: Importing the Law of the West', *Paper at the Workshop: Implications of Enlargement for the Rule of Law and Constitutionalism in Post-Communist Legal Orders*, EUI, 28–29 November 2003.

Elster, J, Offe, C and Preuss, U, *Institutional Design in Post-Communist Europe. Repairing the Ship at Sea* (Cambridge, CUP, 1998).

Engelbrekt, K, 'Installing the *acquis* in Central and Eastern Europe' (2004) available at: http://www.epsnet.org/2004/pps/Engelbrekt.pdf.

—— 'Multiple Asymmetries: The European Union's Neo-Byzantine Approach to Eastern Enlargement' (2002)(39) *International Politics*, 37–52.

Galbraith, J, *The Affluent Society* (London, Hamish Hamilton, 1968).

Heidenhain, S, *Das Verbraucherschutzrecht in Polen und in der Europäischen Union* (Berlin, Springer, 2000).

Holmes, S, 'Can Foreign Aid Promote the Rule of Law?' (1999) (8(4)) *East European Constitutional Review*.

Kozminski, A, 'Consumers in Transition from a Centrally Planned to a Market Economy' (1991) (14(4)) *Journal of Consumer Policy*, pp 351–69.

Łętowska, E, 'Bariery naszego myślenia o prawie w perspektyvie integracji z Europa' (1996) (4–5) *Państwo i Prawo*, pp 44–58.

—— 'Consumer Protection as Public Interest Law' (1999) (1–4) *Droit polonais contemporain*, pp 39–60.

Łętowski, J, 'Verbraucherschutz in Polen, Rechtslage, Wirklichkeit und Zukunft' (1976) *RabelsZeitschrift*, pp 13–41.

Mańko, R, 'The Culture of Private Law in Central and Eastern Europe After Enlargement: A Polish Perspective' (2005) (11) *European Law Journal*, pp 527–48.

Meuwly, D, 'Consumer Policy in Poland: Institutional and Legal Features' (1998) (1) *Review of Central and East European Law*, pp 9–41.

Millan, E and Elliott, R, 'Offensive Advertising, Public Policy, and the Law: The Rulings on the Zagorka Case' (2004)(27(4)) *Journal of Consumer Policy*, pp 475–93.

Micklitz, H-W, 'Verbraucherschutz West versus Ost—Kompatibilizierungsmöglichkeiten in der Europäischen Gemeinschaft–Einige Vorüberlegungen' in: H Heiss (ed) *Brückenschlag zwischen den Rechtskulturen des Ostseeraums* (Tübingen, Mohr Siebeck, 2001), pp 137–82.

Micklitz, H-W (ed) *Rechtseinheit oder Rechtsvielfalt in Europa? Zur Rolle und Funktion des Verbraucherrechts in den MOE-Staaten und in der EG* (Baden-Baden, Nomos, VIEW Band 1, 1996).

Ojala, M, *The Competition Law of Central and Eastern Europe* (London, Sweet & Maxwell, 1999).

Pritchard, J-P (ed) (2000a) *Consumer Protection in Poland* CICPP no 23.

—— (2000b) *Consumer Protection in Bulgaria* CICPP no 17.

Rose-Ackerman, S, *From Elections to Democracy, Building Accountable Government in Hungary and Poland* (Cambridge, CUP, 2005).

Sadurski, W, 'Accession's Democracy Dividend: From Conditionality to Post-Accession' (2004) (10(4)) *European Law Journal*, pp 371–401.

Schimmelfennig, F and Sedelmeier, U, 'Governance by Conditionality: EU Rule Transfer to the Candidate Countries of Central and Eastern Europe' (2004) *Journal of European Public Policy* pp 661–79.

—— (eds) *The Europeanization of Central and Eastern Europe* (Imprint Ithaca, NY, Cornell University Press, 2005).

Skubisz, R, 'Das Recht des unlauteren Wettbewerbs in Polen' (1994) *GRUR Int*, pp 681–9.

Smilov, D, 'EU Enlargement and Judicial Independence in Candidate States', *Paper at the Workshop: Implications of Enlargement for the Rule of Law and Constitutionalism in Post-Communist Legal Orders*, EUI, 28–29 November 2003, available at: http://www.iue.it/LAW/Events/WSWorkshopNov2003.shtml

Stalev, J, 'Verbraucherschutz in Bulgarien' (1976) *RabelsZeitschrift*.

Sunstein, C, *After the Rights Revolution: Reconceiving the Regulatory State* (Cambridge, Mass., Harvard University Press, 1990).

Ullrich, H, 'Anti-Unfair Competition Law and Anti-Trust Law. A Continental Conundrum' (2005) *EUI Working Papers Law* no 2005/01.

Várady, T, 'The Emergence of Competition Law in (Former) Socialist Countries' (1999) (47) *American Journal of Comparative Law*, pp 229–75.

Wiszniewska, I, 'Recht der Werbung in Polen' in Schricker (ed) *Recht der Werbung in Europa* (Baden-Baden, Nomos Verlagsgesellschaft, 1999).

Annual Reports, Bulgarian Commission for Protection of Competition, Sofia, 2001–2003.

OECD Report, The Role of Competition Policy in Regulatory Reform, Hungary (2000).

OECD Report, The Role of Competition Policy in Regulatory Reform, Poland (2002).

Regular Report from the Commission on Bulgaria's Progress toward Accession 1998, 1999, 2000, 2001, 2002, 2003, 2004, 2005 (cited Regular Report Bulgaria, plus year).

Regular Reports from the Commission on Poland's Progress toward Accession 1998, 1999, 2000, 2001, 2002, 2003 (cited Regular Report Poland, plus year).

Regular Reports from the Commission on Hungary's Progress toward Accession 1998, 1999, 2000, 2001, 2002, 2003 (cited Regular Report Hungary, plus year).

COM (2003) 443 final, Proposal for a Regulation of the European Parliament and of the Council on cooperation between national authorities responsible for the enforcement of consumer protection laws ("the regulation on consumer protection cooperation").

2

The Duty of Supreme Courts to Refer Cases to the ECJ: The Commission's Action Against Sweden

PROFESSOR ULF BERNITZ*

1 CONTROLLING MEMBER STATE COURTS UNDER EU LAW[1]

MOST OF THE judicial application of Community law takes place within the national court systems of the Member States. This raises the problem of how to secure a coherent application and uniform interpretation of Community law all over the EU. What are the instruments for controlling the practice of Member State courts under EU law in order to secure national compliance?

In this article I will discuss some of these problems by focusing primarily on the EU Commission's recent action against Sweden targeting the practice of the Swedish supreme courts to refer only few cases to the ECJ for preliminary ruling. This action raises a number of important issues which go right into the core of the structure of the Community court system and the position and responsibilities of national courts in that regard. As far as known, the Commission has never before taken formal action against a member state because its court(s) of last resort have not observed its Treaty obligation to refer cases to the ECJ. Certainly, no such case has ever been tried by the ECJ.

The action taken against Sweden raises complicated and partially new issues of Community law and invites discussion about the best instruments to be chosen in order to enhance the basic aim to secure member state compliance with the European legal system.

* Dr Ulf Bernitz is Professor of European Law at Stockholm University, Sweden and Director, Oxford/Stockholm Wallenberg Venture in European Law, University of Oxford, UK.

[1] The article is partially based on a paper presented by the author at a seminar at Harvard Law School, organised by The Harvard European Law Association (HELA) and The European Law Research Center (ELRC). I thank Professor Daniel Meltzer for valuable comments. A shorter earlier version has been published in Swedish, Kommissionen ingriper mot svenska sistainstansers obenägenhet art begära förhandsavgöranden, ERT (Europarättslig Tidskrift) 2005 p 109 *ff*.

Before presenting the action against Sweden, there are descriptions of some important aspects of the system of preliminary references (section 2), in particular the problem how to define what is a national court of last resort (section 3). On this issue the ECJ decision in the Swedish *Lyckeskog* case[2] is of particular importance as it forms a principal basis for the Commission's subsequent action against Sweden.

The Commission's remarkable action against the practice of the Swedish supreme courts and the Swedish response so far is presented in section 4. In the following sections I will discuss two particularly important legal aspects of the Commission's reasoning, namely the scope of the case before the ECJ, Judgment of 06/10/1982 , CILFIT/Ministero della Sanità (CILFIT), the CILFIT doctrine, on *acte clair* (section 5) and the consequences of ECJ's recent decision in the *Köbler* case[3] on member state liability in damages for decisions taken by national supreme courts (section 6). The article ends with concluding reflections, related to the Commission's action, section 7.

2 THE OBJECT OF THE SYSTEM OF PRELIMINARY REFERENCES

By way of introduction, a few words should be said about the applicable system, albeit familiar to many readers. As is well-known, the relation between Community law and national law in the member states is based on the doctrine of supremacy of Community law, ie the national law of the member states is subordinated.[4] In case of conflict between Community law and national law, the member states courts are obliged to respect the Community law which to a large extent has direct effect in the member states, also in relations between private parties. To considerable extent, this result can be achieved by interpreting national law so that it does not conflict with overriding Community law, something that might require constructive or very narrow interpretation of the national law. However, according to well established case law, if there is an open conflict between Community law and national law, the courts of the member states have to set aside national law and apply Community law. This principle of supremacy of Community law is clearly to be seen as a federal element in the structure of the European Community. Its disputed limits in relation to national constitutional principles need not be discussed here. However, it should be stated from the outset that on this point the attitude of the Swedish

[2] Case C-99/00, *Public Procecutor v Lyckeskog*, [2002] ECR I-4876.

[3] Case C-224/01, *Gerhard Köbler v Austria*, [2003] ECR I-10239.

[4] For general information, reference may be made to Craig-de Búrca, EU Law. Text, Cases and Materials, 3rd edn, Oxford 2003, Douglas-Scott, 'Constitutional Law of the European Union', London 2002, Lenaerts-van Nuffel, 'Constitutional Law of the European Union', 2nd edn, London 2005, Weatherill-Beaumont, EU Law, 3rd edn, London 1999, in Swedish, Bernitz-Kjellgren, Europarättens grunder (The Foundations of European Law), 2 edn Stockholm 2002.

courts has never caused any difficulties of the type well-known from, eg, earlier practice of the French *Cour d'Etat*.[5] The doctrine of supremacy of Community law was accepted loyally by the Swedish supreme courts already shortly after Sweden's accession to the EU from 1 January 1995.[6]

The practical application of the principle of supremacy involves many difficulties. Governments in the member states sometimes try to keep national legislation which is incompatible with the principles of the free movement in the internal market or the Community competition rules and obstruct or at least unduly delay the implementation of Community directives. Member states' courts might at times hesitate to set aside national law provisions, regarded as important in their domestic societal environment, although they do not fully comply with Community law. Also, national courts normally know their own national law far better than Community law. Thus, there are problems not only of tendencies of obstruction at national level but also, and primarily, of insufficient knowledge of Community law. There has been and still is an ongoing struggle to secure the full application of Community law in the member states. This is primarily the task of the Commission, but also the ECJ regards the securing the impact of Community law as an aim of primary importance. Many of the decisions taken by the ECJ are to be understood against this background.

In nations, having a federal structure, it is generally possible to appeal from the highest state court to the federal supreme court as the court of last resort, at least in cases having a constitutional dimension. However, the EU does not have a federal court structure in that sense. For example there is no counterpart within the EU to the American system of federal courts and the notion of federal court jurisdiction as differentiated from state court jurisdiction.[7] The establishment of regional, devolved Community courts has been discussed many times but never introduced. In fact, most of court application of Community law is in the hands of the national courts in the member states.[8]

[5] See, eg, Anderson & Demetriou, References to the European Court, 2nd edn, London 2002 p 177 *ff*, Brown-Kennedy, The Court of Justice of the European Communities, 5th edn, London 2000 p 231 *f*.

[6] The Supreme Administrative Court (Regeringsrätten) clearly accepted the doctrine of supremacy already in the cases RÅ (Regeringsrättens Årsbok) 1996 no 50, Upplands Lokaltrafik and RÅ 1997 No 82 I-II, SÖ Buss and Ancarcrona, see Bernitz, Sverige och europarätten, Stockholm 2002 p 126 *f*. The leading case from the Supreme Court is NJA (Nytt Juridiskt Arkiv) 2002 p 75, *Gharehveran*. See Bernitz, European Law in Sweden—its Implementation and Role in Market and Consumer Law, Faculty of Law, Stockholm University Series of Publications No 70, 2002 p 43 *ff*.

[7] For a comparison, J Cohen, The European Preliminary Reference and the US Review of State Court Judgments: A Study in Comparative Federalism, [1996] 44 Am J Comp L 421 *ff*.

[8] There exists another system for deciding cases in which the Commission has taken a decision directed towards a specific party (appeal to the Court of First Instance [CFI] and from there to the ECJ) but that system can be left aside in this context.

The preliminary reference procedure laid down in Article 234 (formerly Article 177) EC Treaty[9] is the instrument used to secure the control of the interpretation and judicial development of Community law remains in the hands of the ECJ, and is not left to the national courts in the member states. However, as it is in the hands of the national court to decide if a reference should be made or not, the reference procedure has to be distinguished from an appeal procedure; it is never possible for a party to appeal to the ECJ from a national court.

The possible need for reform of the system has been discussed on many occasions but has never resulted in any important change. The Report published in 2000 by a group of 'wise men', *Report by the Working Party on the Future of the European Communities' Court System*[10] has been particularly important because of its close links to the Court itself. The working party was headed by the former President of the ECJ Ole Due and the Report is usually referred to as *The Due Report*. The majority of the members of the working party were or had been ECJ judges or were in other ways closely connected to the Court. The primary object of the Report was to tackle the increasing back-log of cases in the ECJ and make procedure in the Court more expedient. Different issues of reform of the Community court system were contemplated. The Due Report remains an important source although only some of the Report's proposals have been realized.

The Due Report discussed briefly the issue how to remedy a breach of a national court of last resort to observe its obligation to refer cases to the ECJ, in particular when such a breach resulted in a decision which conflicted with Community law.[11] The problem is not covered by any specific Treaty provision. However, the Due Report stated it would be possible for the Commission to bring an action for failure of its obligations against a member state whose court has shown ignorance of Community law. On this point, the Report referred to the Commission's role as the guardian of the treaties and its ability under Art 226 EC Treaty to take actions against member states in breach of EC law and if necessary bring a state before the ECJ. The issue will be further discussed in sections 4 and 7 below.

[9] Art 234 reads as follows:

The Court of Justice shall have jurisdiction to give preliminary ruling concerning:

(a) the interpretation of this Treaty
(b) the validity and interpretation of acts of the institutions of the Community and of the ECB [European Central Bank]
(c) the interpretation of the statutes of bodies established by an act of the Council, where those statutes so provide.

Where such a question is raised before any court or tribunal of a Member State, that court or tribunal may, if it considers that a decision on the question is necessary to enable it to give judgment, request the Court of Justice to give a ruling thereon.

Where any such question is raised in a case pending before a court or tribunal of a Member State against whose decisions there is no judicial remedy under national law, that court or tribunal shall bring the matter before the Court of Justice.

[10] http://europa.eu.int/comm/dgs/legal_service/docs/due_en.pdf

[11] The Due Report p 16.

The Due Report also discussed the relationship between the Community courts (primarily the ECJ) and the national courts.[12] It stressed that these courts are not ranked in a hierarchial relationship to each other but the system is based entirely on cooperation and dialogue between the national courts and the ECJ. According to the Report, a reference for a preliminary ruling is a dialogue between the national court hearing the principal action, which is the only court fully familiar with the case, and the Community court, which is alone capable of securing a uniform interpretation of Community law.

In my opinion, it is not convincing, as is done in *The Due Report*, to describe the relationship between the ECJ and the national courts only as a dialogue or, to use other frequent terminology, partnership or cooperation. For the ECJ, as for the EU in general, it is essential to secure that Community law is fully observed in the member states and applied uniformly. To achieve this, it is of fundamental importance that the control of the development of Community law stays in the hands of the ECJ. For that reason it is necessary to have a well functioning preliminary reference system which respects in practice the leading role of the ECJ. Behind the dialogue and partnership terminology, the primary object of the reference procedure is to secure an efficient control of the uniform application of Community law by the member states' courts.

3 WHAT IS A NATIONAL COURT OF LAST RESORT? THE SWEDISH *LYCKESKOG* CASE IN THE ECJ

As follows from Article 234 (2), any court and tribunal in the Member states *may* refer a case to the ECJ if it raises an issue of Community law. However, according to Article 234 (3) courts and tribunals from which there is no judicial remedy under national law *must* do so, provided the court finds a decision on the question by the ECJ necessary to give judgment.[13]

What is a national court from which there is no judicial remedy? This issue was brought before the ECJ in a Swedish case of great importance for the following discussion, the *Lyckeskog* case.[14] That case was referred to the ECJ by the Swedish Court of Appeal for Western Sweden (*Hovrätten för Västra Sverige*). In substance it dealt with the issue whether the import by a family of a large quantity of rice from Norway (an European Economic Area (EEA) country where the price was cheaper) was to be considered as import for private consumption or smuggling. However, the court of appeal did not only ask the ECJ about that issue but also whether it was a court of last resort under Article 234 (3) in view of the fact that an appeal to the Supreme Court would only be examined as to its substance if the Supreme Court first had found the appeal admissible. With few

[12] The Due Report p 20 *f*.

[13] Art 234 is cited in foot-note 9, above.

[14] See fn 2, above. The opinion in the case by Advocate General Tizzano contains a valuable account of the relevant facts and the observations of various governments.

exeptions, the Swedish Supreme Court admits an appeal only if it finds it important for guidance in the application of the law that the appeal be examined by the Court, ie a supreme court decision in the case has to be of interest as a precedent.[15] Whether the concept of 'the law' refers only to Swedish national law, as was the case before the EU accession, or also to Community law as part of Swedish law has recently been clarified by The Supreme Court, favouring the latter interpretation.[16] With few exceptions, wrongful interpretation or application of the law by the lower court is not in itself sufficient reason to admit an appeal when examining the admissibility. As is easily understood, the question raised by the court of appeal in *Lyckeskog* was of great interest for a number of EU countries using some kind of certiorari system, eg England and the other Nordic countries. Before *Lyckeskog* it was an unsettled and debated issue whether only the highest court in the hierarchy was to be regarded as a court of last resort (the so-called abstract theory) or the highest court fully available to the parties (the concrete theory).[17]

In its judgment, the ECJ made the following statement on the purpose of the preliminary reference system:

> The obligation on national courts against whose decisions there is no judicial remedy to refer a question to the Court for a preliminary ruling has its basis in the cooperation established, in order to ensure the proper application and uniform interpretation of Community law in all the Member States, between national courts, as courts responsible for applying Community law, and the Court. That obligation is in particular designed to prevent a body of national case-law that is not in accordance with the rules of Community law from coming into existence in any Member State.[18]

However, the ECJ favoured the abstract theory and found that decisions of national appellate courts which can be challenged before a supreme court are not decisions within the meaning of Article 234(3) even if the examination on the merits of such appeals is subject to a prior declaration of admissibility by the supreme court. The ECJ remarked that the supreme court will be under an obligation, pursuant to Article 234(3), to refer a question to the ECJ for a preliminary ruling either at the stage of examination of admissibility or at a later stage.

[15] Ch 54 s 10 Code of Judicial Procedure. According to this provision the Supreme Court may grant leave to appeal only if:

(1) it is important for the uniform application of the law that the appeal be heard by the Supreme Court; or
(2) there are particular reasons for hearing an appeal, such as the existence of grounds for review on a point of law, a formal defect, or if the decision by the Court of Appeal manifestly rests on a serious omission or error.

[16] NJA 2004 p 735, Luftfartsverket.

[17] The reporting judge in the Court of Appeals in the *Lyckeskog* case, Judge Hagsgård, had favoured the concrete theory in his PhD-thesis, EG-rätten i nationell rättstillämpning (EC Law in National Court Application), Stockholm 1996.

[18] Para 14 of the decision.

Thus, in Sweden as in many other EU countries with a *certiorari* system, eg House of Lords in England, it is only the supreme court which is regarded as a court of last resort under Article 234(3) in relation to the ECJ. Actually, in line with most continental EU countries, Sweden has two supreme courts, The Supreme Court for private and criminal law in general and The Supreme Administrative Court, on top of the administrative law court system, for administrative law in a broad sense, including social law and tax law.[19]

4 THE COMMISSION'S ACTION AGAINST THE ALLEGED PRACTICE OF THE SWEDISH SUPREME COURTS NOT TO REFER CASES TO THE ECJ

The Commission's action against Sweden is based on the observation that the Swedish courts of last resort, primarily The Supreme Court, seldom refer cases to the ECJ for preliminary ruling.[20] In an exceptional move, the Commission has sent the Swedish Government a Reasoned Opinion on the matter. This is a formal administrative action against a member state, regulated in Art 226(1) EC Treaty, and preceded by informal exchange of opinions. If the member state does not comply with the Reasoned Opinion within a period set by the Commission, the latter may take judicial action against the member state by bringing the matter before the ECJ, invoking Art 226(2) and arguing that there is a breach of Treaty obligations. It the ECJ finds that the member state has failed to fulfil its obligation under the Treaty, the state shall be required to take the necessary measures to comply with the judgment of the ECJ, Art 228(1) EC Treaty.

The Commission normally keeps reasoned opinions secret. However, in this case the Reasoned Opinion has been made public in Sweden under Swedish law on transparency of public documents. I have had access to the Opinion and will give a summary of the essential points raised in this most interesting document.[21]

The Commission takes the *Lyckeskog* case[22] as its point of departure, in particular the remark made by the ECJ in that case that a supreme court is under an obligation to refer a question to the ECJ for a preliminary ruling either at the stage of examination of admissibility or at a later stage. The Commission also refers to the description of the Swedish procedural legislation and its application given by the Swedish court of appeal and the Swedish Government in the *Lyckeskog* case. It is mentioned specifically in the Opinion that until

[19] There can also be specialized courts holding a position as court of last resort. Swedish examples are The Labour Court for labour disputes and The Market Court for competition and commercial practices cases.

[20] See to the following, Schmauch, Lack of preliminary rulings as an infringement of Art 234 EC?. Commission case COM 2003/2161, procedure against the Kingdom of Sweden, European Law Reporter 2005 p 445 *ff*.

[21] Commission docket No 2003/2161, C(2004) 3899, dated 13 October 2004.

[22] Discussed in s 3, above.

31 December 2001 The Supreme Court had only referred two cases to the ECJ[23] and The Supreme Administrative Court ten cases; in 2003 each court referred only one additional case.[24]

In its Opinion, the Commission notes that there is no legislation in Swedish law on the procedure for deciding on referrals of cases to the ECJ and it finds it questionable if the practice applied by the supreme courts is in line with the obligations under Art 234(3).[25] In particular, the Commission finds, the issue of referral does not seem to be taken into regard when deciding whether or not the supreme court will find a case admissible. The Commission notes further that decisions on the admissibility of a case are given without stating the reasons; the supreme court merely states in one sentence no admission is granted. This makes it impossible, eg for the Commission, to check if the court has observed its obligations under Art 234(3). On this point, the Commission cites an example a case in which a Swedish court of appeal (*Göta hovrätt*) had found that Article 82 EC Treaty on misuse of market dominance can form the legal basis for damage claims. In this particular case, the Swedish Supreme Court did not find the case admissible and did not refer the case to the ECJ, no reasons were given by the court. The Commission adds that according to the description of Swedish procedural law given by the court of appeal in the *Lyckeskog* case, incorrect interpretation or application of Community law would not be a reason for The Supreme Court to grant admission.

The case on Article 82 especially mentioned by the Commission dealt with an important and unsettled issue of Community law. The private law consequences under Community law of measures taken by dominant undertakings, amounting to misuse of dominant position, have been much discussed over the years within the EU but have, so far, never reached the ECJ and have remained undecided on Community level. In its decision, which gained legal force, the Swedish court of appeal had found a contractual arrangement basically invalid under Art 82 as constituting a prohibited type of price discrimination and awarded the

[23] The first case referred by The Supreme Court to the ECJ, the *Data Delecta* case, was not much of a success. The Court asked whether the then existing duty for plaintiffs in other member states—but not for Swedish plaintiffs—to furnish security for litigation costs in private law suits was discriminatory. The ECJ found that to be the case, C-43/95, *Data Delecta Aktiebolag and Ronny Forsberg v MSL Dynamics Limited*, [1996] ECR I-4661. However, subsequently, The Supreme Court ruled that the non-discrimination principle was not applicable in cases concerning agreements entered into before Sweden joined the EU, even if the actual litigation occurred after accession, NJA 1996 p 668. However, soon afterwards, the ECJ reached the opposite conclusion in a very similar Austrian case, C-122/96, *Stephen Austin Saldanha and MTS Securities Corporation v Hiross Holding AG*, [1997] ECR I-5325.

[24] Sweden joined the EU on 1 January 1995. Further statistical information is provided in the final part of this section.

[25] There is no Swedish case in which any of the supreme courts has expressed its policy or indicated any guidelines in relation to the practice of the national courts in referring cases for preliminary ruling. This can be contrasted, ia, to the situation in the United Kingdom, where this issue has been discussed in many cases. Primarily are to be noted the restrictive and much criticized guidelines presented by Lord Denning at an early stage and the later, more ECJ friendly guidelines by Justice Bingham, see Weatherill–Beaumont, EU Law, 3rd edn, London 1999 p 334 ff with further references.

other party very substantial civil remedies.[26] Had this case been referred to the ECJ, it would have attracted great interest among competition lawyers all over Europe.

Further, the Commission reminded in its Reasoned Opinion of the interpretation of the obligations under Art 234(3) given by the ECJ in the *CILFIT* case, the *acte clair* principle. This principle will be discussed in section 5, below.

The Commission stated in its conclusion that Sweden has not fulfilled its obligations under Art 234(3) as it has not taken measures against the practice of the supreme courts not to refer cases to the ECJ in connection with their decisions on the issue of admissibility and not required reasons to be given so that the fulfilment of these obligations can be checked objectively. The Commission seems to require new national legislation capable of remedying this situation.

The Commission added it wished to underline that the member state is responsible for Community law to be observed irrespective of which organ in the member state that has caused the violation. Thus, the Commission writes, the independent position of a court of last resort is not jeopardized. On this point the Commission referred to the *Köbler* case, discussed in section 6, below.

It is worth noting that the outcome in the *Lyckeskog* case caused the House of Lords to change the practice of its Appeal Committee not to give express reasons when its reports to the House on petitions for leave of appeal. Since 2003, such reasons are given in cases involving community law in order to ensure proper transparency regarding compliance of the House of Lords with Article 234(3) EC.[27] There is no indication that the Swedish supreme courts discussed a similar change as a consequence of *Lyckeskog*.

What has been the response of the Swedish Government to the Reasoned Opinion of the Commission? The Government has rejected any allegations about breach of Article 234(3). However, in June 2005, the Swedish Ministry of Justice published a proposal for new legislation;[28] the introduction of a completely new, very short legislative Act on Preliminary Rulings of the ECJ. Basically, the proposed act consisted of only one paragraph, addressed to Swedish courts handling cases as a court of last resort. According to the proposed provision, such a court would have to take a reasoned decision, made public, on the issue of referral when a party in the litigation claims the court should refer the case to the ECJ.

[26] The case and the court decision is presented in English in Bernitz, The Arlanda Terminal 2 Case: Substantial Damages for Breach of Art 82, [2003] Competition Law Journal, London p 195 *ff*. See also Bernitz, European and Nordic Competition Law: How well do they Correspond? in A European for All Seasons. Liber Amicorum Sven Norberg, Bruxelles 2006 (forthcoming). However, when one of the parties to the case applied at a later stage to the Supreme Court for relief for a substantive defect, that court, while not granting a new trial, somewhat surprisingly gave reason in its decision why the case could not be referred to the ECJ, NJA 2004 s 735, Luftfartsverket.

[27] House of Lords. Appeal Committee, Session 2002–2003, 38th Report, Petitions for Leave to Appeal: Reasons for the Refusal of Leave, 3 April 2003. The legislation was preceded by negotiations with the Commission.

[28] Förhandsavgörande från EG-domstolen (Preliminary Ruling from the ECJ), Ds 2005:25 (Ministry of Justice), Stockholm 2005.

This Government proposal was not far-reaching but proved to be controversial. When sent for consideration to different courts and other stakeholders, the supreme courts and also several other bodies within the Swedish judiciary opposed the Proposal.[29] As an alternative, The Supreme Court declared itself willing to include a vaguer rule on the matter in its internal procedural rules. Clearly, members of The Supreme Court and The Supreme Administrative Court reacted against the Reasoned Opinion of the Commission, regarding it as an unjustified intrusion. However, the majority of the authorities and organisations heard by the Government supported the proposal, among them the Law Faculties of Lund, Stockholm and Uppsala Universities. Many of the bodies heard criticized the proposed statutory text for limiting the duty to give a reasoned decision on the issue of referral to instances in which a party to the case has raised the matter. They underlined the observance of Article 234(3) is an independent duty of the national court.

However, the Government has decided to disregard the critique put forward by the supreme courts and certain other judicial bodies and in March 2006 a Bill to Parliament based on the Proposal has been presented in the shape of a special statute on referrals of cases to the ECJ.[30] The Bill has been accepted by Parliament and took legal effect from 1 July 2006, applicable also to cases already pending in the courts.[31] It is not known whether or not the Commission will regard the new Swedish legislation as sufficient to remedy the problem raised in its Reasoned Opinion.

It remains to be seen how much impact the new obligation to give reasons will have in the actual practice of the supreme courts. Before presenting the Bill to Parliament the Government heard The Law Council (*Lagrådet*), an advisory body of high standing, mainly composed of judges from The Supreme Court and The Supreme Administrative Court. The Law Council regarded the proposed Bill as unnecessary, warning that the reasons given by the supreme courts, should the legislation be introduced, in many cases probably would be stereotype, closely leaning on the wording of the prerequisites used in Art 234.[32]

How many references have there been from Swedish courts compared to other member states? In total, the ECJ receives per year approximately 250 references for a preliminary ruling. Based on the statistics given in the Annual Report of the ECJ[33] I have counted the number of references from the member states during the ten years 1995–2004 to find out how well Sweden has been far-

[29] The results of the consultations has been presented by the Ministry of Justice in Remissammanställning. Förhandsavgörande från EG-domstolen (Ju2004/9463/DOM).

[30] Government Bill (*proposition*) 2005/06:157.

[31] The Bill was accepted by Parliament without opposition. The Parliamentary Committee on the Judiciary (*Justitieutskottet*) undelined in its Report the importance of full and clear reasons given by the courts, in particular courts of last resort, on the issue of the application of Art 234, Report of the *Justitieutskottet*, 2005/06:JuU39.

[32] The opinion of the Law Council is included in the Government Bill.

[33] Annual Report for 2004 p 185, available at www.curia.eu.int.

Preliminary References from Member States' Courts 1995–2004

	Total number of cases	*Inhabitants in millions*
Belgium	173	10
Denmark	52	5
Germany	686	82
Greece	60	11
Spain	112	40
France	287	60
Ireland	15	4
Italy	480	58
Luxembourg	24	0.5
Netherlands	191	16
Austria	261	8
Portugal	44	10
Finland	38	5
Sweden	50	9
United Kingdom	210	60

ing. During all these years the EU has had 15 member states; Austria, Finland and Sweden having joined on 1 January 1995.

As this table shows, the amount of references differs greatly between the different countries. Naturally, the large member states generate more references than the smaller. But quite visibly, there are also different judicial cultures on this point in the member states. Thus, there are more references from the older member states, primarily the 6 founding states.[34] On the other hand, states in the periphery of the Union tend to have less references, ie the Scandinavian member states, Ireland, Portugal, Spain and Greece. The Austrian practice is remarkable. Having a somewhat smaller population than Sweden, Austria has generated more than 5 times as many references. This particular aspect of Austrian legal culture seems difficult to explain; a considerable number of the Austrian cases seem to concern matters of limited importance. However, if Sweden is compared with Greece and Portugal, there are no big differences. The figures for the 2 other Nordic member states are also fairly similar.[35] Ireland has the lowest number of references, also in relation to its population size.

To conclude, although referrals from Swedish courts have been few, five per year in average, Sweden is not faring particularly badly according to the statistics.[36] However, as a general statement, Swedish courts have been referring

[34] France, Italy, Germany and the Benelux countries.

[35] Similar figures apply to Norwegian references to the EFTA Court. For further information, Sankari, EU Law in Finland and Sweden: A Survey of the Preliminary References, National Jurisprudence and Legal Integration, ERT 2003 p 508 *ff*.

[36] Of the 50 Swedish references, 5 are from The Supreme Court and 14 from The Supreme Administrative Court.

cases for preliminary ruling only with considerable caution and there seems to exist a certain preference within the judiciary for deciding cases involving Community law without consulting the ECJ.

5 THE RELATION TO THE CILFIT PRINCIPLE ON *ACTE CLAIR*

The Reasoned Opinion against Sweden and its justification must be seen in the light of the *CILFIT* principle, as pronounced by the ECJ, and the ongoing discussion about its scope and validity.

It follows from the wording of Article 234(3) that a court of last resort shall bring a case concerning the interpretation of the EC Treaty before the ECJ for a preliminary ruling, if it considers that a decision on the question of Community law is necessary to enable it to give judgment.[37] According to an early decision by the ECJ in the *Da Costa* case, there is no obligation to refer a case to the ECJ when the question raised is materially similar with a question already decided by the ECJ, *acte éclairé*.[38] About 20 years later, the ECJ took a more elaborated position on the scope of the obligation to refer cases in the well-known *CILFIT* case.[39] Albeit the ECJ gave national courts of last resort certain concessions, it was eager to limit the discretion permitted.

The ECJ commenced by stating that 'the correct application of Community law may be so obvious as to leave no scope for any reasonable doubt as to the manner in which the question raised is to be resolved';[40] the notion of *acte clair*. However, the ECJ hedged its notion of certainty around with very far reaching qualifications, ruling:

> Before it comes to the conclusion that such is the case, the national court or tribunal must be convinced that the matter is equally obvious to the courts of the other Member States and to the Court of Justice. Only if those conditions are satisfied may the national court or tribunal refrain from submitting the question to the Court of Justice and take upon itself the responsibility of resolving it.[41]

The ECJ went on to list a number of matters which the national court should bear in mind when assessing whether the question raised can be considered *acte clair*. These include the characteristic features of Community law and the particular difficulties to which its interpretation gives rise, the drafting in different languages, all equally binding, the use of terminology peculiar to Community law, the special meaning of legal concepts in Community law and the fact that every provision must be placed in context and read in the light of Community law as a whole.

[37] The Treaty text is cited in fn 9, above.
[38] Case 28–30/62, *Da Costa en Schaake v Nederlandse Belastingadministratie*, [1963] ECR 31.
[39] Case 283/81, *CILFIT v Ministero della Sanità*, [1982] ECR 3415.
[40] Para 16.
[41] Para 16 continued.

One has to conclude that *CILFIT* allows little room for national courts of last resort for the exercise of judgment as to whether a question must be referred.[42] As it is not the task for supreme courts to handle obvious cases, *CILFIT*, strictly applied, would require supreme courts to refer at least the vast majority of cases they handle that involve an issue of Community law. As is well known, *CILFIT* has been severely critizised over the years; probably it has not been followed literally anywhere.[43] After the many enlargements to the EU and new languages given official status, it is virtually impossible for a court in a member state to access the meaning of the Treaty and statutory texts in all the official languages.[44] Also, the ECJ would have no capacity to decide all the references it would receive if *CILFIT* really were to be followed strictly.

The Due Report suggested changes in the wording of Art 234 (3) to open up for a less restrictive interpretation.[45] It suggested national courts of last resort should be obliged to refer a case to the ECJ 'provided that the question is of sufficient importance to Community law and that there is reasonable doubt as to the answer to that question'. However, the Nice Intergovernmental Conference on Treaty Revision in 2000 did not change Art 234 at all and the proposal now seems to be dropped. The criterion proposed in the Report, 'sufficient importance to Community law', is easily criticized. It is obviously quite vague, could be understood in many different ways and has probably been considered to give national courts of final resort too much leeway to decide for themselves.

Recently, the ECJ has affirmed the CILFIT principle by explicitly referring to it in several new cases. Thus the ECJ made a clear reference to what it had pronounced in *CILFIT* in the *Lyckeskog* case.[46] Even more firmly, the ECJ has stated the validity of the CILFIT principle in the *Köbler*[47] case, decided in 2003, which soon will be discussed on the point of member state liability (section 6). In *Köbler*, the Court pronounced, without indicating any exceptions:

> Moreover, it is, in particular, in order to prevent rights conferred on individuals by Community law from being infringed that under the third paragraph of Article 234 EC

[42] For an analysis of the Court's reasoning in *CILFIT*, Lenaerts—Arts, 'Procedural Law in the European Union', London 1999 p 47 *ff.*

[43] For an account of the discussion with further references, see, eg, Anderson & Demetriou, References to the European Court, 2nd edn, London 2002 p 173 *ff*, Arnull, 'The European Union and its Court of Justice', Oxford 1999 s 65 *ff*, Craig & de Búrca, EU Law, 3rd edn, Oxford 2003 p 445 *ff*, Douglas-Scott, 'Constitutional Law of the European Union', Harlow, England, 2002 p 249 *ff*, Lasok & Miller, Judicial Control in the EU: Procedures and Principles, Richmond, UK 2004 s 173 *ff*, Weatherill & Beaumont, EU Law, 3rd edn, London 1999 p 340 *ff.*

[44] Today, there are 20 official EU languages.

[45] Due Report, above, p 14 *ff.*

[46] *Lyckeskog* case, para 13 and 15. The Swedish Court of appeal had asked explicitly if the CILFIT criteria were applicable, para 9. AG Tizzano's Opinion in Lyckeskog contains a comprehensive assessment of the CILFIT principle.

[47] Cited in fn 4, above.

a court against whose decisions there is no judicial remedy under national law is required to make a reference to the Court of Justice.[48]

Thus, the ECJ does not seem inclined to give up the CILFIT doctrine. To the contrary, the ECJ seems determined to keep control and might distrust the loyalty of national supreme courts and their knowledge of Community law. In this regard, the enlargement as of 1 January 2004 of the EU with ten new member states and thus with ten new national supreme courts might be an important part of the explanation. Probably, the ECJ is afraid of the risk the preliminary reference system be diluted. From a practical viewpoint, the recent decrease in the ECJ's time lag in deciding cases has facilitated this policy.

In its Reasoned Opinion against Sweden,[49] the Commission refers to *CILFIT* as if its principles were beyond any dispute. However, based on the legal discussion that has taken place in judicial circles over previous years, also in circles close to the ECJ itself, the Swedish supreme court judges have had reason to believe they were enjoying a certain degree of discretion in deciding whether or not refer a case for a preliminary ruling. As mentioned, the scope and validity of the *CILFIT* principle were somewhat in doubt for a number of years, however, after *Köbler*, there seems to be much less room for such discussion. The obligation to refer has been tightened up.

6 THE RELATION TO THE KÖBLER DOCTRINE ON MEMBER STATE LIABILITY IN DAMAGES FOR SUPREME COURT DECISIONS

As already mentioned, the Commission underlined in its Reasoned Opinion addressed to the Swedish Government that a member state is responsible for Community law to be observed irrespective of which organ in the member state that has caused the violation. It follows from the Opinion that supreme courts are not considered exempt. The Commission draws this conclusion primarily from the *Köbler*[50] case, to which it refers.

The general principle of member state liability in damages for harm resulting from the breach of its obligations under Community law was established by the ECJ in 1991 in the well-known *Francovich* case.[51] In this case the breach involved the non-implementation of a directive. The ECJ could not base its decision on any specific Treaty provision; the Court referred to the general principles of the Treaty and its own task to ensure that the law is observed in the interpretation and application of the Treaty.[52] The ECJ found the principle of

[48] Para 35, see also paras 55 and 56 and para 118 where the ECJ cites *CILFIT*. See also case C-461/03, *Gaston Schul Douane-Expediteur BV v Minister van Landbouw, Natuur en Voedselkwaliteit*, [2005], not yet reported.

[49] See s 4, above.

[50] Cited in fn 3, above.

[51] Joined cases C-6, C-9/90, *Francovich and Bonifaci v Italy*, [1991] ECR I-5357.

[52] Art 220(1) EC Treaty.

member state liability in damages to be 'inherent in the system of the Treaty' and necessary in order to guarantee the full effect of its provisions. The Court also referred to the general principle of member state loyalty laid down in Art 10(1) EC Treaty, remarking:

> the full effectiveness of Community rules would be impaired and the protection of the rights which they grant would be weakened if individuals were unable to obtain redress when their rights are infringed by a breach of Community law for which a Member State can be held responsible.[53]

Thus, the Community law principle on member state liability is purely judge-made law. The ECJ has clarified the law in some later judgments, primarily the *Brasserie du Pecheur*-case, decided in 1996.[54] Based on these cases the conditions for liability appear to be:

(1) the rule of law infringed must have been intended to confer rights on individuals
(2) the breach must be sufficiently serious
(3) there must be a direct and casual link between the breach of the obligation resting on the State and the damage sustained by the injured parties.

Surprisingly, statutory Swedish tort law is still not in line with the Francovich principle. According to a provision in chapter 3 section 7 of the Swedish Tort Liability Act the general principle of liability of State and local authorities for loss inflicted through fault or negligence in the exercise of public powers cannot be invoked against legislation enacted by the Parliament or the Government. Thus, there is no statutory support for liability of the Swedish State towards individuals claiming damages for loss due to legislation which has implemented directives wrongly or for failure to legislate when that is required in order to implement Community law. However, in recent case law this statutory provision has been set aside in order to honour the principles of Community law.[55] A legislative committee proposed already in 1997 that the provision should be abolished in relation to Community law[56] but, so far, the Government has taken no action. It is remarkable that the misleading statutory text has been kept unaltered.

The *Köbler* case dealt with the issue whether an individual, the Austrian professor Gerhard Köbler, employed by an Austrian state university, could claim damages from the Austrian state because the Austrian Supreme Administrative Court had decided wrongly that the years he had been working in Germany could not be included when calculating whether he was entitled to length-of service increment for professors. This surprising supreme court decision was in

[53] Para 33.

[54] Case C-46/93, *Brasserie du Pecheur SA v Germany*, [1996] ECR I-1029.

[55] The leading case is NJA 2002 p 75, *Gharehveran*, which concerned insufficiant Swedish implementation of the same directive which was at stake in Francovich, Bernitz, European Law in Sweden p 46.

[56] *Statens offentliga utredningar* (SOU) 1997:194, Det allmännas skadeståndsansvar vid överträdelse av EG-regler (The Liability of the State for Breach of EC Law).

clear breach of Community law principles on non-discrimination, freedom of movement and freedom to work in other member states. The fundamental legal problem was that the decision not to award the increment was taken by a court of last resort.

The ECJ found it followed from its earlier case law that the principle of state liability applies to any case in which a member state breaches Community law, whichever is the authority of the member state whose act or omission is responsible for the breach. In light of the essential role played by the judiciary in the protection of the rights derived by individuals from Community rules, the ECJ did not find it possible to exempt courts of last resort. The Court considered different counter-arguments, in particular arguments based on the independence and authority of the judiciary, but found they could not be upheld. The ECJ stated, ia:

> The possibility that under certain conditions the State may be rendered liable for judicial decisions contrary to Community law does not appear to entail any particular risk that the independence of a court adjudicating at last instance will be called in question.[57]

The principle that a member state is to be taken as a single entity seems to be derived from international law. The Court pronounced:

> In international law a State which incurs liability for breach of an international commitment is viewed as a single entity, irrespective of whether the breach which gave rise to the damage is attributable to the legislature, the judiciary or the executive.[58]

However, on the issue whether there was a 'sufficiently serious breach' committed, the ECJ limited the responsibility for national courts to cases in which the breach of Community law is 'manifest'. Taking a particularly lenient attitude, the Court did not find the breach to be manifest in the specific case, although the particular circumstances were remarkable.

The link between the CILFIT principle and the *Köbler* case is obvious. As the ECJ clearly underlines in its *Köbler* judgment, a supreme court in a member state can always avoid the risk of taking decisions in breach of Community law by asking the ECJ for a preliminary ruling. Thus, *Köbler* will most likely have the effect of fortifying the CILFIT principle.

The *Köbler* case has been much discussed; some commentators find it too far-reaching.[59] However, once established, it will in all probability be here to stay, as was the case in the nineties with *Francovich*. For the future, the crucial

[57] Para 42.

[58] Para 32. Interestingly, the ECJ also referred to a decision by the European Court of Human Rights (ECtHR) in which that court found a state liable to pay damages under the ECHR for injury caused to a party by a decision by a national court adjudicating at last instance, para 49 referring to the ECtHR case *Dulaurans v France*.

[59] See for an informed and critical comment Wattel, Köbler, CILFIT and Welthgrove: We can't go on meeting like this, 41 CMLRev [2004] 177 *ff*. For a more balanced discussion, Komárek, Federal Elements in the Community Judicial System: Building Coherence in the Community Legal Order, 42 CMLRev [2005] 9 *ff*.

question will be what is understood by a 'manifest breach' of Community law.[60] It would not be surprising if the ECJ will become less lenient in its application of that concept in future cases, when the national courts can be expected to know of and respect the *Köbler* principle. However, the fundamental principle it is not constitutionally possible for a Government to instruct its courts how they should decide in individual cases puts obvious constraints on how far it would be possible for the ECJ to go. The Swedish constitution contains a clear prohibition against such instructions:

> Neither a public authority nor the *Riksdag* [Parliament] may determine how a court shall adjudicate an individual case or otherwise apply a rule of law in a particular case.[61]

When the general principle of state liability in damages in relation to individuals was introduced in Sweden in 1972 by the Tort Liability Act, The Supreme Court and The Supreme Administrative Court were exempted from such liability, the reason being of a constitutional character.[62] It was not considered appropriate to open up for litigation based on damage claims in which the judgments of the highest courts would be reviewed. However, at least after the decision in *Köbler*, it is clear that this exemption is no longer applicable to the extent such damage claims are based on Community law. The latter will override the provision to the contrary in the Swedish legislative act. The Tort Liability Act should be changed also on this point.[63]

The constitutional importance of the Köbler principle is evident when comparing with American law. Under the Eleventh Amendment to the American constitution, there is state sovereign immunity from being sued in federal courts in damages by private parties.[64] This early amendment, proclaimed already in 1798, was ratified to overrule a decision to the contrary by US Supreme Court in *Chisholm v Georgia*.[65] It is interesting to note that on this point, private actions

[60] A new case based on *Köbler* is presently coming up, *Traghetti del Mediterraneo v Italian Republic* (C-173/03), in which the opinion of Advocate General Léger was made public in October 2005. The background of the case is an Italian competition law (state aid) dispute between two companies. The Italian supreme court found for the defendant without referring the case to the ECJ. Afterwards, the plaintiff has sued the State of Italy for damages, claiming the ECJ would have supported the plaintiff's claim on the basis of well-established Community law, had it been given the opportunity to rule on the case. A lower Italian court has referred this case to the ECJ. According to Italian statutory law, damage caused by court decisions may only be awarded if the decision taken was caused by intention or gross negligence. Interpretation of legal rules and assessment of facts shall never give cause for damages. The ECJ has been asked in the referral to consider if these restrictions in Italian law are in conformity with EC law in light of the *Köbler* case. In his opinion, the Advocate General accepts the first limitation (requirement of intent or gross negligence) but not the latter.

[61] Ch 11 s 2 Instrument of Government (the Swedish constitution).

[62] Ch 3 s 7 of the Swedish Tort Liability Act.

[63] Other flaws of the Tort Liability Act have been discussed above, see at fn 54.

[64] 'The judicial power of the United States shall not be construed to extend to any suit in law or equity, commenced or prosecuted against one of the United States by Citizens of another State, or by Citizens or Subjects of any Foreign State'.

[65] *Chrisholm v Georgia*, 2 US 419 (1793). However, as construed by the US Supreme Court, the Eleventh Amendment allows a federal court suit against a state for injunctive relief. For an overview of the American law on the issue, see eg Baker & Williams, Constitutional Analysis in a Nutshell, 2nd edn, St Paul Minn. 2003.

for state liability in damages, Community law is more far reaching than American law.

7 CONCLUDING REFLECTIONS ON THE COMMISSION'S ACTION

The relation between the ECJ and member states' national courts is complicated and nuanced. On the one hand, the ECJ does not hold the position of a supreme European court in the proper sense, as there are no direct appeals possible from the national court level. On the other hand, to describe the relationship based on the preliminary reference system as one of dialogue or partnership between the two levels would be misleading. Throughout the history of the EU, there have been problems in persuading the member states, some more than others, to transpose, apply and interpret the Community law properly. To assure full, loyal and uniform compliance with Community law in all member states has always been, and still is, an overriding objective for the EU. The ECJ has accepted willingly to play a crucial role in this regard. Cases such as *CILFIT* and *Köbler* are to be understood against this background. Assuring compliance with Community law within the member states is the red thread behind large parts of the case law developed by the ECJ.

From this perspective, the well-functioning of the system of preliminary references is of paramount importance and it is easily understood why the ECJ has been hesitant to allow member states courts of final resort discretion as to whether they should refer cases to the Court or not. As demonstrated in the final part of section 4, above, actual practice when it comes to referring cases to the ECJ varies considerably between the member states, and in all probability many cases are not referred that properly should have been so. One can assume that a number of these cases are decided solely on the basis of national law or by applying or interpreting Community law wrongly. The possibility, confirmed in *Köbler*, for private parties to sue member states for damages caused by non-observance of Community law by national courts, also those of last resort, provides a new weapon in the Community legal arsenal.

Still, it might be questionable if the weapons available to assure compliance with Community law by member states courts are sufficient. It is against this perspective, one has to view the Commission's Reasoned Opinion on the alleged practice of the Swedish supreme courts not to refer cases to the ECJ to the extent so should have been done. It is interesting to note that the Commission in its Reasoned Opinion does not refer to any specific case or cases in which it finds that the Swedish courts have applied Community law wrongly or, even worse, tried to protect Swedish interests against overriding Community law to the contrary. The Commission limits its critique to lack of a sufficient number of references and lack of reasons given for decisions taken not to refer. The Commission is able to base its claims on good arguments; clearly, Swedish courts have been and still are fairly reluctant to refer cases to the ECJ. As mentioned in section 4, new Swedish legislation compelling courts of last resort to state the reasons for their decision to refer or not to refer a case under Article 234(3) is in place from 1 July 2006. It seems likely that this new legislation will form the basis for a negotiated settlement between the Commission and the Swedish Government.

Suppose, on the other hand, no settlement would be reached and the Commission starts an infringement proceeding against Sweden in the ECJ based on its Reasoned Opinion. Would the Commission win that case? Most likely, and breaking new ground, the ECJ would accept that the Commission is entitled to bring such a case against a member state and examine the substance of it. The outcome would probably be in line with the *Köbler* reasoning of the Court, under which member states are responsible vis à vis the EU for decisions taken by their courts, also those of final resort. On this point, reference can be made specifically to the conclusions drawn in *The Due Report*.[66] There is also support in legal doctrine, written already before the judgment in *Köbler*, for the principle that an infringement action by the Commission would lie against a Member State whose courts of final resort were in breach of their obligation under Article 234(3).[67] In my opinion, the ECJ would probably apply a restrictive test along the lines chosen in *Köbler,* possibly relying on principles of manifest error or bad faith, in order to maintain the general notion of dialogue and not humiliate the national supreme courts.

However, this being said, the relations between the ECJ and the national supreme courts of the Member States need to be based on cooperation and confidence in order to function well and assure compliance and mutual trust. After all, the large bulk of cases involving Community law are handled by national courts and not by the Community courts. As the former British ECJ Judge David Edward has pointed out, the national courts are the 'powerhouse' of Community law.[68] More needs to be achieved in that direction. Non observance of Community law by national courts is normally not a matter of bad faith but of lack of sufficient knowledge and understanding of a complicated legal system, different from national law. National judges often do not find themselves comfortable with Community law and might not grasp the full significance of a case when viewed in a broader European legal perspective. This seems to be a principal explanation behind the reluctant attitude towards the application of Community law among many national judges, at least in Sweden and the other Nordic countries.

This attitude should be overcame by means of promoting improved education, further contacts and increased understanding of the EC legal system, and

[66] See s 4, above.

[67] See, eg, Schwarze in Schwarze (ed), EU-Kommentar, Baden-Baden 2000 p 2008, Brown & Kennedy, The Court of Justice of the European Communities, London 2000 p 231, Lenaerts—Arts, 'Procedural Law of the European Union', London 1999 p 52. However, the latter find proceedings in the ECJ to enforce Art 234 (3) 'inappropriate', Brown & Kennedy take the same view 'except for a flagrant breach'.

[68] Edward, National Courts—the Powerhouse of Community Law, The Cambridge Yearbook of European Legal Studies, 5 [2004] 1 *ff*.

only as a very last resort by the Commission starting infringement proceedings against national Governments. The full acceptance of Community law in fairly new member states is a matter of time, learning and maturity and, not the least, the upbringing of a new generation of lawyers and judges. Actually, very recent decisions by the Swedish Supreme Court to refer several cases to the ECJ might indicate the Commission's action to issue its Reasoned Opinion, discussed in this article and certainly much observed within the Swedish judiciary, already might have achieved much of its intended effect.

In its reasoned opinion, the Commission has not discussed how important the Swedish cases referred to the ECJ have been or how well they represent the problems related to the application of Community law in Sweden. Actually, most of the cases referred have dealt with specific Swedish statutory provisions of a restrictive or prohibitive character, likely to involve discrimination on grounds of nationality or hindering or impeding the free flow of goods, services or capital. Very few cases have dealt with general principles of law or other issues of broader Community interest; the *Lyckeskog* case being the most important exception. No case has dealt with competition law; however, two advertising law cases referred from Sweden have attracted general attention.[69] In sum, the Swedish contribution to the development of Community case law has been rather scanty so far.[70] If the Commission's action, discussed in this article, will bring about a change on this point and spark increased Swedish activity, it has served its purpose well.

BIBLIOGRAPHY

Anderson, D, Demetriou, M, *References to the European Court*, 2nd edn, London 2002.

Arnull, A, *The European Union and its Court of Justice*, Oxford 1999.

Baker, TE and Williams, JS, *Constitutional Analysis in a Nutshell*, 2nd edn, St Paul, Minn 2003.

Bernitz, U, 'The Arlanda Terminal 2 Case: Substantial Damages for Breach of Article 82', [2003] *Competition Law Journal* p 195 *ff.*

—— 'European Law in Sweden—its Implementation and Role in Market and Consumer Law, Faculty of Law'. *Stockholm University Series of Publications No 70, 2002.*

—— 'European and Nordic Competition Law: How well do they Correspond?, A European for All Seasons'. *Liber Amicorum Sven Norberg*, Bruxelles 2006 (forthcoming).

[69] The *De Agostini* case, C-34–36/95, *Konsumentombudsmannen v De Agostini (Svenska) Förlag AB and TV-shop i Sverige AB*, [1997] ECR I-3843, the Gourmet case, C-405/98, *Konsumentombudsmannen v Gourmet International Products AB*, [2001] ECR I-1795

[70] The Finnish experience is very similar, Ojanen, The Impact of EU Membership on Finnish Constitutional Law, [2004] 10 European Public Law 561 *ff.* He mentions as the only Finnish preliminary ruling case of general importance C-513/99, *Concordia Bus Finland Oy Ab v Helsingin kaupunki and HKL-Bussiliikenne*, [2002] ECR I-7213, known as the Helsinki bus case. In this public procurement case, the ECJ found environmental factors could be taken into consideration although the relevant directive was silent on the issue.

—— 'Kommissionen ingriper mot svenska sistainstansers obenägenhet att begära förhandsavgöranden', *ERT* 2005 p 109 *ff*.
—— *Sverige och europarätten*, Stockholm 2002.
Bernitz, U and Kjellgren, A, *Europarättens grunder*, 2nd edn, Stockholm 2002.
Cohen, J, 'The European Preliminary Reference and the US Review of State Court Judgments: A Study of Comparative Federalism', [1996] *Am J Comp L* 421 *ff*.
Craig, P and de Búrca, G, *EU Law, Text, Cases, and Materials*, 3rd edn, Oxford 2003.
Brown, N and Kennedy, T, *The Court of Justice of the European Communities*, 5 edn, London 2000.
Douglas-Scott, *Constitutional Law of the European Union*, London 2002.
Edward, D, 'National Courts—the Powerhouse of Community Law', *Cambridge Yearbook of European Legal Studies*, 5 [2004] 1 *ff*.
Hagsgård, A, *EG-rätten i nationell rättstillämpning*, Stockholm 1996.
Komárek, J, 'Federal Elements in the Community Judicial System: Building Coherence in the Community Legal Order', 42 *CMLRev* [2005] p 9 *ff*.
Lasok, KPE and Miller, T, *Judicial Control in the EU: Procedures and Principles, Richmond*, UK 2004.
Lenaerts, K and van Nuffel, P, *Constitutional Law of the European Union*, 2nd edn, London 2005.
Lenaerts, K and Arts, D, *Procedural Law of the European Union*, London 1999.
Ojanen, T, 'The Impact of EU Membership on Finnish Constitutional Law', [2004] 10 *European Public Law* 561 *ff*.
'Report by the Working Party on the Future of the European Communities' Court System [The Due Report]', http://europa.eu.int/comm/dgs/legal-service/docs/due_en.pdf.
Sankari, S, 'EU Law in Finland and Sweden: A Survey of the Preliminary References, National Jurisprudence and Legal Integration', *ERT* 2003 p 508 *ff*.
Schmauch, M, 'Lack of Preliminary Rulings as an Infringement of Article 234 EC?', [2005] *European Law Reporter* p 445 *ff*.
Schwarze, J (ed), *EU-Kommentar*, Baden-Baden, 2000.
Wattel, PJ, Köbler, 'CILFIT and Welthgrove: We can't go on meeting like this', 41 *CMLRev* [2004] 177 *ff*.
Weatherill, S and Beaumont, P, 'EU Law', 3rd edn, London 1999.

3

Ten Years within the EU—Labour Law in Sweden and Finland following EU Accession

NIKLAS BRUUN* AND JONAS MALMBERG†

ABSTRACT

THE AIM OF this article is to evaluate the impact of EU membership on Swedish and Finnish labour law during the ten-year period 1995–2004.

Sweden and Finland applied to join the EU in July 1991 and March 1992 respectively. The negotiations were completed in March 1994 and both countries acceded to full EU membership on 1 January 1995. These membership negotiations took place in parallel with negotiations on establishing the EEA which were already in progress and were completed in May 1992, with the EEA Agreement coming into effect on 1 January 1994. Hence, the fact of being bound by that Agreement meant that Sweden and Finland were actually covered by the social dimension of European cooperation from 1994 onwards.

At the time when the two countries applied for membership, EU labour law was relatively limited in scope. Apart from a number of Directives regulating issues of health and safety at work, it essentially consisted of two Directives in

* Niklas Bruun is a Professor of EU Labour Law at Hanken, Swedish School of Economics and Business Administration. Professor Bruun is author and co-author of several books mainly within Labour Law and Intellectual Property Law. He has participated in several Nordic labour law projects and is co-author of several books on Nordic Labour Law. He has been a member of several state committees within the field labour law in both Sweden and Finland (sex discrimination, Employment Contracts, Employee inventions, Annual leave) and intellectual property law and several Expert Commissions for ILO, EU Authorities (European Commission, European Parliament) and for the Swedish and Finnish Governments.

† Jonas Malmberg is a Professor of Labour Law at the National Institute for Working Life, Sweden. He is an expert in Nordic and European Labour Law and has for instance published 'Effective Enforcment of EC Labour Law' (Kluwer 2003), 'Stability and Change in Nordic Labour Law' (Scandinavian Studies in Law vol 43) and 'The Evolution of Labour Law in Sweden and Finland'. He has been an expert of several state comittees in Sweden and for the European Commission.

the field of equal opportunities (the Equal Pay Directive 75/117/EEC; and the Equal Treatment Directive 76/207/EEC, subsequently amended by Directive 2002/73/EC) and three Directives on employee rights in the event of company restructuring (the Collective Redundancies Directive 75/129/EEC, subsequently repealed by consolidated Directive 98/59/EC; the Transfer of Undertakings Directive 77/187/EEC, subsequently amended by Directive 98/50/EC and consolidated by Directive 2001/23/EC; and the Insolvency Directive 80/987/EEC, subsequently amended by Directive 2002/74/EC).

The preconditions for developing this social dimension of European cooperation had been created by the Treaty on EU that was signed in Maastricht on 7 February 1992. The Protocol on Social Policy annexed to the Maastricht Treaty enabled the United Kingdom to opt out from the more far-reaching cooperation in the social field, using Community institutions and procedures, which was envisaged for the then eleven other Member States under the Agreement on Social Policy signed by them and itself annexed to the Protocol. This Agreement gave the Community (or *de facto* eleven Member States) increased competence in the field of labour law. It also extended the range of measures that could be decided by qualified-majority voting. Furthermore, it recognized a formal role for the European social partners (that is trade unions and employers' organizations at EU level) as regards law-making in the field of labour law. In brief, the process known as social dialogue signifies that, before submitting proposals for new Directives, the Commission must first consult the social partners. The latter can then, if they so wish, take over the initiative from the Commission and themselves negotiate and conclude a collective agreement on the matter in hand. If they reach such an agreement, they can either request that it should be adopted as a Directive or decide that it is to be implemented 'in accordance with the procedures and practices specific to management and labour and the Member States'. From 1997 onwards, under the Treaty of Amsterdam, the whole of the Agreement on Social Policy was reincorporated into the EC Treaty. At the same time a new Title on Employment was also introduced, with the Nordic countries—particularly Sweden—playing an active part in its creation.

Thus, although during the negotiations on the accession of Sweden and Finland the scope of EU labour law was still somewhat limited, the foundations for the development of the social dimension had already been laid by the Agreement on Social Policy.

1 EXPECTATIONS PRIOR TO EU ACCESSION

For most of the time while the membership negotiations were in progress the political situation was relatively similar in Finland and Sweden. During the period 1991–1994 Sweden had a conservative-majority government led by Prime Minister Carl Bildt, while Finland had a conservative-majority government led by Prime Minister Esko Aho from 1991 to 1995. In both countries relations between the government and the trade union movement were extremely strained, and on the domestic-policy front there were numerous conflict-prone issues relating more particularly to labour law.

In both cases it was clear from an early stage that the question of EU membership was to be settled through a referendum. It was also clear that a referendum was unlikely to yield a 'yes' vote unless strong union backing for membership could be mobilized. This explains why the issue of the EU's social dimension—labour law and the labour market, equal opportunities and social policy—featured in the membership negotiations with what was perhaps disproportionate prominence, and why both negotiators and government exhibited keen awareness of union wishes during this stage.[1]

The official perception in both Finland and Sweden was, quite justifiably, that the EU was at a dynamic stage as regards labour law. It was also felt that things had not yet progressed all that far and that there were unlikely to be any problems in adapting their own more highly developed national systems of labour law to the requirements of Community law.

In *Sweden* one aspect that attracted considerable interest was the feasibility of 'safeguarding the Swedish model of industrial relations in the context of EU integration'.[2] Probably the main concern in this respect was the feasibility of regulating matters by means of collective bargaining in preference to legislation. The central thrust of efforts from the Swedish side was to ensure the possibility of implementing EU Directives in the field of labour law through collective agreements rather than through legislation. There was broad consensus on this point, both among the political parties and among the social partners.[3]

The issue received early attention during the membership negotiations themselves. In an exchange of letters between Sweden and the Commission the competent Commissioner at the time, Pádraig Flynn, expounded his view on the implications of the Agreement on Social Policy for the Swedish model of industrial relations. Commissioner Flynn pointed out that matters relating to pay, the right of association and the right to strike or to impose lockouts were expressly excluded from the scope of the Agreement. He also emphasized that the Agreement resembled the prevailing Swedish system in so far as it provided for the possibility of allowing European-level collective agreements to take the place of legislation. In short, he indicated that the Agreement did not call for any

[1] This is the background underlying the following statement made by Sweden's EC Minister Ulf Dinkelspiel in Brussels on 1 February 1993 in a speech on the starting-points for the Swedish accession negotiations:

> We welcome the Protocol on Social Policy annexed to the Treaty on European Union, including the greater role envisaged for the social partners in the elaboration and implementation of common measures in the area of the labour market. We assume that this signifies the recognition of Swedish collective agreements as an adequate means of implementing EC Directives.

[2] Bill, Proposition 1994/95: 19, p 218.

[3] See, for example, EEA Committee Report 1992/93 EU1, p 124.

kind of change in Swedish practice as regards labour-market matters. In the final event, the Act of Accession accompanying the Treaty of Accession included an annexed Declaration by Sweden on social policy, referring to this exchange of letters and stating that it had received assurances with regard to Swedish practice in labour-market matters and notably the system of determining conditions of work in collective agreements between the social partners.

The debate in *Finland* was similar to that in Sweden except that there were not the same fears of the collective-bargaining system potentially being undermined, because from 1971 onwards Finland had introduced the system whereby certain collective agreements have *erga omnes* applicability—originally under the 1970 Contracts of Employment Act (*Työsopimuslaki*) and nowadays under chapter 2 section 7 of the new Contracts of Employment Act (adopted in 2001 as Law No 55/2001), even non-organized employers must observe the minimum terms and conditions of employment laid down in the national collective agreement considered to be representative in the industry or profession concerned.

In a way, the membership negotiations actually came to the rescue of the trade union movement in the early 1990s in terms of legal policy. During the deep economic recession in which Finland was plunged at the start of the 1990s many employers were calling for the system of *erga omnes* applicability to be abolished on the grounds that it prevented small businesses from lowering wages and thereby surviving the recession. However, criticisms levelled against the system petered out somewhat when it emerged that the system was mirrored in a number of countries of continental Europe and that it could serve as a viable instrument for the implementation of EU legislation.

2 NATIONAL INFLUENCE ON EU LEGISLATION

2.1 General

The paradoxical starting-point of EU cooperation is that, while in both Finland and Sweden there is support for the idea of exerting an influence, in practice 'influence' often appears to mean no more than warding off any EU rules that might entail changing something in their own systems of national legislation. Neither Finland nor Sweden is, however, unique in this respect. Most Member States are engaged in 'selling' a form of harmonization whereby individual countries are able to keep their own system intact and change as little as possible.

The Member States exert an influence on EU legislation through the various formal channels and at various stages in the legislative process. This takes place, firstly, through consultation with the Commission and its working bodies before it puts forward its proposals. There is a widespread perception that since 1995 the Directorate-General for Employment and Social Affairs, the department within the Commission responsible for Directives in the field of labour law, has acquired both a good knowledge of Nordic labour markets and labour-law traditions and an understanding of the great importance that is attached to the latter in the Nordic countries, whereas in other parts of the Commission there appears to be both less knowledge of and less understanding of those traditions. National governments also exert an influence in the working groups of the Council of Ministers and during negotiations within the Council on proposals actually put forward by the Commission.

In addition to these channels, there are a number of other ways in which influence can also be exerted. One example is the possibility of instituting legal proceedings before the ECJ for the annulment of an EU act on the ground that the EU is not competent to legislate on the matter in hand. Although such measures are rarely resorted to, in 2002 Finland brought an action against the European Parliament and the Council for the partial annulment of Directive 2002/15/EC on the organization of the working time of persons performing mobile road transport activities, in so far as it relates to drivers who are self-employed persons. Spain also brought a similar action challenging the same Directive. Finland submitted that neither Article 71 EC nor Article 137(2) EC constitutes a sufficient legal basis for the Community to adopt rules applying to self-employed drivers. Not entirely surprisingly, however, Finland lost the case.[4]

Where legislation takes place by the collective route, through European-level agreements concluded by the social partners, it is the national confederations of trade union and employers' organizations that are able to exert influence, via their respective European organizations. Here, the Finnish and Swedish social partners on both sides have participated actively in the negotiating process and also contributed to the development of systematic rules of the game on the conduct of that process with proper recognition of their negotiating mandate, etc.[5]

2.2 Sweden

Preservation of the Swedish model was also at the heart of the debate on how Sweden was to act within the framework of European cooperation. At the time when the EEA Agreement was being concluded, the Social Democratic government then in power stressed that Sweden should work towards the development of the social dimension.[6] The conservative government which succeeded it, and which had done the preparatory work leading up to the overarching legislation giving rise to Sweden's accession to the Union, was more cautious on this point. It emphasized that membership gave increased opportunities for playing an active part and influencing Community legislation in this field, and the importance of

[4] See the ECJ judgment in Joined Cases C-184/02 and C-223/02 *Spain and Finland v Parliament and Council* [2004] ECR I-7789.

[5] SK Andersen (ed) *EU og det nordiske spil om lov og aftale* SALTSA Report No 2:2003 (Stockholm, 2003), p 22 *et seq*.

[6] See, for example, EEA Committee Report already cited (n 3 above), p 113.

safeguarding the Swedish model.[7] The same thinking was reiterated when the Social Democratic government that came into power in 1994 spelled out Sweden's EU strategy in the field of labour law. The overall aim was stated to be one of safeguarding the Swedish model of industrial relations and ensuring that the social partners and collective bargaining continue to have a meaningful role in the labour market. The government also specified, among other things, that Sweden would endeavour to advocate the incorporation of semi-discretionary rules in Directives as a means of enabling each country to implement Directives in whatever manner is natural for it and to indicate the possibilities of taking industrial action.[8]

Our general impression is that since Sweden's accession to the EU the government has consistently followed a line of promoting the development of the EU's social dimension while at the same time safeguarding the Swedish model. One example is provided by the Information and Consultation Directive (2002/14/EC), on which political agreement was arrived at in June 2001 during the Swedish presidency. In principle, the Swedish government supported the Commission's Proposal for the Directive during the negotiations within the Council of Ministers. However, one reservation shaping the government's stance was that in point of fact Sweden's 1976 Co-Determination Act (*Medbestämmandelagen* (MBL))[9] and other provisions in force already meet all existing needs for information and consultation within businesses. Another reservation was that the often differing traditions and practice of the various individual countries had to be borne in mind when drafting the Directive. This was particularly true as regards taking account of collective agreements between the social partners. These considerations led Sweden to oppose the inclusion in the Directive of a proposed provision whereby the legal effect of any decision taken by the employer without due consultation was to be postponed indefinitely, which was thought to be alien to Swedish labour law. In the event, the final version of the Directive contained no such provision.

2.3 Finland

Throughout the period since its accession, Finland's lines of approach to the EU have been stamped by a remarkable degree of consensus. The main focus of efforts in Finland has been to ensure that as regards both the drafting and the implementation of EU legislation a joint position is arrived at, as far as possible, in tripartite negotiations between the social partners and the government.

[7] Bill already cited (see n 2 above), p 218.

[8] 'Arbete i Europa', Departmental Report Ds 1995:64.

[9] Abbreviated title commonly used (as are therefore the initials MBL) for the 1976 Act on Employee Consultation and Participation in Working Life. The widely accepted English name 'Co-Determination Act' is, however, misleading in that it suggests equivalence to German-type *Mitbestimmung*, which is not the case.

Efforts have also been made to involve the Finnish Parliament in the drafting process.

This consensual starting-point, together with the fact that during the period 1995–2003 Finland had a 'great' coalition government that included both the Social Democratic Party and the Conservative Party (Kokoomus in Finland), may explain why Finland's activities were devoted more to seeking to reconcile disagreements between other countries than to forcefully or actively pursuing initiatives or issues of its own.

However, EU membership appears to have prompted the central trade union and employers' confederations in Finland to intensify their cooperation, and the extensive national programme of legislation carried out in the field of labour law has to a certain extent striven to take account of and anticipate EU legislation. Examples of this include the legislation on personal privacy in working life and the regulation of the hiring-out of labour.

Finland has taken a relatively positive stance towards granting the EU increased competence in labour-law matters. At the most recent Intergovernmental Conference one of the lines pursued was that the usual legislative procedure, whereby a qualified-majority decision is sufficient for an act to be adopted, could be extended to the areas of job security and cooperation at workplace level.[10]

3 CHANGES IN NATIONAL LEGISLATION AND COLLECTIVE AGREEMENTS

3.1 Legislation

3.1.1 Introduction

In the mid-1930s the view became established in Sweden that regulation of the labour market was a matter of joint responsibility for the social partners themselves and that the state should refrain from intervening by passing legislation in this field. Over the next few decades this apportionment of roles was accepted by both the Parliament and the social partners. Such labour legislation as was adopted was modest in scope and chiefly aimed at ironing out differences in the treatment of different groups of employees as regards aspects including annual holidays and working hours, while by contrast numerous issues such as employee participation in decision-making through works councils, and a certain degree of employment protection, were the subject of regulation by collective agreement. From the start of the 1970s onwards there was an abrupt change of direction, with the former lack of intervention in the field of labour law by

[10] See Report of the Cabinet to Parliament on the outcome of the Convention and preparations for the Intergovernmental Conference, SRR 2/2003, p 70.

the government authorities being replaced by the adoption of a lengthy series of new laws. The most important of these were the 1974 Employment Protection Act (the *Lagen om Anställningsskydd* (LAS), since replaced by a 1982 version) and the 1976 Co-Determination Act (the MBL see note 10 above). The implementation of this new legislation led to considerably reduced opportunities for cooperation and the joint assumption of responsibility by the social partners themselves, and remains controversial to this day. The Employment Protection Act has, for example, been the subject of five Government Committees. Nevertheless, the labour legislation of the 1970s is still essentially unchanged.

Since the mid-1990s yet another lengthy series of legislative provisions in the field of labour law has been adopted. The main triggering factor for this 'second wave of legislation' has been Sweden's membership of the EU.[11]

In the case of Finland, the state has traditionally played a dominant role in the labour market and there is no equivalence with the tradition of self-regulation that is characteristic of Denmark and Sweden. This means that in terms of legislation Finland is closer to continental Europe, with a special Act on the individual contract of employment (*Työsopimuslaki*) and mandatory legal rules on the *erga omnes* applicability of collective agreements.

For a long time, industrial relations in Finland were shaped by the competitive relationship that prevailed between the Communists and the Social Democrats within the labour movement. It was not until the 1970s that Finland adopted something resembling the Nordic model of industrial relations.[12]

In Finland too, joining the EU has left its mark on the development of labour law. The implementation of EU labour law has, however, been accompanied by a systematic modernization of Finnish labour law taking place in parallel. The Working Time Act (*Työaikalaki*), Health and Safety Act (*Työturvallisuuslaki*), Company Medical Service Act (*Työterveyshuoltolaki*) and Contracts of Employment Act (*Työsopimuslaki*) have all been renewed. And more recently, a Bill proposing a new Annual Holidays Act (*Vuosilomalaki*)[13] has been debated by the Finnish Parliament, while the Cooperation Act (*Yhteistoimintalaki*), which regulates employee participation in decision-making at workplace level, is undergoing total revision within a specially appointed committee. However, this programme of reform signifies little that is fundamentally new; it demonstrates, rather, that the collective bargaining system is functioning effectively.

In many cases adaptation to the EU has constituted a natural part of the cooperation described above. When the new Contracts of Employment Act came into force in 2001 it introduced a number of EU-based rules, and in several respects the Bill proposing the new Annual Holidays Act was designed to meet

[11] R Fahlbeck 'Lex Laboris—Quo Vadis? The Swedish Experience' in R Blanpain & M Weiss (eds) *Changing Industrial Relations and Modernisation of Labour Law. Liber Amicorum in Honour of Professor Marco Biagi* (The Hague/London/New York, Kluwer Law International, 2003), pp 127–38 at p 128.

[12] See N Bruun *et al*, *The Nordic Labour Relations Model* (Dartmouth, Aldershot, 1990) p 8.

[13] Government Bill Reg. proposition 283/2004. The Act came into force on 1 April 2005 (Law 162/2005).

EU requirements regarding the equal treatment of various categories of employee (part-time workers, etc).

3.1.2 Increased importance of fundamental rights

The most striking indication of the Europeanization of their respective legal orders since the 1980s is the new status nowadays accorded to fundamental rights in both Finland and Sweden.

Traditionally, fundamental rights have been upheld in Europe in Conventions concluded by the Council of Europe, among which the 1950 European Convention for the protection of Human Rights and Fundamental Freedoms (also known as the European Convention on Human Rights (ECHR)) has been by far the most significant. A number of important social rights are also contained in the Council of Europe's 1961 European Social Charter, as revised in 1996.

Although within the EU itself fundamental rights have not as yet been explicitly incorporated in the Treaty, they have been accorded great importance in the case-law of the ECJ. For one thing, the Court has referred to the constitutional traditions common to the Member States as representing a relevant source of law and, furthermore, relied on international Conventions that have been ratified by all of the Member States, especially the ECHR. Next, certain Treaty provisions such as Article 141, which recognizes the principle of equal pay for men and women, have gradually taken on something of the nature of fundamental rights.

For many years there has been an active body of opinion within the EU advocating that fundamental rights should be explicitly guaranteed under the Treaty. In 1989 approval of a Community Charter of Fundamental Social Rights of Workers was successfully achieved in the form of a non-binding solemn proclamation. The Maastricht Treaty introduced a special Article F requiring the Union to respect fundamental rights, as guaranteed by the ECHR and as they result from the constitutional traditions common to the Member States, as general principles of Community law. These texts were given added authority in the Treaty of Amsterdam. Then in 2000 a special EU Charter of Fundamental Rights was adopted in the form of a separate declaratory instrument. The Charter contains a number of pertinent fundamental rights relating to social and labour-law matters. The Member States in 2004 proposed that the Charter should be made an integral part of the new EU Constitution. However, after the referendum in France and the Netherlands in 2005 it seems clear that the new Constitution will not be ratified.

As in many other European countries, the importance of fundamental rights has also increased at national level in both Finland and Sweden.[14]

[14] See, for example, S Sciarra (ed) *The Evolution of Labour Law (1992–2003)* (2004) Available at: http://europa.eu.int/comm/employment_social/labour_law/docs/generalreport_en.pdf

After having already incorporated the ECHR into domestic law in 1990, *Finland* carried out a constitutional reform in 1995 whereby a new chapter on fundamental rights was added to the original republican constitutional instrument of 1919 (*Suomen hallitusmuoto*) still in force at the time. These rights were then inserted, unchanged, into the entirely new Constitution which was adopted in 2000, with the result that in Finland a number of important fundamental rights are constitutionally safeguarded. The right to protection of private life, the right of assembly and freedom of association, the right to equality, the right to work and social security are all guaranteed by the Finnish Constitution. The right to work encompasses, inter alia, a rule prescribing that nobody may be dismissed from an employment relationship without just cause.

This reform has had several major consequences for labour law. For a start, the importance of the fundamental rights argument has increased considerably outside the state domain as well. The starting presumption is that fundamental rights can also be relied on as between individuals, although there is still some uncertainty as to the precise implications of this. In addition, the fact of being recognized as a fundamental right means that, as a general rule, exceptions to or restrictions of the right in question can be established only by parliamentary statute. Furthermore, fundamental rights are considered to have a not inconsiderable influence as an interpretative factor where judgment is being passed on situations in which constitutionally protected values are at stake.

In practice, the new Constitution has had an influence on the rules of labour law in several ways. Firstly, the protection against unjust dismissal for certain groups which do not fall within the purview of ordinary employment protection as laid down by statute has been regulated. Public servants at local-government level probably represent the most important group in this respect. Second, greater importance has been accorded to fundamental rights in the new Contracts of Employment Act, and a special Act on Personal Privacy Protection in Working Life (*Laki yksityisyyden suojasta työelämässä*) has been passed. Protection of the individual's private life and personal privacy and protection in relation to the processing of personal data are anchored in the Constitution and, like the right to protection against discrimination, come under the heading of human rights.

By international standards, the *Swedish Constitution* has been of remarkably little significance in the field of labour law, but a somewhat changed approach can perhaps be detected in more recent case-law. Under chapter 2 section 17 of the Instrument of Government (*Regeringsformen*, the most important of the legal instruments which make up Sweden's Constitution) trade-unions and employers and employers' organizations enjoy the right to take industrial action, failing any provision to the contrary laid down by law or agreement. In Labour Court judgment AD 46/2003 the Court took the view that this provision prohibits it, as a matter of principle, from introducing via its case-law any restrictions on the right to take industrial action which are not authorized by law or agreement. This judgment may be contrasted with an earlier one (AD 120/1989) whereby the Labour Court upheld certain restrictions on the right to take industrial action in circumstances not covered by a valid collective agreement, without any discussion of the import of the relevant constitutional provision. The importance of fundamental rights has, obviously, increased as a result of the incorporation of the ECHR into Swedish law in 1994. One of the main motives for doing this was Sweden's forthcoming EU membership. As already mentioned, the ECHR forms part of EU law and as such must axiomatically be applied by Swedish courts in the application of EU law. Explicitly incorporating the Convention into domestic law avoided the situation whereby the courts would have had to apply it only in cases where they were ruling on EU law but not in other cases.[15] In its case-law the Labour Court has taken the view that the ECHR can, as a matter of principle, be relied on in disputes between individuals. The Convention has had a measure of influence as regards, inter alia, the negative freedom of association (ie the right of an employee or employer not to belong to a trade union or employers' organization) and personal privacy in working life—see as respective examples Labour Court judgments AD 17/1998 and AD 3/2001. In the legislative context, the fact that a particular right has fundamental-right status has frequently served to justify tight legislation. This is particularly true in the area of discrimination.[16]

3.1.3 Direct EU influence on national legislation

EU labour law is mainly laid down in the form of Directives. Generally speaking, Directives are not directly applicable in the Member States until the latter have adopted such laws or taken such measures as are necessary to ensure that the provisions of the Directive in question have been transposed into national law. Both before and after accession to the EU, a number of amendments have been made to existing laws and several special laws have been adopted in order to implement EU Directives in Finland and Sweden. The following table gives an overview of the legislative changes that have been carried out pursuant to EU Directives in the field of labour law.

It can be seen from the table (below) that EU Directives in the field of labour have occasioned extensive legislative changes at national level—and this without even counting changes made as a result of EU rules on freedom of movement for workers and the comprehensive regulation of health and safety at work, which have not been included. It is no exaggeration to say that in both countries EU-based legislation has dominated the legislative agenda during this period, although the impression is more striking in the case of Sweden than in Finland. The picture also demonstrates that the EU, in its law-making capacity, was very

[15] I Cameron *Introduction to the European Convention on Human Rights* (4th edn, Iustus, Uppsala, 2002), p 155.

[16] See, for example, Bill, Proposition 1997/98:177, p 119.

Legislation to implement EU labour-law Directives

Major EU Directive	*Sweden*	*Finland*
Article 141 EC (ex 119) and the Equal Pay Directive (75/117/EEC)	Amendments to the Equal Opportunities Act in, inter alia, 1991 and 2000	Amendments to the Equality Act (Law 86/609, amended 1995/196 and 2005/232)
Equal Treatment Directive (76/207/EEC, as amended by 2002/73/EC)	Amendments to the Equal Opportunities Act in, inter alia, 1991 and 2000	Amendments to the Equality Act (Law 1995/196)
Collective Redundancies Directive (75/129/EEC, as amended by 92/56/EEC and consolidated in 98/59/EC)	Amendments to the MBL and the Employment Promotion Act	Amendments to the Contracts of Employment Act (new Law 2001/55) and the Cooperation Act
Transfer of Undertakings Directive (77/187/EEC, as amended by 98/50/EC and consolidated in 2001/23/EC)	Amendments to the MBL and the Employment Protection Act	Amendments to the Contracts of Employment Act and the Cooperation Act
Insolvency Directive (80/987/EEC, as amended by 2002/74/EC)	Amendments to the Pay Guarantee Act	Amendments to the Pay Guarantee Act (new Law 1998/866)
Proof of Employment Contract Directive (91/533/EEC)	Amendments to the Employment Protection Act	Amendments to the Contracts of Employment Act
Working Time Directive (93/104/EC)	Amendments to the Working Time Act in 1996 and 2005	New Working Time Act (Law 1996/605)
European Works Council Directive (94/45/EC) 1996/614)	European Works Councils Act (Law 1996:359)	Amendments to the Cooperation Act (Law
Parental Leave Directive (96/34/EC)	Entitlement to Time Off for Urgent Family Reasons Act (Law 1998:209)	New chapter inserted in the Contracts of Employment Act
Posted Workers Directive (96/71/EC)	Posting of Workers Act (Law 1999:678)	Posted Workers Act (Law 1999/1146)
Burden of Proof Directive (97/80/EC)	Amendments to the Equal Opportunities Act	No changes
Part-Time Work Directive (97/81/EC)	Act Prohibiting Discrimination Against Part-Time Workers and Fixed-Term Workers (Law 2002:293)	New rule inserted in the Contracts of Employment Act (Law 2001/55)
Fixed-Term Work Directive (99/70/EC)	Act Prohibiting Discrimination Against Part-Time Workers and Fixed-Term Workers (Law 2002:293)	New rule inserted in the Contracts of Employment Act (Law 2001/55)

Racial or Ethnic Discrimination Directive (2000/43/EC)	Amendments to the 1999 Act Against Ethnic Discrimination in Working Life and introduction of the Act Prohibiting Discrimination (Law 2003:307)	Equal Treatment Act (Law 2004/21)
General Framework for Equal Treatment Directive (2000/78/EC)	Amendments to the 1999 Act Prohibiting Discrimination in Working Life based on Sexual Orientation and the 1999 Act Prohibiting Discrim ination Against Disabled Persons in Working Life, and introduction of the Act Prohibiting Discrimination (Law 2003:307)	Equal Treatment Act (Law 2004/21)
Employee Involvement in the European Company (SE) Directive (2001/86/EC)	Employee Involvement in the European Company (SE) Act (Law 2004:559)	Employee Involvement in the European Company (SE) Act (Law 2004/758)
Information and Consultation Directive (2002/14/EC)	Amendments to the MBL	Amendments to the Cooperation Act

much focused on something other than the type of measures known as 'soft law'.

In our opinion the relevant Directives have, for the most part, been implemented correctly. One exception is the implementation of the Working Time Directive in Sweden. The Directive was supposed to have been implemented in 1996. In setting about its implementation in Sweden, in 1995 a Working Time Committee prepared a radical overhaul of the Working Time Act (*Arbetstidslagen*). Pending its final report, the Committee presented a proposal for the provisional implementation of the Directive. In its interim report the Committee started from the presumption that, although certain differences existed, the Act guaranteed employees just as good protection as the Directive; it suggested an amendment to the Act (which was duly introduced) whereby no collective agreement or administrative decision granting exemption from the Act's provisions may have the effect of creating conditions less favourable to employees than the minimum standards laid down in the Directive. In its final report, which contained a proposal for a completely new Working Time Act, the Committee suggested further changes to the system of regulation in the light of the Directive. This proposal, however, was never carried through, mainly owing to political disagreement on issues other than implementation of the Working Time Directive. As a result, the amendment to the Act which in 1996 was intended to be purely provisional became permanent. In 1996 the European Commission opened infringement proceedings against Sweden for failure to comply adequately with the Directive. In June 2004 the Commission then brought an action against Sweden before the ECJ, submitting in its application that the Directive's rules on the daily rest period (ie the unbroken period of rest between successive working days) and working hours for night work had not been incorporated and that the provision on maximum weekly working hours had been incorporated misleadingly. Sweden conceded the Commission's case, and at the same time the government presented a Bill to Parliament on amendments to the Working Time Act effecting a 'more explicit implementation of the EU's Working Time Directive'.[17] The amendments to the Act were adopted in February 2005. In May 2005 the ECJ declared that Sweden had failed to fulfil its obligations under the Directive.[18]

In the case of Finland, an obvious example of failure to comply explicitly with a Directive can be found in the implementation of the European Works Council Directive. The Directive was transposed into Finnish law by inserting a few new paragraphs in Finland's Cooperation Act (*Yhteistoimintalaki*).[19] The actual process of 'implementation' took place in the Act's *travaux préparatoires*, where explanations were given of what was laid down in the Directive and what were seen as its implications. The formal aim of the total revision of the Cooperation Act currently under way is to 'spell out' the process of implementation. In practice, however, most issues relating to European Works Councils have probably been resolved through negotiation and the lack of explicit implementation has therefore not really had any serious consequences.

3.1.4 Interplay between EU level and national level

The fact that the bulk of legislative activity in the field of labour law has been about implementing EU Directives by no means implies that the national legislatures have not influenced the direction followed by the legislation in question.

Firstly, instances can be found where changes to the law are a consequence not just of an adjustment to EU rules but also of a response to national political calls for tighter regulation. The most high-profile example is the way in which discrimination legislation has developed in Sweden. Since 1991 the provisions of the Equal Opportunities Act (*Jämställdhetslagen*) have been tightened on repeated occasions. In addition, statutory protection against discrimination has been widened to take in more grounds for discrimination: ethnic origin, disability and sexual orientation. Although this trend has been partly driven by the need to comply with EU law, in many cases the Swedish legislators have anticipated or gone further than those requirements—as witness the fact that

[17] Bill, Proposition 2003/04:180.

[18] Case C-287/04 *Commission v Kingdom of Sweden*, judgment of 25 May 2005 (unpublished).

[19] See Government Bill, Reg. proposition 99/1996.

Sweden's three statutes on discrimination on the grounds of ethnic origin, disability and sexual orientation were adopted prior to the corresponding EU Directives. There is also the point that the obligation to take active measures to promote equality which is laid down in the Equal Opportunities Act and the Act Against Ethnic Discrimination in Working Life (*Lagen om åtgärder mot diskriminering i arbetslivet på grund av etnisk tillhörighet, religion eller annan trosuppfattning*) has no equivalent at all in EU law. In one instance the Swedish legislature's endeavour to achieve gender equality has been deemed contrary to EU law.[20]

In Finland, the rules on the hiring-out of labour which were introduced in the Contracts of Employment Act in 2001, but on which we are still awaiting an EU Directive, can be regarded as a similar example.

Second, EU Directives allow national legislators quite considerable freedom in choosing precisely how they are to be implemented. To start with, this is because Directives in the field of labour law are normally confined to laying down purely minimum standards of employee protection and do not prevent individual Member States from adopting more far-reaching rules. They also leave 'gaps' to be filled in at national legislative level (as regards sanctions, for example). In addition, the more detailed purport of EU law is often unclear. This means that, failing any clarification provided by ECJ case-law, national legislators have the opportunity of interpreting and defining the content of EU law. Consequently, the legislative process whereby EU Directives are implemented encompasses not just 'application of the law' entailing the interpretation of EU law but also scope for national choices. It is not possible, in the context of the present report, to explore in more detail how this scope has actually been utilized by the Swedish and Finnish legislators.[21] One likely hypothesis, however, is that the tendency has been to encroach as little as possible on existing legislation, particularly as regards issues that can be said to relate to what is perceived as the Nordic model of industrial relations.

One instance that can be cited as an example of this strategy is the implementation of the Posted Workers Directive (96/71/EC), which took place in Sweden through the Posting of Workers Act (*Lagen 1999:678 om utstationering av arbetstagare*). One of the Directive's main objectives is to counteract social dumping, but the method it stipulates is different from that traditionally used in Sweden. Whereas the task of counteracting low-pay competition in Sweden has traditionally rested with the unions, the Directive is based on the notion that it is for the state to determine which rules are to apply to employees not directly covered by Swedish law or Swedish collective agreements. Against this background it is not surprising that in implementing the Directive the legislators opted for a relatively minimalist strategy, made particularly noticeable by the

[20] ECJ Case C-407/98 *Abrahamsson and Anderson v Fogelqvist* [2000] ECR I-5539 (concerning positive action in the appointment of university professors).

[21] Pernilla Lundblad, of the Arbetslivsinstitut, is currently engaged on a project dealing with this issue.

fact that they refrained from taking up the possibility of making Swedish collective agreements applicable to employees posted to Sweden (on the basis of Article 3(8) and 3(10) of the Directive), even though in the negotiations leading up to the adoption of the Directive Sweden had actively collaborated in ensuring the introduction of this possibility. In the statement of grounds one of the reasons cited was that the means used today by the social partners to counteract social dumping in Sweden, ie the conclusion (under threat of industrial action) of collective agreements with foreign employers, is sufficient to prevent social dumping in the Swedish labour market.[22]

3.1.5 Impact on individual and collective labour law

How has the implementation of Directives influenced labour legislation? It is primarily in the domain of individual labour law that implementation of the EU Directives relating to labour law has taken place. Sweden has witnessed the introduction of several special statutes to that end, namely the Entitlement to Time Off for Urgent Family Reasons Act (*Lagen 1998:209 om rätt till ledighet av trängande familjeskäl*), the Posting of Workers Act (*Lagen 1999:678 om utstationering av arbetstagare*) and the Act Prohibiting Discrimination Against Part-Time Workers and Fixed-Term Workers (*Lagen 2002:293 om förbud mot diskriminering av deltidsarbetande arbetstagare och arbetstagare med tidsbegränsad anställning*). In addition, the EU perspective has been a strong influencing factor in the revision of several key statutes such as the Equal Opportunities Act (*Jämställdhetslagen*) and the three anti-discrimination statutes of 1999. A number of amendments to the Employment Protection Act (LAS) have been occasioned by the Transfer of Undertakings Directive and the Proof of Employment Contract Directive. As a result of these legislative changes, a lengthy series of individual rights has been created that had no equivalent under previous law. In the case of Finland, corresponding regulation has been introduced predominantly in the Contracts of Employment Act (*Työsopimuslaki*) and the Equality Act (*Tasa-arvolaki*) and in addition a special Posted Workers Act (*Laki lähetetyistä työntekijöistä*) has been adopted.

Collective labour law has been affected by the changes only to a lesser degree. The Transfer of Undertakings Directive and the Collective Redundancies Directive contain rules on information and consultation. These entailed only marginal changes to the Swedish model of employee participation as provided for under the MBL. Although the existing Swedish provisions in this area were certainly on a level corresponding to the Directive's requirements, the process of implementation has to some extent resulted in a strengthening of employee participation in workplaces not covered by a collective agreement. The same can be said about the implementation of the Information and Consultation Directive.

[22] Government Committee SOU 1998:52, p 84 *ff*, especially p 90, and Bill, Proposition 1998/99:90, p 26 *et seq*.

Implementation of the European Works Council Directive has, on the other hand, brought increased opportunities for employee participation at international level.

3.1.6 *Indirect EU influence on legislation*

Alongside the impact inherent in the fact that Sweden and Finland have implemented actual labour-law Directives, what might be termed an indirect influence is also discernible where legislative measures which affect labour law have been motivated either by EU rules in other policy areas or as consequences of an integrated European market.

One example of this kind of indirect EU influence is to be found in the rules on public procurement, on which the question of how much room the rules on the award of contracts leave for social considerations has been the subject of an ongoing debate in Sweden ever since accession, and on which the legislature has also made certain cautious statements.[23]

Another such example can perhaps be inferred from the increased interest in wage formation displayed by the legislature. Issues relating to wage formation and industrial action have traditionally been seen mainly as the responsibility of the social partners themselves. During the 1980s and 1990s the process of wage formation failed to function satisfactorily. Sweden experienced higher nominal pay increases than other countries representing its trading partners and competitors, which drove up inflation and undermined real earnings. Despite pay rises of the order of 150 per cent, real earnings did not increase at all between 1980 and 1995. In order to protect the level of employment Sweden was forced into a series of devaluations, which in their turn drove up the rate of inflation. In 2000, with a view to improving the possibilities of combining moderate increases in real earnings with low unemployment and stable prices, new rules on mediation were introduced. These new rules can also be viewed as a preparatory measure leading up to Sweden's then projected participation in EMU.

3.2 EU impact on national collective agreements and collective bargaining systems

3.2.1 *General trend in the collective bargaining system*

Despite the fact that labour legislation has increased in volume, in both Finland and Sweden the key instrument for regulating pay and other terms and conditions of employment is still the collective agreement. In the case of Sweden,

[23] See, for example, Government Committee SOU 2001:31, 'Mera värde för pengarna'. Final Report of the Procurement Committee (2001), especially Annex 3, 'Sociala hänsyn vid offentlig upphandling', pp 441–57.

collective agreements contain virtually wall-to-wall regulation of the various issues that can arise in an employment relationship and it is estimated that a good 90 per cent of all employees are covered. Over the past few decades the major change in the collective bargaining system has been a greater degree of decentralization, manifested in two main ways. Firstly, a decline in the importance of negotiations between the trade union and employers' confederations at central national level. Second, a change in the content of national sectoral agreements, with a shift away from detailed regulation towards more of the nature of framework or procedural agreements leaving greater scope for regulation at local level.[24] In the latter case, regulation may take place between the individual employer and either local union representatives or directly with the employees concerned (possibly assisted by union representatives), and the issues which are nowadays handled at local level more frequently than was formerly the case typically include pay and working hours. Developments of this kind are probably most marked with regard to white-collar workers, and local bargaining is always subject to the peace obligation. This trend is regarded as having taken place quite independently of EU involvement. The same trend is also evident in Finland, although in terms of decentralization and pay determination it has not gone so far as it has in Sweden.

3.2.2 Direct consequences of labour-law Directives

There has been no really significant degree of change in the content of collective agreements as a direct consequence of EU Directives relating to labour law.

The only such Directives which have led directly to changes in existing agreements are probably the Part-Time Work Directive and the Fixed-Term Work Directive, which prohibit discrimination against part-time and fixed-term workers as reflected in their terms and conditions of employment.[25] In the Swedish labour market it was formerly common for collective agreements to prescribe differences in employment conditions between full-time and part-time workers in particular, but fixed-term workers were also subject to special treatment. As a corollary of the implementation of the two Directives, these agreements have been the subject of negotiations between the parties leading to substantially improved employment conditions for part-timers and those

[24] See K Ahlberg and N Bruun 'Sweden: Transition through collective bargaining' in (T Blanke and E Rose eds) *Collective Bargaining and Wages in Comparative Perspective. Germany, France, The Netherlands, Sweden and the United Kingdom* (Kluwer Law International, 2005) pp 117–143.

[25] It may be noted that these two Directives were first negotiated between the social partners at European level before being subsequently accorded legislative status. On the advent and content of the Fixed-Term Work Directive, see C Vigneau *et al Fixed-term work in the EU—A European Agreement against discrimination and abuse* (Arbetslivsinstitutet: Stockholm, 1999).

[26] Ahlberg, above, p 33 *ff*.

employed under fixed-term/temporary contracts.[26]

3.2.3 National implementation of EU Directives through collective agreements

As mentioned earlier, in the run-up to EU membership there was some debate surrounding the possibility of implementing Directives through collective agreements of the Swedish/Danish type. The central problem here is that it follows from previous ECJ case-law that, although collective agreements may be used as a means of implementing Directives, this presupposes that the agreements in question are applicable to all employees throughout the country—something which is not the case in Sweden and Denmark. At the time, Sweden concluded from an exchange of letters with Pádraig Flynn (see section 2 above) that it had been given guarantees that it would be possible to implement EU Directives through Swedish-type collective agreements. Just how legally tenable Flynn's guarantees are is a matter of controversy which will not be examined in detail here.[27]

Following earlier discussions on the possibility of the collective-agreement route as an alternative or complement to legislation in connection with implementation of the European Works Council Directive, when no such collective regulation materialized and legislation was adopted instead,[28] when it came to implementation of the Part-Time Work Directive and Fixed-Term Work Directive the Swedish government made strenuous efforts to persuade the social partners to conclude agreements on the matter. Yet again, however, no collective regulation materialized. Thus, despite the great weight placed by Sweden during the membership negotiations on the possibility of implementing Directive through collective agreements, this means of implementation has never once been tried, either with or without supplementary legislation.

It is perhaps apposite in this connection to draw a comparison with the situation in Denmark. During the 1990s a central and recurring theme in Danish labour-law debate was precisely that of how EU labour law should be incorporated into the Danish model. In the case of Directives relating to terms and conditions of employment, a procedure has evolved over the years whereby the social partners begin by concluding the collective agreements necessary in order to implement the Directive in question in their respective industries or professions. Then the legislators supplement these collectively agreed rules to ensure that the Directive also applies to workplaces not covered by collective bargaining. The notion that EU Directives can be implemented in Denmark through collective agreements alone, without supplementary legislation, nowadays seems to have been abandoned. Various legislative techniques have been used for this type of supplementary legislation. In a number of cases, such as implementation of the Working Time Directive and the Fixed-Term Work Directive,

[27] See, for example, B Nyström *EU och Arbetsrätten* (Stockholm, Norstedts, 2002), p 66 *ff.*
[28] Government Committee SOU 1995:115, p 27.

'semi-discretionary' legislation was used, ie laws which can be derogated from by collective agreement. This presupposes that the collective agreement concerned fulfils the Directive's requirements. A different technique was used for implementing the Part-Time Work Directive, where it was decided, instead, to adopt a special law under which major collective agreements were invested with *erga omnes* effect.[29] The way in which EU labour-law Directives have been implemented in Denmark means that, unlike what has been the case in Sweden, the social partners have been able to exert a strong joint influence on how the rules of labour law are shaped.

It may be asked what reason there is for opting to have Directives implemented by the social partners through collective agreements, possibly supplemented by legislation.

The most salient reason is that this system allows the social partners to gain control over how the rules are adjusted and applied. This brings us to a difference that can be pointed out between Denmark and Sweden. In Denmark, when the rules are incorporated through provisions in collective agreements disputes over their application can be settled via the 'industrial' (*fagretlige*) system, ie through lengthy negotiation procedures and, ultimately, by an industrial arbitration tribunal or the Labour Court. Disputes over interpretation of statute law, on the other hand, are dealt with by the ordinary courts, without any need to pass through preliminary negotiation procedures. In Sweden, things are different: disputes are handled via the Swedish equivalent of the 'industrial' system (ie collective negotiation on grievances and an action before the Labour Court) directly a dispute of rights arises between an employer and employee bound by the same collective agreement, irrespective of whether the dispute concerns a collective agreement, individual employment contract or statute. This means that the incentive for the social partners to conclude agreements is far greater in Denmark than it is in Sweden.

3.2.4 Collective agreements as a barrier against low-pay competition. Industrial action

The fact that any rules relating to pay and employment conditions give rise to costs for the employer is a fundamental problem in the field of labour law. Employers who apply lower levels of protection are able to gain competitive advantages as a result. It is also an accepted fact that the existence of employers who apply low levels of pay or protection makes it difficult for others to maintain or raise the level of protection for their own employees. In these circumstances, a key issue is how protective labour-law rules can be made applicable in a way that prevents certain employers from gaining competitive advantages by applying lower levels of protection.

In Europe there is a prevailing presumption that a standard floor of minimum

[29] See, for example, R Nielsen 'Europeanization of Nordic Labour Law' *Scandinavian Studies in Law* 43, 2002), p 51 *ff*.

labour standards must be maintained by all employers in a given industry or profession, regardless of whether they have concluded collective agreements or not. The methods used to achieve this vary, however. In some Member States there is legislation on minimum wages. In many Member States there are systems for extending collective agreement, making the general applicable or, in other words, giving them *erga omnes* effect.

In Sweden and Denmark there are neither systems for general applicable collective agreements nor any minimum wages regulation. Instead, another method is used which might be denominated the *autonomous collective agreements model*. According to this model it is de facto the responsibility of the trade unions to uphold a general level on wages and employment conditions. The trade unions try—where necessary, by threatening industrial action—to conclude collective agreement with national or foreign employers who do not belong to any employers' organization. If the outside or non-organised employer refuses to sign a collective agreement the normal procedure is that the trade union, which concludes agreements in the particular branch, will declare a boycott against the outside employer. The content of the boycott is that the members of the trade union shall refuse to be employed by the outside employer. To make the action more effective, the primary boycott is combined with sympathy (secondary) actions. These actions may be taken by the trade union itself, or by other trade unions. The sympathy actions are usually aiming at stopping deliveries to and from the outside employer. It is considered a legitimate trade union interest to ensure that a collective agreement covers all businesses in the industry or profession concerned. At the same time, there is a borderline where efforts to counter social dumping go beyond the aim of establishing a level playing-field for all businesses and turn into pure protectionism. Exactly where this borderline lies is, however, unclear.

In the autonomous collective agreements model an extensive right to take industrial action against employers who are outside the collective bargaining system is of key importance.

During the past decade it is possible to discern a certain shift in the apportionment of roles that has traditionally prevailed between legislators, courts and social partners as regards the scope of the right to take industrial action in situations not regulated by any collective agreement.

The right to take industrial action is constitutionally guaranteed in chapter 2 section 7 of the Instrument of Government. In accordance with this provision the right to take such action may be restricted by law or agreement. The principle statutory restriction is to be found in sections 41–2 of the MBL, dealing with the peace obligation which ensues from a collective agreement. There are only a few provisions on industrial action against employers not bound by a collective agreement. One such rule is the prohibition of industrial action against sole

[30] See, for example, Bills Proposition 1999/2000:32 and Proposition 1999/2000:AU5. For an overview of earlier debates, see Government Committee SOU 1988:49, p 151 *ff*.

traders and family businesses (section 41b of the MBL). Otherwise, despite repeated debates the legislators have refrained from specifying the limits to what industrial-action scenarios are permissible.[30] Nothing equivalent to the rules which exist in other countries stipulating that such action must be in support of an interest relating to a union's natural domain, or must be in reasonable proportion to the objective pursued, has been introduced. Ever since the 1930s the starting presumption of the legislators has been, rather, that it is primarily up to the social partners themselves to assume responsibility for seeing that the right to take industrial action is not abused. In the last resort, however, the government authorities have reserved their right to intervene legislatively in order to bring ongoing industrial action to an end, although very little use has been made of this possibility.

Sweden's Labour Court has also—with some exceptions[31]—been markedly cautious about developing principles which restrict the possibilities for the social partners to take industrial action in situations not regulated by any collective agreement.[32] This line is of course consistent both with the constitutional rule laid down in the Instrument of Government that the right to take industrial action may be restricted only by law or collective agreement and with the apportionment of roles between legislature and social partners as expressed by the legislators. It is in striking contrast to the 'peace obligation-friendly' line traditionally upheld by the Court where a collective agreement is in force between the parties.[33]

In Finland, the Supreme Court has cautiously introduced in its case-law what is referred to as a general peace obligation, signifying that forms of industrial action which have an unlawful purpose or are conducted in a manner deliberately intended to cause harm to persons or property can be prohibited even during an interval without a collective agreement (eg when a previous agreement has expired before a new one has been concluded). The penalty in such cases can be liability in damages. Otherwise, it is predominantly industrial action directed against a current agreement that is prohibited during the agreement's period of validity.

To give the impression that instances of industrial action which are not specifically prohibited are actually accepted in Sweden would be misleading. Historically speaking, it is more accurate to say that the legislature has refrained from intervening so long as the social partners do not abuse the trust it has

[31] See, in particular, Labour Court judgment AD 120/1989.

[32] See, for example, Labour Court judgments AD 113/1986, AD 143/1989 and AD 15/1993. See also AD 94/1980, where the Court ruled in favour of an employer withholding due pay as a form of industrial action. The judgment prompted the Swedish Parliament to prohibit such action (s 41a of the MBL). The Minister stressed that this should not be seen as a departure from the principle that the detailed control of industrial action is a matter for the social partners (Bill Proposition 1983/84:165, p 14 *ff*).

[33] See, for example, Labour Court judgment AD 15/1980. See also, for example, H Göransson 'Hidden Clauses in Collective Agreements: The Case Law of the Swedish Labour Court' *Scandinavian Studies in Law 34* 1990, p 93–113.

placed in them. It is therefore a question of self-regulation of the type that also exists in other areas of society. And it should be emphasized that their track record shows that the social partners have essentially lived up to that trust. There are a number of arrangements in place aimed at preventing abuse of the right to take industrial action, and in this respect we need only point to the Saltsjöbaden Agreement between the Confederation of Swedish Enterprise (SAF) and the LO (the Swedish Confederation of Trade Unions), which restricts certain types of industrial action, and to the fact that in accordance with the internal rules of sectoral trade union or employers' organizations the right to decide to take industrial action is normally reserved to the central executive of the organization concerned.[34] In Finland, too, there is collectively agreed regulation of the rules of the game in dispute situations.

Thus, both in Sweden and in Finland the social partners have in the past *de facto* enjoyed a kind of immunity against legal control of the use of industrial action. The Europeanization of labour law has to some extent pierced this immunity.

Article 11 of the ECHR implies certain, albeit narrow, restrictions on the right to take industrial action against a non-organized employer. The Article in question protects not only the positive freedom of association but also, to some extent, the negative freedom of association. For example, industrial action taken for the direct purpose of pressurizing an employer into joining an employers' organization is probably contrary to the Convention and hence to Swedish and Finnish law.[35] The issue may be the subject of further judicial scrutiny.

Further, there are for the time being two cases pending before the ECJ which concerns the relationship between industrial actions and EU law.

The first one of these cases has its roots in Sweden and concerns industrial action undertaken in Vaxholm, a place situated not far from Stockholm. Accordingly it has been called '*the Vaxholm case*' or '*the Laval-case*'. In the case a Swedish trade union has taken industrial action against the Latvian company *Laval un partneri Ltd* which hires out labour from Latvia to companies carrying out work in Sweden. Another Swedish trade union has taken secondary action against the Latvian company. The Company is not bound by a collective agreement with any of the Swedish trade unions. It is, however, bound by two collective agreements with a Latvian trade union. The dispute in the case concerns the issue of whether the industrial action and supporting secondary action taken against the Company is lawful or not. The Company has claimed that the industrial action mentioned is in breach of Community law, which the employee parties dispute. On the 15 September 2005 the Swedish Labour Court made a reference for a preliminary ruling to the ECJ (ECJ case C-341/05). The reference by the Labour Court consists of two rather complex questions, which concern

[34] See also, for example, Government Committee SOU 1984:19, p 9 *ff*.

[35] ECtHR decisions of 25 April 1996 and 30 July 1998 in the case between Torgny Gustafsson and Sweden, and Labour Court judgment AD 17/1998.

three problem areas. The first one has to do with the relationship between the EC Treaty provisions on free movement of services and its relationship to the right or freedom to undertake industrial action. The second one is related to the Posting of workers Directive and its relevance for the present case. The third issue at stake is whether section 42(3) and other provisions of the 1991 amendment to the MBL popularly known as *Lex Britannia* may be regarded as contravening the EC Treaty rules on, in particular, the free movement of services according to the EC Treaty. A Labour Court judgment of 1989 (AD 120/1989) established that industrial action aimed at *replacing or altering an existing collective agreement* applicable to a given workplace is prohibited even if those taking the action are not bound by the agreement concerned (the Britannia principle, so called because the case involved M/S Britannia, a ship flying a flag of convenience). Through the subsequent amendment to section 42 of the MBL introduced in 1991, the legislature then made it clear that this principle does not hold good where a union takes industrial action in connection with employment relationships to which the MBL is not directly applicable, eg in cases where a foreign company sends individuals to perform work temporarily in Sweden. In these circumstances a Swedish union may, notwithstanding the Britannia principle, take industrial action in order to replace the collective agreement already concluded by the employer. The effect of *Lex Britannia* is in practice that the prohibition to take industrial action according to the Britannia Principle is not applicable to industrial action against a foreign undertaking which is temporarily active in Sweden and which brings its own workforce.

The second case—the *Viking case* (C-438/05)—is related to the maritime sector and concerns the possible future reflagging of the ship 'Rosella' owned by the Finnish company Viking Ltd from Finnish to Estonian flag. Viking had brought legal action in London against the International Transport Federation and the Finnish Seamen's Union in order to get an injunction according to which all kind of industrial action that might have an adverse impact on the reflagging process and the replacing of the Finnish crew with a (cheaper) Estonian crew is forbidden by EU-law especially the right to free movement for workers and the freedom of establishment. Viking succeeded in getting an injunction in the London first instance commercial court in June 2005, but the judgment was set aside by the appeal court in November 2005, which referred a series of questions of legal interpretation of EC law to the ECJ.

In these cases the ECJ will have to address the question on how to balance the free movement of services and the right of establishment, on the one hand, and the right to industrial action, on the other. The criteria the Court will lay down for this balancing of interests will potentially have a huge impact for the future of not only the Nordic but also the European model of industrial relations.

All this means that the immunity against legal control formerly enjoyed by the social partners has been pierced to a certain extent. In the final analysis, however, any such legal control is exercised neither by the Swedish Parliament or by the Swedish Labour Court, but by the ECJ in Luxembourg and the European

Court of Human Rights (ECtHR) in Strasbourg. That being so, it must nevertheless be stressed here that the case-law emanating to date from these two courts does not gainsay the notion that it is a legitimate function of the unions to counter social dumping by keeping a close watch on employment conditions in the labour market as a whole and not merely to look after their own members' interests directly by influencing the latter's terms and conditions of employment. The supervisory role of the courts is deemed to be confined to ensuring that the unions do not abuse the powers which they have traditionally enjoyed in this respect.

4 THE COURTS AND EU LABOUR LAW[36]

4.1 Interpretation and application of implemented Directives. EU-consistent interpretation

During the first ten years the impact of EU law on Finnish and Swedish labour law as it appears from its application by the courts has been more a matter of theory than of practice. The labour-law system of dispute resolution has, for the most part, been preserved intact and has continued to survive as it was before, safely unaffected by the changed scenario of sources of law and complicated structure of legal remedies. When we calculate the proportion of EU-relevant cases in the Swedish and Finnish Labour Courts and other national courts, they represent only a small fraction of the total corpus of case-law produced during the period.

The main area in which Finnish and Swedish courts have come into contact with EU labour law is in the interpretation and application of national legislation that implements labour-law Directives. When applying such national law, the courts are obliged to interpret it in the light of the wording and purpose of the Directive concerned in order to achieve the result envisaged in the Directive ('EU-consistent interpretation').

In Sweden, it is primarily the Labour Court that has been called on to interpret and apply EU labour law. The Court has examined issues relating to the EU Directives in some 40 cases. The Labour Court has placed great weight on the interpretation given to the underlying Directives in the case-law of the ECJ. This has given the range of legal materials it uses as sources of law a new and more international slant. Its judgments frequently contain detailed accounts and analyses of ECJ case-law.

In Finland, the jurisdiction of the Labour Court is more limited than that of its counterpart in Sweden. The Finnish Labour Court is not competent to apply

[36] This section constitutes a shortened version of N Bruun & J Malmberg 'Finska och svenska domstolar som arbetsrättsliga gemenskapsdomstolar' in B Nyström *et al* (eds) *Liber amicorum* (Lund, Reinhold Fahlbeck, Juristförlaget, 2005).

either the Contracts of Employment Act (*Työsopimuslaki*, Law 2001/55) or the Equality Act (*Tasa-arvolaki*, Law 1986/609). The EU labour-law dimension in the work of the Finnish Labour Court arises predominantly in the form of questions on whether the rules in collective agreements meet the requirements laid down by EU rules. Do the pay and other provisions of collective agreements meet the requirement to be non-discriminatory? Do the procedures applied in the event of business transfers meet the requirements of EU law?, etc. In examining questions of this kind the first step, naturally, is to establish what a correct interpretation of the EU law concerned implies and how conformity between EU Directives and provisions in individual collective agreements can be achieved through EU-consistent interpretation.

In cases relating to transfers of undertakings the Finnish Supreme Court has systematically availed itself of, and referred to, the case-law of the ECJ. When reviewing the work of the Supreme Court it is useful to point out that, since it is a court of last resort, many of the cases it dealt with in the second half of the 1990s concerned events which occurred before the EU Directive on the subject, ie the Transfer of Undertakings Directive, had been implemented in Finnish law.[37] But in cases relating to the period after 1 January 1994 the Court systematically refers to the Directive and the impact of its interpretation on Finnish law.[38] The same also applies to lower courts. However, EU law is seldom used as an interpretative basis or support when considering general matters. In its judgment HD 2004:103, which set a fundamental precedent as regards application of the principle of equal treatment as enshrined in Finland's Contracts of Employment Act, the Supreme Court essentially opted not to refer to EU law, despite the fact that in several Directives the ban on discrimination is based on a principle of equal treatment.[39]

4.2 Preliminary rulings

4.2.1 Introduction

Article 234 EC enables Member State courts to make references for a preliminary ruling on, inter alia, the interpretation of the Treaty and of secondary EC law (Directives, for example). Where a question concerning interpretation of the Treaty or secondary law is raised before a national court and the latter considers that a decision on the question is necessary to enable it to give judgment on the matter the national court *may* request the ECJ to give a preliminary ruling. If the question is raised before courts of last resort against whose decisions

[37] See Finnish Supreme Court judgments HD 1996:142, HD 1997:30 and HD 1997:105.

[38] See Finnish Supreme Court judgments HD 1999:48a, HD 1999:69, HD 1999:70, HD 1999:71, HD 2000:7, HD 2001:12, HD 2001:44, HD 2001:48, HD 2001:49, HD 2001:72 and HD 2002:54.

[39] See R Nielsen *Employers' prerogatives—in a European and Nordic perspective* (Handelshøjskolens Forlag, 1992).

there is no judicial remedy under national law, those courts *must* request a preliminary ruling from the ECJ. Accordingly, while lower courts can choose whether to request a preliminary ruling, it is obligatory for courts of last resort to submit a preliminary reference of this kind.[40] Generally speaking, in both Finland and Sweden the courts have been relatively restrictive in deciding when to submit such references.[41]

4.2.2 Swedish experience

It has frequently been commented in the literature that the Swedish Labour Court has been restrictive as regards submitting references for a preliminary ruling from the ECJ.[42] It has on a number of occasions rejected a request from one of the parties in a case that such a reference should be made (see, for example, Labour Court judgment AD 134/1995), and has only twice requested a preliminary ruling from the ECJ (in connection with its judgment AD 66/1998 and AD 49/2005, the Laval case, see above section 3.2.4). What is more, the Supreme Court, the Stockholm District Court and the Universities Appeals Board have each submitted preliminary references.[43] It may well be asked how the Labour Court sets about assessing whether a preliminary reference should be submitted or not.

It follows from ECJ case-law that courts of last resort are not obliged to request a preliminary ruling where *the interpretation of EU law is not necessary to enable them to give judgment in the case in hand*. In its judgment AD 69/1997 the Labour Court states that, in general, a preliminary ruling ought not to be requested from the ECJ in a matter which is not of decisive importance in any event to the final outcome of the case. The Court therefore appears to be on the lookout for possible ways of deciding disputes on the basis of rules other than 'unclear rules of EU labour law'. It may be pointed out here that the issue on which the Labour Court requested a preliminary ruling in connection with its judgment AD 66/1998 turned out not to be decisive for the case when judgment was finally delivered. The case, brought by JämO (the Equal Opportunities Ombudsman), related to pay discrimination and the employer side objected, inter alia, that the two midwives who felt that they were discriminated against

[40] 59 On the obligation to request a preliminary ruling see, for example, ECJ Case 283/81 *CILFIT* [1982] ECR 3415 and Case C-99/00 *Lyckeskog* [2002] ECR I-4839.

[41] S Sankari 'EU law in Finland and Sweden: A survey of the preliminary references, national jurisprudence and legal integration' (2003) (3) *Europarättslig tidskrift*, pp 508–34 (2003), sketches a useful picture of practice in Finland and Sweden during the period 1995–2001.

[42] See, for example, U Bernitz & A Kjellgren *Europarättens grunder* Stockholm, (Norstedts, 1999) p 152; D Eliasson *et al* 'Community Directives: Effects, Efficiency and Justiciability in Sweden' (1998) (3) *Svensk Juristtidning*, p 212–29 p 219 *et seq*; and K Karlsson & F Hägglund 'En kartläggning av Sveriges fem första år med EG-rätt' (1999) (3) *Europarättslig tidskrift,* p 457*et seq.*

[43] Respectively Case C-441/99 *Gharehvaran* [2001] ECR I-7687, Case C-321/97 *Wåkerås-Andersson* [1999] ECR I-3551 and Case C-407/98 *Abrahamsson* [2000] ECR I-5539. See also the judgment of the EFTA Court of 20 June 1995 in *Samuelsson* (Case E-1/95), where the Varberg District Court requested a 'preliminary ruling' from the EFTA Court.

were not paid less than the male clinical technician cited as a comparison (since other factors, such as their shorter working hours, had to be taken into account). In its preliminary ruling (Case C-236/98 [2000] ECR I-2189), the ECJ rejected the objection put forward by the employer, who therefore withdrew it. When Labour Court judgment was finally delivered, the Equal Opportunities Ombudsman's case was dismissed on different grounds (relating to the age differences between the clinical technician and the two midwives, the labour market situation and the fact that the Provincial Council showed that the pay differentials had no connection with the sex of the employees). It can therefore be concluded, in retrospect, that the question which the Labour Court referred to the ECJ was not necessary in order to settle the dispute, and the situation illustrates how difficult it can be to assess in advance which questions will eventually turn out to be decisive for the outcome of a case.

Another situation where it is possible to avoid applying unclear rules of EU labour law is where national law is more extensive in scope than EU law. In situations of this kind the case can be decided on the basis of national law, without any need for the court concerned to interpret EU law (see Labour Court judgment AD 76/2001).

A different type of case where it is possible for national courts to dispense with requesting preliminary rulings is where the matter in hand is one that is expressly left to them to decide. It is not unusual for ECJ case-law to establish that certain matters connected with the interpretation of EU law are for the national courts to decide even though they involve questions of law rather than questions of fact. For example, it follows from ECJ case-law, and now also from the Transfer of Undertakings Directive, that for the purposes of the Directive the concept of an employee is to be interpreted as encompassing any person who is protected as an employee under national law.[44] The question of who is covered by the Directive is therefore a matter for the national courts to decide on the basis of national law. Similarly, in its earlier case-law the ECJ has emphasized that it is for the national courts to make an overall assessment, in the light of what are known as the *Spijkers* criteria, as to whether the circumstances in a given case are such as to constitute a transfer of economic activity.[45] It also follows from ECJ case-law that in determining whether indirect discrimination existed it is the task of the national courts to examine whether the grounds invoked are admissible, and also whether the explanations given for the employer's pay practices are commensurate with objective reasons connected with the employer's business and whether they are appropriate and necessary in order to achieve the result pursued. Such examples show that to some extent the

[44] See, eg Case 105/84 *Danmols Inventar* [1985] ECR 2639.

[45] See, eg Case 24/85 *Spijkers* [1986] ECR 1119; Case 101/87 *Bork* [1988] ECR 3057; and Case C-209/91 *Rask* [1992] ECR I-5755. In more recent case-law there are instances where the ECJ has declared that a certain transaction constitutes a transfer within the meaning of the Directive; see, for example, Case C-172/99 *Liikenne* [2001] ECR I-745.

ECJ upholds a kind of subsidiarity principle, in the sense that the interpretation of certain legal concepts is left to the national courts. In so far as the legal issues in disputes relate to those concepts, national courts of last resort need not request preliminary rulings. This argument was advanced by the Swedish Labour Court in its judgments AD 134/1995, AD 13/2001 and AD 15/2002.

It likewise follows from ECJ case-law that a national court of last resort is not normally required to request a preliminary ruling before issuing an interim order in interlocutory proceedings.[46] There was therefore no obligation on the Swedish Labour Court to submit a preliminary reference before its interim order in judgment AD 111/2004: it was, rather, the task of the Court to apply EU law independently in reaching its decision.

Lastly, in accordance with what are referred to as the *CILFIT* criteria[47] the national court has the discretion not to request a preliminary ruling if:

(1) an interpretation of the point of Community law in question has already been provided in previous decisions of the ECJ (*acte éclairé*)
(2) the correct application of Community law is so obvious as to leave no scope for any reasonable doubt (*acte claire*).

With regard to the second criterion, the ECJ has warned in its case-law that national courts must bear in mind the special nature of Community law, the particular difficulties that its interpretation entails (inter alia, its multilingual nature and the fact that all the different language versions are equally valid) and the risk of conflicting bodies of case-law within the Community. Before concluding that it need not request a preliminary ruling the national court of last resort must be convinced that the matter is equally obvious to the courts of the other Member States and to the ECJ. Only if that is the case may it decide the case in its own right.

As it stands on the basis of ECJ case-law, the requirement as to when national courts of last resort must request a preliminary ruling would appear unrealistic.[48] If all courts of last resort were to submit preliminary references to the extent indicated by a strict interpretation of the *CILFIT* criteria, the ECJ's case load would increase so much that it would not be able to give preliminary rulings within an acceptable period of time. Moreover, the rules governing the preliminary rulings procedure take no account of the interest of the parties

[46] Cases 35–36/82 *Morson* [1982] ECR 3723 and Case 107/76 *Hoffmann-La Roche* [1977] ECR 957. See also the Swedish Supreme Court decision *Nytt Juridiska Arkiv I* (1995), p 635.

[47] See Case 283/81 *CILFIT* [1982] ECR 3415. The ECJ has not altered the *CILFIT* criteria since 1982. What is more, it has very rarely had occasion even to restate its stance on them. See, however, Case C-393/98 *Gomes Valente* [2001] ECR I-1327, in which the ECJ declared that the fact that the Commission has discontinued infringement proceedings against a Member State concerning a piece of legislation does not relieve a national court of the obligation to request a preliminary ruling from the ECJ.

[48] See, for example, G Bebr 'The Reinforcement of the Constitutional Review of Community Acts under Article 117 EEC Treaty' (1988) (25) *Common Market Law Review*, pp 667–91.

concerned in having their dispute settled within a reasonable period of time, but are predominantly aimed at ensuring uniform application of the law. In 2003, the average length of time taken for the ECJ to give a preliminary ruling was a good two years.[49] This means that proceedings before the ECJ incur considerable delays and costs for the parties involved. As established in ECJ case-law, however, the rules leave no scope for giving priority to the dispute-resolution function of judicial proceedings, which in other contexts is viewed as central.

In the light of all this, it is not surprising that the national courts of last resort do not request preliminary rulings to the extent that might be expected. On the contrary, the available statistics indicate that they avoid doing so wherever they can. During the period 1995–2003 the Swedish and Finnish courts of last resort have requested preliminary rulings on four and five occasions respectively; the corresponding figures for the Swedish Supreme Administrative Court and the Finnish Supreme Administrative Court were thirteen and ten respectively. In 2003 requests for preliminary rulings in cases relating to social policy from all Member State courts combined amounted to only twelve,[50] whereas during the same year the Swedish Labour Court alone applied EU labour-law Directives in six cases. These statistics suggest that the strict view, as established in ECJ case-law, of when courts of last resort are required to request a preliminary ruling is not upheld in practice. It may be inferred that the national courts of last resort do not request preliminary rulings in anything like the numbers they would if the criteria established by the ECJ were actually complied with. This is probably not something specific to courts in the area of labour law or to courts in the Nordic countries.[51]

There are only three cases in which the Swedish Labour Court has found that the *CILFIT* criteria were not fulfilled. In two of them, as already mentioned, the Court requested a preliminary ruling (judgment AD 66/1998 and AD 49/2005), while in the other it considered it unnecessary to submit a preliminary reference since it was possible to give judgment on other grounds (judgment AD 69/1997: see above). It seems clear that the Swedish Labour Court—like other national courts of last resort—uses a more extensive application of the *CILFIT* criteria than that ordained by the ECJ (for example, Labour Court judgment AD 61/2001). It may perhaps be fair to speculate that the Labour Court is inclined to request a preliminary ruling only if, after a penetrating analysis of EU law, it feels unable to predict with a high degree of probability how the ECJ itself would have decided the case.

[49] Statistical Information of the ECJ (2003): see http://europa.eu.int/cj/en/instit/presentationfr/rapport/stat/st03cr.pdf (1 December 2004).

[50] *Ibid.*

[51] See, for example, T Tridimas 'Knocking on Heaven's Door: Fragmentation, Efficiency and Defiance in the Preliminary Reference Procedure' (2003) (40) *Common Market Law Review*, pp 9–50, here p 17; O Due 'Danish Preliminary References' in O'Keeffe & Bavasso (eds) *Judicial Review in European Union Law. Liber Amicorum in Honour of Lord Slynn* (TheHague/London/New York, Kluwer, 2000), pp 363–75. See also J Shaw *Law of the European Union* (3rd edn, Hampshire, Palgrave, 2000), p 410 *et seq*.

As indicated above, in our view it makes good sense for national courts to exercise some measure of caution in requesting preliminary rulings, and it is reasonable for them to interpret EU law themselves to a certain extent. That notwithstanding, it has to be asked whether it is appropriate to refrain from requesting preliminary rulings in cases where opinion in a court is divided as regards the interpretation of a particular provision of EU law and this division of opinion is unconnected with the evidence presented. In its judgments AD 81/1997, AD 124/1998 and AD 15/2002 the Labour Court was divided not only as to whether a preliminary reference should be submitted to the ECJ but also as to how the provision in question should be interpreted. In a situation of this kind the Court lays itself open to criticism. If the dissenting minority of members have any good reason at all for their interpretation of EU law the provision in question is, almost by definition, not obvious (according to the *CILFIT* criteria). When the interpretation is not obvious to all members of one and the same court, it can hardly be obvious to the courts of all Member States (*cf* the ECJ definition above). If, on the other hand, the majority of members are right in their view that the interpretation of the provision in question is obvious (according to the *CILFIT* criteria), the minority must have been advocating an application that clearly conflicts with the law.

4.2.3 Finnish experience

The Finnish experience as regards preliminary rulings in the field of labour law is little different from what has been the case in Sweden. In Finland, the Labour Court has never once to date requested a preliminary ruling from the ECJ, the Supreme Court has requested preliminary rulings in the field of labour law on probably two occasions and there has been one request each from a lower court and from the Social Insurance Court (the court of last resort for social-security matters).[52]

The Finnish Supreme Court submitted a preliminary reference in the *Liikenne* case.[53] It took two years to obtain the preliminary ruling, the events with which the case was concerned took place in 1995 and final judgment was eventually pronounced in 2001. It goes without saying that a time horizon of this scale is not all that practical for typical labour-law disputes.

As far as Finnish practice is concerned there is also a marked reluctance to deliberate on the question of requesting a preliminary ruling. In many cases it is not discussed at all unless the argument has been raised. And where a party has

[52] Of these, the request from the Social Insurance Court concerned the question of pensionable ages and the applicability of Treaty Art 141 to certain state pensions (see ECJ Case C-351/00 *Niemi* [2002] ECR I-7007). Two of the cases (from the Supreme Court and the Tampere District Court) are still pending before the ECJ and concern the relationship of the rules on health and safety at work to control the market (see Cases C-470/03 and C-40/04). The Supreme Court's request in Case C-172/99 *Liikenne* [2001] ECR I-745 is discussed below.

[53] Supreme Court judgment HD 1999:48a, by which the decision to request a preliminary ruling was issued; the final judgment is HD 2001:44.

asked for a preliminary ruling to be requested the answer given is often merely to the effect that the matter in hand does not involve a situation of the kind envisaged in Article 234 EC:

> The case does not necessitate interpretation of Community law as envisaged in Article 234 of the Treaty establishing the European Community. Consequently, giving judgment on the case does not presuppose submitting a reference for a preliminary ruling from the Court of Justice of the European Communities.[54]

However, just exactly what is meant by this reasoning remains unclear: Is it primarily a matter of interpreting national law, a matter which is left to the national courts to decide or a matter which is not unclear under EU law?

4.2.4 Available remedies against failure to submit a reference for a preliminary ruling

It can be seen from what has been said above that both the Swedish and the Finnish courts have been restrictive as regards submitting references for preliminary rulings from the ECJ. In the circumstances, it may be useful to say something about the remedies that are available against national-court decisions as regards requesting a preliminary ruling.

The opportunities for parties to contest decisions relating to preliminary references on the basis of national rules are extremely limited.

A decision made in the course of legal proceedings by a Swedish district court not to request a preliminary ruling cannot be appealed against separately; it can only be appealed against in the context of an appeal against the judgment as a whole. If a district court decides to request a preliminary ruling, this can be appealed against in particular where that decision can mean that the case is delayed unnecessarily (chapter 49 section 7 of the Swedish Code of Judicial Procedure: see Labour Court judgment AD 67/2001). In Finland a corresponding situation can hardly arise in the Finnish Labour Court, since it is not an appellate court. There is no rule in Finland's Code of Judicial Procedure corresponding to the above-mentioned provision in the Swedish Code.

No ordinary legal remedies are available to contest decisions by the Swedish and Finnish Labour Courts on whether or not to request a preliminary ruling. One alternative open to parties who are dissatisfied with the failure to request a preliminary ruling is to apply to the Supreme Court to have the Labour Court's judgment set aside on the ground of miscarriage of justice. Under chapter 59 section 1 of the Swedish Code of Judicial Procedure a judgment must, on application, be set aside on the ground of miscarriage of justice if in the course of legal proceedings there has been a gross defect in procedure which may be presumed to have affected the outcome of the case (in Finland the corresponding provision is in chapter 31 section 1 of the Code of Judicial Procedure). Generally speak-

[54] See, for example, Finnish Supreme Court judgment HFD 4 November 2004, Drnr 233/1/03.

ing, it will probably be easier for a party to succeed with an allegation that the failure to request a preliminary ruling was a manifest procedural defect, rather than prove in an application for retrial that the application of law underlying the judgment was manifestly contrary to law (*cf Nytt Juridiska Arkiv* 2003 C 36).

To some extent, the failure by national courts to submit a reference for a preliminary ruling can be contested on the basis of rules of EU law. Purely as a matter of principle, there is nothing to stop the European Commission from instituting *infringement proceedings* under Article 226 EC on the ground that in particular cases a court has interpreted the *CILFIT* criteria incorrectly, although probably no such example exists. In practice, a situation of this kind is more likely as regards failure to implement a Directive correctly or non-compliance with EU law.

Parties to disputes who consider that national courts of last resort have wrongly decided not to request a preliminary ruling are not able to institute infringement proceedings against the State. On the other hand, they can in principle institute an action for damages against the State on the ground that the State has caused them damage through infringement of Community law. The *Köbler* judgment established that the principle whereby Member States are liable in damages for infringements of Community law is also applicable where the alleged infringement stems from a decision of a court adjudicating at last instance.[55] The preconditions for receiving damages are, however, obviously narrow. Firstly, the rule of Community law infringed must be intended to confer rights on individuals. Second, the infringement must be sufficiently serious and there must be a direct causal link between the infringement and the damage sustained by the injured parties. Furthermore, if the infringement stems from a court of last resort that infringement must be manifest. According to the ECJ the factors to be taken into account in assessing this include, in particular: the degree of clarity and precision of the rule infringed; whether the infringement was intentional; whether the error of law was excusable or inexcusable; the position taken, where applicable, by a Community institution; and non-compliance by the court in question with its obligation to submit a reference for a preliminary ruling under the third paragraph of Article 234 EC. In addition, an infringement of Community law is in any event deemed sufficiently serious if the decision concerned was made in manifest breach of the case-law of the ECJ in the matter in hand.

In the light of all this it is conceivable for a party who has lost a case in, for example, the Swedish Labour Court in which the latter declined to request a preliminary ruling, to institute an action for damages against the State before a district court. The grounds for the claim can be that the losing party has sustained damage as a result of the Labour Court's failure to request a preliminary ruling in manifest contravention of the third paragraph of Article 234 EC and that if a

[55] See ECJ Case C-224/01 *Köbler* [2003] ECR I-10239. For a critical and thought-provoking analysis of the judgment, see PJ Wattel '*Köbler*, *CILFIT* and *Welthgrove*: We can't go on meeting like this' (2004) (41) *Common Market Law Review*, pp 177–90.

reference for a preliminary ruling had been submitted the outcome of the case would have been a different one.

5 CONCLUSIONS

It is not altogether easy when attempting to assess the mark left by EU labour law on Finnish and Swedish labour law over the past decade, to give an overall picture summing up the situation. There are, furthermore, radically differing views expressed among labour lawyers on the impact of EU labour law. Many think that in substantive terms the changes are relatively small and that the national systems have successfully held their ground, while others think that we have undergone something of a system shift and that the scope for specifically national solutions has more or less vanished. Both viewpoints are justified to some extent—much depends on the perspective adopted and the yardstick used to measure changes. Not entirely surprisingly, a balanced overall view almost certainly lies somewhere midway between these two extremes. That said, we nevertheless believe that the changes are greater than they seem at superficial level when we look at the multitude of new rules, legal actions, disputes or negotiations.

5.1 Internationalization aspects

It is worth noting, to start with, that purely national law is succumbing to internationalization. More and more situations are arising in the domestic labour market where companies or employees from more than one country are involved. Instances of this kind can include Swedish–Finnish companies in the banking, pulp and paper, energy or telecommunications sectors. Situations can arise which involve the temporary posting of workers or relocation, and many others. The employer may be established in other countries, etc. It is clear that situations in which more than one country's legislation comes into play in one way or another have increased and will increase radically. We now have new supranational forms of company such as the European Company (SE), which is also influencing labour law in a new way as it becomes more common. All this means that we are encountering new problems and disputes which our traditional labour-market mechanisms are not particularly well-suited to coping with. The reason is that we have arrived at the stage where the internal market is no longer a purely academic concept but is now becoming a reality, for good or ill. Added to this, the enlargement of the EU, attended as it is by differences in the standard of living and cost structures between the various countries, means that the pace of this internationalization is being accelerated and its effects are being made more noticeable.

5.2 The 'system shift' in labour law

In our view there are at least three respects in which labour law has undergone revolutionary changes as a result of its Europeanization and of EU membership: national control of the industrial relations system; the relationship between labour law and economic law; and the question of the importance of legislation as compared with case-law and, associated with this, the importance of fundamental rights within the context of labour law.

One revolutionary change in the Finnish and Swedish labour-law system is that the final decision-making authority and control no longer reside at national level. Ultimately, it is international courts that decide what is feasible and permitted in our system. We recently obtained clarification in a judgment from the ECtHR in Strasbourg, by five votes to two, that Sweden's Labour Court is a court which can be permitted to continue its adjudicative activity in its existing composition.[56] The question of the lawfulness of certain forms of industrial action that have traditionally been accepted in Finland and Sweden is questioned in the Vaxholm and Viking-cases (above section 3.2.4). Similarly, the permissibility of parts of our labour legislation may be examined by international courts. There is also considerable scope within the EU for so-called *forum shopping*. A party can choose to pursue a legal action in a particular Member State where the prospects of winning the case are good and then demand that the judgment be enforced in another country on the basis of the Brussels Regulation.[57] None of this means that all authority has been transferred to these international courts, which critics of the EU sometimes maintain in debate as there is still a significant degree of influence left at domestic level. What has changed is that the national courts and ultimately the legislature are no longer able, on their own, to control the game plan close to home. Control takes place within the framework of a complicated system of influence and interaction between numerous national, foreign or supranational decision-makers and actors in which none possesses sovereign authority to make, alone, the final and more overarching decisions. We have to expect, in such a system, more elements of surprise and inconsistencies than in a traditionally hierarchical, nation-state legislative and judicial system.[58]

[56] ECtHR judgment of 24 October 2004, *Kellerman v Sweden* (Application No 41579/98).

[57] Council Reg (EC) No 44/2001 on jurisdiction and the recognition and enforcement of judgments in civil and commercial matters.

[58] T Wilhelmsson 'Jack-in-the-Box Theory of European Community Law' in Eriksson & Hurri (eds) *Dialectic of Law and Reality. Readings in Finnish Legal Theory* (Publications of the Faculty of Law, University of Helsinki, 1999).

During the postwar period labour law in Finland and Sweden grew into a relatively idyllically protected discipline. Once it had established a basis of its own, it was able to build on this undisturbed and develop a functioning system of protection for employees in various problematic situations. Labour law had a more or less well-defined territory of its own which was not called into question. Nowadays, this state of affairs has been radically altered. In the shadow of the internal market a territorial struggle is in progress over where labour law ends and economic rules take over. Exposure to competition, privatization of services, control of operating results, regulation of insider dealing and free movement of goods, services and capital are all phenomena which are in at least a relationship of tension with, if not directly clashing with, the rules of labour law. We know that the relationship between competition law and labour law has been controversial both nationally and at EU level.[59] The endeavour to create guarantees that labour-law requirements are complied with or will be complied with in public procurement has entailed a prolonged tug-of-war which is still going on. A recent judgment of the ECJ concerns the issue whether the general secretary of a trade union is entitled to receive information that a major bank is to undergo a merger or whether a union representative on the board of the bank ought not to disclose a matter of this kind to the union's general secretary, even though it may have a decisive impact on the livelihood and future of thousands of employees.[60] In the *Vaxholm* and *Viking* cases the relation between industrial action and the free movement of services is at stake. The debate on the current Directive on Services concerns essentially the same question. Should compliance-enforcement and control mechanisms based on labour law be scrapped in favour of an ideologically conditioned country-of-origin principle?[61] This territorial struggle represents a significant change for labour law, an upheaval and a challenge for the actors of industrial relations, even though there is of course no cause to try to enlarge the territory of labour law beyond what is reasonable. We merely wish to emphasize here that a sensibly conducted territorial struggle is an important task for governments and unions, but also in certain cases for the employers at international and national level. Consequently, the European-level social partners were indeed making common cause when they criticized the unrealistic ideas about how employment relationships in, for example, the building industry can be controlled from a country other than the one in which the work is performed which are mirrored in the European Commission's Proposal for a Directive on Services.

It is clear from developments to date that the relevant legislation has become increasingly supranational and harmonized. However, in a heterogeneous EU soon to include thirty Member States there are no grounds for nursing any par-

[59] N Bruun & J Hellsten *Collective Agreement and Competition Law in the EU* The Report of the COLCOM Project (Copenhagen, DJOEF Publishing, 2001).

[60] Case C-384/02 *Grøngaard and Bang*, judgment 22 November 2005, not yet reported.

[61] See N Bruun Employment issues, memorandum *European Parliament Public Hearing. On the Proposal for a Directive on Services in the Internal Market* 11 November 2004.

ticularly high expectations that the legislative process in the field of labour law will function speedily and effectively. There is also good reason to question whether the upward harmonization towards an increased level of employee protection as envisaged by the Treaty, which up till now has taken place, can continue. The call for a relaxation of labour law is already making itself strongly felt as regards, for example, the revision by the EU of its Working Time Directive. As a result of all these factors the main focus in legal developments is shifting towards case-law, at both national and international level. Case law is a balancing factor which can protect social interests in the internal market. In this respect the fundamental rights of employees also come into the picture. If and when the EU's new Constitution comes into force, fundamental rights may in the future prove to be an important factor in the application of the law. The rights falling under this heading of course include not only the right to equal treatment or non-discrimination but also the right to information and consultation, the right to bargain collectively and the right to take industrial action. Naturally, social fundamental rights do not solve all of the problems and, furthermore, have to be balanced against economic rights, but when all is said and done they can play a positive part in a trend in the law which is in many respects steered by liberal market thinking.

BIBLIOGRAPHY

Ahlberg, K and Bruun, N, 'Sweden: Transition through collective bargaining' in (T Blanke and E Rose eds) *Collective Bargaining and Wages in Comparative Perspective. Germany, France, The Netherlands, Sweden and the United Kingdom* (Kluwer Law International, 2005).

Andersen, SK, (ed) *EU og det nordiske spil om lov og aftale* SALTSA Report No 2:2003 (Stockholm, 2003).

Bebr, G, 'The Reinforcement of the Constitutional Review of Community Acts under Article 117 EEC Treaty' (1988) (25) *Common Market Law Review*.

Bernitz, U and Kjellgren, A, *Europarättens grunder* Stockholm, (Norstedts, 1999).

Bruun, N, Employment issues, memorandum *European Parliament Public Hearing. On the Proposal for a Directive on Services in the Internal Market* 11 November 2004.

—— *et al*, *The Nordic Labour Relations Model* (Dartmouth, Aldershot, 1990).

—— and Hellsten J *Collective Agreement and Competition Law in the EU* The Report of the COLCOM Project (Copenhagen, DJOEF Publishing, 2001).

—— and Malmberg J 'Finska och svenska domstolar som arbetsrättsliga gemenskapsdomstolar' in B Nyström *et al* (eds) *Liber amicorum* (Lund, Reinhold Fahlbeck, Juristförlaget, 2005).

Cameron, I, *Introduction to the European Convention on Human Rights* (4th edn, Iustus, Uppsala, 2002).

Due, O, 'Danish Preliminary References' in O'Keeffe & Bavasso (eds) *Judicial Review in European Union Law. Liber Amicorum in Honour of Lord Slynn* (TheHague/London/New York, Kluwer, 2000).

Eliasson, D, *et al* 'Community Directives: Effects, Efficiency and Justiciability in Sweden' (1998) (3) *Svensk Juristtidning*, p 212–29.

Fahlbeck, R, 'Lex Laboris—Quo Vadis? The Swedish Experience' in R Blanpain & M Weiss (eds) *Changing Industrial Relations and Modernisation of Labour Law. Liber Amicorum in Honour of Professor Marco Biagi* (The Hague/London/New York, Kluwer Law International, 2003).

Göransson, H, 'Hidden Clauses in Collective Agreements: The Case Law of the Swedish Labour Court' *Scandinavian Studies in Law 34* 1990.

Karlsson, K and Hägglund, F, 'En kartläggning av Sveriges fem första år med EG-rätt' (1999) (3) *Europarättslig tidskrift*.

Nielsen, R, *Employers' prerogatives—in a European and Nordic perspective* (Handelshøjskolens Forlag, 1992).

—— 'Europeanization of Nordic Labour Law' *Scandinavian Studies in Law* 43, 2002.

Nyström, B, *EU och Arbetsrätten* (Stockholm, Norstedts, 2002).

Sankari, S, 'EU law in Finland and Sweden: A survey of the preliminary references, national jurisprudence and legal integration' (2003) (3) *Europarättslig tidskrift*.

Sciarra, S, (ed) *The Evolution of Labour Law (1992–2003)* (2004) Available at: http://europa.eu.int/comm/employment_social/labour_law/docs/generalreport_en.pdf.

Shaw, J, *Law of the European Union* (3rd edn, Hampshire, Palgrave, 2000).

Tridimas, T, 'Knocking on Heaven's Door: Fragmentation, Efficiency and Defiance in the Preliminary Reference Procedure' (2003) (40) *Common Market Law Review*.

Vigneau, C, *et al Fixed-term work in the EU—A European Agreement against discrimination and abuse* (Arbetslivsinstitutet: Stockholm, 1999).

Wattel, PJ, '*Köbler*, *CILFIT* and *Welthgrove*: We can't go on meeting like this' (2004) (41) *Common Market Law Review*.

Wilhelmsson, T, 'Jack-in-the-Box Theory of European Community Law' in Eriksson & Hurri (eds) *Dialectic of Law and Reality. Readings in Finnish Legal Theory* (Publications of the Faculty of Law, University of Helsinki, 1999).

Bill Proposition 1983/84:165.

Bill, Proposition 1994/95: 19.

Bill, Proposition 1997/98:177.

Bill, Proposition 1998/99:90.

Bill Proposition 1999/2000:32.

Bill, Proposition 2003/04:180.

Bill Reg. proposition 283/2004.

Proposition 1999/2000:AU5.

Government Bill, Reg. proposition 99/1996.

Government Committee SOU 1984:19.

Government Committee SOU 1988:49.

Government Committee SOU 1995:115.

Government Committee SOU 1998:52.

Government Committee SOU 2001:31.

'Arbete i Europa', Departmental Report Ds 1995:64.

EEA Committee Report 1992/93: EU1, p 124.

Report of the Cabinet to Parliament on the outcome of the Convention and preparations for the Intergovernmental Conference, SRR 2/2003.

Statistical Information of the ECJ (2003): see http://europa.eu.int/cj/en/instit/presentationfr/rapport/stat/st03cr.pdf (1 December 2004).

4

Damages for Violations of ECHR Rights: the Swedish Example

IAIN CAMERON*

ABSTRACT

ARTICLE 13 OF THE ECHR (or 'the Convention') requires the provision of effective remedies at national level for anyone alleging that his or her Convention rights have been breached. The extent to which damages remedies should be available for ECHR rights violations, particularly the right to trial in a reasonable time, are topical issues in a large number of European states. In this article the Swedish experience will be described and analysed.

1 SOMETHING ON THE LEGAL-CULTURAL AND CONSTITUTIONAL BACKGROUND

1.1 Rights skepticism?

Sweden is one of the first countries in the world to have given individual rights protection at the constitutional level in its Freedom of the Press Act of 1766. However, this protection was limited to the right of freedom of expression. It was 1976 before Sweden included a catalogue of individual rights in its new

* Iain Cameron is Professor in Public International Law at the University of Uppsala. His research interests lie in human rights, international criminal law and civil liberties. He is a member of inter alia the Advisory Board of the Nordic Journal of International Law, and a Rapporteur for the Journal European Public Law. He holds an LLD and an LLM in International Law. He has published extensively in the fields of international law and constitutional law, particularly on international criminal law and human rights issues. He was an expert adviser to the Badinter Commission and to a number of Swedish government commissions of inquiry proposing legislation. He is a member of the Commission on Democracy through Law (Venice Commission) of the Council of Europe. His most recent books are National Security and the ECHR (Kluwer, 2000) and an Introduction to the ECHR (5th edn Iustus, 2006).

Instrument of Government, *Regeringsformen* (RF).[1] However, at the risk of some simplification, the pragmatic Swedish legal culture combined with the Swedish emphasis on the democratic political process has meant that the rights provisions of RF have only relatively rarely been applied by the Swedish courts. It is fair to say that there has been a certain degree of suspicion of rights which has been regarded by the centre and left wing political parties as attempts to trump the political process. Rights have not been regarded by many as necessary in a generous welfare state. The revelatory experience of the value of rights which can be brought by foreign oppression has (thankfully) passed Sweden by. Until very recently, little support can be found for a more activist approach in legal theory. Among Swedish legal philosophers, has had a tradition of regarding talk of constitutional rights as wooly metaphysical thinking.

1.2 The Incorporation of the Convention and its Status under Swedish Law

A skeptical approach to rights is also reflected in the Swedish approach to the ECHR. Although Sweden was one of the first member states of the Council of Europe to ratify the ECHR, it was 1995 before the Convention became part of Swedish law.[2] The incorporation of the Convention was a 'rush job' and, moreover, something of an afterthought to EU membership which also became operational on 1 January 1995. A commission of inquiry was responsible for the report proposing incorporation.[3] This report was superficial and badly researched, skating over problems rather than identifying them and proposing solutions. By contrast to the procedural approach to rights that characterizes the common law, very little attention was devoted in the *travaux préparatoires* to the question of *remedies* for violations of the Convention. The approach was taken that fulfilling the Convention rights would cause few problems for Swedish administrative agencies and courts, and the commission devoted only two pages to the issue of remedies.[4]

[1] When reference is made to RF the chapter and section number is given. It should be noted that this article is primarily intended for an English speaking audience, albeit not necessarily lawyers from common law systems. Reference as much as possible to English language sources will be made. The British (English/Scottish) legal system has had more experience of the use of damages to remedy Convention violations under the Human Rights Act, 1998. For this reason a number of analogies between Sweden and the UK are drawn.

[2] Lag (1994:1219) om den europeiska konventionen angående skydd för de mänskliga rättigheterna och de grundläggande friheterna [Act on the ECHR]. Translations are my own unless otherwise noted. As regards citation, references to the Swedish statute book (*Svensk författningssamling*, SFS) are by year followed by the relevant number. The law was amended with the incorporation of Protocol 11 (Prop. 97/98:107).

[3] SOU 1993:40. References to *travaux préparatoires* are either to the number of the commission responsible for investigating the law, SOU and the year of its report, or the draft bill put before parliament together with its accompanying documentation, (*proposition,* prop) or the report of the Parliamentary Committee on the Constitution on the bill (KU).

[4] *Ibid*, pp 73–4. To be fair, the commission did at least *raise* the question as to whether the Tort Liability Act (below) was adequate.

Unlike the United Kingdom, Sweden chose to incorporate the whole Convention, and its protocols, rather than simply the substantive rights and the general limitation provisions.[5] There is little explanation for this in the *travaux préparatoires*. The main reason appeared to have been that the other Nordic states had incorporated the whole treaty or were planning to do so.[6] In any event, there are no specific remedies explicitly connected to the incorporation law.[7]

The incorporation law provides that the Convention is to have the status of an ordinary statute. In order to avoid the situation where this statute came into conflict with other statutes, an amendment was made to RF providing that 'a law or other regulation shall not be issued in conflict with Sweden's obligations under [the Convention]' (RF 2:23). This does not, as such, give the Convention constitutional status. Nor does it, formally speaking, create a new category of laws midway between the Constitution and ordinary laws (although this is the position in practice). Formally the provision means that a law or other regulation which conflicts with the Convention, also conflicts with the Constitution.

Swedish social democracy is especially cautious about giving the courts power to annul or change political decisions, and constitutional review is particularly sensitive in the Swedish system. Constitutional review is very rare in Sweden and, it is fair to say, in all the Nordic states. There is a restriction in the Instrument of Government, RF 11:14, which provides that where an inferior norm in primary legislation or a government ordinance conflicts with a higher norm, then for the courts or administrative agencies to refuse to apply the inferior norm, the conflict with the higher norm must be 'manifest'. Accordingly, the effect of RF 11:14 together with RF 2:23 is that where statutes or ordinances conflict with the Convention but do not manifestly conflict with it these should be applied. No restriction applies to constitutional review of rules lower down in the hierarchy of norms, ie regulations promulgated by administrative agencies or local authorities. The 'manifest breach' requirement obviously risks creating situations which are at odds with the idea behind incorporation—solving problems at the national level, without the need to go to Strasbourg.[8] The Swedish courts have, sensibly, not engaged in overt constitutional review but have instead attempted to avoid conflicts by applying the principle of treaty conform construction and interpreting Swedish law in accordance with case law, even if this means going against opinions expressed in the *travaux préparatoires* to a statute.[9] This source

[5] Sweden has ratified protocols 4, 6, 7 and 13 but has not signed protocol 12.

[6] SOU 1993:40 p 126.

[7] For the legislation on the subject of compensation in cases of wrongful arrest and detention see below.

[8] For more detailed criticism see I Cameron 'The ECHR in Sweden after incorporation' in A Boyle, C Himsworth, A Loux, and H MacQueen (eds) *Human Rights and Scots Law: comparative perspectives* (Oxford, Hart publishing, 2002) pp 105–40.

[9] See in particular, RH 1995:66, RÅ 2000 ref 65, RÅ 2000 ref 66 I (Volvo), RÅ 2000 ref 66 II (Din Bil Örebro AB), NJA 2001, s 409, NJA 2001, s 563, NJA 2004, s 336. NJA 2005, s 462, NJA 2005, s 805. Cases from the Supreme Court are cited from the semi-official series, *Nytt juridisk arkiv* (NJA) cases from the courts of appeal, from the official series *Rättsfall från hovrätterna* (RH) cases

of interpretative data is otherwise considered very faithfully by the Swedish courts which often follow a subjective or historical approach to statutory interpretation.

On the other hand, the ECtHR, like the ECJ, applies a teleological interpretative method. The requirements of the Convention are concretised by the ECtHR and can grow over time. The obligation which contracting states undertake in Article 1 to 'secure to everyone within their jurisdiction the [Convention] rights' is thus of a continuing nature. The Convention case law is at present growing at the rate of some 1,100 judgments and 28,000 admissibility decisions per year. There is no requirement to have regard to this case law in the Swedish incorporation statute.[10] On the other hand, such a requirement is made clear in the *travaux préparatoires* to the act of incorporation where it is stated that ECtHR cases are a source of law to be applied by the Swedish courts.[11] The Supreme Court and Supreme Administrative Court have often referred to Convention case law and so encouraged the lower courts to follow suit. The higher courts have also, generally speaking, faithfully attempted to understand and apply the ECtHR case law.

Nonetheless, the wording of Swedish legislation obviously sets the limits for the interpretative powers of the courts which cannot interpret a provision *contra legem*. And the legislature has not encouraged more activism on the part of the courts. This is made very plain in the *travaux préparatoires* to the incorporation statute where it was repeatedly stated that the primary responsibility for ensuring compliance with the Convention was with the legislator. It might then, have been expected that steps would be taken to ensure that legislation, and subordinate legislation, which raises issues under the Convention is not passed without first having undergone expert scrutiny. This is not the case. There is no group, or person, in the Foreign or Justice Ministries given the job of checking whether a new case may cause problems for Swedish law and there is no formal 'Strasbourg proofing' of new legislation. On the other hand, the normal legislative process being long and rather open, ought to identify potential breaches. In particular, the directive given to the departmental or parliamentary commission of inquiry which is usually established to prepare new legislation should focus attention on the implications of the Convention case law. Having said this, mistakes have been made in the past. For example, the commission of inquiry established to bring Swedish tax law into line with the *Funcke* case[12] chose, despite

from the Labour Court from the official series *Arbetsdomstolens domar* (AD) and cases from the Supreme Administrative Court from the official series *Regeringsrättens årsbok*, RÅ. Supreme Administrative Court cases regarded as more important are found in the reference (ref) section, others in the note (not) section.

[10] *Cf* s 2 of the British Human Rights Act which requires courts and tribunals to have regard to the Convention *acquis*.

[11] Prop. 1993/94: 117 s 37. See also Ds 1997:25 s 49, produced as a result of the *Holm* case.

[12] SOU 1996:116. *Funke v France*, A/256-A, 25 February 1993. I refer to the series A and the date of judgment for ECtHR cases before 1996, and the number of the case and the date of judgment, or the case citation in the reports series for cases after 1996.

strong evidence to the contrary, to continue to classify tax penalties as administrative in nature, rather than as 'criminal' within the meaning of Article 6, and Protocol 7, Article 4. The refusal to change to the law ended up causing considerable problems for the Swedish courts.[13] A later commission of inquiry into tax penalties drew the correct conclusion that the teleological interpretative method most often applied by the ECtHR means that Swedish commissions of inquiry recommending legislation should not 'balance on the border' of what is permitted by the Convention.[14] Such an approach can only serve to postpone problems, shifting them to the courts.

After ten years experience of incorporation, and at the risk of simplification, it can be said that the main effect the Convention has had in Sweden has been in administrative law, especially administrative procedure and tax law, although criminal and civil procedural law has also been affected. This is not surprising as the Convention is primarily aimed against state abuse of power and the state will invariably act through its public servants (police, social workers etc). However, although the main judicial forum for considering complaints against the state are the administrative courts, these courts are unable to award damages. Only the ordinary courts in Sweden may do this.

1.2 Which Bodies are Bound by the Convention?

Against whom or what may an injured person bring an action for damages? The Convention binds the state[15] vis-a-vis individuals and legal persons and the state acts through public authorities. Unlike, eg the United Kingdom, little consideration was given in Sweden at the time of incorporation to the question of *which* public authorities were bound by the Convention.[16] The majority of public administration in Sweden is performed by elected local authorities (*kommuner*) and authorities at the county level; centrally appointed county administrative boards (*länsstyrelser*) and elected county health boards (*landsting*). Central administrative functions are performed by a large number of independent administrative agencies, varying greatly in composition, functions, size and importance. The vast majority of administrative agencies are subordinate to the government (RF 11:6)[17] but the Swedish system separates the administration from the government; administrative agencies have the constitutionally protected freedom to interpret and apply the law in individual cases (RF 11:7).

[13] See the judgments of the Supreme Court in NJA 2000 s 622 and the Supreme Administrative Court in RÅ 2000 ref 66.

[14] SOU 2001:25, p 331.

[15] In Sweden the term *det allmänna* is used to denote all central and local bodies exercising public power.

[16] The requirement in HRA s 6 is that all 'public bodies' have regard to the Convention. See also the discussion on horizontal effect below and in the concluding comments.

[17] A very few, such as the Ombudsman, are subordinate to Parliament.

However, there is no general definition in Swedish law of an administrative authority. Instead, a number of criteria have been developed in doctrine for identifying an administrative authority: whether the authority exercises *public power* (*myndighetsutövning*), whether its mandate, composition etc is regulated in statute or subordinate legislation rather than private law forms, whether it is financed from public funds etc.[18] The first of these is the most important criterion as far as rights are concerned, especially when the exercise of public power involves creating entitlements or duties for individuals. There is also Convention case law to the effect that it is the exercise of public power which is decisive factor.[19]

As there was little discussion of the authorities which were bound by the Convention, it is not surprising that there was no discussion at the time of incorporation of any *drittwirkung* or 'horizontal' effect the Convention might have between individuals. This is a disputed subject. At international law, the Convention is a treaty regime, albeit of a special character, compliance with which functions, as with all treaties, on the basis of the rules of state responsibility. This basic relationship is not altered by the fact that the nature of the obligations contained in certain articles in the Convention sometimes requires the contracting parties to provide for rights for individuals which are exercisable against other individuals.[20] The most obvious example of this is the right of access to a court to determine a dispute concerning civil rights or obligations, but even other rights can oblige states to engage in positive action for the benefit of some individuals (and, sometimes, the creation of corresponding duties for other individuals). This is sometimes known as 'indirect *drittwirkung*'.

Having said this, the Convention, once it has been incorporated into national law, is a national legal instrument. As a matter of constitutional law it is the national parliament, together with the national courts, which determine whether or not the incorporated Convention is to be given any horizontal effect, direct or indirect. But there is no evidence in the *travaux préparatoires* that the Swedish parliament intended any such effect. Thus, the Swedish courts have no explicit mandate to go further than the case law of the ECtHR, which, at most, requires positive action on the part of the state, rather than direct *drittwirkung*.

[18] See, eg L Marcusson *Offentlig förvaltning utanför myndighetsområdet* (Uppsala, Iustus, 1989), pp 108–66.

[19] See, eg Finska församlingen in *Stockholm and Teuro Hautaniemi v Sweden*, No 24019/94, 85 DR 94 (1996) and *Municipal Section of Antilly v France*, No 45129/98, ECHR 1999-VIII.

[20] See generally, AR Mowbray *Development of positive obligations under the European Convention on Human Rights by the European Court of Human Rights* (Oxford, Hart publishing, 2004).

2 DAMAGES UNDER SWEDISH LAW

The subject of Swedish tort law is obviously very large. However, I do not—thankfully—have to go into any great detail on the subject.[21] The main statute in the area is the Tort Liability Act (*Skadeståndslagen*, SkL)[22] although there are also special statutes regulating eg environmental law. Chapter 2 section 1 (2:1) SkL provides for damages for physical injury to persons or damage to property (*person och sakskada*) and consequential financial losses arising from a personal injury or physical damage to property (called in doctrine *allmän förmögenhetsskada*). However, financial losses can obviously arise from a tort not involving physical injury or damage to property. This is referred to as pure economic losses (*ren förmögenhetsskada*) and is limited under SkL 2:2 to losses arising as the result of the commission of a crime. There are exceptions to this in various other statutes, eg relating to copyright law.

Swedish law also provides for non-pecuniary damages (*ideellt skadestånd*) for 'suffering' but under SkL 2:3 only when this has resulted from a crime against personal freedom or integrity (eg unlawful imprisonment or rape) or reputation (eg defamation).[23]

There are special rules for public authorities and these are obviously of most interest as far as human rights violations are concerned. Interestingly, bearing in mind the historical development in the common law of private law remedies (trespass etc) against public servants, the Swedish rules on public authority liability are of relatively recent vintage. Before 1972, the remedy for abuse of power by a public servant was a personal claim against the person responsible (perhaps combined with a criminal prosecution for misuse of office).

Public authorities are liable to pay damages for physical injury to persons or damage to property and consequential financial losses arising from *negligent acts in the exercise of public power* (SkL 3:2). They are also liable to pay damages for suffering caused in the circumstances set out in 2:3 above. Finally, if special reasons exist, they are liable to pay damages for pure economic losses arising out of a situation in which the public authority negligently gave inaccurate information or advice (SkL 3:3). In adjudging whether such special reasons exist, account is to be taken of the nature of the information or advice, the connection this advice or information had with the functions of the public authority and the circumstances in which the information or advice were given.

One special damages rule applicable to the Convention relates to the specific requirement of compensation for unlawful detention under Article 5(5).[24]

[21] For a brief description in English see B Bengtsson 'Torts and Insurance' in M Bogdan (ed) *Swedish Law* (Stockholm, Norstedts, 2000). As a Scottish lawyer, I would normally refer to 'delict' law, but as the majority of readers of this yearbook are not likely to be Scottish, I will use the common law terminology.

[22] 1972:207.

[23] See below concerning recent changes in the law in this respect regarding discrimination.

[24] 1998: 714, replacing an earlier statute, 1974:515.

Under section 5 of the Act on Compensation for Detention and other Coercive Measures, for compensation to be payable it must be clear that the decision to detain a person was based on erroneous grounds. For detentions lasting longer than tewnty four hours, the state has a strict responsibility. But in both cases, compensation is only payable to the person detained, not the losses to a third party. This means that where a person is self-employed, acting through a juridical person (eg a company), the loss of business the company suffers as a result of the detention is not able to be compensated, although the fact that the detainee is unable to take out salary during the period of detention is.

In SkL 3:7 there is a special rule providing that an individual has no standing to claim damages for a 'decision of the parliament, the government, the Supreme Court or Supreme Administrative Court unless the decision has been annulled or changed'. This special rule is motivated by the same considerations as the previously mentioned restriction on constitutional review in RF 11:14. There is some dispute in doctrine as to whether 'decision' also includes the enactment of legislation or an ordinance.[25] There is, however, an older case from the Supreme Court, prior to the incorporation of the Convention, ruling that an individual has no standing regarding complaints about a failure to enact legislation or an ordinance.[26]

It should be pointed out here that neither under the Convention régime, nor under Swedish law, is it possible for an individual to complain about legislation *in abstracto*. Under the Convention régime, an individual must be a victim of the legislation, although in certain circumstances it is enough that the legislation exists, combined with a likelihood of its application against the individual in question.[27] And it follows from the Code of Procedure (*Rättegångsbalken*, RB) chapter 13, section 2 that an individual cannot invoke a Convention right *in abstracto*, but only in the context of a concrete dispute.[28]

The special problems caused by EC law have given rise to discussions as to whether this special rule can be maintained. It is clear that the Swedish legislature can, and occasionally will, legislate, or fail to legislate, in a manner that is in conflict with EC law. A commission of inquiry produced a report in 1997 recommending the repeal of SkL 3:7.[29] This issue is, however, closely linked to the

[25] See B Bengtsson *Det allmännas skadestånd enligt skadeståndslagen* (Stockholm, Norstedts, 1996, 2nd edn) pp 131–2, Marcusson, above. pp 67–71, T Andersson 'Remedies for Breach of EC Law Before Swedish Courts' in J Lonbay and A Biondi (eds) *Remedies for breach of EC law* (New York/Chicester, John Wiley, 1997) pp 211–4.

[26] In NJA 1978, s 125 the plaintiff alleged that domestic law was not line with Sweden's commitments under, inter alia, the UN Covenant on Civil and Political Rights, 1966, 993 UNTS 3.

[27] For example in the areas of criminalisation of homosexual conduct or secret surveillance. See Harris D J Harris, M O'Boyle and C Warbrick *Law of the European Convention on Human Rights* (London/Dublin/Edinburgh, Butterworths, 1995), pp 635–6.

[28] Although the 'legal interest' an individual needs will, of course vary depending on the nature of the dispute. Standing is very wide in some areas, eg, any person resident in a local authority area is entitled to apply for judicial review of allegedly ultra vires acts of the local authority (*legalitetsprövning*).

[29] De allmännas skadeståndsansvar vid överträdelse av EG-regler [State liability for damages for breach of EC rules] SOU 1997:194.

question of constitutional review which, as already mentioned, is politically sensitive. In order to avoid making a legislative change, the position was therefore taken that the transfer of competence which was made to the EC at the time of accession under RF 10:5[30] allows Swedish courts to act directly upon EC law in awarding damages for breach of EC law. In fact, so far, the majority of such problems have been solved not by the courts but by a peculiarly Swedish institution, the Chancellor of Justice (*Justitiekanslern,* (JK)), who can be described as the 'government's ombudsman'. One of the functions of the Chancellor of Justice is to represent the state in court proceedings involving damages claims against the state, but individuals can also apply directly to this official alleging that they have suffered losses as a result of state action contrary to SkL or other applicable tort rules. The Chancellor of Justice then assesses whether the claim is justified, calculates the individual's losses and awards damages payable out of public funds. The award can be appealed to the ordinary courts, but is usually accepted without demur—a system which would probably be regarded as charmingly innocent in many other countries. Thus, when legislation, or a failure to enact legislation, entails infringements of individuals' rights under EC law, the Chancellor of Justice awards damages.[31]

There have also been a few JK cases concerning Convention rights, of which more below. But even prior to incorporation of the Convention, the practice of the Chancellor of Justice recognised in exceptional cases the duty to pay compensation to a person who suffered financial loss because his or her Convention rights were violated, even without a claim having been made to the Strasbourg organs, as long as the violation was clearly established.[32]

3 DAMAGES UNDER THE CONVENTION

3.1 Just Satisfaction

There are two issues which need to be explained as regards damages and the Convention: the first is the ECtHR's practice as regards 'just satisfaction' in Article 41, the second is the ECtHR's development of the 'effective remedies' requirement of Article 13 to mean that *national* courts are obliged to provide a remedy in damages for violation of certain Convention rights.

[30] For a short discussion, see I Cameron 'Swedish Parliamentary Participation in the Making and Implementation of Treaties' (2005) (74) *Nordic Journal of International Law* pp 429–83.

[31] For a recent example see JK Beslut 2005-11-11, Dnr 2690-02-44. There has been some discussion as whether the JK practice as regards friendly settlement of EC cases on omission to legislate is outside JK's competence.

[32] See J Sundberg *Human Rights in Sweden: the Annual Reports 1985* (Stockholm, 1987) at pp 56–7, who notes the case of Arne Andersson who benefitted indirectly from the Court's judgment in *Sporrong and Lönnroth v Sweden*, A/52, 23 September 1982. Andersson was part owner of one of the houses which had been subject to the *same* expropriation order found to be in breach of Art 1, Protocol 1 in the Sporrong and Lönnroth case. On the other hand, later claims made to JK by other property owners who had been subject to *similar* expropriation orders were dismissed.

Even though, as explained further below, there is a link between the two issues, it is important to keep them separate and the second issue is more important as far as the present article is concerned. I will, in any event, keep my discussion of the first issue relatively brief and instead refer the reader to thorough studies of the subject made by Shelton and by the Scottish and English Law Reform Commissions.

Under Article 41, the ECtHR can award 'just satisfaction' to an applicant whose Convention rights have been breached.[33] The wording and *travaux préparatoires* of Article 41 seemed to indicate that a state found in breach of the Convention could 'cure' this breach simply by the payment of a sum of money to an individual applicant. However, the Court soon went further than this and stated that the legal consequences of the ECtHR finding a violation are that there is a legal obligation on the respondent State 'to put an end to the breach and make reparation for its consequences in such a way as to restore as far as possible the situation existing before the breach'.[34] This development has now reached fruition in 2004 with the cases of *Assanidzé v Georgia*[35] where the Court ordered the release of a detained person and *Broniowski v Poland*[36] where the Court specified legislative measures to be taken to correct structural violations.

In making monetary awards under Article 41, the ECtHR has distinguished, not always very clearly, between economic losses and non-pecuniary damages. As the Scottish and English Law Reform Commissions note,[37] damages under Article 41 have been awarded by the ECtHR for a variety of economic losses, eg for loss of earnings and of pension rights,[38] medical expenses,[39] unlawfully expropriated property[40] and to reimburse fines paid.[41]

Non-pecuniary awards have included compensation for pain, suffering and psychological harm or trauma,[42] distress,[43] frustration,[44] anxiety,[45]

[33] The origins of the provision lie in similar provisions in arbitral treaties, see the separate opinion of Judges Holmbäck, Ross and Wold in *De Wilde, Ooms and Versyp v Belgium*, A/12, 18 June 1971. As Martens notes, this is something which makes it inappropriate to the European ordre publique the Convention has become, Martens, p 273.

[34] *Papamichalopoulus v Greece*, A/330B, 31 October 1995, para 34.

[35] No 71503/01, 8 April 2004

[36] No 31443/96, 22 June 2004. Committee of Ministers Resolution DH(2004)3

[37] Scottish and English Law Reform Commissions, pp 27–8.

[38] For example *Young, James and Webster v UK* A/55 (Art 50), *Smith and Grady v UK*, Nos 33985/96 and 33986/96, 25 July 2000.

[39] eg *Aksoy v Turkey*, No 21987/93, 18 December 1996, *Ilhan v Turkey*, No 22277/93, 27 June 2000

[40] eg *Papamichalopoulos v Greece* A/260-B, 24 June 1993, A 330-B (1995) (Art 50).

[41] eg *Baskaya and Okçuoglu v Turkey* Nos 23536/94 and 24408/94, 8 July 1999.

[42] eg *Aydin v Turkey*, No 23178/94, 25 September 1997, *MC v Bulgaria*, No 39272/98, 4 December 2003, para 194.

[43] eg *H v France* A/162, 24 October 1989.

[44] eg *Van der Leer v Netherlands*, A/170, 21 February 1990.

[45] eg *Lopez Ostra v Spain*, A/303-C, 9 December 1994. See also *Massey v UK*, No 14399/02, 16 November 2004, para 34 'distress and frustration'.

inconvenience,[46] humiliation,[47] loss of reputation[48] and 'loss of relationship' (ie loss of love, companionship and support).[49] There appears to be no conceptual limit on the categories of loss which may be taken into account, and the EctHR seems often prepared to assume such loss, without direct proof.[50]

Companies are also entitled to claim damages for non-pecuniary losses. In *Comingersoll S.A. v Portugal*[51] the Court stated that in deciding whether to award damages under this head, account should be taken of a number of factors, namely:

> the company's reputation, uncertainty in decision-planning, disruption in the management of the company (for which there is no precise method of calculating the consequences) and lastly, albeit to a lesser degree, the anxiety and inconvenience caused to the members of the management team.[52]

As Shelton notes, it is difficult to discern any coherent principles underlying the ECtHR's application of Article 41.[53] There are a number of explanations for this.[54]

(1) the ECtHR does not apply a strict doctrine of precedent. The Court is obviously keen to build up a predictable body of case law interpreting the Convention, and so it is reluctant to overrule or diverge significantly from an earlier judgment. But this motivation is less pressing as regards the monetary award made under Article 41
(2) there are diverse traditions within Europe on judicial assessment of damages: in some countries, such as the UK, Sweden, Germany and the Netherlands, this follows relatively detailed rules, in other countries such as Belgium and France this is regarded as a matter of fact for the judge of first instance[55]

[46] eg *Olsson v Sweden* (No 2) A/250, 21 November 1992.

[47] eg *Young, James and Webster v UK* (Art 50) above.

[48] eg *Sakik and others v Turkey*, Nos 23878–23883/94, 26 November 1997.

[49] See eg *H v UK*, A/121 8 July 1987, A/136-B (just satisfaction), *W v UK* A/121, 8 July 1987, A/136-C (just satisfaction).

[50] Scottish and English Law Reform Commission, p 27. See eg *Abdulaziz, Cabales and Balkandali v UK*, A/94 28 May 1985 para 96 where the EctHR stated 'By reason of its very nature, non-pecuniary damage of the kind alleged cannot always be the object of concrete proof. However, it is reasonable to assume that persons who, like the applicants, find themselves with problems relating to the continuation or inception of their married life may suffer distress and anxiety'. See also *Assanidzé v Georgia* above, para 200, for a similar stance as regards unsubstantiated pecuniary damage.

[51] No 35382/97, 6 April 2000.

[52] At para 35.

[53] D Shelton Remedies in international human rights law (Oxford, Oxford University Press, 2005), p 68. See also Lester of Herne Hill and D Pannick (eds) *Human Rights Law and Practice* (London, LexisNexis, 2004, 2nd edn), who state that this case law is 'little more than equitable assessments of the facts of the individual case . . . there is a danger of spending time attempting to identify principles that do not exist' (para 2.8.4). Grosz, Beatson and Duffy, (2000) state that '[c]ourts and tribunals are . . . likely to be largely frustrated in their search for those principles applied by the ECtHR' at p 144.

[54] *Cf* Scottish and English Law Reform Commissions, pp 19–22.

[55] This is a large subject. See generally U Magnus (ed) *Unification of tort law: damages* (the Hague/London, Kluwer Law International, 2001).

(3) the ECtHR's function of doing justice in a particular case is undoubtedly seen by many of its judges as secondary to its quasi-constitutional function of laying down minimum European rules. This primary function has become even more prominent in recent years with the massive increase in the Court's case law.

3.2 Effective Remedies Generally

The second issue—under what circumstances the Convention requires the provision of a damages remedy at *national* law—has, like every other Convention obligation, developed slowly, and somewhat haphazardly. The Court's case law on Article 13 was underdeveloped and unpredictable for a long time and this related to fact that the Court's views were heavily dependent on the facts of the particular case,[56] which in turn related to the Court's conception of its role as an international rather than constitutional law remedy.[57]

The Court decided in *Klass and others v FRG* in 1978 that where a national authority does not take sufficiently into account, or is not capable of taking into account, the substance of an individual's arguable *claim* that his or her Convention rights have been breached then there has been a breach of Article 13.[58] The Convention organs have, subsequent to *Klass v FRG*, also confirmed that a remedy under Article 13 must be available to the applicant personally.[59] However, Article 13 also has a subsidiary character in that an effective remedy means only a remedy which is as effective as can be having regard to the circumstances.[60] In other words, where a state limitation in a material right is compatible with the Convention, Article 13 should not be interpreted so as to undermine that limitation. One might imagine that, where the Court ruled that a material right was breached, then it would also rule that Article 13 was breached. But the subsidiary character of the article was also apparent in that the Court did not usually proceed to find such a violation. And the Court was careful to stress that Article 13 does not *generally* require any particular form of remedy. In other words, Article 13 sets out an obligation of *result* and states

[56] See Harris, O'Boyle and Warbrick, above, p 444.

[57] For a detailed analysis see JG Merrills *The Development of International Law by the European Court of Human Rights* (Manchester, Manchester UP, 1993, 2nd edn), pp 9–62 and I Cameron 'Protocol 11 to the ECHR: the European Court of Human Rights as a Constitutional Court?' (1996) (15) Yearbook of European Law, pp 219–60.

[58] A/28 6 September 1978.

[59] See, eg *Plattform 'Ärzte für das Leben' v Austria*, No 10126/82, report of 12 March 1987 at paras 97–8.

[60] *Ibid*, para 69. The Court considered that the aggregate of a number of remedies ineffective in themselves could nonetheless constitute an 'effective remedy'. Such a view is only possible to accept where the ineffective remedies act to complement each other, so as to allow *some* form of redress, in practice, and not simply in theory. Where, on the other hand, the individual effect of every supposed remedy is zero in practice, it is difficult to see how five, or ten, times zero is anything other than zero.

have a margin of appreciation as to how they interpret their obligations under the article.[61]

Thus, notwithstanding the wording of Article 13, for a long time, in many contracting states, including Sweden, the primary remedy for an individual who alleged a breach of his or her Convention rights was to apply to the Court in Strasbourg. However, with the incorporation of the Convention into the national legal orders of all the contracting states, the growing number of these states and the vast expansion in complaints to the Court, the Court's international law approach has gradually changed in favour of a more 'constitutional' approach. In 1996 the Court found for the first time a breach of Article 13 where it had not ruled that breaches of other articles had occurred.[62] Moreover, without departing from its case law that states have a margin of appreciation in how they apply Article 13, the Court also began stressing that more 'important' rights, eg Article 3, require stronger remedies.[63]

3.3 Kudla and Subsequent Cases

In 2000, in the landmark case of *Kudla v Poland*,[64] the Court took the opportunity to reconsider its earlier case law to the effect that, when an applicant complains under both Article 6 and Article 13 about the ineffectiveness of a judicial remedy, the complaints under the latter article are 'subsumed' within the former, as Article 6 has been deemed to set out stricter requirements in this regard.[65] The Court now recognised that there is no overlap between the two articles when the violation of Article 6 concerns the length of proceedings, as this is a separate issue from the question of the *availability* of an effective remedy to *complain* about lengthy proceedings. The Court noted the link between the requirement of exhaustion of local remedies in Article 35(1) and Article 13. The former requirement presupposes that there is an effective national remedy. Finally, the Court stressed the need to interpret the Convention in a way which improved its effectiveness. As the protection provided by the Convention can only ever be of a subsidiary nature, an effective national remedy is a necessity.[66]

The Court was careful to restrict the precedent effect of the *Kudla* judgment. It reiterated that there will be cases, such as complaints relating to the absence or remedies to vindicate civil rights or the adequacy of an existing appellate or

[61] See, eg *Kaya v Turkey*, No 22729/93, 19 February 1998, para 106

[62] *Valsamis v Greece*, No 21787/93, 18 December 1996.

[63] See eg *Chahal v UK*, No 22414/93, 15 November 1996 and below on the Z and others case.

[64] No 30210/96, 26 October 2000.

[65] See, eg, *Bouilly v France*, No 38952/97, 7 December 1999. The reason for reconsidering the earlier case law was the 'continuing accumulation of applications before it in which the only, or principal, allegation is that of a failure to ensure a hearing within a reasonable time in breach of Article 6' and that 'excessive delays in the administration of justice' were a danger to the rule of law (at para 148).

[66] At para 152.

cassation procedure in criminal cases, where the safeguards of Article 6(1) absorb those of Article 13.[67] Moreover, it was careful to stress that there are inherent limits on Article 13, in particular, that it cannot be read as requiring states to allow complainants to challenge before national courts primary legislation as being in violation of the Convention.[68] The Court, in fact, went out of its way to say that this particular inherent limit meant that Article 13 '*cannot be read* as requiring the provision of an effective remedy that would enable the individual to complain about the *absence* in domestic law of access to a court as secured by Article 6(1)'.[69]

At more or less the same time, the Committee of Ministers of the Council of Europe responded to the massive growth in Court case law by adopting, first, a recommendation stressing the need for member states to allow re-opening, following judgments of the Court and second, the Rome resolutions on subsidiarity of human rights protection and the need for improved supervision of the Court's judgments.[70] These non-binding political documents encourage the creation of improved national Convention remedies.

Encouraged by the above political expressions of approval and its own growing work load, the Court has gone on to find explicitly in a number of other cases that there is a need for a national damages remedy. In *Z and others v UK*,[71] a local authority, despite receiving warnings from schools, the police and social services, as far back as October 1987, failed to take into care three children until June 1992, when they were placed in emergency foster care at the request of their mother. It had thus failed to prevent the appalling and repeated mistreatment of the applicant children by their parents over a period of four and a half years. An action for damages was later brought against the local authority on behalf of the three children. This failed, the English courts ruling that public policy considerations were such that local authorities should not be held liable in negligence in respect of the exercise of their statutory duties safeguarding the welfare of children.

The Court found a violation of Articles 3 and 13. It stressed that where alleged failure by the authorities to protect people from the acts of others was concerned, there should be available to the victim or the victim's family a mechanism for establishing any liability of State officials or bodies for acts or

[67] See, eg, *Brualla Gómez de la Torre v Spain*, No. 26737/95, 19 December 1997, para 41 and *Kamasinski v Austria*, A/168, 19 December 1989, para 110.

[68] See the earlier attempt to read Art 13 in this way, disproved in the case of *James and others v UK*, A/98, 21 February 1986, para 85. However, as shown below, the Court's statement in Kudla is somewhat misleading. Where the Convention requires a damages remedy, then the ECtHR considers that national courts have a duty to interpret national law in such a way as to provide one. The boundary line between the creation of a remedy and the expansion of an existing remedy is fluid and depends upon the national legal culture.

[69] Para 151 (my emphasis).

[70] No R (2000) 2. Resolution I concerns institutional and functional arrangements, Resolution II concerns respect for human rights, democratic stability and cohesion. They can be found in Human Rights Information Bulletin, no 50 and the council website (www.coe.int).

[71] No 29392/99, 10 May 2001.

omissions involving the breach of their rights under the Convention. Furthermore, the Court stated, in the case of a breach of Articles 2 and 3, which ranked as 'the most fundamental provisions of the Convention . . . compensation for the non-pecuniary damage flowing from the breach should in principle be available as part of the range of redress'.[72]

The case of *TP and KM v UK*,[73] was the reverse side of the coin in that it concerned a negligent decision by a local authority to take a child into care. The mother and child later brought a claim for damages on the basis that they had suffered psychologically on account of their enforced separation from each other for a year. Their claim went, eventually, to the House of Lords where it was rejected on the same basis as the *Z and others* case, namely that public policy considerations were such that local authorities should not be held liable in negligence in respect of the exercise of their statutory duties safeguarding the welfare of children. The Court unanimously found a violation of Article 8 and also of Article 13 because the applicants should have had available to them a means of claiming that the local authority's handling of the procedures was responsible for the damage which they suffered and obtaining compensation for that damage. The Court thus accepted the applicants' argument that the tort of negligence was the only remedy in national law capable of determining the substance of their complaint and which (but for the alleged immunity) would closely match the requirements of the Convention. Here the Court went beyond its formulation in *Z and others* and stated that:

> where an arguable breach of one or more of the rights under the Convention is in issue, there should be available to the victim a mechanism for establishing any liability of State officials or bodies for that breach. Furthermore, in *appropriate cases*, compensation for the pecuniary and non-pecuniary damage flowing from the breach should *in principle* be available as part of the range of redress.[74]

There have subsequently been a number of Turkish cases involving deaths or disappearances allegedly caused by the security forces, where the Court has also found that damages claims should in principle be available for such very serious violations of Article 2.[75] But even for deaths caused by negligence the Court has now stressed that a damages action should be available in cases of accidental deaths. This requirement to make available at national law a remedy in damages in such cases has not limited allegations of negligence by a state official, eg a policeman or doctor employed in a public hospital, but also applies as regards such allegations directed against private parties.[76]

[72] At para 109.

[73] No 28945/95, 10 May 2001.

[74] At para 107 (my emphasis).

[75] These cases have usually also involved the adequacy of criminal prosecution of the alleged offenders.

[76] *Öneryildiz v Turkey* No 48939/99, 18 June 2002. See also *Calvelli and Ciglio v Italy*, No 32967/96, 17 January 2002, where the Grand Chamber ruled that (in the context of medical negligence) that the positive obligation to protect life does not always require a criminal law remedy, but can be satisfied by a civil law remedy in cases of unintentional infringement of the right to life.

So it should have been clear to the Swedish government by 2001 that the Swedish system for non-pecuniary damages would not always be adequate in the light of this new ECtHR case law.[77] Nonetheless, in 2003, the Swedish government, rather cynically perhaps, tried to stave off a finding of a violation of Article 13 by the ECtHR by arguing that the Swedish courts were able to develop SkL to provide adequate remedies for a breach of Convention rights (in this case, the right to property, caused by an incorrect decision to declare a company bankrupt). But the ECtHR pointed out, correctly, that generally speaking, where there is no crime or serious negligence on the part of a public authority, then SkL provides no remedy in damages and it saw no evidence—in 2003—of such a willingness or ability to develop SkL in this way.[78]

Having criticised the Swedish government, I should add that, notwithstanding the above quote from the *TP and KM* case, it is still by no means clear whether damages should be available for breaches of *all* Convention rights, and if not, what criteria should be applied to identify those situations in which a remedy in damages should lie. So far, we can only say for certain that there are three situations in which national damages remedies must exist. First, breaches of Article 2, 3 generally. Secondly, certain violations of Article 8 in situations similar to those of *TP and KM*. Thirdly, violations of the right to trial within a reasonable time.

The first category can be explained by the position of these rights in the hierarchy of Convention rights and the nature of the injury suffered. The suffering of a person tortured, or the relatives of a person who has been unlawfully killed, cannot be healed by compensation. However, this, together with the prosecution of the perpetrator and undertakings to try to ensure that similar cases do not occur in the future, is all the state can offer. The second category can be explained by the level of suffering of an individual wrongfully deprived for a number of years of his/her family life. A child may have become permanently estranged from one or both of its parents. Again, this cannot be repaired. The third category can be explained either by the importance of a well-functioning judicial remedy for all civil rights and/or, more cynically, by the ECtHR's desire to cut down on the massive number of reasonable time cases.

It is, however, very important to note two points as regards damages remedies for violations of Article 6. Firstly the *Kudla* judgment does not specifically refer to the need for a remedy in damages. As already mentioned, Article 13 sets out an obligation of result and other forms of remedy can be more appropriate for certain types of proceedings. Comparative material indicates that states have one or other, or a combination of, four types of action for dealing with delayed proceedings.[79] These are, remedies for speeding up proceedings, remedies allowing for discontinuance of proceedings or mitigation of sentence, damages remedies and disciplinary

[77] As to why nothing was done, see below.

[78] *Stockholms Försäkrings- Och Skadeståndsjuridik AB v Sweden*, No 38993/97, 16 September 2003.

[79] Venice Commission, 2005.

proceedings. ECtHR case law after *Kudla* makes it clear that the first three of these, so long as they fulfill the criteria of effectiveness set by the Court, will satisfy the requirements of Article 13. A remedy must be effective in both law and practice. For example, where a damages remedy exists, but a national court awards significantly lower sums than the ECtHR has done for similar periods of delay in similar circumstances, as the Italian courts had begun doing in so-called 'Pinto' (delay) proceedings, the ECtHR stated in *Scordino* and subsequent cases that it does not regard the remedy as 'effective'.[80] As Italian cases take up an unncessarily large amount of the time of the Court, it came as no surprise that the Court in the *Zullo* case later set out detailed guidelines for when and how much damages should normally be payable.[81] But assuming that the remedy is effective, the first three types of action will usually be alternatives, although in some special cases *both* a speeding up remedy and a remedy in damages might be necessary.[82] The fourth is not regarded as an effective remedy as it will not result either in speeding-up of lengthy proceedings, or in an adequate redress for the delay.[83]

Secondly, while the Convention requirements on what is an effective remedy for delay is becoming successively clearer with the ECtHR case law, the same cannot (yet) be said for what is the appropriate national response to other violations of Article 6. For example, in a case where a national court is not impartial within the meaning of the ECtHR case law, a plaintiff might claim that but for the Convention violation found the outcome of the proceedings would probably have been different and more favourable to the him/her. More problematically, he/she might claim that the violation deprived him/her of an opportunity to achieve a different result which was not in all the circumstances of the case an opportunity without value. What is an 'effective remedy' in such cases? The Court in any event has, generally speaking, not been easily persuaded that a structural violation of Article 6 justifies the making of an award of just satisfaction under Article 41.[84]

[80] *Scordino v Italy*, No 36813/97, 17 March 2003, confirmed in the judgment of 29 July 2004. The Italian Court of Cassation subsequently affirmed in its judgment no 1340 of 26 January 2004 proceedings the principle that:

> the determination of non-pecuniary damage by courts of appeal in accordance with section 2 of Law no 89/2001, although inherently done on an equitable basis, must move within the confines of a legally defined context since regard must be made to the amounts awarded in similar cases by the Strasbourg Court.

[81] *Zullo v Italy*, No 64897/01, 10 November 2004.

[82] See, eg *Djangozov v Bulgaria*, No 45950/99, 8 October 2004, para 47.

[83] *Kormacheva v Russian Federation*, No 53084/99, 29 January 2004, para 64.

[84] eg in *Kingsley v UK*, No 35605/97, 7 November 2000, para 43, the Grand Chamber stated:

> In all the circumstances, and in accordance with its normal practice, in civil and criminal cases, as regards violations of Article 6(1) caused by failures of objective or structural independence and impartiality, the Court does not consider it appropriate to award monetary compensation to the applicant in respect of loss of procedural opportunity or any distress, loss or damage allegedly flowing from the outcome of the domestic proceedings.

The question of a national damages remedy in Article 6 structural violation cases was discussed by the British House of Lords in *Greenfield, R (on the application of) v Secretary of State for the Home Department* [2005] UKHL 14 (16 February 2005).

Finally, as regards how far we can interpret the *TP and KM* cases I should note that the Committee of Ministers adopted in 2004 a further recommendation, again stressing the subsidiarity of the Convention system. Member states are to:

> ascertain, through constant review, in the light of case-law of the Court, that domestic remedies exist for anyone with an arguable complaint of a violation of the Convention, and that these remedies are effective, in that they can result in a decision on the merits of the complaint and adequate redress for any violation found.[85]

The recommendation stops short of requiring damages remedies, but does mention these as a 'best practice'.

4 THE SWEDISH CASES ON CONVENTION DAMAGES

The restrictions placed by the Tort Liability Act upon awards of economic and non-pecuniary damages meant that it was not long after incorporation of the Convention before the question arose as to whether the incorporation Act, which makes even Articles 13 and 41 a part of Swedish law, can be used as a statutory basis for awarding damages.

The first case to my knowledge where the issue arose in a higher court was the *Kellerman* case before the Labour Court.[86] The plaintiff company was in dispute with a trade union which wished it to join a collective agreement, or otherwise accept a specially drafted substitute agreement. This, the company's owner argued, was in violation of his employees's rights of non-association under Article 11. He also argued that the state was under an obligation under Article 6 to allow him a judicial remedy in cases where trade union action was allegedly disproportionate. The Labour Court noted that there were no explicit rules in Swedish law on sanctions for breaches of the Convention the matter. It found on the facts no violation of Article 11, and stated that since the Labour Court could consider the alleged lack of proportionality of the trade union measures—a hotly disputed issue I should add—there was no breach of Article 6 either. If the plaintiff had won the case, the issue would have arisen as to what the courts could or should do about the matter. Kellerman would have wanted first an

[85] Rec (2004) 6 on the improvement of domestic remedies. States should also:

> II. review, following Court judgments which point to structural or general deficiencies in national law or practice, the effectiveness of the existing domestic remedies and, where necessary, set up effective remedies, in order to avoid repetitive cases being brought before the Court; III. pay particular attention, in respect of aforementioned items I and II, to the existence of effective remedies in cases of an arguable complaint concerning the excessive length of judicial proceedings.

The recommendation is appended to the Declaration of the Committee of Ministers 'Ensuring the effectiveness of the implementation of the European Convention on Human Rights at national and European levels' (adopted by the Committee of Ministers on 12 May 2004, at its 114th Session). available at http://www.coe.int/T/E/Human_rights/ib62e_web.pdf.

[86] AD 1998 no 17.

injunction against the trade unions preventing them from taking further blockade action and secondly damages for his losses. It is in general possible for an administrative authority or court to order a private party to refrain from taking action in breach of the law and to attach a financial penalty for non-compliance with the order (*vitesförläggande*).[87] Disputes regarding the execution of the penalty are determined by the courts. But, in the absence of a specific statute authorising this, it is uncertain whether an injunction can be ordered in circumstances where damages are not also recoverable for the conduct in question.[88] The two issues, injunction and damages, are thus linked in this respect. If, however, the incorporation statute is itself seen as authorising the courts to issue an injunction, then there is no need to link the issues of damages and injunctions.

As regards doctrine, I believe I was the first person who expressed the opinion in the Swedish debate that Article 13 could provide a statutory basis for making damages claims in certain special circumstances. However, I committed the fatal error—as I do now—of putting my thoughts in English rather than in Swedish.[89] As an academic lawyer writing in the field of constitutional and international law, one must, sooner or later come to the bitter conclusion that legal development rarely if ever hinges upon, revolves around, or is even remotely affected by one's writings. So, I was not surprised that there was no immediate reaction. It was the *Kudla* case which sparked off the discussion properly. In a number of cases before district courts, the argument began to be made that, first, certain breaches of the Convention, in particular, violations of the reasonable time requirement in Article 6 were 'negligence' within the meaning of the Tort Liability Act and secondly, that Article 13 and/or Article 41 created an independent basis for awarding damages against the state.[90] The first case in which a district court awarded non-pecuniary damages on the basis of Article 13 was in 2002.[91] Interestingly, it was one of the last cases presided over by the then president of the court, which I think says something about the, in general, considerable reluctance of the Swedish lower courts to stick their necks out in controversial issues connected to rights.

The initial reaction of JK was negative.[92] JK argued that Article 41 did not provide a basis for damages claims. Although Article 41 was a part of Swedish law, only the ECtHR could award 'just satisfaction'. The ECtHR was thus a 'special court' within the meaning of the forum rule in RB 10:17. This rule

[87] Act on Conditional Fines (1985:206), Execution Code, ch 2, s 15.

[88] F Schmidt, R Eklund, H Göransson, K Källström and T Sigemann *Facklig arbetsrätt* (Stockholm, Juristförlaget, 1997), p 236. It should be pointed out here that, in Sweden as in many other jurisdictions, damages and injunctions are often alternative remedies. Injunctions can be issued in deportation cases. Following *Cruz Varas v Sweden*, A/201, 20 March 1991, an amendment was made to the Aliens Act (ch 8 s 10a) allowing the government to issue a stay of execution in deportation cases where the ECtHR requests this.

[89] See I Cameron 'A Survey of ECHR Case law and the question of remedies' in I Cameron and A Simoni (eds) *Dealing with Integration*, vol 2 (Uppsala, Iustus, 1998), pp 47–52.

[90] See eg Uppsala tingsrätt, dom 8 June 2000, Mål no T 3326-97 (unreported).

[91] Stockholms tingsrätt, dom 8 March 2002, Mål no T17442-00 (unreported).

[92] Published in pointlex 30 August 2002.

excluded the ordinary courts from taking up claims to be brought before a special court. This argument was accepted in a number of cases.[93]

In another case, NJA 2002, section 88, the issue was whether a lower court had committed a procedural error in allowing a lay judge who could be suspected of a lack of impartiality to participate in a case. Part of the claimant's argument in the case was based upon the case law of the ECtHR on impartial tribunals to which the claimant alleged the lower court had negligently failed to have regard.[94] The Supreme Court agreed that there was a duty on courts to have regard to the case law of the ECtHR, but that, as there was no case directly on point, and as only manifest errors by a court can give rise to tortuous liability, the claim for damages must fail.[95]

The Supreme Court then proceeded in NJA 2003, section 217 to take up a case concerning a tax penalty which the claimant alleged violated his right to trial within a reasonable time. The Court of Appeal had dismissed the case on the basis that only the Tort Liability Act provided for damages. While this statute should, as far as possible be interpreted in conformity with the Convention, the wording of SkL 3:2 clearly required negligence on the part of state officials. Although case law accepts that as far as bureaucratic decision-making is concerned, negligence can be 'cumulative' in the sense that a series of minor errors, acceptable in themselves, can add up to negligence,[96] the claimant had failed to substantiate his claim that there had been any such negligence in his case. The Supreme Court considered that JK's argument on Article 41, on which the Court of Appeal had based part of its reasoning, was correct. However, without deciding the issue, it stated that it had been procedurally wrong for the Court of Appeal to dismiss out of hand that part of the application which built upon Article 13 as an independent ground for obtaining damages. At around the same time, the Supreme Court ruled that a violation of the right to trial within a reasonable time in a criminal case where the accused had been convicted could be corrected by means of a reduction in sentence.[97]

Shortly after NJA 2003, section 217, JK accepted that a violation of the Article 6 right to trial within a reasonable time could give rise to damages, but on the basis that this qualifies as negligence under SkL 3:2.[98]

[93] See eg Svea Court of Appeal, beslut 20 August 2002, Mål no T 1509-02 (unreported), Södergren, 2002, p 669.

[94] The independent and impartial tribunal requirement in Art 6 had been considered in *Holm v Sweden*, 25 November 1993, A/279-A. The government response to the case was that when impartiality was at issue, the courts should interpret the general rules on impartiality in RB 4:13 in conformity with the ECtHR case law, particularly *Hauschildt v Denmark*, A/154 24 May 1989. See prop. 97/98:43, s 129–35. See also Prop. 1992/93:25, s 19 and 22. For cases see eg RH 1996:58 and RH 1996:68.

[95] The Supreme Court dismissed another damages claim, this time brought against appeal court judges for violation of the right to an impartial trial, but on the basis that the claim was not 'serious' and thus did not fall within Art 6 at all. NJA 2003, s 527.

[96] B Bengtsson and E Strömbäck *Skadeståndslagen. En kommentar* (Stockholm, Norstedts, 2002), pp 78–9; H Andersson 'Europakonventionen som parallell respektive fristående skadeståndgrund' (PointLex, 21 June 2005), p 14.

[97] NJA 2003, s 414.

[98] JK drn 1916-02-41, beslut 10 October 2003.

The most recent, and most significant case is NJA 2005, section 462. In this case, the plaintiff, an accountant, claimed damages for breach of his rights under Article 6 to trial within a reasonable time. He had been informed on 29 January 1992 that he was suspected of involvement in economic crime. He was formally charged on 16 June 1995 and his trial commenced on 5 November 1998. He was acquitted in December 1998. The proceedings had thus lasted almost seven years. He applied for both economic and non-pecuniary damages on two grounds:

(1) he alleged that the prosecutor had been guilty of fault or negligence in the exercise of public power, first by informing him that he was under suspicion when the evidence of his committing an offence was insufficient, secondly, by charging him with an offence and thirdly, by failing to drop the prosecution when it became evident after additional inquiries that there were insufficient grounds for concluding that that he had committed an offence
(2) his Convention rights under Article 6 had been violated.

The Supreme Court dismissed the first ground for complaint without discussion. Public policy reasons can be assumed to lie behind this. In any system, charges will be brought which are not found proven in court proceedings. Moreover, the Swedish system is based on the principle of legality, which allows the prosecutor only limited grounds for discretion in not bringing a prosecution.

It then considered whether the plaintiff's rights under Article 6 had been breached and came to the conclusion that they had. It again dismissed the argument that Article 41 could serve as an independent statutory basis for damages. It now explicitly stated, however, that Article 13 *did* impose a duty to provide effective remedies, but that this did not necessarily mean a duty to provide a remedy in damages. In line with the now usual judicial approach to the Convention, the Supreme Court first examined whether the Tort Liability Act could be interpreted in conformity with the Convention. It considered that unacceptable delays could constitute negligence. Although the *travaux préparatoires* indicate that the state should be able to avoid damages in such a situation where the delay has arisen because of a lack of administrative resources, the Supreme Court noted that this possibility is very limited in practice.[99] As the ECtHR does not accept such an argument for delays, it must be assumed that the court's reference to the principle of treaty conform construction means that the contrary statements in the *travaux préparatoires* must be disregarded as far as delays in Article 6 cases are concerned.

The Supreme Court proceeded to examine whether there was an adequate causal connection between the delay and the plaintiff's alleged injury. As mentioned, the Swedish case law allows 'accumulation of errors' in that a series of minor errors, each excusable in itself, can together add up to negligence. However, one could argue that the injury the plaintiff was complaining about—

[99] The Court referred to Bengtsson, above, pp 89–90.

the damage to his reputation, with consequent difficulties in being re-employed—had already occurred with the bringing of the prosecution. The delay had not added much to this injury. On the other hand, one can argue that the injury is continuing, and the delay has lengthened the period of the injury before he was cleared of all suspicions.[100]

If delay is seen through the prism of an injury to reputation, this implies that, in most cases where a person is convicted, then the tarnished reputation will usually be justified, and so there *is* no injury. But the Supreme Court emphasized that, in principle, the injury exists whether a person is convicted or not. Thus, the Supreme Court does not consider that loss of reputation is a necessary element in proving the tort. Instead, as shown below, the loss of reputation is a factor affecting the *assessment* of the economic *and* non-pecuniary damages. The Supreme Court found that there was a causal connection between the suspicion of crime, and loss to the plaintiff's income. It fixed the date at which the unacceptable delay had started at 1 January 1997 and accordingly awarded damages for economic loss for the period of about two years, plus a one year 'transitional' period. The latter period was based on the fact that reentry to the labour market would take time: the damage to his reputation could not have been said to have disappeared immediately. In this respect it can be noted that the Supreme Court referred to the ECtHR's case law on 'loss of opportunities' and seemed to consider that this pure economic loss was taken into account by adding on the transitional period of one year. It however halved the damages payable for loss of income on the basis that all the delay in the case could not be attributed to the state—an adjustment which it supported by reference to established principles of Swedish tort law.[101]

The question remained as to whether there was any basis on which to award him non-pecuniary damages. The negligence (delay) shown by the prosecutors in the case was not of the level of a crime (misuse of office), and so no such duty to pay compensation could be based on SkL. The Supreme Court noted that according to established principles of Swedish tort law, non-pecuniary damages should only be awarded on the basis of a statute. Without explicitly concluding that the incorporated Article 13 constituted the necessary statutory authority, the Supreme Court stated that 'strong reasons' existed for a Swedish court being able to award such damages.[102] It added that in assessing such claims for non-

[100] H Andersson, above, p 16.

[101] For an illuminating discussion, see *ibid*, pp 17–18. Andersson points out that, arguably, this is to allow the state to profit from its own wrong. In the circumstances, he considers that the compensation was not generous. In common law terms one could see this type of argument as a variant of estoppel. See also the 'eggshell' argument made by the plaintiffs in the English case of Anufrijeva, below n 115. The state should act on the basis that certain classes of people, such as asylum seekers, are often vulnerable and, because of their experiences, more susceptible to mental suffering. Where a miscarriage of justice occurs, this can 'set off' other factors. In such circumstances it should not be open for the state to escape liability, or reduce it, on the basis that the human rights breach (delay or mistake of law or fact) is only partially responsible for the injury (mental suffering).

[102] As to why it took this stance, see the discussion in the concluding comments below.

pecuniary damages, it was 'a natural point of departure' to take account of the case law of the ECtHR interpreting just satisfaction under Article 41, 'even if there was no exact duty in the Convention to do so'. It assessed these damages on the basis of the *Zullo* case, which as already mentioned, calculates damages on the basis of the whole period awaiting trial. This more generous method of assessment goes some way to compensating for the downward adjustment of the economic losses.

The Supreme Court has had one further case in 2005 on ECHR damages.[103] Here the plaintiff was a taxi driver who had been convicted of robbery at first instance and sentenced to imprisonment for one year but acquitted in the court of appeal. In Sweden, the court of appeal in criminal cases generally grants a new trial of both law and fact. He was not jailed pending the appeal, but his taxidriver's licence was recalled. Almost sixteen months had elapsed between the conviction and the judgment in the court of appeal. He argued that the case should have been given priority and that he was entitled to damages under either SkL and/or the ECHR. The Supreme Court rejected his claims, ruling that the period of sixteen months was insufficient to violate the Convention requirement of trial within a reasonable time.

5 CONCLUDING COMMENTS

5.1 Difficulties Involved in Creating Remedies

There are a number of points to be made in conclusion. To begin with, the Swedish court should not have been put in the position of having to create new remedies. This should have been done by the legislature. The incorporation act is no ordinary statute, but rather the insertion into Swedish law of a large body of principles. The process of applying these principles can be described as one of concretization rather than 'interpretation'. For a pragmatic judiciary, rights need to be completed with remedies, otherwise they are meaningless. In the area of procedural law, existing remedies can often be interpreted in accordance with the principle of treaty conform construction. But in other Convention areas, it is not simply a question of applying a pre-existing remedy to correct the wrong, but creating one, or at least, developing creatively an existing remedy. However, the Swedish courts, especially the lower courts, are unused to doing this. The Swedish cases in fact illustrate the difficulties a bureaucratic judiciary applying a primarily subjective (legislative history) approach to law interpretation have in adapting existing national remedies to comply with a case law system applying a teleological interpretative method. The first reaction of most of the lower courts in the cases sketched out in the preceding section was to reject any types of damage claim that could not be fitted into the existing matrix of damages only for economic loss.

[103] HD mål nr T 923-02, 3 November 2005.

One might be surprised at this, bearing in mind the fact that Sweden has had a catalogue of constitutional rights since 1976. As already mentioned, individual rights in RF have not really been regarded by the courts as 'operational' and this has meant that there has been little tradition of judicial rights reasoning to build upon. Admittedly, the influence of EC law means that Swedish courts are increasingly having to reason independently from the parliament's *travaux préparatoires* to legislation, or even contrary to these. As shown above, the ECHR can also have this effect. But the lower courts are obviously still uncomfortable with having to develop the law in this way. The débâcle of the tax penalty cases, with parallel judgments reaching different conclusions in different courts of appeal and courts of administrative appeal around the country shows this clearly.

There are other similarities between the damages cases and the tax penalty cases. It can be recollected that emphatic statements were made in the *travaux préparatoires* to the incorporation statute that the primary responsibility for ensuring continuing compliance lay with the parliament. But here was another area in which the courts were left on their own. According to what has been heard, the Foreign Ministry in fact, brought the *Kudla* case to the attention of the Ministry of Justice which in turn raised the issue as to whether a commission of inquiry should be appointed to investigate the issue. Apparently, the Ministry of Finance vetoed this idea, a decision supposedly taken at the highest political level.This does seem plausible. Politicians of any political complexion, but especially, bearing in mind the Swedish context, Social Democratic politicians, have little interest in creating new rights to sue the state for damages.

5.2 The relationship between Articles 13 and 41

The Swedish debate in doctrine has been largely driven by practicing lawyers who have done a good job in publicizing the ECtHR case law.[104] However, they are, naturally, interested in maximizing the situations in which damages should be available for violating Convention rights. Two views have been expressed by these practicing lawyers:

(1) the ECtHR's statements in the *TP and KM* case have been interpreted as requiring, in principle, compensation for the pecuniary and non-pecuniary damage flowing from a breach of *any* Convention right, even if they accept that not all such breaches in practice need be remedied by damages.

[104] See C Crafoord 'Inhemsk gottgörelse för kränkningar av Europakonventionen' (2001 (4)) *Europarättslig tidskrift*, pp 519–47; J Södergren 'Axplock II ur svensk konventionstillämpning' *Europarättslig tidskrift* (2002 (5)), pp 659–82; J Södergren 'Axplock III ur svensk konventionstillämpning' *Europarättslig tidskrift* (2003 (6)), pp 706–25; J Södergren 'Rätt till skadestånd i Sverige direkt på grundval av Europakonventionen' *Juridisk Tidsskrift* (2004–2005), pp 762–75.

(2) arguing from the principle of subsidiarity, the amount of damages available should be assessed on the basis of ECtHR case law on Article 41.[105] In other words the position has been taken that the ECtHR considers that there is, in general, an obligation to provide a remedy in damages at the national level, and that the ECtHR considers that the calculation of damages payable by the national court should be made applying the principles which can be derived from the EctHR case law on just satisfaction

What support can be found for these positions? Undoubtedly, one can argue that if the ECtHR makes a monetary award to a victim of a rights violation in a situation where a Swedish court would not, then there is a clear risk that the victim will apply to the ECtHR, thus undermining the purpose of incorporation of the ECHR.[106] It is also true that the Court has refused to accept a respondent government's argument that a plaintiff should not be awarded more in just satisfaction than he or she would have received in a similar case before a national court.[107] Furthermore, as already mentioned, the ECtHR has stated in the *Scordino* and subsequent cases that damages awards for delay must not significantly deviate from the awards the Court itself would make under Article 41.

I agree that the category of rights for which national damages remedies must exist is open-ended. It will become clear—and larger—through the ECtHR's case law. But, as already mentioned, so far, the ECtHR has only said in three situations that damages remedies are definitely required at the national level. While new situations can, and undoubtedly will, be added by the ECtHR it is important to distinguish the situation of national courts applying the incorporated Article 13 and the ECtHR applying Article 41. In the latter situation, a violation has occurred of an international obligation, leading to an injury occurring to an individual.[108] There is state responsibility for this violation and as regards the measures of damages, the ECtHR, the guardian of pan-European values, naturally could not, and should not, say that a life in, eg, Turkey is worth less than a life in, eg, Sweden.

By contrast, there *is* no violation of international law if a national court provides an effective remedy. If there *had* been an effective remedy available and applied in the case, then the ECtHR would not have taken up the case and found a violation. The issue before the national courts is thus the *effectiveness of the remedy*. The fact that the ECtHR has awarded damages under Article 41 in a case cannot automatically be interpreted to mean that a national court should award damages in a similar case, because, up till the reform of the ECtHR's case

[105] See Crafoord, *ibid*, pp 541, 545.

[106] Södergren, 2003 *ibid*, 708.

[107] eg *Ogur v Turkey*, No 21594/93, 20 May 1999, para 98. Although the reverse has also applied—the ECtHR has taken into account high levels of damages available in the UK for other torts, to justify a high award of just satisfaction, *Z and others v UK*, para 128.

[108] For an interesting discussion of recent Supreme Court case law from a public international perspective see G Lysén 'Två rättsfall från HD: förvirrade käpphästar eller en brytningstid?!' (2005) *Europarättslig tidskrift* pp 645–61.

law in 2004 on reopening and on structural violations, damages were all the ECtHR *could* award.

It should thus be understood that, even though the ECtHR rarely goes on to find a separate violation of Article 13, the finding of a substantive rights violation and award under Article 41 by the ECtHR *presuppose* that there has been no effective remedy in the case at the national level. Any damages award made available at the national level should thus not *automatically* apply the ECtHR's award made in a similar case which has made it all the way to Strasbourg, but should deduct the 'value' to the plaintiff of any non-damages remedy which could be, or might have been, made by the national court. This value can be anything between 0 per cent and 100 per cent of the Strasbourg award of just satisfaction. This, I submit, is not in contradiction with the *Scordino* case. The *Scordino* case can be explained by the fact that the ECtHR, in order to cut down on its case load, deliberately restricted states' margin of appreciation as regards damages remedies for delays. As far as delays are concerned, the ECtHR has now made it very clear that the assessment of damages must conform with the criteria set out in the *Zullo* case. In other cases, I submit that the margin of appreciation is still relatively wide, and states have considerable discretion as to which remedies, or combination of remedies, they are to provide to meet the standard of effectiveness in Article 13. In any event, the ECtHR has recently stated that compensation which has been granted that is lower than the amount usually awarded for comparable delays by the Court itself may nevertheless be considered 'adequate' in the light of the specific circumstances of the case, the standard of living in the State concerned, the promptness of the finding and award by the national court as well as the promptness of the payment within the national legal system.[109]

5.3 But are there other Effective Remedies?

This will depend on the area of law in question as: different areas are governed by different statutes. An overview of such a large area will not be attempted here, but I will simply make a number of general comments. It seems that, inter alia the impact of European law, has led to the subject of administrative remedies becoming fragmented and incoherent and ripe for an overhaul. Having said that, the main area of concern for individuals is likely to be the area of social benefits, but it should be remembered that many social benefits will fall outside of the area of application of Article 6 or even, for states such as Sweden which have not ratified Protocol 12, the Convention as a whole. Where this is so, then there is accordingly no Convention duty to provide effective remedies to correct erroneous administrative decisions refusing to award or wrongly calculating benefits.

[109] See *Bako v Slovakia*, No 60277/00, 15 March 2005.

In general, administrative proceedings and judicial proceedings are to be conducted expeditiously (Administration Act, 1986:223, section 7). As regards remedies for erroneous decisions in administrative law generally speaking an administrative agency has a duty to reconsider a decision it has made should new facts come to light, or where circumstances otherwise call for this, and this can be done quickly and simply and without any disadvantage to an individual (Administration Act, section 27). Reopening in administrative cases is thus relatively easy. As regards administrative courts, reopening of their decisions is possible under section 37b of the Administrative Procedure Act (1971:291) where, 'because of particular circumstances, there are special reasons for doing so'. This possibility of reconsidering/reopening will often suffice for most cases of Convention violations committed by the state, although as noted there are special problems in child custody cases, where it is no longer in the best interests of the child to reunite the natural family. In criminal cases, violations of the 'reasonable time' requirements of Article 6 can often be taken into account by drawing off time at the sentencing stage, if and when the victim has been convicted.[110] In both civil and criminal proceedings, a party who is of the opinion that the processing of the case has been unnecessarily delayed by a decision of a district court may file an interlocutory appeal against the decision (RB 49:7).[111] If the Court of Appeal finds that the appeal is meritorious it may quash the disputed decision. Reopening in civil and criminal cases is more awkward, depending on the circumstances, but bearing in mind the explicit encouragement to do so from the Committee of Ministers, it may, conceivably, be possible to interpret existing Swedish provisions in RB to permit this in at least some cases.[112]

In some cases, then, I think that reopening will, and should, be the primary remedy, but a victim might be expected to want damages as a supplementary remedy. Thus, something should be said about the *role* of damages in the overall system of control of public power, ie both preventive controls and remedies. It should be recognized that damages play different roles in public and private law[113]

[110] See, eg RH 2000:96, RH 2000:98.

[111] Although see, in this respect, *Eskelinen v Finland*, No 7274/02, 3 February 2004, where the ECtHR did not consider that this remedy worked in practice and so rejected the Finnish claim of non-exhaustion.

[112] These are complicated issues of procedural law. See generally, Cameron, 1998 above, pp 53–64.

[113] With this in mind, the British judge, Lord Woolf (2000) suggested eight possible principles to guide the English courts in deciding whether to award damages for Convention violations. These were not followed by the House of Lords in the Greenfield case (see above, n 84), but they are nonetheless of interest and can be summarized in the following way (1) If there is any other remedy in addition to damages, that other remedy should usually be granted initially and damages should only be granted in addition if necessary to afford just satisfaction. (2) The court should not award exemplary or aggravated damages. (3) An award should be 'of no greater sum than that necessary to achieve just satisfaction'. If it is necessary for a decision to be retaken, the court should wait and see what the outcome is; (4) The quantum of the award should be 'moderate', and 'normally on the low side by comparison to tortious awards' (5) The award should be restricted to compensating the victim for what has happened 'so far as the unlawful conduct exceeds what could lawfully happen'. (6) Failure by the claimant to take preventative or remedial action will reduce the amount of damages. (7) There is no reason to distinguish between pecuniary and non-pecuniary loss. What matters is that the loss

something which is accepted in EC law.[114] The money for the damages comes from the same 'pot' as the provision of public services and litigating on damages will usually be a very inefficient way of making public policy.[115] Simply put, the more money paid to some people in damages, the less which is available for other people, perhaps even more needy. The state is not deterred in the same way by damages as a private actor may be.[116] Sweden is a welfare state where individuals, moreover, also tend to be covered by private insurance. Although abuse of state power is not something which can be insured against, and in that sense it is obviously *necessary* for individuals to have a remedy in damages against the state, the extent to which they experience a need to *use* this remedy will depend on a large number of different factors, in particular how well people perceive that preventive mechanisms against abuse of power are working. At the risk of considerable simplification, Sweden is generally speaking not a very 'litigatious' society and there is little tradition of public interest litigation. Where society is generous with benefits, as Sweden traditionally has been, and where labour law is generally enforced by collective mechanisms the need for individual litigation to assert rights is undoubtedly less. Another factor is political abuse of power. While this undoubtedly exists in Sweden as in every other state, transparency and safeguards on the independence of public servants in making decisions in individual cases (as already mentioned, constitutionally protected in Sweden, RF 11:7) means that there is not the same need for the courts to intervene to prevent the government steering the administrative system for party political reasons. Where public servants nonetheless abuse power, there are alternative methods of discouraging this. These include complaints to the Ombudsman and—more rarely used—prosecution of public servants (eg of police officers for excessive use of force). However, Sweden, like all other societies in Europe is undergoing rapid change, and some or all of these preventive factors may be weakening, thus strengthening the need for a remedy in damages.[117]

Obviously *whether* a remedy counts as effective must naturally be judged in the light of the ECtHR case law. But the *measure* of effectiveness will also depend upon the national legal culture and socio-economic conditions. It should be remembered that the Convention organs have gone so far as to dismiss cases

should be 'real [and] clearly caused by the conduct contrary to the Act'. (8) Domestic rules as to costs will probably cover any costs or expenses incurred by the complainant.

[114] See, eg C-178–9, 188, 190/94, *Dillenkoffer and others v Germany* (1996) ECR I-4845.

[115] The costs of the litigation in legal aid in a leading English damages case, *Anufrijeva v Southwark* London Borough Council [2003] EWCA Civ 1406, [2004] QB 1124 led the Court of Appeal to lay down guidelines to attempt to avoid such litigation in future (at paras 79–81).

[116] For an interesting discussion of this issue from US perspective see JJ Park 'The Constitutional Tort as Individual Remedy' (2003 (38)) Harv. CR-CL LR pp 393–453.

[117] See W Warnling-Nerep 'Skadeståndstalan mot staten—en allt vanligare företeelse?' (2004–2005) *Juridisk Tidsskrift*, pp 170–80, for a brief discussion. A recent illustration of the expanded concept of 'suffering' is that the Swedish law on sexual discrimination has been changed to allow for the award of non-pecuniary damages, SFS 2003:307, amended by SFS 2005:480, Prop. 2004/05:147.

in the past where the applicant had received a partial remedy, holding that he was no longer a victim.[118]

Thus, my conclusion is that while the Article 41 case law can certainly provide some *guidance* for a national court, there will be many situations in which a damages remedy need not be offered and, even when a damages remedy is available, then apart from the special area of delays, the measure of damages applied by the national courts need not be the same as that applied by the ECtHR in Article 41 cases.[119]

5.4 Some Problems for the Future

The cases so far which have reached the Supreme Court have been relatively straightforward. The assessment of damages for delays in the right of fair trial is comparatively simple, now that the ECtHR has, in an effort to rid itself of primarily Italian cases, laid down easy to follow scales in the *Zullo* case. It is more difficult to apply ECtHR case law in assessing whether damages should be payable in a situation where, eg a court is not impartial, or where action has been taken (or not taken) resulting in an infringement of personal integrity. And the Swedish case law so far cannot be interpreted to mean that a breach of any Convention right—even an obvious breach—automatically means that a state official has committed negligence within the meaning of SkL 3:2. A special problem exists as regards the already mentioned issue of 'horizontal rights'. Some advocates are already advancing the position that the Convention requires the state to provide a damages remedy against a private actor (company etc) which has infringed an individual's rights to privacy. They have based such arguments partly on *von Hannover v Germany*,[120] where the respondent state was found to have violated Article 8 by not providing Caroline of Monaco a remedy before its courts to complain about breaches of her rights of privacy, committed by *paparazzi* selling photographs to the German press. Here, however, it should be noted that it was not a question of the EctHR requiring the creation of a new right of action under German law. The right of privacy is already protected under German law, including protection by means of actions for injunctions and damages, but the German courts, including the Federal Constitutional Court had, according to the ECtHR, interpreted the right of privacy too narrowly in the concrete case. Nonetheless the horizontal dimension, direct or indirect, may partly explain the reluctance of the Supreme Court to state explicitly that Article 13 was sufficient statutory authority for making a damages claim

[118] Harris, O'Boyle and Warbrick, above, pp 636–7.

[119] The situation is different for UK courts where s 8(4) HRA provides that 'In determining—(a) whether to award damages, or (b) the amount of an award, the court *must take into account* the principles applied by the ECtHR in relation to the award of compensation under Article 41' (my emphasis).

[120] No 59320/00, 24 June 2004.

against the state in NJA 2005, section 462. If it can be invoked directly against the state, then why not, they might argue, against the state for failing to provide a remedy in damages?

Another troublesome issue which will arise again, sooner or later is the question of damages for the promulgation of rules that are in breach of the Convention. Such cases will not be common, as one will have to show 'proximate causality', ie prove a chain of causation from the enactment of, or failure to enact, a statute or ordinance and the loss suffered. Nonetheless, JK has indicated that there are several areas where problems can arise.[121] There is no difficulty as regards rules promulgated by administrative authorities, whether of central or local government. However with statutes and ordinances an anomalous situation can arise that a Swedish court may be able to refuse to apply a statute or ordinance it finds to be in violation of the Convention, but it may not be able to award damages to an individual who has suffered economic loss as a result of this violation. The legislature will have to do something about the issue soon, even if it is politically sensitive.

Although I have expressed some skepticism in the preceding section, I can sympathise with the practicing lawyers attempts to kick start the lower courts into activity. Even though I think they exaggerate the need to provide damages remedies and the likely level of damages payable, it will be the case that damages remedies will sometimes be necessary. It seems to me that the lower Swedish courts are badly equipped to develop the case law. They will, I fear, wait for Swedish cases directly on point. JK has stated, reasonably enough, that since the Supreme Court has interpreted the duty to pay damages narrowly he will do the same but, with the exception of delays in court proceedings, there will rarely *be* any Swedish cases directly on point. Thus, the tendency will be for JK and the lower courts not to award any damages. It will take a determined litigant to take the issue to the Supreme Court. The lower courts are not trying to undermine the Convention. They are simply not creative enough to develop it actively and the Supreme Court has not felt it can *require* creativity. While, as already mentioned, the Supreme Court and Supreme Administrative Court have definitely encouraged the lower courts to have regard to the Convention, the Supreme Court has *not* stated that failure to be aware of, and have regard to, relevant ECtHR case law is a *clear* error of law, so that damages can be payable under SkL.[122] This is understandable as the problem is not so much that the lower courts have refused blatantly to take the Convention into account (with the possible exception of the right to oral hearings in administrative courts). Rather it is that they have made an attempt to understand what is required in a given situation but have failed to do so. The situation is easier under EC law where, as already mentioned, there is both a constitutional basis and a relatively simple rule—non-discrimination—to latch onto.

[121] G Lambertz 'Det allmännas skadeståndsansvar i framtiden—trender och utvecklingsmöjligheter' (2004–2005) *Juridisk Tidsskrift*, pp 1–24.

[122] See NJA 2002, s 88, noted above.

It can be said that the problems experienced by Sweden are far from being unique in Europe. Indeed, the comparative material available shows that in many states, the remedies available on paper for Convention breaches, particularly delays, are not effective in practice.[123] Nor are the problems of lack of judicial creativity on the part of the lower courts peculiarly Swedish. While the ECtHR has praised national supreme courts' development of the existing law on delays to provide for effective remedies, it has indicated also that it knows that this power of development has its limits.[124] Demands of legal certainty call for clear legislation, not simply a vague encouragement to the courts to apply the principle of treaty conform construction. Also, as regards the question of Convention remedies in damages in general, only the legislature is capable of taking a coherent approach spanning the whole field of torts committed by the state, and fitting into this 'human rights torts'. Moreover, the requirements of democracy and subsidiarity mean that such important issues should not be left only to the courts, or the ECtHR. As far as Sweden is concerned, it is for the Swedish parliament to attempt to lay down principles to be applied by the Swedish courts setting the 'value' of a breach of human rights, even if the law will have to be 'open-ended' to allow for further developments in the light of new Strasbourg case law on damages.

BIBLIOGRAPHY

Andersson, H, 'Europakonventionen som parallell respektive fristående skadeståndgrund' (PointLex, 21 June 2005).

Andersson, T, 'Remedies for Breach of EC Law Before Swedish Courts' in J Lonbay and A Biondi (eds) *Remedies for breach of EC law* (New York/Chicester, John Wiley, 1997).

Bengtsson, B, *Det allmännas skadestånd enligt skadeståndslagen* (Stockholm, Norstedts, 1996, 2nd edn).

—— and Strömbäck, E, *Skadeståndslagen. En kommentar* (Stockholm, Norstedts, 2002).

—— 'Torts and Insurance' in M Bogdan (ed) *Swedish Law* (Stockholm, Norstedts, 2000).

Cameron, I, 'A Survey of ECHR Case law and the question of remedies' in I Cameron and A Simoni (eds) *Dealing with Integration,* vol 2 (Uppsala, Iustus, 1998).

—— 'Protocol 11 to the ECHR: the European Court of Human Rights as a Constitutional Court?' (1996) (15) Yearbook of European Law, pp 219–60.

—— 'The ECHR in Sweden after incorporation' in A Boyle, C Himsworth, A Loux, and H MacQueen (eds) *Human Rights and Scots Law: comparative perspectives* (Oxford, Hart publishing, 2002) pp 105–40.

—— 'Swedish Parliamentary Participation in the Making and Implementation of Treaties' (2005) (74) *Nordic Journal of International Law* pp 429–83.

[123] Venice Commission 2005.

[124] *Rachevi v Bulgaria*, No 47877/99, 23 September 2004, para 64.

Crafoord, C, 'Inhemsk gottgörelse för kränkningar av Europakonventionen' (2001 (4)) *Europarättslig tidskrift*, pp 519–47.

Harris, DJ, O'Boyle, M and Warbrick, C *Law of the European Convention on Human Rights* (London/Dublin/Edinburgh, Butterworths, 1995).

Lambertz, G, 'Det allmännas skadeståndsansvar i framtiden—trender och utvecklingsmöjligheter' (2004–2005) *Juridisk Tidsskrift*, pp 1–24.

Lester of Herne Hill and D Pannick (eds) *Human Rights Law and Practice* (London, LexisNexis, 2004, 2nd edn).

Lysén, G, 'Två rättsfall från HD: förvirrade käpphästar eller en brytningstid?!' (2005) *Europarättslig tidskrift* pp 645–61.

Magnus U (ed) *Unification of tort law: damages* (the Hague/London, Kluwer Law International, 2001).

Marcusson L *Offentlig förvaltning utanför myndighetsområdet* (Uppsala, Iustus, 1989).

Merrills JG *The Development of International Law by the European Court of Human Rights* (Manchester, Manchester UP, 1993, 2nd edn).

Mowbray AR *Development of positive obligations under the European Convention on Human Rights by the European Court of Human Rights* (Oxford, Hart publishing, 2004).

Park JJ 'The Constitutional Tort as Individual Remedy' (2003 (38)) Harv. CR-CL LR pp 393–453.

Schmidt, F, Eklund, R, Göransson, H, Källström, K and Sigemann, T, *Facklig arbetsrätt* (Stockholm, Juristförlaget, 1997).

Shelton, D, *Remedies in international human rights law* (Oxford, Oxford University Press, 2005).

Sundberg, J, *Human Rights in Sweden: the Annual Reports 1985* (Stockholm, 1987).

Södergren, J, 'Axplock II ur svensk konventionstillämpning' *Europarättslig tidskrift* (2002 (5)), pp 659–82.

—— 'Axplock III ur svensk konventionstillämpning' *Europarättslig tidskrift* (2003 (6)), pp 706–25.

—— 'Rätt till skadestånd i Sverige direkt på grundval av Europakonventionen' *Juridisk Tidsskrift* (2004–2005), pp 762–75.

Venice Commission (2005), Report on National Remedies in Respect of Excessive Length of Proceedings, Study no 316/ 2004.

Warnling-Nerep, W, 'Skadeståndstalan mot staten—en allt vanligare företeelse?' (2004–2005) *Juridisk Tidsskrift*, pp 170–80.

5

The Free Movement of Services in Conflict with Swedish Industrial Relations Model—or was it the Other Way Around?

ÖRJAN EDSTRÖM*

ABSTRACT

THIS CHAPTER DEALS with the free movement of services founded on the EC Treaty in relation to national regulations protecting domestic workers. This issue is dealt with referring to a Swedish case concerning the free movement of services and some basic elements in the Swedish industrial relations model on the labour market. Collective bargaining and collective agreements are important for the regulation of the Swedish labour market, and the parties' right to take industrial action in the bargaining process is fundamental. When a collective agreement has been concluded the law will secure industrial peace between the parties in the collective agreement. However, a foreign employer performing temporary services in Sweden will not be in receipt of industrial peace, although he is bringing with him employees from the State of origin and even if he is bound to a collective agreement in that State. The reason is that the Swedish regulations on industrial peace do not embrace working conditions to which Swedish law is not directly applicable. Hence, the crucial issue is if the free movement of services in fact is restricted if an undertaking from another Member State is subject to industrial action in order to establish a

* Örjan Edström is professor and Dr in labour law at the Department of Law, Umeå University. He has published a number of books and articles on labour law, EC law especially concerning the free movement of workers, and on immigration and asylum law. In labour law he has published books and articles concerning co-determination and employment security in the knowledge-based society together with contributions to text-books in labour law. He has been Swedish reporter to the free movement of workers network in 1996–2002 set up by the European Commission, a work that since 2004 is carried out through the European observatory on the free movement of workers. Further, he is a member of the Academic network for legal studies on immigration and asylum in Europe.

collective agreement with a Swedish trade union, even if the employer is bound to a collective agreement in another Member State where he is established. Different arguing strategies to deal with the legal problem in the Swedish debate are analysed, and finally conclusions and a proposal on how to resolve the incongruence between EC law and Swedish labour law are presented.

1 INTRODUCTION

The free movement of services is one of the fundamental freedoms within the EU and is regulated in Articles 49–55 of the EC Treaty. This chapter will mainly deal with Article 49 which prohibits restrictions on the freedom to provide services in Member States in relation to the national protection of domestic workers in labour law. This general problem regarding the free movement of services and restrictions founded in labour law is dealt with referring to the *Laval* case before the Swedish Labour Court (Arbetsdomstolen; case 2005 no 49). A characteristic feature in the Swedish industrial relations system is that labour market conditions to a far extent are regulated in collective agreements. Between labour market parties that are not bound to each other by a collective agreement, there is a mutual right to take industrial action in order to force the other party to an agreement. Such industrial conflicts may under certain circumstances interfere with EC law and the free movement of services.

The *Laval* case involves Swedish trade unions which took industrial actions against an undertaking established in Latvia and providing temporary services in Sweden. The dispute of interest was mainly concerning the workers' wage level. The most important issue in the Labour Court was the right to take industrial action against a foreign employer, when the employer is not bound by a collective agreement concluded with a Swedish trade union. Regarding this, the Swedish Labour Court has addressed two questions to the ECJ, and waiting for the ECJ's decision an extensive debate on the matter has started.

1.1 The aim of the study

The crucial issue is the relationship between Article 49 and the Swedish national system for industrial relations, especially regulations on the right to take industrial action and the peace obligation between parties in collective agreement. Different solutions to resolve a possible incongruence between Swedish law and EC law have been suggested in the Swedish debate.

The aim is to analyse different arguing strategies dealing with Swedish labour law and the right to take industrial action in relationship to EC law and the free movement of services, especially in situations when an undertaking from another Member State is posting workers in Sweden for the performance of temporary services. Further, another aim is to make an analysis if there are contradictions between EC law and Swedish labour law on this matter, and if so to outline a proposal on how to resolve the conflict.

I will analyse different arguing strategies on the matter in a critical way in order to find the potential with different strategies. An outline of EC law on the matter and give a brief introduction to the Swedish industrial relations model, which is challenged in the *Laval* case will be given. Further, an argument for a solution to the uncertainty in the relationship between EC law and the regulations concerned in Swedish labour law—if there is such a problem will ensue.

1.2 The problem behind

The dispute in the *Laval* case touches upon the general issue on what employment conditions should apply to the employment relationship in the host Member State when a service providing undertaking is posting workers in another Member State. Basically, the underlying reason to the occurrence of the problem is that the costs for wages etc are considerable lower in the new Member States in 2004, compared with the corresponding costs in the 'old' Member States. Then the service provider from a Member State with a low cost level is considered to have a comparative advantage on the host State's market. Hence, jobs for domestic workers in the host Member State will be threatened and the posted workers will probably have comparatively worse employment conditions than national workers on the labour market in the host State. Both aspects are relevant in a social dumping perspective.

Before an account of the *Laval* case is given there is an outline the basic position in EC law concerning the free movement of services and the posting of workers and, further, a brief introduction to the Swedish industrial relations system. Thereafter, discussions of different kinds of strategic arguing in order to find a solution to the problem of the relationship between the free movement of services, the Swedish industrial relations and the regulation of posted workers' employment conditions. Finally, there are some conclusions concerning the future dealing with the matter.

1.3 Demarcations

Regarding demarcations on the matters dealt with, there are also other categories to which EC law on transnational services should apply, for instance service providers from other Member States who offer services as self-employees, sometimes established in a host Member State referring to Article 43.[1] There will be

[1] Compare Numhauser-Henning 'Freedom of movement and transfer of social rights' (2002) *VII European Regional Congress, Labour Law Congress 2002.* (Reports, Stockholm) p 200 and Pennings 'Co-Ordination of Social Security on the Basis of the State-of-Employement Principle: Time for an Alternative?' (2005) (42) *Common Market Law Review,* p 82 *ff.*

no comment on problems in connection with these categories. Article 49 also includes people who receive services as visitors in another Member State and also this category will not be commented on. Thus, analysis will be restricted to the situation where an employee is posted in Sweden for temporary work as an employee in the posting undertaking established in another Member State.

2 THE FREE MOVEMENT OF SERVICES

2.1 Discrimination and nationality

The free movement of services often implies that the service provider performing services in another Member State—referring to Article 49 of the EC Treaty—will bring with him employees who are employed in the State where the service provider is established.[2] The problems that may arise in connection with the posting of workers will also concern the principle of non-discrimination and the right to equal treatment, which regarding services is expressed also in Articles 50 and 54.[3] Further, even the EC Treaty, Article 12, explicitly bans discrimination on grounds of nationality, although this Article should apply only if the measure is not covered by another Article of the Treaty. This follows from the legal situation which means that the ban of discrimination expressed in Article 50 (and Articles 43 and 50), should be considered as *lex specialis* vis-à-vis the ban of discrimination based on Article 12.[4]

A fundamental precondition for the ban on discrimination to apply is that a national from a Member State has moved to the territory of another Member State utilizing his right to free movement. A situation when a person is making use of his 'free movement entitlements' will not be considered discriminatory etc, if the person in question has not moved from another Member State, although he was otherwise in the same situation. The latter situation is considered to be 'internal' and will not fall under the scope of Article 49.[5] The example shows how so called reverse discrimination could occur, basically dependent on whether there is a free movement perspective or not.[6]

In the case-law from the ECJ, the Court has reacted on direct discrimination on the grounds of nationality.[7] Concerning discrimination, direct discrimination

[2] For general comments on the free movement of services, see eg Barnard *The Substantive Law of the EU: the Four Freedoms* (Oxford, Oxford University Press 2004).

[3] Concerning the right to equal treatment, see also the EC Treaty, Art 39.2, regarding workers, and Art 43, regarding the right to establishment.

[4] Ingmanson *Erkännande av yrkeskvalifikationer inom EU* (Umeå, Skrifter från juridiska institutionen vid Umeå universitet no 11/2005, 2005) p 94.

[5] As sententiously expressed by Shuibhne '. . . no movement, no free movement protection'. Shuibhne 'Free Movement of Persons and the Wholly Internal Rule: Time to Move On?' (2002) (39) *Common Market Law Review*, p 731.

[6] A 'classical' case from the ECJ is Case 175/78 *Saunders* [1979] ECR 1129. For further analysis, see Shuibhne *ibid*.

[7] Regarding judicial practice, see eg Case 2/74 *Reyners* [1974] ECR 631.

is mostly not the main problem from a judicial point of view. Indirect discrimination, which occurs when apparently nationality-neutral requirements in practice lead to disadvantages for nationals from other Member States, is often a more complicated matter to deal with.[8]

2.2 Justification

Discriminatory measures could be justified by referring to certain derogations such as public policy, public security and public health. Such a restriction must be based on 'objective considerations' and the principle of proportionality must be fulfilled; the measures taken must be 'proportionate to the legitimate aim pursued by national law'.[9]

The *Gebhard* case is the most elaborated and well known case in which the ECJ stated the requirements for restrictions on the right to establishment and the free movement of services.[10] Hence, the national measures to be tried must:

(1) be applied in a non-discriminatory manner
(2) be justified by imperative requirements in the public interest
(3) be suitable for securing the attainment of the objective which they pursued
(4) not go beyond what is necessary to attain the objective.[11]

In the 'service case' *Gouda* it was added that 'it must not be possible to obtain the same result by less restrictive rules'.[12]

Regarding the public interest, further requirements were developed in among others the *Gouda* case, for instance concerning professional rules aiming to protect the recipients of services, protection of intellectual property and more.[13] A requirement of certain interest for the present work is the protection of workers.[14] Beyond these examples, further criteria have been developed by the ECJ.[15]

Another important aspect is that Article 49 of the EC Treaty has a direct effect against both the host Member State and the State of origin.[16] In case *Walrave and Koch* it was suggested that Articles 39 and 49 have both vertical and horizontal effect and that the ban on discrimination also embrace collectively regulated conditions in employments and services.[17] Further, in case *Angonese* concerning discrimination it was confirmed that Article 39, which deals with the

[8] See eg Case 152/73 *Sotgiu* [1974] ECR 153.
[9] Case C-340/89 *O'Flynn* [1996] ECR I-2617. See also Bernitz 2005.
[10] Case C-55/94 *Gebhard* [1995] ECR I-4165.
[11] Case C-288/89 *Gouda* [1991] ECR I-4007.
[12] Case C-288/89 *Gouda* [1991] ECR I-4007.
[13] Barnard, above, p 241 *f*.
[14] See for instance Case 113/89 *Rush Portuguesa* [1990] ECR I-1417.
[15] Barnard, above, p 242.
[16] *Ibid*, p 261.
[17] Case 36/74 *Walrave and Koch* [1974] ECR 1405. See Barnard, above, p 262.

free movement of workers, also has horizontal direct effect in individual decisions taken by an employer.[18]

2.3 A paradigmatic shift

The judicial practice from the ECJ shows that in the Court's dealing with different barriers to the free movement of services, the right to market access has been more emphasized. Although this development is founded on the principle on national treatment—regarding services expressed in the EC Treaty, Article 50—it is considered to go beyond a pure discrimination perspective.[19,20]

The development represents a shift in perspectives—moving away from a 'discrimination model' towards a model based on 'market access'—which has been considered to be the most important development in the case-law of the ECJ on these matters.[21] Compared with the accentuation of the principle of non-discrimination, the tendency to focus on obstacles to free movement of services is expected to have a greater impact on the Member States' legislative autonomy.[22]

2.4 The proposal for a Directive on services

In connection with the free movement of services based on the EC Treaty, there is a proposal for a Directive on services on the internal market.[23] In principle, the proposal is aiming to open up for cross-border services on the internal market including the facilitating of the right to establishment. The proposal has been much criticized and is subject to further considerations. A disputed matter is the application of the country-of-origin-principle.

In accordance with the proposal for a Directive a service provider is suggested to be subject 'only to the law of the country in which he is established and Member States may not restrict services from a provider established in another Member State'. However, concerning the posting of workers for temporary services in another Member State, the proposal contains derogation from the country of origin principle.

[18] Case C-281/98 *Angonese* [2000] ECR I-4139. Concerning horizontal direct effect and the free movement of services, see Baquero Cruz 1999.

[19] See for instance Case C-384/93 *Alpine Investments* [1995] ECR I-1141 and Case C-415/93 *Bosman* [1995] ECR I-4921.

[20] Barnard, above, p 238 and Ingmanson, above, p 96.

[21] Barnard, *ibid*, p 263.

[22] *Ibid*, p 263.

[23] Proposal for a Directive of the European Parliament and of the Council on services in the internal market. COM/2004/0002 Final/3.

3 THE DIRECTIVE ON THE POSTING OF WORKERS

3.1 Social dumping

In order to counteract the imbalances that could follow from the different levels of costs, employment conditions and more in Member States, the Directive 96/71/EC concerning the posting of workers was taken in 1996.[24] An underlying line of thought was obviously that the foreign service provider should in principle not be able to compete on the market in a host Member State by offering worse working conditions than those that should apply to domestic undertakings in that State. In other words the directive aims at counteracting social dumping on the labour market in the host Member State. Concerning the issues discussed in the present article, the Article 3(1)(c) on minimum wages is of vital interest.

Regarding posted workers in a host Member State the Directive stipulates that 'a "hard core" of clearly defined protective rules should be observed by the provider of the services' (Article 3(1) and the preamble point 14). Hence, in principle temporarily posted workers with some exceptions should be entitled to the same basic rights as workers in the host State.[25] Further, the directive provides directions for the dealing with certain working conditions that are important for a foreign undertaking's competitiveness, especially concerning wages and some other costs.

3.2 Implementation methods

The directive assigns different methods for the Member States to use when implementing the entitlements that should apply to posted workers' employment contracts in a host Member State. In accordance with Article 3(1) a Member State should comply with the directive through regulations on terms and conditions of employment laid down in (1) law, regulation or administrative provision, and/or (2) collective agreements or arbitration awards which have been declared universally applicable (with some exceptions).[26] The

[24] Dir 96/71/EC concerning the posting of workers of the European Parliament and of the Council of 16 December 1996 concerning the posting of workers in the framework of the provision of services. Official Journal L 018, 21/01/1997, pp 1–6.

[25] Some exceptions concerning minimum wages and in 'clearly defined cases of assembly and/or installation of goods, the provisions on minimum rates of pay and minimum paid annual holidays do not apply' (preamble point 15). Further, 'when the length of the posting is not more than one month, Member States may, under certain conditions, derogate from the provisions concerning minimum rates of pay or provide for the possibility of derogation by means of collective agreements; whereas, where the amount of work to be done is not significant, Member States may derogate from the provisions concerning minimum rates of pay and the minimum length of paid annual holidays' (Art 3.1.b; the preamble point 16).

[26] See for instance Case C-113/89 *Rush Portuguesa* [1990] ECR I-1417. Compare Sigeman 2005b, pp 466 *f*.

directive does not prevent employment conditions for posted workers that are more favourable than those conditions stipulated in the host State.

Concerning 'collective agreements or arbitration awards which have been declared universally applicable', there are further regulations in Article 3(8). If the Member State does not have a system for declaring collective agreements etc to be universally applicable, the Member State can—in accordance with Article 3(8)—make use of collective agreements which are generally applicable to:

> all similar undertakings in the geographical area and in the profession or industry concerned, and/or . . . collective agreements which have been concluded by the most representative employers' and labour organizations at national level and which are applied throughout national territory, ...

The collective agreements referred to in Article 3(8) are agreements that 'must be observed by all undertakings in the geographical area and in the profession or industry concerned'. However, the wording in Article 3(8) is considered to satisfy Member States such as Sweden and Denmark, where collective agreements do cover close to all employers on the labour market, and should facilitate the introducing of regulations to be applied on foreign employers providing temporary services in for instance Sweden.

3.3 The Rome Convention and the Directive

According to the Rome Convention—ratified by Sweden in 1998—the parties to a labour agreement have the right to agree on which legal order to apply.[27] If no such choice has been agreed upon, the contract is to be governed by national law of the country in which:

> (a) . . . the employee habitually carries out his work in performance of the contract, even if he is temporarily employed in another country; or (b) if the employee does not habitually carry out his work in any one country, by the law of the country in which the place of business through which he was engaged is situated, unless it appears from the circumstances as a whole that the contract is more closely connected with another country, in which case the contract is to be governed by the law of that country; . . ..

Regarding the application of the Rome Convention it should be noted that in accordance with the Directive 96/71/EC, the terms of contract that should apply to the employment will apply 'whatever the law applicable to the employment relationship' (Article 3(1)). Hence, regarding the application of the 'hard core' of national labour law, the directive is stipulating an exception from the country-of-origin-principle, otherwise to be maintained in accordance with the

[27] Concerning the Swedish ratification of the Convention, see Law (1998 no 167) on applicable law concerning agreed obligations. Amendments in Swedish law have been proposed, meaning that the new Member States in 2004 will be embraced by the application of the law mentioned following the extended application of the Rome Convention. See Government proposition 2005/06:14.

Rome Convention and in line with the previously mentioned proposal for a directive on services in the internal market.

4 THE SWEDISH INDUSTRIAL RELATIONS SYSTEM

4.1 Self-regulation, collectivism and substantial law

In order to make the discussion in Sweden comprehensible to a foreign reader I will give a brief analysis of the industrial system in Sweden. The industrial relations system in Sweden could in the main be characterized as a collectivist system founded on the parties' autonomy.[28] The workers and the employers on the labour market are to a comparatively large extent organized in trade unions and employers' associations respectively. There are many explanations for the emergence of the current situation. When the basic structures on the labour market were established in the 19th century the state ideology was very liberal. The state was not to interfere in the parties' dealings, although there were important exceptions for instance regarding strikes. Following this, the parties themselves have developed the procedures for collective bargaining and the basic structure for the regulation of the labour market.

The Swedish industrial relations system has been described as developed through self-regulation. Later on, the procedures for collective bargaining developed by the parties have been laid down in law. Today the fundamental regulations on collective bargaining, industrial action and more are found in the Co-determination Act (1976:580; Medbestämmandelagen). However, during the 1970s substantive labour law was developed gradually. Later on, following the impact from EC law especially discrimination law in working life has been developed.

4.2 Constitutional rights

Comparatively, in general the Swedish Constitution does not put much emphasize on trade union rights as basic constitutional rights, although in practice these rights are well-founded and recognised in the labour market.[29] However, the right to take industrial action is protected by the Constitution chapter 2 section 17.[30] This right to take industrial action belongs to trade unions and

[28] For brief comments, see for instance Edström 2004, Fahlbeck 2002, and Hasselbalch 2002. Concerning the characterizing of the system as 'collectivist', see Edström 2005.

[29] Bruun *Fackliga och grundläggande rättigheter i EU* Stockholm, TCO, 1999

[30] Concerning judicial practice, see the Labour Court Case 2003 no 46. A Turkish vessel in a Swedish harbour was subject to industrial action by a Swedish trade union. The employer was not bound to any collective agreement and the trade union insisted on that an agreement should be concluded. Regarding the legality of the trade union's action the Labour Court stated that referring to the Constitution chapter 2 s 17, there was no legal base to ban the action.

employers' association. Hence, it is not an individual right and restrictions could be found in law or collective agreements.[31]

Beside the right to take industrial action a constitutional provision on the freedom of association is found in the Constitution chapter 2 section 1.5. This right includes the right to organize trade unions. Both regulations concerning the right to industrial action and the right to association—which both the employers and the trade unions enjoy—are regulated in the Co-determination Act.

Since 1 January 1995, the ECHR is an integrated part of Swedish law. The freedom of association is regulated in Article 11 of the Convention and even the individual worker's right in the relationship vis-à-vis the employer is accentuated by Article 11. Also, the individual's right *not* to join an association is considered to be protected by the Convention.[32]

4.3 The Co-determination Act and collective bargaining

The general right to collective bargaining is regulated in the Co-determination Act (1976:580) section 10. Employers, employers' associations and trade unions have a mutual right to collective bargaining. In practice collective bargaining within the framework of section 10 mainly deals with working conditions, such as wages and general terms of employment, to be laid down in collective agreements.

Basically, the procedure for collective bargaining is regulated in sections 15–17 of the Co-determination Act. In accordance with sections 15, a party that has the duty to bargain must appear to a negotiation meeting. Further, the party is obliged to present and state his motive for a suggestion concerning the matter that is subject to the bargaining. Bargaining orders making the duty to bargain more elaborated are stipulated in the collective agreements.

The right to bargain for one party means an obligation to bargain for the other party. The duty to bargain is called forth when a party presents a proposal for a bargaining or negotiation (section 16). The subject for the bargaining must be presented in the proposal, which, on request from the other party, must be written. Finally, the bargaining procedure must be conducted in a 'speedy manner'. If a party that has the duty to bargain refuses to attend a bargaining meeting or in any other respect does not fulfil his obligation to bargain, the

[31] Compare the non-binding but important EU Charter of Fundamental Rights, Art 28, which is stating that 'Workers and employers, or their respective organisations, have in accordance with Union law and national laws and practices, the right to negotiate and conclude collective agreements . . . and, in cases of conflicts of interest, to take collective action to defend their interests, including strike action'. Compare also Art 6.4 of the non-binding European Social Charter taken by the members of the Council of Europé, which recommends workers' right to collective action, which could be interpreted as an individual right to industrial action.

[32] See The European Court decisions 25/4 1996 and 30/7 1998 (both *Torgny Gustafsson v Sweden*) and the Swedish Labour Court Case 1998 no 17.

Labour Court can find the party guilty of breach of the duty to bargain. Such a violation of the duty to bargain is sanctioned by general damages.

Negotiations in legal disputes are basically to be conducted in accordance with the regulations in the Co-determination Act if the parties cannot agree on another procedure. In practice the negotiations are conducted in accordance with the basic agreements on the labour market. The Labour Court is the instance for the final settling of conflicts on these matters. The parties can also agree on that the dispute will be dealt with in an arbitration board or a corresponding committee.

Before the Court deals with a legal dispute, it is to be dealt with in negotiations between the involved parties (see the Act 1974 no 371 on litigation in labour disputes chapter 4 section 7). This 'barrier rule' is of vital importance and the parties themselves resolve in negotiations the overwhelming number of disputes in accordance with the procedures stipulated by the collective agreements. If the parties in a legal dispute fail to settle the dispute, the conflict is transmitted from the area of self-regulation to the pure judicial arena.

The Co-determination Act is optional in most parts, and in almost all lines of business and on the public sector, there are collective agreements on the procedures for collective bargaining in interest disputes, joint decision, legal disputes and more. Hence, the basic structure for collective bargaining etc is founded in law, but in practice the parties elaborate the collective bargaining procedures through collective agreements.

Collective agreements are concluded within the framework of law. Substantive law many times stipulates a basic level for matters that could be subject to regulations in collective agreements. For instance, the length of the holiday period with pay is stipulated in the compulsory Holidays Act section 4, and the number of days stipulated in collective agreements can be more—but not less—than what is stipulated in law. The meaning is that substantial law thus fulfils the function to guarantee a certain standard to be maintained.

4.4 Industrial action and *lex Britannia*

In a collective bargaining perspective it is important to keep in mind that in connection with the right to collective bargaining in interest disputes there is a right to take industrial action. When the parties have concluded a collective agreement, industrial peace must be maintained in accordance with the Co-determination Act section 41. Hence, in connection with a negotiation in a legal dispute there is no right to industrial action. An important issue is concerning the preconditions for the section 41 to apply when an employer is bound to a collective agreement in another Member State where the employer's undertaking is established.

The regulation which is central to the concrete matter dealt with is in particular the Co-determination Act section 42, where the ban on illegal industrial actions is expressed. The crucial issue is if temporary work performed in

Sweden by a service providing firm established in another Member State, should fall under the scope of the ban on illegal actions or not. If not, the question is if such an exception will mean a breach of the principal on equal treatment and if the exception is contrary to EC law?

Section 42 was amended in 1991 and in the following it is referred to as *lex Britannia*. The background to the amendment was the Labour Court Case 1989 no 120. A trade union had taken an industrial action against a foreign employer—a shipping company and owner to the vessel named M/S Britannia. The aim was to repress a foreign collective agreement concluded between the employer and the employees' trade union. The Court found the Swedish trade union's industrial action unlawful referring to the Co-determination Act section 42 (hereby establishing the so-called Britannia principle). The reason was that the action aimed at obtaining a removal or a change in an existing collective agreement between the employer and another trade union.[33]

The Labour Court's decision led to a debate and later on an amendment of the Co-determination Act was taken by the Riksdag. The amendment of the Co-determination Act section 42 and more—*lex Britannia*—was in force in 1991.[34] The important part of *lex Britannia* that I will put the light on is found in the last sentence of the Act section 42, where it is stated that the ban of industrial actions violating legislative provisions or collective agreements 'shall only apply where an organisation resorts to industrial action as a consequence of a working condition *to which this Act is directly applicable*'. (Italics made by the author.)

Compared with the previous legal situation—when the final decision was taken in Case 1989 no 120—the amendment in 1991 meant that industrial action could be lawfully taken concerning temporary work performed by foreign undertakings in Sweden. Regarding the motivation for this amendment the Riksdag stated that the trade unions must have the possibility to work for a situation on the Swedish labour market, where all employers offer the wages and employment conditions that are customary in Sweden. Thus, a basic thought is that an employer that offers working conditions etc that are not covered by the Co-determination Act, should not be entitled to the law's protection against industrial actions.[35]

In a public investigation presented in 1994—before the Directive 96/71/EC had been adopted by the Council—*lex Britannia* was assumed not to be contrary to EC law, even though the regulation meant a special treatment of foreign undertakings performing temporary services in Sweden.[36] The main reason for

[33] Compare Labour Court Case 2004 no 96. A trade union had taken industrial action against an employer bound by a collective agreement with another trade union, but in this case the fighting trade union claimed that a collective agreement should be concluded only concerning those who were members in that trade union. Hence, the industrial action was not unlawful.

[34] Government proposition 1990/91:162.

[35] *Ibid*, pp 5 *f*.

[36] Official report Ds 1994:13.

this conclusion was that a special treatment of a foreign undertaking should be considered as allowable if it could be justified referring to EC law, by example if the treatment aimed to counteract social dumping on the labour market. At the same time an interrogation mark was made by the investigator if all stipulations in collective agreements had such an effect. On the other hand, the investigator argued, a foreign contractor could bring the matter before the Court if he considered the collective agreement in any part being too far going in relation to the interest of avoiding social dumping.

4.5 The implementation of Directive 96/71/EC

The Directive 96/71/EC concerning the posting of workers is implemented in Sweden through law 1999:678 (Utstationeringslagen).[37] In section 5 of the Act there is a detailed list of regulations that should apply to posted workers. In section 6 some exceptions are mentioned, for instance concerning the application of the Holiday Act when the work is of short duration. In section 7 an important notification is made; when the posting employer has concluded a collective agreement with a Swedish trade union section 41 of the Co-determination Act should apply.

The implementation of the directive in Swedish law has been questioned. There are no regulations concerning minimum wage in Sweden and, further, there is no legal basis for the extension of collective agreements in order to make them 'universally applicable'. Hence, is the directive satisfactorily implemented in Swedish law and what does it mean if the answer to that question is no? For instance, the ECJ might come to the conclusion that Swedish law does not provide any guarantees that all employees on the labour market sector respectively will be embraced by the protective netting implied by the Directive.[38]

In practice also another problem appears. How do trade unions know what employment conditions that apply in a foreign undertaking performing temporary services in Sweden and when is there a risk for social dumping to occur?

[37] Government proposition 1998/99:90.

[38] Compare Case C-287/04 *Commission v Sweden*. The fact that collective agreements on the Swedish labour market do not apply to work places where the employer is not bound to a collective agreement was a main argument when the ECJ rejected the Swedish implementation of the working time Directive 93/104/EC. See judgment on 26 May 2005, published in French on http://curia.eu.int/jurisp/cgi-bin/form.pl?lang=en&Submit=Submit&alldocs=alldocs&docj=docj&docop=docop&docor=docor&docjo=docjo&numaff=C-287%2F04&datefs=&datefe=&nomusuel=&domaine=&mots=&resmax=100 (web site 12 October 2005). The Directive dealt with in Case C-287/04 was Council Directive 93/104/EC of 23 November 1993 concerning certain aspects of the organization of working time. Official Journal L 307, 13/12/1993, pp 18–24. (The directive has later on been replaced by Dir 2003/88/EC of the European Parliament and of the Council of 4 November 2003 concerning certain aspects of the organisation of working time. Official Journal L 299, 18/11/2003, pp 9–19). Further, compare Sigeman 'Fri rörlighet för tjänster' (2005) (8) *Europarättslig tidskrift*, pp 483 *ff*, and a discussion on the Directive 96/71/EG and horizontal direct effect.

The control of employment conditions is crucial and a public investigation was presented in 2005.[39] The primary thought was that the trade unions should be entitled to make inspections concerning the application of the collective agreement in undertakings, where the employer is bound to a collective agreement even though the trade unions do not have any members among the employees. The aim was to counteract wage levels and other conditions that do not fulfil the requirements stipulated in the collective agreement. However, referring to a recommendation from labour market parties, the Minister for Employment has declared that there will not be any legislation on the matter (see below, section 6.3).

In September 2005 a similar proposal for an amendment of Finnish law has been put on the table, aiming at the completion of the industrial relations system in Finland.[40] In accordance with the proposal the undertaking which is posting workers in Finland should leave information concerning the activity to the competent State authority, investigate which terms of employment contract should apply, and in addition to that the employer should have a representative competent to bargain and more in Finland. Exceptions are suggested if the work is of short duration. A starting point to take notice on is that in Finland collective agreements are declared universally applicable in accordance with the Employment contracts Act 1970/320.

5 THE *LAVAL* CASE

5.1 The dispute in the Labour Court

In a case in 2004 the Swedish Labour Court dealt with the matter if it was allowed for a Swedish trade union to take industrial action against an undertaking performing temporary services in Vaxholm, a local society at commuting distance to Stockholm.[41] The contractor's undertaking was established in Latvia and the employer performed the temporary services with his own employees under a contract between a local community and another service providing firm established in Latvia. The workers were Lettish and they were bound by a collective agreement between the parties in Latvia.

A Swedish trade union took industrial action against the employer and claimed that the employer should sign a collective agreement with the Swedish trade union. Further, other trade unions took industrial actions supporting the trade union involved in the primary conflict. In Case 2004 no 111 the Labour Court stated that the employer could not show that there were probable reasons to break off the ongoing industrial actions. Regarding the employer's claim that

[39] Official report SOU 2005:89.

[40] Government proposition 2005, proposition from the Finnish Government concerning the amendment on Act 1146/1999 on posting of workers.

[41] Case 2004 No 111 first provisional ruling of the *Laval* Case.

the industrial actions should be interrupted, the Court—referring to *lex Britannia*—took the decision that by that time there was no obvious legal reason to break the actions against the employer.

A marginal note is that the first provisional ruling from the Labour Court (Case 2004 no 111) caused the employer to bring the case before the Supreme Court. The employer claimed that the Labour Court had committed a miscarriage of justice when not asking the ECJ on the legal situation regarding EC law. The Court agreed to the position that EC law ought to be taken into consideration, but the employer's claim regarding the Labour Court's provisional ruling was rejected.[42]

When the Labour Court later on—in April 2005—again dealt with the *Laval* case, the Court found that the trade unions' action aimed to set aside the Lettish collective agreement to which the employer was bound and to replace it with a Swedish collective agreement.[43] The Court did not agree to the trade unions' position that the industrial actions were not aimed to supersede the Lettish agreement; this question—the trade unions meant—was separated from the question if the actions taken should be considered lawful.

5.2 Questions addressed to the ECJ

The Court's standpoint raised the question whether *lex Britannia* was in accordance with EC law, since the industrial action taken was legally founded on *lex Britannia*. Thus, referring to Article 234 of the EC Treaty, the Labour Court took the decision to ask the ECJ for a preliminary ruling on the matter. The questions which the Labour Court addressed to the ECJ were in short:

(1) if it is in accordance with the EC Treaty (the free movement of services and discrimination on grounds of nationality) and the Directive 96/71/EC on the posting of workers, for a trade union to take industrial action in order to make the employer to sign a collective agreement, when there are no explicit regulations in Swedish law on the application of working and employment conditions in collective agreements, and

(2) if the EC Treaty and the Directive 96/71/EC constitute an obstacle to the application of *lex Britannia*.

5.3 A delicate matter

In the following debate the questions addressed by the Labour Court have been criticised for going beyond what is necessary for a decision on the basic issue (presupposing that the aim with the industrial actions was legitimate). Objections have also been raised claiming that the questions should have been

[42] The Swedish Supreme Court, Case No Ö 82-05 judgment delivered in February 22, 2005-11-13.

[43] Labour Court Case 2005 No 49.

more detailed or that it was not necessary to ask the ECJ on the whole (the latter position presupposing that EC law does not regulate industrial action at all).[44]

The comprehensive debate with reference to the *Laval* case and the Labour Court's decisions shows that the matter is rather delicate. The case point at basic features in the Swedish industrial relations model, and many people think that the questions to the ECJ are challenging the basic principles of the Swedish industrial relations system, and, further, even the social dimension approach in general in the EU.[45]

6 ARGUING STRATEGIES FOR MAKING SWEDISH INDUSTRIAL RELATIONS COMPATIBLE WITH EC LAW

It is obvious that there is some uncertainty as regards the relationship between Article 49, the Directive 71/96/EC and MBL section 42. This is the case especially when a trade union takes industrial action in order to establish a collective agreement relationship between the union and a foreign undertaking, which is performing temporary services in Sweden, and possibly already is bound to an agreement in a Member State where the undertaking is established. It is not evident what the discussion and the ECJ's dealing with the Laval case will end up to, and further, what will be the consequences for the industrial relations model in Sweden on this crucial issue.

Different strategies to handle the situation, highlighted in the Labour Court Case 2005 no 49, have crystallized in the debate. I will deal with these positions by dividing them into four categories of strategies for arguing on the matter:

— EC law does not apply to the right to industrial action and more
— The Swedish model is just a variant of implementation method
— Collective bargaining should be used to deal with contradictions between the Swedish industrial relations model and EC law
— Swedish labour law should be made in order to make Swedish industrial relation compatible with EC law.

6.1 EC law does not apply

One arguing strategy regarding the right to industrial action is that EC law does not interfere with national legislation concerning industrial actions.[46] The argu-

[44] Concerning the debate on the matter, see *Lag & avtal* vol 2005.

[45] See for instance the General Secretary of the ETUC 2005; a communication to the President of the European Commission, concerning certain statements made by Commissioner McCreevy talking about protectionism expressed in the Swedish debate.

[46] That was the position taken by the Swedish Riksdag when adopting the *Lex Britannia* legislation in 1991. (Government proposition 1990/91:162, p 28.) Compare Lag & avtal 2005 (contribution from Hamskär & Holke, published in 28 January 2005).

ment refers to Article 137(5) of the EC Treaty and Directive 96/71/EC, the preamble point 22, where it is stated that the directive is without prejudice to laws in Member States concerning 'collective action to defend the interests of trades and professions'.

Is there a reason to presume that an exception from the application of Article 137 in general on the right to strike and more means that the EC Treaty does not interfere with the right to take industrial action in Member States? First, the wording of point 5 does only exclude the provisions in Article 137, which implies Council decision taken by qualified majority on certain matters, from the application on the right to strike etc. Secondly, even so, probably Article 137(2) does not exclude the possibility for the Council to take unanimous decisions for instance concerning industrial action.[47]

The first objection mentioned above is in line with the Labour Court decision in Case 2004 no 111. The Court claimed that when judging if *lex Britannia* is in conformity with the free movement of services, a distinction should be made between trade union claims that are too far going in relation to the goal to counteract social dumping and trade union claims that are in line with this purpose.

A consequence of the Labour Court's statement is that there are industrial actions that could be too far-reaching in relation to EC law and the free movement of services. The meaning is that—despite the regulation in Article 137—there are actions that could be contrary to the free movement of services. It also means that the permission of industrial actions must be judged in the light of the trade unions' demands that are supported through the industrial action. Further, as pointed out, another consequence of the position taken by the Court is that the traditional immunity against legal control of trade union demands by this to some extent has been breached.[48]

Also the so called Monti Regulation 2679/98 regulating the free movement of goods and industrial actions has been adduced as an argument for the strategy that EC law should not apply to industrial actions.[49] In accordance with the Regulation, Article 4(1)(a), a Member State should 'take all necessary and proportionate measures so that the free movement of goods is assured in the territory of the Member State . . .', but at the same time the application should not affect the exercising of 'fundamental rights as recognised in Member States, including the right or freedom to strike'. (Article 2).

According to my opinion the word 'proportionate' is a keyword when judging the legitimacy aspects of laws on industrial action. In principle, I do not find it contrary to the Regulation 2679/98 to take the position that an action taken

[47] Sigeman *Yttrande om tillämpning av artikel 234 EG* (2005).

[48] Bruun & J Malmberg 'Arbetsrätten i Sverige och Finland efter EU-inträdet. Kerstin Ahlberg ed, Tio år med EU—effekter på arbetsrätt, partsrelationer, arbetsmarknad och social trygghet' (2005:5) *Arbetsliv i omvandling*, p 33.

[49] Council Reg (EC) No 2679/98 of 7 December 1998 on the functioning of the internal market in relation to the free movement of goods among the Member States. Official Journal L 337, 12/12/1998, pp 8–9.

could interfere with the free movement of services. However, there is no judicial practice from the ECJ on the matter and the legal position is not clear.[50]

Another argument for that EC law should not evidently apply on the right to take industrial action, is that the right to take industrial action is protected by the Swedish Constitution chapter 2 section 17.[51] This circumstance may in practice lead to carefulness when drawing one conclusion or another. The ECJ have tried the free movement of services before in relationship with constitutional rights and it is a delicate balance to make.[52] However, restrictions on the right to industrial action in accordance with the Swedish Constitution can be regulated in law or collective agreements. Then, is the assumption that the EC Treaty cannot have the corresponding effect reasonable?

6.2 Focus on the implementation method and the equal treatment principle

Another arguing strategy is also built on the position that there is not a conflict between EC law and Swedish industrial relations, especially the Co-determination Act section 42. The Directive 96/71/EC does not in detail lay down in what way a Member State should regulate the matters concerned. In Sweden the same result will be the outcome within the framework of *lex Britannia*, since the trade union through collective bargaining—and if necessary by using industrial action—will establish equal working conditions for workers posted to Sweden as those who apply to employees in Swedish undertakings. Hence, for instance the minimum wage policy expressed in the directive is considered to be implemented through *lex Britannia*, giving the trade unions a right to industrial action in order to drive through such wage conditions and hereby fulfilling the aim with the Directive.

This arguing is in line with the directive's aim in so far that social dumping should be encountered. However, this argument strategy could have bearing in this perspective, but then the spokesman must disregard the fact that the directive is rather clear regarding the criterion to which collective agreements should apply (the agreement should have been declared universally or at least apply to all employers in the business concerned etc).

Another aspect is that—referring to the practice from the ECJ—there is a tendency in the Court's practice to emphasize market access when judging cases on the free movement of services. Then the argument that the right to take industrial action in accordance with *lex Britannia* aims at fighting social dumping

[50] Sigeman *Yttrande om tillämpning av artikel 234 EG*, above, p 5.

[51] Lag & Avtal, above, contribution from Hamskär & Holke, published in 28 January 2005.

[52] Two cases from the ECJ are Case C-112/00 *Schmidtberger* [2003] ECR I-5659 and Case C-159/90 *Grogan* [1991] ECR I-4685. The first case dealt with the free movement of goods (a legal demonstration blocking a motorway) and the second case with the free movement of services (the Irish ban on abortion founded in the Constitution and information concerning legal abortion in the UK).

may be too one-sided. To correspond with EC laws I think the spokesmen also have to consider the market access aspect on the matter.

Further, presuming that *lex Britannia* is judged to be of public interest etc, it could be questioned if the *lex Britannia* approach would be considered as proportionate in order to fight social dumping, when using the Gebhard test. Is it reasonable to treat foreign employers with collective agreements concluded in another Member State different from employers having collective agreements concluded with a Swedish trade union in Sweden? Would it not be a more immediate solution to declare the Swedish collective agreement to be universally applicable in accordance with the directive?

Finally, what will be the situation if a Swedish trade union fails to carry through, for example a guarantee that the minimum level regarding wages will be observed? In such a situation it is the Member State concerned that should secure the terms to be followed. Two other Nordic countries—Finland and Norway—already have introduced different models for making collective agreements universally applicable. In Finland collective agreements are automatically declared universally applicable in accordance with the Employment contracts Act 1970/320.[53] In Norway a certain Act on universally declaration of tariff-regulations in collective agreements (Act 4.6 1993/58) is in force since 1994. A State committee (Tariffnemnda) can declare certain parts of a collective agreement to be universally applicable on the request from any of the parties to the agreement.[54]

An argument that focuses on the equal treatment aspect also takes as the starting point in the position that Swedish law industrial action is not contrary to EC law was expressed by a trade union associated member of the Labour Court taking the decision in Case 2005 no 49. He argued that a Swedish employer—within the framework of the law—should have been subject to the same treatment as the Lettish employer, if the former had not been bound by a collective agreement with a Swedish trade union.[55] The meaning is that such an employer would have been subject to industrial action. Hence, both employers would be subject to equal treatment independently on in which State the employer is established.

Accordingly this arguing strategy makes a crucial distinction between foreign employers bound to a collective agreement in the State where the employer is established, and foreign employers bound to an agreement with a Swedish trade union. The first category of employers could be subject to industrial action but not the second category, which would be protected against industrial actions by Swedish law. Hence, the distinction is built on the nationality of the trade union

[53] A precondition is that the collective agreement is representative concerning the line of business and applied nation-wide for the actual work.

[54] A precondition to declare regulations in a collective agreement universally applicable, is that foreign workers' wages and employment conditions are obviously worse, compared with Norwegian workers' employment conditions.

[55] Dissident opinion in the Labour Court Case 2005 No 49.

that is part in the collective agreement, and an agreement with a trade union in another Member State does not enjoy the protection in Sweden. This fact will in principle constitute an unequal treatment regarding the application of *lex Britannia* if industrial actions are taken.

6.3 Using the collective agreement model

The arguing strategy above deals with the effect of collective agreements and nationality. Now analysis of arguing strategies that advocate the use of collective agreement between the parties on the Swedish labour market in order to avoid a clash between the Swedish industrial relations system, *lex Britannia* and EC law will ensue. In line with this strive suggestions have been put forward that the parties on the Swedish labour market should agree on not to take industrial action against employers from other Member States that are utilizing the free movement of services if the trade union claims goes beyond what is stipulated in the posting of workers directive.[56]

Another arguing strategy obtains a solution directly involving the foreign employer from another Member State, providing temporary services in Sweden, as a party to the Swedish industrial relations system. Thus, the foreign employer should be offered a temporary membership in a Swedish employers' association.

Such a solution has been agreed upon by the LO and the Confederation of Swedish Enterprise (Svenskt Näringsliv).[57] In an arrangement the parties state a joint recommendation to their sectoral affiliates to accept a temporary affiliation of foreign undertakings performing temporary services in Sweden to an employers' association in Sweden.

The legal effect of such an affiliation to a Swedish employers' association, which is a part in collective agreements, is that the foreign employer as a member of the association will be bound by the collective agreement concluded between the employers' association and the trade union for the actual kind of work. Hence, the ban on industrial action, referring to the Co-determination Act section 41, will embrace the foreign employer's activity on the same terms as other members of the employers' association.

A practical example where the labour market parties have considered to follow the recommendation is on the industry sector. The employers' Association of Swedish Engineering Industries has offered the trade unions to sign an agreement expressing a positive will concerning temporary membership in the employers' association. A foreign contractor providing services not longer than twelve months in Sweden should apply for a temporary membership in the organisation.[58]

[56] Lag & Avtal, above, contribution from Nycander, published in 16 June 2005.

[57] The joint recommendation was signed on 30 August 2005. On 6 September 2005, a similar agreement was concluded concerning the private sector and white collar work. (The European industrial relations observatory on-line 2005.)

[58] Lag & Avtal, above (information published 23 February 2005).

The foreign employer should be committed to apply the collective agreement concluded between the Association of Swedish Engineering Industries and the trade unions, then the foreign employer is obliged to apply at least the minimum wage stipulated in the collective agreement. But at the same time a trade union concerned—the Swedish Metal Workers Union—has expressed scepticism referring to the risk for social dumping when the minimum wages should apply, since the individual wages for Swedish workers are beyond the minimum level.[59]

Even if this kind of solution in practice would legitimate lower wages for posted workers in comparison with the average in Sweden, it could hardly be considered as social dumping to apply minimum wages stipulated in the collective agreements (although the term minimum wages in collective agreements many times may be indistinct).

This way to deal with the matter is that Swedish undertakings paying wages on an average level beyond the minimum level, will find themselves in an unfavourable position in the competition with foreign service providing undertakings, who beside this fact will be protected against industrial actions. On the other hand the foreign undertakings will always have additional costs for the posting of workers in another country.

6.4 Amendments of the Co-determination Act

Suggestions have been lodged that the *lex Britannia* regulation in section 42 of the Co-determination Act should be amended in a way that the ban against industrial action, in order to repress an existing collective agreement, should include all collective agreements as long as the agreement in question keeps up with the general standards on the Swedish labour market concerning conditions that are covered by the Directive 96/71/EC.[60] The first concluded agreement, independent of if it is concluded in Sweden or another Member State, should apply before an agreement concluded thereafter, as long as the first agreement fulfils the requirements. Further, it is suggested that the conditions applied in the line of business concerned or on the actual place should be used to fix the minimum levels concerning wages etc that should apply. The great advantage would be that all collective agreements concluded in Sweden or in another Member State would be treated equally.

Another strategy that also has been mentioned by the same author is described as a 'partial extension regulation'.[61] The ambition is to find a solution in connection with Article 3(8) of the Directive 96/71/EC. A collective agreement that is generally applied in the line of business concerned, even if not by 100 per

[59] See the collective agreement between the Association of Swedish Engineering Industries and the Swedish Metal Workers Union for the period 1 April 2004–31 March 2007. The wages should be set individually but the collective agreement stipulates a minimum wage level.

[60] Sigeman 'Fri rörlighet för tjänster', above, p 494.

[61] *Ibid*, p 477.

cent of the domestic employers, should apply to foreign employers. Thereby, the posted workers' social protection would be safeguarded in line with the directive.

The crucial objection to the two suggestions above is based on the equal treatment principle in EC law, and the author calls attention to this shortcoming.[62] If not all domestic employers are parties in the employers' association, and if the employer has not concluded a local collective agreement, then the employer will not be embraced by the collective agreement. Hence, domestic undertakings will be treated different compared with foreign undertakings, which will be contrary to EC law.

Finally, an arguing strategy, which is in conformity with EC law and the Directive 96/71/EC, is that Swedish law should be amended by introducing a possibility to declare collective agreements universally applicable.[63] This would minimize the scope for social dumping and create stability and predictability regarding what wages to apply etc for foreign undertakings offering temporary services in Sweden.

7 CONCLUSIONS

The dispute in 2004–2005 involving a Lettish undertaking performing temporary services in Sweden and Swedish trade unions, has highlighted indistinctness in the relationship between EC law including the free movement of services and the Swedish industrial relations model. The debate in Sweden on the matter and in which several arguing strategies have been formulated confirms that conclusion. Further, the different arguing strategies almost consistently turned out to express a great national unity in defending the basic features constituting a Swedish model for labour market relations.

7.1 Two main positions

The inventive debate in the wake of the *Laval* case has been showing that regulations in law concerning minimum wages or a state decree, imposing other parties than those who have signed a collective agreement to apply the agreement, are contrary to the ideology of the autonomy of the parties that is fundamental on the Swedish labour market.

The argument strategies show a great variation. In principle there are two main positions. The first one is that there is no incongruence between EC law and Swedish labour law on the matter. The second that there is a real problem

[62] Sigeman 'Fri rörlighet för tjänster', above, p 479.

[63] Ö Edström 'Svensk arbetsrätt i ett europeiskt perspektiv' in Falkenhall & Rauhut (eds). *Arbetsrätt, rörlighet och tillväxt* (Östersund, Institutet för tillväxtpolitiska studier (ITPS), 2005).

but there are two different ways to deal with the situation, either within the framework of the Swedish industrial relations system or by making crucial principal changes of that system.

Even if they disagree, the spokesmen for both lines take a starting point in a legal point of view; dealing with the problem shows a high level of juridification while the jurist profession has dominated the debate. This might conceal the fact that there is an extensive support to an industrial relations model built on self-regulation and that law should not be used to regulate labour market relations, while the *Laval* case touches upon the fundamental issue in that respect.

7.2 The political perspective

An initiative in October 2005 from the Swedish Minister for Industry and Trade, was a shot from the political arena in line with the basic values expressed in the judicial debate. In a statement the Minister frankly declared that if Sweden will be counteracted by the Commission in the *Laval* case, this will affect the Swedish Government's possibility for constructive cooperation with the European Commission concerning the proposal for a Directive on services! The statement was made in awareness of the political situation; the Commission shows great anxiety to have an understanding between Member States concerning the proposal, while the Swedish Government is very keen not to make principal changes in the industrial relations model.

The statement from the Minister also shows that the Government wants to open up a bargaining process with the Commission regarding the implications of the *Laval* case. The initiative also indicates that the problems raised through the *Laval* case should not be resolved without considering the political aspects and that a solution will go beyond what a pure judicial approach will impose.

The Minister of Industry, Employment and Communications in the present Government—dominated by the Social Democrats, who traditionally have a strong connection to the trade union movement—could not be expected to take any other position than to support the basic fundaments in the Swedish model. However, even representatives from other political parties have not raised objections or argued for any other standpoint in the Laval case. This is because practically all political parties represented in the Riksdag are dedicated to an industrial relations model based on the autonomy of the labour market parties, although the politicians often disagree regarding matters that could displace the power relations in working life in one direction or the other.

7.3 Designing a compromise

There is indisputable incongruence between EC law and the Swedish industrial relations model regarding the application of the Co-determination Act section

42 demonstrated in the *Laval* case. Hence, those who advocate the arguing strategy that EC law does not apply to industrial actions (see above, section 6.1) may be in error as may those who argue for a solution where minimum wages should be regulated in law. Considering both the legal and political aspects, arguments for a solution to the incongruence between EC law and labour law in Sweden taking the starting point in the established model for industrial relations will be made.

First the strategy to use the collective agreement in order to minimize the conflict between Swedish labour law and EC law will be argued. The starting point for the proposal is in line partially with the suggestions from Nycander (see above section 6.3). The labour market parties should conclude a collective agreement committing them to a self-restriction of the possibility to take industrial action towards undertakings that are established in other Member States and performing temporary services on the Swedish market.

In principal this solution means that the labour market parties—primarily trade unions—should commit themselves not to take industrial action towards a third party. Such an agreement would be in conformity with the Swedish tradition meaning that the parties are committed to take on the responsibilities for labour market conditions through self-regulation. The advantage would be that the State referring to such an agreement could abstain from taking legislative initiatives that would challenge the industrial relations model. The parties involved could be expected to accomplish the arrangement since they have a common interest not to give the State a reason to intervene through legislation. Finally, the labour market parties are aware of that if the commitment is not respected, then the State is obliged to take measures in order to secure the Directive's objectives, which would restrict the labour market parties' autonomy and the scope for self-regulation.

It should be noted that an arrangement in principle fulfilling a similar function has worked for many years between the parties on the public sector. In 1976 they agreed on the Special Basic Agreement for the Public Sector, which contains rules relating to political democracy. The parties agreed not to use collective actions when there is a conflict between the bargaining issues and the principal that the public sector should be ruled by the principal of political democracy. In the Basic Agreement for State Employment the parties there are provisions on industrial conflicts that could endanger important functions in society, and on the local government sector there is a corresponding Basic Agreement for Local-Government Employment. Further, the parties on the sector respectively have established certain committees assigned the task to examine if industrial actions could be considered to interfere with important functions in society and to give recommendations on the matter.

Following these examples on the public sector, the parties in an agreement concerning industrial actions against undertakings established in another Member State and performing temporary services in Sweden, could agree on a joint committee that in advance should examine trade union demands and notice of industrial actions in order to appoint if the action is in conformity with EC law. Regarding this question, the crucial matter for the committee to deal with is if the aim of the industrial action to be taken is to counteract social dumping or not, and, further—referring to EC law—to elaborate the criterion on social dumping, especially concerning wage levels. On this matter it is in one way or another necessary to introduce a right for such a committee to have information concerning the employment conditions that a foreign employer will apply (see above, section 4.5).

Further, the committee should be assigned the task to examine if an industrial action fulfils the requirement of being 'proportionate', and finally the committee should issue a recommendation on the matter. Indirectly this dealing with the contradictions regarding industrial actions and foreign undertakings would mean that the position of the collective agreement in different lines of businesses would be strengthened.

The suggested approach is a pragmatic solution founded on the established industrial relations model, built on the labour market parties' autonomy. In order to enjoy industrial peace the employer must bargain and conclude a collective agreement or run the risk of collective actions. The same effect would arise if the foreign employer joined an employers' association already bound to a collective agreement, but it should be up to the employer to take a decision to apply for membership, and both employers from another Member State and Swedish employers have to make the same choice.

Nevertheless, in accordance with my suggestion the foreign employer has a more favourable position in comparison with a Swedish employer, since the former can receive protection against industrial actions referring to a recommendation from the suggested joint committee. Regarding the Swedish employer such a situation is an 'internal situation' that will not fall under the scope of Article 49 (see above, section 2.1).

Following my proposal, a weak point is that in principle, and from a pure legal point of view, *lex Britannia* still could be questioned from an EC law perspective. Normally, it is the State that is supposed to—direct or indirect—take the normative decisions on for instance which minimum wages that should apply. A possibility to bring the suggestion closer to EC law in this respect, is that the labour market parties should nominate the members of the joint committee to be appointed by the State, and the joint committee should be a State body to which the competence to fix the criterion on social dumping etc is delegated.[64] Then, formally the decision taken by the committee would be taken by a State body, which would be in conformity with EC law.

If necessary, in order to bring *lex Britannia* explicitly in accordance with EC law also the suggestion—dealt with above in section 6.4—to amend the

[64] There are many State bodies where professional and industrial organizations are nominating members to be appointed by the State, for instance personnel representatives in State authorities' boards and the majority of the members of the Swedish Labour Court.

Co-determination Act should be considered.[65] The meaning is that the first concluded collective agreement should be respected, independent of if it is concluded in Sweden or in another Member State where the undertaking is established. The precondition is that the agreement fulfils the requirements based on the Directive 96/71/EC, but in order not to violate the equal treatment principle the minimum wage level should be settled in line with my suggestion above.

An alternative strategy to the proposal as was mentioned above, is to make it explicitly possible in law to declare the crucial matters in collective agreements universally applicable. If so, the extension of the collective agreement should be restricted to issues regulated in the Directive on 96/71/EC, including minimum wages. This is a pure legal solution, but even this way out has an important connection to the collective bargaining system, since the agreement to be declared universal is an agreement between the parties. Thus, the solution is closely linked to the collective bargaining strategy and it will secure the application of collective agreements.

However, to declare collective agreement universally applicable through State intervention is undermining the parties' autonomy. The ideological resistance towards such an amendment is very extensive, both among the parties on the labour market and on the political arena. The reason is that law would be used for the regulation of matters that traditionally have been regulated between the labour market parties themselves. At the same time the parties in practice are used to regulation of working life through law. In fact Sweden has many labour laws and before, trade unions especially have not hesitated to make request for legislation in working life when the parties have not managed to find a joint bargaining settlement.

An amendment in law making it possible to declare collective agreements universally applicable is an instrument for the State to use which infringes upon the labour market parties' autonomy. However, the thought behind it is to make the result of the collective bargaining universally applicable. It is not up to the State to fix for instance the wage level that should apply (regarding this the State has other measures to make use of). In principle such a system making collective agreements universally applicable could be looked upon as a variant on a model for self-regulation.[66]

7.4 The great challenge

A solution to the problems highlighted in the *Laval* case might focus more or less on the legal aspects or more or less the political and more pragmatic point of

[65] Sigeman 'Fri rörlighet för tjänster', above.

[66] Numhauser-Henning 'Lagstiftning eller självreglering i arbetsrätten? Svaret är både ock' (2001) (3) *Svensk Juristtidning*, p 322.

view. The underlying practical problem that a legal solution must tackle, is the discrepancies of the costs of wages and more in different Member States. The challenge is to deal with this matter balancing the free movement of services with wage structures and more in other Member States when a service providing undertakings established in another Member State utilizes the right to free movement of services.

EC law is providing different solutions to be utilised by Member States. However, regarding Sweden the kind of solutions offered within the framework of EC law and the Directive 71/96/EC, are not fully compatible with the Swedish industrial relations system. A crucial dividing line is concerns the autonomy of the labour market parties. The adaptation of the industrial relations system is necessary, and possibly such an adaptation should take-off in the institutions that are well-founded in society. The best working solution is if the existing industrial relations model itself is used to make the parties committed to voluntarily self-restriction. Therefore the parties' on the labour market must take the initiative in order to anticipate another solution that either the parties or most of the politicians prefer. That is the great challenge!

BIBLIOGRAPHY

Barnard, C, *The Substantive Law of the EU: the Four Freedoms* (Oxford, Oxford University Press, 2004).

Bruun, N, *Fackliga och grundläggande rättigheter i EU* (Stockholm, TCO, 1999).

—— and Malmberg, J, 'Arbetsrätten i Sverige och Finland efter EU-inträdet. Kerstin Ahlberg ed, Tio år med EU—effekter på arbetsrätt, partsrelationer, arbetsmarknad och social trygghet' (2005:5) *Arbetsliv i omvandling*, pp 7–45.

Edström, Ö, 'Svensk arbetsrätt i ett europeiskt perspektiv' in B Falkenhall & D Rauhut (eds) *Arbetsrätt, rörlighet och tillväxt* (Östersund, Institutet för tillväxtpolitiska studier (ITPS), 2005), pp 241–81.

Government proposition 1990/91:162 Vissa fredspliktsregler.

Government proposition 1998/99:90 Utstationering av arbetstagare.

Government proposition (2005) Regeringens förslag till Riksdagen om lag om ändring av lagen om utstationering av arbetstagare. (Helsinki September 23, 2005) (Amendment on the Finnish Act 1146/1999 on posting of workers).

Ingmanson, S, *Erkännande av yrkeskvalifikationer inom EU* (Umeå, Skrifter från juridiska institutionen vid Umeå universitet no11/2005, 2005).

Lag & avtal Vol 2005.

Maier, L, *Utstationering av arbetstagare och det svenska kollektivavtalssystemet* (Stockholm, SACO, 2005)

Numhauser-Henning, A, 'Lagstiftning eller självreglering i arbetsrätten? Svaret är både ock' (2001) (3) *Svensk Juristtidning*, p 322.

—— 'Freedom of movement and transfer of social rights' (2002) *VII European Regional Congress, Labour Law Congress 2002*. (Reports, Stockholm.)

Official report Ds 1994:13 *Lex Britannia*.

Official report SOU 2005:89 Bevakning av kollektivavtals efterlevnad.

Pennings, F, 'Co-Ordination of Social Security on the Basis of the State-of-Employement Principle: Time for an Alternative?' (2005) (42) *Common Market Law Review*, pp 67–89.

Shuibhne, N, 'Free Movement of Persons and the Wholly Internal Rule: Time to Move On?' (2002) (39) *Common Market Law Review*, pp 731–71.

Sigeman, T, *Yttrande om tillämpning av artikel 234 EG* (2005).

—— 'Fri rörlighet för tjänster' (2005) (8) *Europarättslig tidskrift*, pp 465–95.

The European industrial relations observatory on-line (4 October 2005) *Social partners agree on treatment of foreign employers in Sweden*. The European Foundation for the Improvement of Living and Working Conditions. http://www.eiro.eurofound.eu.int/2005/09/feature/se0509102f.html

6

Restrictive Use of Award Criteria in Public Procurement

LARS HENRIKSSON*

ABSTRACT

SOCIAL REQUIREMENTS AND environmental considerations are areas of great concern and procuring entities have as significant buyers a possibility to influence tenderers in order to achieve their own objectives in this field. It is, however, doubtful whether such concerns can or should be used as award criteria unless they are directly related to the contract at hand. This chapter focuses on the legality of various award criteria and the area of interest is therefore what criteria can be used for evaluating tenders against each other.

Permissible award criteria under the EC public procurement directives are limited to either the lowest price or to criteria aimed at identifying the economically most advantageous tender. The legal limits of the latter criteria have, however, been imprecise both in case law and more detailed guidance are scarcely found in the legal literature. The discussion relates mostly to the admissibility of non-economic factors as award criteria and the inclusion of 'soft values' such as environmental aspects and social considerations into the evaluation phase of the procurement process. In recent years it has been advocated for a wider interpretation of permissible award criteria. In this chapter it is, however, submitted that a more restricted approach should be adopted in formulating award criteria as it otherwise would bestow contracting entities tasks that lie outside the subject matter of the contract.

* Lars Henriksson, LL D, B Sc Econ, is an associate professor at the Stockholm School of Economics, department of accounting and business law. He is also active at Centre for Law at the Economic Research Institute, EFI. The main area of research is business law in general and public procurement law, competition and antitrust law in particular.

1 INTRODUCTION

Pursuant to the EC directives on public procurement,[1] it is a firmly established principle that contracts should be awarded based on objective criteria only. Such criteria must ensure that the procurement procedure is conducted in compliance with the principles of transparency, non-discrimination and equal treatment. In Sweden, public procurement must be performed according to the principle of good business practice. As such, award of public contracts must be arranged to take due advantage of existing competition and the award procedure must be conducted in accordance with good business practice. Unwarranted considerations that may affect treatment of tenderers, candidates or tenders are not allowed.[2] The principle originates from a recommendation by a commission of inquiry in the early 1970s, according to which public procurement should be well adapted to its purpose, namely to base purchasing on economic terms and not to consider aspects of general public policy about commerce, employment and the like, which were unrelated to the contract at hand. No reference to such a principle can be found in the EC procurement directives. Although the actual meaning of the principle has been subject to different interpretations over the last three decades, it should however be viewed as incorporating the aforementioned principles of transparency, non-discrimination and equal treatment.

The overall objective for public procurement legislation is to guarantee that tenders are assessed in the light of effective competition. As a result, only two award criteria are allowed in the EC procurement directives as well as in Swedish legislation; either the lowest price, or the most economically advantageous tender. The lowest price criterion is best suited for well defined, standardised services or commodities, in situations where no evaluation of different levels of quality, service levels etc is required. In practice, however, the value of many procured products and services cannot be appraised on price alone. Also, procuring entities may want to have some discretion in their choice of the product or service. For most contracting authorities, therefore, other considerations in addition to a low price may be of equal or even greater significance such as quality, time factors etc. Hence, the use of the criteria the economically most advantageous tender is commonly used amongst contracting entities. A short list of permissible sub-criteria to the latter criterion is provided in the directives. However, only scarce guidance regarding the application of these criteria can be found in the articles and the recitals of the directives.

[1] Dir 2004/17/EC of the European Parliament and of the Council of 31 March 2004 coordinating the procurement procedures of entities operating in the water, energy, transport and postal services sector, OJ L 134/1 and Dir 2004/18/EC of the European Parliament and of the Council of 31 March 2004 on the coordination of procedures for the award of public works contracts, public supply contracts and public services contracts, OJ L 134/114. Both directives are provides for identical award criteria, although some examples differ. Hereinafter they are referred to jointly.

[2] s 4 of the Act on Public Procurement, SFS 1992:1528.

Procuring entities have traditionally enjoyed considerable freedom about what and when to buy. In recent years, matters of public concern such as environmental aspects, social considerations on unemployment and the like have become increasingly important for the legislator, both on the community and national level. As will be shown below, the usage of such considerations in formulating award criteria have been subject to assessment by the ECJ. Based on inter alia those rulings it has in some cases been advocated in the legal literature that permissible award criteria should encompass a wider area of decisive factors, accommodating evaluation of issues more remotely related to the subject-matter of the contract at hand.

It is submitted in this chapter that EC-legislation does not allow for such a wider interpretation of permissible award criteria and may risk, in fact, conferring procuring entities responsibilities that are not within their competence and infringe community law. Even if 'soft' values can be considered in a procurement process, it will be demonstrated in this chapter that these factors have only limited importance in the evaluation of submitted tenders.

According to the preambles of the directives, economic and qualitative award criteria in terms of environmental and social requirements may enable the contracting authority to meet the needs of the public *concerned*. This implies, as a proper starting point, that it is neither the public nor society in general that is in centre of interest; only the needs of the contracting entity.

Only those award criteria that are aimed at identifying the economically most advantageous tender are permitted by community law.

An award criterion may be considered unlawful for two main reasons. First, an inherently lawful criterion may be formulated in such a way that the award procedure would be arbitrary. Secondly, although a criterion is well formulated, measurable and allows for comparisons of submitted tenders it may be still outside the four corners of the contract and thereby unrelated to procurement at hand. This warrants an analysis of what factors are acceptable as award criteria and what limitations must be observed.

In order to show the necessity of limiting the application of award criteria and to adopt a restrictive approach in formulating award criteria, it is required to establish the specific permissible characteristics and the boundaries of award criteria. It is indispensable in this analysis to first consider what criteria are indeed lawful in order to contrast those with criteria that are unacceptable. Hence, the article will be structured as follows:

(1) principles that govern and limit the choice of award criteria in general are ascertained;
(2) economic criteria are analysed. Although economic criteria in general are commonly used, and accepted, as award criteria, they still need to be sufficiently related to the contract at hand;
(3) aspects of non-economic nature will be examined, which also include an assessment of the treatment of 'soft' considerations in the award procedure.

Under this section, it is demonstrated that even though soft values can be considered in public procurement their use as decisive factors in the evaluation of tenders are still limited; and lastly,

(4) a special section is devoted to establishing the boundary between award criteria and contract performance conditions.

2 PERMISSIBLE CRITERIA UNDER EC LAW—GENERAL PRINCIPLES

In comparison to the Government Procurement Agreement (GPA) regime,[3] EU law does not prescribe that contracts should be awarded to the tenderer that submits the most advantageous offer, but more specifically to the *economically* most advantageous tender. The GPA regime therefore allows a wider discretion for the contracting authorities in applying the criteria that it deems to be advantageous. It is not necessary to prove any direct or indirect economic advantage.

The directives on public procurement do, however, leave it open to the procuring entities to decide if a service, product or works should be procured or not. Under the old and current directives it is neither mandatory for the procuring entity to procure at all, nor do the directives—if the procuring entity decides to procure—prescribe what should be procured.

If a contracting entity decides to put out a contract for tender, the ECJ has underlined that contracting authorities have in fact a wide discretion in assessing what factors should be taken account of as award criteria when formulating an invitation to tender. The judicial review of this is limited to verifying that there have been no serious or manifest errors.[4] Whilst Community law on the one hand thereby leaves it open to contracting authorities to choose relevant criteria, on which they decide to base the award of the contract, the ECJ held in *SIAC* on the other hand that the choice of award criteria of adjudicating authorities is, however, limited to only those that are aimed at identifying the most economically advantageous offer (para 36).[5] In reality, therefore, the discretion of choice of award criteria is limited to those linked to contract at hand and to factors that contribute to the economic value of the tenders submitted.

In order to identify tenders that fulfil these criteria, the ECJ held in *Commission v Italy* that the contracting authority enjoys discretion to formulate qualitative and quantitative sub-criteria that vary according to the contract

[3] The Government Procurement Agreement (GPA), is one of the plurilateral agreements annexed to the WTO Agreement.

[4] To that effect, see Case 56/77 *Agence Européenne d'Intérims v Commission* [1978] ECR 2215, para 20, Case T-19/95 *Adia Interim v Commission* [1996] ECR II-321, para 49, Case T-129/99 *AICS v Parliament* [2000] ECR II-2849, para 39, Case T-145/98 *ADT Projekt Gesellschaft der Arbeitsgemeinschaft Deutscher Tierzüchter mbH v Commission* [2000] ECR II-387, para 147, Case T-169/00 *Esedra SPRL v Commission* [2002] ECR-II 609, para 95 and Case T-183/00 *Strabag Benelux NV v Council of the European Union* [2003] ECR II-135.

[5] See also Case 31/87 *Gebroeders Beentjes BV v State of the Netherlands* [1988] ECR-4635, para 19.

at hand.[6] As a point of departure in the analysis below this would appear natural as different sub-criteria may vary in significance and relevance according the subject-matter of the contract. Also, an individual sub-criterion may be more important than another criterion in determining the definitive value.[7]

Therefore, it also follows from the freedom of choice given to the contracting authorities that they enjoy considerable leeway in determining the relative weighting of each sub-criterion, at least as long as the weighting permits an overall appraisal to be made of the criteria applied in order to identify the economically most advantageous tender.[8]

The current directives on public procurement stem from the older directives that date back to the 1970's. In principle, the permissible award criteria remain unchanged, although the interpretation has changed over the years and the ECJ has in several cases identified some essential limitations to freedom of choice conferred to the contracting entities. Notwithstanding the fact that the award criterion laid down in the directives can be construed widely so as to encompass several factors, the scope of discretion is still restricted. The ECJ held in *Concordia Bus*[9] that award criteria are subject to several constraints that in connexion with the *EVN*-case[10] can be summarized as follows:

(1) the award criteria chosen by the contracting entity must be linked to the subject-matter of the contract
(2) the criteria chosen must not confer an unrestricted freedom of choice on the contracting authority
(3) the criteria must be expressly mentioned in the contract documents or the contract notice
(4) comply with all the fundamental principles of Community law
(5) the award criteria must be verifiable.

These essential principles will be analysed in turn below.

[6] Case 274/83 *Commission v Italy* [1985] ECR-1007, para 25.

[7] In practice, many award procedures are performed through the allowance of relative points on several sub-criteria according their importance to the contracting authority, eg 1–5 points, where the tenderer, whose offer performs best on a criterion, eg offers highest quality, gets the highest amount of points on that particular area. A tenderer, who in relation to other tenderers offers the second best quality, would accordingly be awarded a lower scoring on such a quality criterion. The points attained for each individual sub-criteria are thereafter summarized after having considered the relative weighting of each individual criterion. An offer, which scores the highest total points, shall be deemed to be the economically most advantageous tender.

[8] Case C-448/01 *EVN AG, Wienstrom GmbH v Republik Österreich, Stadtwerke Klagenfurt AG and Kärntner Elektrizitäts-AG* [2003] ECR I-14527, para 39. The weighting of 45 per cent did not, according the ECJ, appear to present an obstacle to an overall evaluation of the criteria applied in order to identify the most economically advantageous offer (para 42). See also the judgment of the Swedish Supreme Administrative Court in the case RÅ 2002 ref. 50 where the Court emphasized that award criteria must be formulated so that a contractor shall be able determine what importance the contracting authority attaches to each criterion.

[9] Case C-513/99 *Concordia Bus Finland Oy Ab v Helsingin kaupunki, HKL-Bussiliikenne* [2002] ECR I-7213.

[10] Case C-448/01 *EVN*.

2.1 Link to the subject matter of the contract

In *Concordia Bus*, the ECJ held that as a tender necessarily relates to the subject-matter of the contract it also follows that the award criteria must themselves likewise be linked to the subject matter of the contract (para 59). In that case, the city of Helsinki had called for tenders for operating the urban bus network within the city of Helsinki. Regarding quality of the vehicle fleet, a tenderer could receive additional points if the undertaking that submitted the tender were to use buses with nitrogen oxide emission and external noise levels below certain values. The Court found that these criteria were indeed linked to the subject matter of the contract, namely the provision of urban bus transport services (para 65). Advocate General Mischo suggested that emission criteria are irretrievably linked to the configuration of bus fleet, which, the authority wished to see operate the bus service. He argued that:

> a contracting authority cannot be prohibited from requiring the use of a fleet having state of the art characteristics, even if it gives prime importance to one of the qualities of such a fleet, namely its characteristics in relation to gas emission and engine noise (para 77).

As Arnould points out, the Court did not make any extensive qualification to the linkage requirement.[11]

The question of linkage between the award criteria and subject-matter of the contract was further developed in the *EVN*-case. The subject-matter of the contract was the supply of a specific amount of electricity, originating from renewable resources, to the contracting authority that corresponded to its expected annual consumption. According to one of the award criteria, however, it was required by the tenderers to state the capacity of delivery of such electricity to a non-defined group of other consumers, independent of the authority. The maximum number of points on that award criterion was allocated to whichever tenderer stated the highest amount. In addition hereto, the amount of electricity should correspond to capacities in excess of the expected volume needed by the authority. The Court found that such a criterion had no link to the subject matter of the contract in question. One could argue that the stated capacity to some extent would mirror reliability of supply. However, such a criterion ceases to be relevant to the subject-matter of the contract and the authority when the reliability exceeds 100 per cent. According to Dischendorfer, the *EVN*-case shows that the linkage must relate to a *concrete need* of the procuring authority. How much of a product or a service those tenderers are able to deliver to other customers in addition to an assured volume to the contracting entity is therefore irrelevant.[12] If

[11] J Arnould 'Environmental criteria and the EC procurement directives: a note on the Concordia Bus Finland case' (2003(1)) *Public Procurement Law Review*, p 3–8.

[12] M Dischendorfer 'The Rules of Award Criteria under the EC Procurement Directives and the Effect of Using Unlawful Criteria: the EVN Case' (2004 (3)) *Public Procurement Law Review*, p 74–84.

a criterion is applied in this way, it will be discriminatory against those tenderers that are fully capable to meet the maximum requirements, which are linked to the subject-matter of the contract. As such, the award criteria in *EVN* could, in the view of the Court, have the effect of thwarting the very objective of the procurement directives, namely the opening up of markets to competition.[13]

The requirement of a link between the criteria used for awarding contracts is now, based upon the development of case law, expressly stated in the new procurement directives. It should be borne in mind that the general principle following the judgments in *Concordia Bus* and *EVN*, as Arrowsmith holds, is that the requirement of a link to the subject matter of the contract in many cases rules out criteria that are related to secondary policies, like environmental protection and social considerations.[14] However, these examples have been subject much debate in the legal literature, which shall be analysed further below.

2.2 Restricted freedom of choice

A second requirement laid down by the ECJ is that under any award criteria chosen the contracting authority must not bestow on such an entity an 'unrestricted freedom of choice as regards the award of the contract to a tenderer' (para 61).[15] In *Beentjes*[16] the ECJ held that national legislation on public procurement, which, in effect, confers the authorities awarding contracts *unlimited freedom of choice* in awarding contracts to a tenderer, is incompatible with community law (p 26). Whether the provision in national legislation has this effect depends on the interpretation under national law. The national legislation in the case at hand stipulated that the contract should be awarded to the tenderer whose tender appeared 'the most acceptable to the awarding authority'. Although such a provision is not equal to the criterion provided for in community legislation, it may still be compatible with community law. This could be the case if such legislation can be interpreted as allowing the contracting authorities, firstly, to compare different tenders and, secondly, to accept the economically most advantageous tender based upon such objective criteria provided for in relevant directives on public procurement (para 27). In *Concordia Bus*, the ECJ held that awarding additional points to tenders that meet certain specific and objectively quantifiable environmental requirements did not confer the contracting entity an unrestricted freedom of choice (para 66).

[13] Case C-448/01 *EVN*, para 66–71.

[14] S Arrowsmith *The Law of Public and Utilities Procurement* (London, Sweet & Maxwell 2005, 2nd edn).

[15] See also Case 31/87 *Beentjes*. The ECJ ruled that the any award criteria that would confer on the contracting authorities 'unrestricted freedom of choice' regarding the award of the contract would be incompatible with Community law (para 26).

[16] *Ibid*.

2.3 Procedural aspects

A third requirement, which was reconfirmed by the ECJ in *Concordia Bus* as a well established principle, is that any award criterion must be applied in correspondence with all the procedural rules stipulated in the directives (para 62). Special emphasis lies upon the rules of advertisement (to that effect, see more under 2.4.2 below).

In the *ATI*-case[17] a notice concerning a public contract for passenger transport were published. The contracting authority had decided to award the contract to the bidder offering the economically most advantageous tender. Four award criteria were laid down and each criterion were allocated a maximum number of points. First of all, there were two different criteria on cost per kilometre (max 60 and 10 points respectively). The third criterion covered organisation procedures and support structures (max 25 points) and the last one was possession of a certificate of conformity (max 5 points). As to the third criterion, five different sub-criteria were published, however no sub-points or weighting were assigned to those sub-criteria. During the evaluation of the submitted tender the contracting authority assigned different numbers of points to each sub-criterion, however the sum of these were equal to the main criterion (25 points). In referring to established case-law, the ECJ held that it is important that potential tenderers are aware of all the features to be taken into account of the contracting authority in identifying the economically most advantageous tender, and their relative importance (para 24).[18] However, in the case at hand the ECJ held that the old procurement directives did *not* preclude a contracting entity to attach specific weight to the subheadings of an award criterion, which are defined in advance. This is, nonetheless, subject to that it may not alter the criteria for the award of the contract set out in the contract documents or the contract notice, and it may not contain elements that could have affected the preparation of the tender, if they hade been known at the time the tenders were prepared. Lastly, this procedure may not be adopted so that it will be discriminatory against one of the tenderers (paras 26, 28, 30).

The new procurement directives require that the contracting authority, when lowest price is not used as award criterion alone, must specify the relative weighting that it gives to each and every criterion on that it has chosen to determine the most economically advantageous tender. Such weighting can be expressed by a range of adequate maximum spreads. The directives provide only one exception from this requirement. In cases where weighting is not possible for *demonstrable reasons*, the procuring entity shall indicate the criteria in descending order of importance. The general rule is therefore that award

[17] Case C-311/04 *ATI EAC Srl e Viaggi di Maio Snc, EAC Srl and Viaggi di Maio Snc v ACTV Venezia SpA, Provincia di Venezia and Comuna di Venezia (ATI)*, [2005] (not yet published).

[18] To that effect see also Case C-87/94, *Commission v Belgium* [1996] ECR I-2043, para 88 and Case C-470/99 *Universale Bau and others (Universale Bau)*[2002] ECR I-11617, para 98.

criteria must be weighted, unless it is not possible to do just that. *E contrario* the wording of the directives implies that whenever it is, in fact, possible to give weighting to criteria, the contracting authority has an obligation to do so. Only in those cases when the contracting entity is able to show reasons why weighting is impossible are they allowed to indicate the criteria in descending order of importance.

Advocate General Colomer went further than the Court in the *ATI*-case and argued that when it is not possible to rank the award criteria according to their importance in the notice or the contract documents it should not be compatible with the old procurement directives to attach specific weight to sub-criteria after the tenders have been submitted. This position is correct under the new directives because the procedural rules on weighting and ranking have been materially changed, also, the directives nowadays do not leave any discretion to the entities in this respect. Although the *ATI*-judgment was just recently decided, it must be viewed in the light of the specific question referred to the Court for preliminary ruling. As this comprised an interpretation of the old directives only, it appears doubtful whether ECJ had arrived at the same conclusion under the new directives.

The directives remain silent on the issue of how non-compliance through absent importance rating shall be handled. A prudent interpretation of the legislation could imply that in such a case all award criteria must be presumed to have equal weight. It cannot, however, always be taken for granted that all tenderers have presumed equal weighting/ranking. Therefore, in agreeing with Arrowsmith, there seems to be only two possible options to handle such a situation.[19] First, the entity cannot proceed until it has been explicitly stated that the criteria indeed have equal weight. Yet, this does not offer adequate guarantees that all potential tenderers have not been excluded as time limits may have been passed. Therefore, and secondly, in order to ensure compliance with the principle of equal treatment and that it must be ensured that this does not affect any potential tenderer, it may require the procedure to be cancelled and re-started. After all, if the directives prescribe an obligation at least to rank criteria in descending order there is no room for the entity not to comply with this.

2.4 Compliance with essential principles of Community law

Any award criteria must comply with all the fundamental principles of Community law. This can be regarded as an overall requirement on the whole procurement procedure and the ECJ has laid particular emphasis on that award criteria may not violate the principle of non-discrimination. This obligation on the contracting authorities implies inter alia that the right to establishment and

[19] S Arrowsmith *The Law of Public and Utilities Procurement* above.

the freedom to provide services may not be jeopardized when formulating award criteria.[20]

Arrowsmith underlines also that the provisions on free movement contained the EC Treaty has an essential impact on public procurement, which require thorough knowledge and understanding of basic EC principle. This is clearly evident when assessing matters of non-discrimination.[21]

2.4.1 Principle of equal treatment and non-discrimination

In *BFI Holding*, the ECJ emphasized that the overall aim of Community law on public procurement and the procedures for the award of contracts is to increase competition amongst competitors throughout the Union by eliminating barriers to the freedom to provide services and products across the borders of the Member States.[22]

Also, the directives aim at avoiding the risk of favouring national tenderers or applicants whenever a contract is awarded by the procuring authority. Furthermore, bodies financed or controlled by the Member States, regional or local authorities or other entities governed by public law may not be guided by considerations other than economic ones.[23] Consequently, it is the interest of a trader, who is established in a Member State and wishes to offer products and services to a contracting authority in another Member State, which is protected by the directives.[24] In a note about the purpose to regulate the award of public contracts, Advocate General Jacobs held in *SIAC* that public funds should be spent 'honestly and efficiently on the basis of a serious assessment and without any kind of favouritism or *quid pro quo* whether financial or political' (para 33). In the *Storebaelt*-case the contracting authority required that the contractor was obliged to the greatest extent to use Danish material, consumer goods, labour and equipment in the construction of the bridge across the Western channel of the Great Belt. This requirement was annulled before signature of the contract with the winning tenderer. Still, in the ECJ's opinion, the procurement procedure was based upon a clause that was unlawful and the clause was inherently likely to affect alliances amongst the contracts and the terms they would submit (para 26).

The ECJ underlined in *Storebaelt* that the principle of equal treatment lies at the very heart of the directives, albeit the duty to observe that principle is not

[20] Case C-513/99 *Concordia Bus*, para 63. See also case 31/87 *Beentjes*, para 29 and case C-225/98 *Commission v France (Nord-Pas-de-Calais)* [2000] ECR I-7445, para 50.

[21] S Arrowsmith 'The Application of the E.C. Treaty Rules to Public and Utilities Procurement' (1995) *Public Procurement Law Review*, p 225–80.

[22] Case C-360/96, *Gemeente Arnhem, Gemeente Rheden v BFI Holding* [1998] ECR I-6821, para 41.

[23] See Case C-44/96 *Mannesman Anlagenbau Austria and Others v Strobal Rotationsdruck* [1998] ECR I-73, para 33 and C-360/96, *Gemeente Arnhem*, para 42.

[24] Case C-380/98 *The Queen v H.M. Treasury, ex parte The University of Cambridge* [2000] ECR I-8035.

expressly mentioned in the old directives on public procurement. Otherwise, it would be very hard to ensure the development of effective competition regarding public contracts.[25] Therefore, in protecting intra-community trade, the principle of non-discrimination is of fundamental importance. The ECJ highlighted in *SIAC* that the principle of equal treatment entails that tenderers must be equally treated both at the stage when they formulate their tenders, and, at the subsequent stage, when the contracting authority is assessing the tenders.[26]

2.4.2 Principle of transparency

According to the ECJ's ruling in *SIAC*, an outflow of the principle of equal treatment is the obligation on the procuring entities to observe transparency in order to be able to verify compliance with the aforementioned principle.[27] In *Unitron Scandinavia and 3-S* the ECJ held that a contracting authority must observe the principle of transparency in order to be able to assure compliance with the principle of non-discrimination on grounds of nationality.[28] The principle of equal treatment must be ensured throughout the whole procurement procedure so that all tenderers will have equal opportunities in formulating the tenders.[29] In practical terms, and more specifically, this implies that any award criteria, regardless of whether it appears in the contract documents or in the contract notice, must be formulated 'in such a way as to allow all reasonably well-informed and normally diligent tenderers to interpret them in the same way'.[30] An example of a violation of this principle is when the contracting authority in *EVN* did not determine the time period in respect of which tenderers should state the amount of electricity to be supplied from renewable resources. It was, in essence, impossible for the tenderers to determine the exact scope of the criterion in question and, thereby, to interpret the criterion in the same way.[31]

Also, contracting authorities may not change the way they interpret the award criteria throughout the entire procurement procedure. Another aspect is that tenders should not be allowed to deviate from the basic terms stated in procurement documents or notices. The directives explicitly make it possible to take account of *variants* of award criteria,[32] but the possibility for the contracting authority to consider variants is restricted to those which have been expressly mentioned in the contract document or in the tender notice.[33] Upon

[25] Case C-243/89 *Commission v Denmark* [1993] ECR I-3353, para 33.

[26] Case C-19/00, *SIAC Construction Ltd. v County Council of the County of Mayo* [2001] ECR I-7725, para 34. See also case C-87/94, *Commission v Belgium*, para 54.

[27] See to that effect, case C-470/99 *Universale Bau*, para 91 and Case C-324/98 *Telaustria and Telefonadress* [2000] ECR I-10745, para 61 and case C-92/00 *HI* [2002] ECR I-5553, para 45.

[28] Case C-275/98 *Unitron Scandinavia A/S and 3-S A/S, Danske Svineproducenters Serviceselskab v Ministeriet for Fødevarer, Landbrug og Fiskeri* [1999] ECR I-8291, p 31.

[29] See inter alia, case C-470/99 *Universale Bau*, para 93 and case C-87/94, *Commission v Belgium*, para 54.

[30] Case C-19/00, *SIAC*, para 42.

[31] Case C-448/01 *EVN*, para 58.

[32] Arts 36 and 24 of the procurement directives.

[33] Case C-87/94, *Commission v Belgium*, para 89.

taking account of variants, the contracting authority must also indicate any minimum or specific requirements that would have to be met by the contractors.

2.5 Verifiable and measurable award criteria

In case law, the principle of verifiability has been emphasized as a crucial aspect to consider when formulating award criteria. In *EVN*, the contracting authority admitted that it did not have the technical ability to verify whether electricity supplied to it actually hade been generated from renewable resources. Furthermore, it did not require from the tenderers to supply any proof of origin of the electricity generated. The ECJ found that the authority in question neither had the intention nor the ability to verify the accuracy of the information supplied by the tenderers and the Court therefore held that this infringed the principle of equal treatment as a criterion of this sort did not ensure transparency and objectivity in the tender procedure. Hence, unverifiable award criteria are deemed to be contrary to Community law.[34] In the current procurement directives, it is now explicitly stated in the preambles that the award criteria chosen must allow for an assessment of the performance on each criterion offered by each tenderer in light of the object of the contract. Therefore, it must be possible to measure the value offered by a tenderer on each criterion. Absent this requirement, there is a clear risk for arbitrary and subjective assessments.

The requirement laid down by the Court should not, as Arrowsmith correctly emphasises, be construed as an absolute requirement and that detailed, full verification is needed in every situation.[35] Until it has been clarified how far this requisite on the entities stretches, it appears prudent to say that verification should be done as far as this is reasonable and realistically achievable.

2.6 General legal consequences of unlawful criteria

A relevant matter for consideration is the consequences for the procurement at hand that follows as a result of choosing unlawful or undisclosed sub-criteria to the criterion economic most advantageous tender.

One way of correcting such criteria would be to amend them prior to awarding the contract. Arrowsmith emphasizes, however, that it follows from the equal treatment principles that any changes, which constitute a material change, imply that the procuring entity must stay the procedure and revert to the point of the award procedure necessary, where it can be ensured that no potential tenderer is excluded from the award procedure.[36]

[34] Case C-448/01 *EVN*, para 44–52.

[35] S Arrowsmith *The Law of Public and Utilities Procurement* above.

[36] *Ibid.*

2.6.1 Disregarding unlawful criteria

Another method of handling unlawful criteria would be to disregard them altogether. However, this would risk shifting the relative balance between the criteria and thereby materially changing the award decision. For example, if an award criterion on high quality was deemed unlawful and thereby disregarded, while leaving other criteria like price and service, tenderers that offer high quality may be disfavoured in relation to those, who offer a low price at the expense of good quality. If the high quality tenderer initially had been aware of the exclusion of quality as award sub-criterion he might have submitted a different offer. Likewise, potential low-price tenders may have been excluded from submitting a tender as the initial inclusion of high quality may have discouraged them for participating in the procurement procedure. In support of this view, Dischendorfer maintains that if an authority would re-evaluate a tender without regard to an unlawful criterion, this would infringe EC law, as it would first be incompatible with the principle of transparency because tenders would be evaluated on basis of award criteria not known to the tenderers and, secondly, it would also violate the principle of equal treatment since the award criteria are in fact altered.[37]

Hence, in my view, disregarding unlawful criteria will in most cases in fact materially change the award decision and thereby violate the principle of equal treatment.

2.6.2 Substituting unlawful criteria for lowest price

Another possibility is that all sub-criteria to economically most advantageous tender are unlawful, rendering the main criterion itself unlawful. In such a case, can lowest price be used as a supplemental award criterion? The answer has been in the affirmative by some commentators and also in national case law. In the case *Heby Kommun*,[38] the Swedish Supreme Court found that a procuring entity had formulated an unlawful award criterion giving the entity unlimited discretion to choose among the tenders. It was not possible from the contract documents to determine the factors to which the entity attached importance, apart from the offered price. The Supreme Court held that in such a case, the entity was obliged, according to section 6:12 of the Swedish Act on Public Procurement, to accept the tender offering the lowest price, *regardless* of the fact that the entity had explicitly advertised that lowest price was not solely decisive. Falk contends that the Supreme Court judgment is in line with the ECJ case law.[39] However, in this author's opinion, an entity cannot continue the award procedure and apply lowest price instead of what has been advertised. After all,

[37] M Dischendorfer 'The Rules of Award Criteria under the EC Procurement Directives and the Effect of Using Unlawful Criteria: the EVN Case' above.

[38] Swedish Supreme Court judgment of 23 December 1998, Case NJA 1998 s 873, *Heby Kommun*.

[39] J-E Falk 'Miljökrav vid upphandling' Europarättslig tidskrift, 2002(1) p 45–56.

although the criteria chosen for economically most advantageous tender were indeed badly formulated, it should have been obvious that the contracting authority had *at least* made it clear that it did *not* intend to use lowest price as the sole award criterion. This fact would make usage of lowest price as an award criterion just as badly chosen as amending a faulty sub-criterion to economically most advantageous tender. It must be presumed that the procuring entity's formulation had influenced the tenderers so that they at least had formulated their tenders so to meet the requirement that lowest price was not solely decisive. For the reasons previously presented, it is submitted that this reasoning is erroneous and may indeed violate the principle of equal treatment. In order to ensure compliance with this fundamental principle of EC law, the correct procedure should have been to cancel the tender process and start a new award procedure.

Arrowsmith holds that in the event that no criteria at all have been disclosed, the procuring entity *must* use lowest price as award criterion, as it is impossible to use undisclosed criteria.[40] A similar conclusion was drawn by Advocate General Darmon in *Beentjes* where on the issue of when no criterion for awarding a contract had been validly advertised it was claimed that it appeared that '. . . only the criterion of the lowest price may be applied' (para 38). This point of view appears to be derived from the ECJ statement in *Beentjes*, which reads:

> [. . .] it is clear from the wording of Article 29 (1) and (2) of the directive that where the authorities awarding the contract do not take the lowest price as the sole criterion for awarding the contract but have regard to various criteria with a view to awarding the contract to the most economically advantageous tender, they are required to state these criteria in the contract notice or the contract documents. Consequently, a general reference to a provision of national legislation cannot satisfy the publicity requirement (para 35).

As well as case law in Sweden, Arrowsmith shows that the subsequent cases before the ECJ, *Evans Medical* and *Walloon Buses*, have been construed by national courts in the UK so as where these assessment criteria are undisclosed to bidders, then it would be a violation of the rules not to apply the lowest price criterion.[41] Strange as it may seem, though, the ECJ has not in the referred cases explicitly laid down such a requirement on the procuring entities and it appears to be a far-reaching interpretation on the general obligation to clearly state the criteria chosen.

Consequently, the standpoint of an obligation to always use lowest price when the alternative criterion is ill-formulated—or absent—presupposes the far-fetched scenario that in the unlikely event of an entity putting out a contract for tender without disclosing any information whatsoever regarding the basis

[40] S Arrowsmith *The Law of Public and Utilities Procurement* above.

[41] S Arrowsmith 'United Kingdom: Further Developments in the Luck Litigation Under the U.K. Public Services Contracts Regulations: The Decision of McDuff J in *Luck v London Borough of Tower Hamlets*', (2002 (5)) *Public Procurement Law Review*, p 105–13.

for awarding the contract, tenderers are required to always presume that silence or bad formulation on the choice of award criteria implies lowest price. This can indeed create odd results as has been shown above. Whereas the new directives provide for two alternative, mutually exclusive, award criteria and no preference is given to either of them, it is inappropriate to infer from mere silence in the notice or contract documents lowest price as the presumed choice. Thus, cancelling the award procedure appears also in this situation to be a better choice.

To conclude, material changes to unlawful criteria, disregard of them or using lowest price as a supplemental criterion will all have the same effect, namely that there is a evident risk that the principle of equal treatment is violated. Arrowsmith holds, though, that it does not have to be an absolute necessity to commence a new award procedure if the circle of tenderers is unaffected by the presence of the unlawful criterion.[42]

Dischendorfer applies a similar reasoning in his comments on the *Traunfellner*-case.[43,44] In that case, questions were raised by the Austrian Bundesvergabeamt in an application for a preliminary ruling regarding inter alia what legal consequences of unlawful award procedure should apply to the conclusion of that procedure. The questions related to the legal consequences when a publication of award criteria and minimum specification for the appraisal of different tender variants did not meet legal requirements. More specifically, the Bundesvergabeamt asked for a ruling by the ECJ on the question whether the procedure could be concluded, when variants were permissible, although the award criteria remained unspecified and, in such a case, if the variant containing the lowest tender should be accepted. Albeit the ECJ for procedural reasons declared the questions inadmissible on grounds that they were hypothetical, Advocate General Alber still commented on the issue and underlined that the principles of equal treatment and transparency required the entity to cancel the proceedings and to re-tender the contract, as all award criteria must been made known to all tenderes (para 81–2). Dischendorfer appears to agree with GA Albert in principle but argues that procedures should not be cancelled where minor infringements—like too short time limits—are at hand. AG Alber did not either accept the notion of accepting lowest price as entities are not allowed to change the award criteria during the procedure (para 83).[45]

Although the facts that Arrowsmith and Dischendorfer describe in the last two paragraphs above may be true in some cases, it is still submitted that the general rule should be to cancel the award procedure during these circumstances.

[42] S Arrowsmith *The Law of Public and Utilities Procurement* above.

[43] Case C-421/01 *Traunfellner GmbH v Österreichische Autobahnen- und Schnellstraßen-Finanzierungs-AG (Asfinag)* [2003] ECR I-11941.

[44] M Dischendorfer 'The Assessment of Variants under the EC Public Procurement rules: the Traunfellner Case' (2004 (3)) *Public Procurement Law Review*, p 67–73.

[45] Advocate General Mischo held in *EVN* that 'the award criteria must remain the same throughout the entire tendering procedure', Case C-448/01 *EVN*, para 122. To that effect, see also Case C-19/00, *SIAC*, para 43 and Case C-87/94, *Commission v Belgium*, para 88–9.

Treumer expresses the firm view that lowest price could not be substituted for an unlawful formulation of economically most advantageous tender and that the entity is not only entitled to cancel the award proceeding in circumstances where an unlawful criteria has been or when a criteria has not been properly notified, but even has a duty to do so.[46] In my opinion, bearing in mind the consequences that otherwise would occur as has been shown above, this view is correct.

3 ANALYSIS OF CRITERIA CHARACTERISTICS

The directives indicate several examples of different sub-criteria that individually or taken together would constitute the most economically advantageous tender. Most of the examples of sub-criteria stated in the directive are of economic nature such as quality, running costs, delivery or completion date/period, running costs, cost-effectiveness, functional characteristics, after-sales service and technical assistance, commitments with regard to parts, security of supply and, naturally, the price. Such criteria all have in common that they generally are easily translated into measurable economic terms that would allow for an objective comparison between the different tenders.

It is clear, however, already from the wording of the articles on contract award criteria that the list is not exhaustive, which read 'such as . . .'. The ECJ has also ruled that the directives do not exhaustively list those criteria which may be accepted as the decisive factors for what constitutes the most economically advantageous tender.[47]

A relevant question is whether the directives allow for other criteria, which may not be of a purely economic nature. The non-exhaustive listed examples include aesthetic and environmental characteristics, which is a clear indication that this most probably is the case. Moreover, the EC treaty stipulates in Article 6 that environmental protection requirements and sustainable development must be integrated into the definition and implementation of the Community policies and activities referred to in Article 3 EC. Therefore, a relevant question is whether criteria that are related to the preservation of the environment or for that matter—other 'soft' considerations—are widening the scope of permissible award criteria to encompass other objectives than those related to the contract? Although such aspects are explicitly mentioned in the procurement directives, this author maintains that the use of such aspects as award criteria is still limited. In the analysis below, though, an adequate starting point appears to be criteria of economic nature, quantifiable criteria and such criteria that could easily be translated into an economic value. Thereafter, more complicated matters will be dealt with.

[46] S Treumer, *Ligebehandlingsprincippet i EU's utbudsregler* (Jurist- og Økonomforbundets Forlag, 2000).

[47] Case C-19/00 *SIAC*, para 35. The finding of the ECJ regarded Art 29(1) of the old directive 71/305, as amended, but the ruling must certainly be applicable to the new directives as well.

3.1 Quantitative criteria

Among quantitative decisive factors, price is certainly the most common criteria. Prices are easy to compare on an objective basis. Other criteria of quantitative nature may be for example different kind of well defined costs (eg price of spare parts), warranty periods, expected lifetime, number of previous identical contracts (quantitative dimension of experience), number of units offered if the price is fixed etc. They all have in common that they can prima facie be quantified and thereby objectively compared. Generally, therefore, quantifiable criteria do not require a subjective assessment. However, there is no requirement in the directives that all criteria must be objectively measurable.

3.1.1 Unknown contract volumes

A special problem arises when it is not possible for the contracting authority to establish precise quantities of the product/service to be procured prior to the beginning of work. These problems do not relate to the appropriateness or legality of the award criteria as such but could create arbitrary evaluations if not handled correctly.

When constructing eg sewage systems it can be difficult to determine how many parts are to be used. For such contracts, many unforeseen adjustment are likely to be made and so called measure-and-value contracts can be used to overcome the problem. Under such contracts, a bill of quantities is used and the tenderers fill in a rate for each item in the bill and also a total price for the estimated total quantity. What the amount the contracting is eventually going to pay will thereafter be determined by a new measurement of actual quantities used upon completion of the work. In case law, award criteria that relate to these kind of elements that will be known only after the contract has been awarded—or for that matter completed—has not been considered to confer an adjudicating authority unrestricted freedom of choice.[48] From a practical point of view, this would otherwise yield unreasonable outcomes, as it would be impossible for public bodies to procure services and products when it, for obvious reasons, is impossible to specify the exact size or scope of a project.

However, certain evaluation problems may arise if a tenderer zero-rates individual items in the bill of quantities and only submits a total all-inclusive sum. This may complicate the evaluation of this tender in relation to another tender that specifies individual items and a total price. Which contract would yield the lowest ultimate cost if the final size of the work were to be larger? This may call for a professional opinion of an expert, who is capable of assessing different tenders. It has been deemed permissible for a contracting authority to award the contract to the tenderer whose offer, in the opinion of an expert, is the lowest in terms of ultimate cost and thereby representing the most economically

[48] Case C-19/00 *SIAC*, para 38.

advantageous tender. The legality hereof is, however, subject to that the award criteria has been clearly announced and that the expert's opinion is delivered on grounds of objectivity and that the expert's assessment can be considered to be good professional practice, relevant and appropriate to the assessment that is to be made.[49]

3.2 Qualitative criteria

The economic value of a tender does not necessarily have to be quantifiable but instead require an assessment, ranking the tenders relative to one another. It may be eg be very hard to objectively assign an absolute and objective numeric value to quality, type of experience, technical competence, familiarity with the kind of work covered by the contract documents, quality of sub-contracts etc. It should be made clear that these factors may be relevant during different stages of the award procedure and it is important to bear in mind that although the same kind of experience/quality is analysed the object of the analysis and the rules that govern selection and award phase differ. For example, experience and technical competence may be used as criteria during the qualification stage in order to exclude those tenderers that do not meet minimum requirements on financial standing and technical capability.

All these factors may also, however, have a direct link to the economic value of the contract and can therefore also be used as criteria during the award phase. Higher product quality may reduce maintenance cost; better experience can reduce execution time and thereby avoid costs for additional work etc. Although it may be impossible to assign absolute numerical values to qualitative criteria, such factors will in many cases, nevertheless, have a significant effect on the *value* of a tender. After all, in the words of the recital of the directives, the task is to determine which undertaking offers *the best value for money*. Moreover, the overall objective is to determine the economic and quality criteria, which, *taken together*, constitute the most economically advantageous tender. The analysis during the award stage is in nature different to the qualification stage as the task at hand is not to establish if a tenderer is qualified but to establish the which tender offers the best value for money.

Notwithstanding the problems connected to quantification of these factors, tenders may still be ranked against one another in terms of qualitative aspects. Tenders may therefore be given a relative value. It follows from the directives that such criteria are indeed permissible. Although qualitative factors are accepted as award criteria it can be argued that criteria such as experience and competence are too vague as they can be too difficult to evaluate. Any vague criteria always imply a risk for arbitrariness and subjective evaluation. However, the Court of First Instance (CFI) held in *Renco* that such aspects indeed could

[49] Case C-19/00 *SIAC*, para 46.

be applied objectively, uniformly and specifically in order to *compare* tenders and that they undeniably were relevant for identifying the economically most advantageous tender.[50] The problem is not that these criteria are unsuitable as grounds for evaluation, but poorly or vaguely formulated criteria may render tenders incomparable. It should be pointed out that the judgment in *Renco* is somewhat confusing in that it does not underline the distinct difference between the two stages in the award procedure. Braun holds that this, however, merely suggests a mistake by the CFI and not a change in law.[51]

3.2.1 Obligation to assess qualitative factors solely related to the tender at hand

In some cases, current suppliers may have an advantage in relation to other tenderers when a contracting authority is renewing contracts and requesting new tenders. Incumbent suppliers can claim to have more experience for the contract in question and thereby also higher quality in relation to other tenderers, who may be inexperienced with the particular contracting authority and may also, upon submitting the tender, lack certain specific assets and staff necessary to the completion and quality standards of the contract. In *TQ3*,[52] the CFI emphasized that the quality of a tender should be assessed based solely upon the tenders themselves and not on the tenderers previous experience gained from previous contracts with the contracting authority. Also, the quality of a tender may not be assessed on basis of a selection criterion—eg technical capacity of the tenderer—as this criterion already has been used in the phase of qualification when selecting applications and cannot thereafter be used again to compare the tenders submitted by qualified tenderers.[53] This is however, not to say that a criterion used for selecting tenderers is irrelevant to the award procedure. The use of selection criteria is, however, governed by different rules in the directives. Experience of past deliveries may, for example, be relevant to assess in order to establish the technical capability of a tenderer. The number of past deliveries could therefore be considered. Such past experience may tell the contracting authority something about the value of the tender. However, the fact that the tenderer has experience does not say anything about the quality of the experience. The tenderer may indeed be capable and have technical capacity, but simple facts like number of deliveries and to who deliveries have been made say very little about eg customer satisfaction with those deliveries. In the award procedure, evaluation would therefore require a different analysis than the one done

[50] Case T-4/01 *Renco SpA v Council of the European Union* [2003] ECR II 171, para 68–9.

[51] P Braun 'The Use of Qualitative Award Criteria and the Difference between Award and Qualification Criteria: A Note on T-4/01, *Renco SpA v Council of the European Union*' (2003) *Public Procurement Law Review*, p 116–19.

[52] Case T-148/04 *TQ3 Travel Solutions Belgium SA v Commission* of 6 July 2005 (not yet published), para 86–90.

[53] To this effect, se case T-148/04 *TQ3 Travel Solutions Belgium SA v Commission* of 6 July 2005 (not yet published), para 86, Case T-169/00 *Esedra SPRL v Commission* [2002] ECR II 609, para 158 and case 31/87 *Beentjes*, para 15.

during the selection phase. Assessing experience requires a qualitative analysis, which in turn requires award criteria that are aimed at assessing the value of experience rather than just establishing the presence of it.[54]

3.2.2 Excessive limiting of potential tenderers through high quality standards

Contracting authorities may decide to pursue objectives that indirectly would require tenderers to undertake investment, large-scale recruitments or the like. In *Concordia Bus*, the possibility of meeting the criterion of reducing the level of nitrogen oxide emissions and the noise level, were in practice very limited, unless the contractor had access to natural gas powered buses. Only the winning tenderer had access to such buses. Thus, Concordia held that the award criteria in question were inadmissible as only one tenderer had possibility of offering services eligible for points according to these award criteria. The ECJ held, however, that the fact that only a small number of undertakings were able to satisfy award criteria was not enough to constitute a breach of the principle of equal treatment.[55] Higher environmental standards will necessarily limit the number of potential undertakings that can satisfy the demands of the contracting entity. In *Concordia bus*, the complainant actually won the tender for a route on the Helsinki urban bus network despite that the gas-powered vehicles was required on that route. Furthermore, it was not established in the case that the winning tenderer in fact was the only remaining alternative when applying the award criteria on environmental aspects. As the Court based its decision of this 'factual context' the question remains whether award criteria are permissible if they lead to that only one undertaking will be able to meet the standards required. On the one hand it follows from *Fracasso and Leitschutz* that the contracting authority is not required to award the contract to the only remaining tenderer that is regarded to be suitable. On the other hand, if the award criteria were formulated so that only one tenderer could satisfy the objectives, the contracting authority would not be in a position to compare different bids and this would be contrary to the very subject of the procurement directives, which is to ensure sufficient genuine competition. Hence, award criteria leading up to the effect of only one remaining tenderer would not be allowed.[56] This position taken by the ECJ needs to be analysed further and is without doubt accepted if the singling out other tenderers is a result of eg requirements similar to those in the *Storebaelt* case (ie factors that would in fact favour national tenderers). The award of points relating to reduction of nitrogen oxide emissions and noise

[54] See case 31/87 *Beentjes*, para 16 and case C-315/01 *Gesellschaft für Abfallentsorgungs-Technik GmbH (GAT) v Österreichische Autobahnen und Schnellstraßen AB (ÖSAG)* [2003] ECR I 6351, para 58–67.

[55] Case C-513/99 *Concordia Bus*, para 85.

[56] See case C27/98 *Metalmeccanica Fracasso SpA and Leitschutz Handels- und Montage GmbH v Amt der Salzburger Landesregierung für den Bundesminister für wirtschaftliche Angelegenheiten* [1999] ECR I-5697, para 27–34.

levels are not in themselves discriminatory. It is in fact possible for any tenderer to acquire vehicles that meet these standards and each tenderer then have equal opportunity of scoring high points on such a criterion. In *Concordia Bus*, the only reason to why the tenderers were treated differently was that one was able to offer the requested standard, whereas another was not. Thus, in effect, there was only one tenderer remaining. This fact alone cannot imply that the award criteria are contrary to the directives. If that would be the case, the formulating of award criteria would be dependent on the present technical capability standing of different tenderers and would in fact hamper the possibilities of taking advantage of new technology. The contracting authority would then have to abstain from using any criteria that *a priori* cannot be satisfied by more than one contractor. Also, a contracting authority should in theory be able to award extra points to contractors that could supply highest standard although only very few will be able to deliver it. Suppose that it is technically possible to deliver the requested standard, but this would call for investments. The standard could apply to quality, delivery time, environmental aspects etc. If no tenderer can meet the standard when the procurement notice and documents are drafted this cannot be regarded as discriminatory. If any tenderer was able to meet this higher standard this would offer the contracting entity a higher value for the money to be spent on the contract. In that situation, surely it would be unreasonable to demand the abolishment of criteria just because there is one undertaking that can meet the standard already. That would in fact be counterproductive and create negative incentives for undertakings to invest in better but more expensive technology. Conversely, undertakings that for some reason are able to meet new, higher, standards are thereby discouraged from investing in future technology regardless of this aims at better quality, better services, reduction of polluting emissions. All in all, it appears unreasonable that contracting authorities should be prevented from taking advantage of technical progress just because currently only one undertaking can deliver the requested technology. This would in fact, as Advocate General Mischo pointed out in *Concordia Bus*, strip the contracting entities of the freedom of choice of award criteria and could in essence lead to indirect discrimination as undertakings capable of submitting better quality tenders would be denied points for the extra value this could give the contracting authority (see para 153–4).

3.2.3 Timing factors relating to access to key assets

It follows from the reasoning above that time factors are also of great significance when evaluating the quality of a tender. In case law, the CFI has established that it cannot be required that the tenderer must have all necessary staff at the time of submitting the tender. The assessment of quality criteria—eg number of staff or access to certain assets, machinery etc should be done on basis of the tender only. In turn, this requires that the tenderer must have access to the necessary staff at the time when for example services according to the contract are be to provided, but not before that time. The ability to recruit staff and acquire necessary assets is primarily a question related to the selection process (the overall suitability of a tenderer from an economic and technical standpoint) and has little to do with the quality itself of the tender. Any such requirement would in fact considerably favour all incumbent suppliers and thus counteract the main purpose of the tender procedure, namely that to ensure the best value for money by giving the opportunity to qualified applicants to submit tenders.[57]

3.2.4 The reliability of supplies

Companies that are capable of delivering on time or having the capacity of offering supplies on a continuous basis may reduce costs for the contracting authority. Steady and secure deliveries may for example enable the contracting authority to cut back on items in stock and can be beneficial in terms of cash-flow and interest and waste of perishable or non-durable goods. Thus, such aspects can clearly be economically advantageous and may therefore be used as award criteria.[58] As Advocate General Lenz rightly pointed out in *Evans Macfarlan*, a very attractively low priced tender may prove to be quite costly for the contracting authority if the contractor is unable to guarantee future deliveries.[59] Moreover, even if these criteria are forward-looking by their nature, security of supply is nowadays one of the exemplified permissible criteria in the directives. Reliability must, though, be linked to the very subject-matter of the contract in question. Hence, the relevance of supply reliability may not concern other supplies than those to the contracting entity. Otherwise, the award procedure could become arbitrary and take into account factors that have very little or nothing to do with the value of the tender at hand.

3.3 Other aspects of criteria of economic nature

A contracting authority may wish to take account of the full cost of an investment, ie not merely the initial investment but also maintenance costs. The life-cost or ultimate cost of an investment is often relevant to consider. It must be argued that such criteria are basic economic nature is thereby naturally a permissible award criteria. Brown emphasizes that it would indeed be perverse not

[57] Case T-148/04 TQ3, para 90. The Commission's procuring of services is governed by Council Reg No 1605/2002 on the financial regulation applicable to the general budget (OJ L248/1, 16 September 2002) and the implementation rules laid down in Council Reg No 2342/2002 (OJ L357/1, 31 December 2002), however the findings of the CFI should apply to other contracting authorities as well.

[58] Case C-324/93 *Evans Medical and Macfarlan Smith* [1995] ECR I-563, para 44.

[59] Advocate General Lenz opinion in Case C-324/93 *Evans Medical and Macfarlan Smith*, para 77.

to account of the ultimate cost when deciding which tender is the economically most advantageous one.[60]

As long as the contracting authority lists all relevant factors that are included in the notion of ultimate costs, this would not give raise to any concern. However, this can prove to be quite a difficult task. The expected ultimate cost is determined by a number of factors that in most cases are interrelated. For example, higher product quality may reduce maintenance cost, high quality products may prove to be more durable and reliable and thereby causing low indirect costs when standing idle for repairs. Combinations of relevant factors may therefore yield unforeseeable results in cases where the decisive aspects of each factor are not clearly specified.

4 NON-ECONOMIC CRITERIA

The ECJ held in *Concordia Bus* that in order to establish the value of a tender from the point of view of the contracting authority, the award criteria does not necessarily have to be of pure economic nature (para 55). Already the old directives referred expressly to aesthetic characteristics. It can be very difficult to assign an objective economic value to such a criterion, which implies that not all criteria need to have pure economic aspects in order for the authority to determine economically most advantageous tender.

It has been a firmly rooted opinion of the Commission that award criteria must satisfy the condition they must demonstrate a direct economic advantage to the contracting authority.[61] It cannot, however, be argued that all criteria—like environmental aspects—must be economic in nature. Neither can it be argued that each and every award criterion must show a demonstrable, direct or indirect, economic benefit to the authority. How does one, for example, assign a value to architecture? One has to take a broader view to the contract in question. The contract must be viewed in relation to the task the contracting authority is assigned to perform and the requirements laid down by its principals. This will naturally constitute the basis for the contract and thereby the choice of award criteria.

In essence, the situation would be the same for every undertaking. Consider for example a firm that is selling groceries and have a home delivery system. Upon renewing its fleet of small distribution vehicles the firm decides to purchase gas-operated trucks. This would, in fact, dramatically increase the cost for the firm by at the same time, hopefully, create goodwill and contribute positively to the firm's reputation as environmentally conscious, which in turn in can enhance sales of its 'green' products. It may be very difficult to establish the

[60] A Brown 'Award Criteria under the E.C. Procurement Directives: A Note on the SIAC Construction Case' (2002) *Public Procurement Law Review*, p 25–9.

[61] See eg Case C-513/99 *Concordia Bus*, para 52.

actual value of the goodwill gained, especially a priori. Furthermore, from an economic point of view, the decision to purchase these particular vehicles can perhaps—at face value—not be regarded as sound business practice.

Similar aspects apply to authorities. The city of Helsinki could surely have found a cheaper alternative than the one eventually chosen, however that could have implied the use of more noisy buses with higher emissions. Also, as general advocate Mischo pointed out, it could even be hard to justify the usage of more expensive low-floor buses (providing better accessibility for certain passengers) from a pure economic standpoint (para 107). Arnould agrees with this notion and underlines that the cost for easy access on buses may be hard to recoup solely on the revenues from the disabled people, who will have access to buses or from other passengers.[62] This is not a matter of cost-effectiveness but rather one objective that a public local transport authority is assigned to fulfil. The relevant question is which tenderer will be able to offer the best value for money in relation to the task the contracting authority shall perform, eg which undertaking will be able to offer best price/quality ratio not on buses in general but on those buses well adapted to the needs of passengers in general *and* disabled persons. Consequently, these aspects are indeed directly related to the subject-matter of the contract.[63]

Therefore, the directives on public procurement cannot be construed to impose obligations on the contracting authorities that would counteract the main purpose of their activities or the way they are pursuing their objectives laid by governments or their respective principals. The permissibility of different award criteria in order to determine the economically most advantageous tender must be viewed in light of the task the contracting entity has been assigned to perform and also other objectives that shall be met in doing so. Also, in *EVN* the ECJ confirmed that Community legislation does not generally preclude a contracting authority to take ecological criteria into consideration. More specifically, it was deemed permissible in the context of assessing the economically most advantageous tender for a contract for the supply of electricity to use an award criterion requiring that electricity supplied should be produced to renewable resources ('green electricity'), subject to the general conditions laid down in *Concordia Bus*.[64] Bovis argues that the discretion conferred on the contracting authorities permits an extensive array of different factors to be considered as award criteria, without having to show a direct economic advantage attributable to each and every award factor.[65] Likewise, Falk goes even farther and contends that any criteria can be used at the award phase of the procure-

[62] J Arnould 'Environmental criteria and the EC procurement directives: a note on the Concordia Bus Finland case' above.

[63] See also J Arnould 'Secondary Policies in public procurement: the innovation of the new directives' (2004) *Public Procurement Law Review*, p 187–97.

[64] Case C-448/01 *EVN*, para 34.

[65] C Bovis 'The new public procurement regime of the European union: a critical analysis of policy, law and jurisprudence' (2005 (30(5))) *EL Rev*, 607–30.

ment provided there is a link between the subject-matter of the criteria, that the criteria are non-discriminatory, non-restrictive of intra-community trade, proportionate and relevant.[66]

The discussion of non-economic values is closely related to the actual meaning of *economically* most advantageous tender. Does this notion imply cost-effectiveness in a very narrow sense, ie to always go for the cheapest tender or is it possible to take other—'soft'—values such as labour market, social policy, equality question into consideration? According to the reasoning above, the wording 'economically' must be viewed in the relevant context. There are naturally several ways of interpreting the concept 'economic'; Krüger *et al* say that even under a very narrow interpretation of the directives, which wording on award criteria stems from the first directives in 1970s, an cost-effectiveness approach within the four corners of the contract at hand may justify the inclusion of 'soft values'.[67] If the contracting entity eg fails to meet ex-statutory demands, this may turn out to be costly for the entity in the long run.

Factors of a non-economic nature are normally not assessed under a short-time cost-minimization. For example, life-cycle-costing considerations are inherently long-term oriented. Hence, as the long-term approach is commonly used when assessing economic factors it appears desirable that contracting authorities should be permitted to the same regarding other criteria as well.

Although one should always bear in mind that the contracting authority is free to decide exactly what it wishes to procure, the question remains how far they may go in their specifications of the object that is to be purchased. The obligation to uphold the link between award criteria and the subject-matter of the contract inevitably raises the question how broad the link can be. The matter would be driven to its extreme when considering requirements related to production processes and methods (PPMs) and externalities. These factors can have very little impact of the end product. Consider, for example, the *Concordia Bus*-case. The emissions of the buses were indeed related to the contract and the services provided, but what if the authority were to decide to just purchase the buses the operate the vehicles themselves and at the same time require of the bus manufacturer that the buses should be manufactured using electricity from renewable resources only and give a higher scoring in the evaluation of tenders to that tenderer that could offer the best PPM. This would have a positive effect on the environment, but very little to do with characteristics of the end-product—the buses. The Commission has up to now—in my view for good reasons—been restrictive in its approach to these factors and have said that requirements on PPMs may be required by contracting authorities 'if its helps to specify the performance characteristics (visible or invisible) of the product or service'.[68]

[66] J-E Falk 'Miljökrav vid upphandling' above.

[67] K Krüger, R Nielsen and N Bruun *European Public Contracts in a Labour Law Perspective* (Copenhagen, Djøf Publishing, 1998).

[68] The interpretative notice p 1.2.

Kunzlik argues that the Commission's narrow interpretation of the wording 'economically most advantageous' does not necessarily have to be correct.[69] Instead, it is suggested that the criterion can be construed as not being limited to economic benefits for a particular procuring entity. Economic benefits for society as a whole should, according to this view, also be possible to consider. Widening the area of interpretation would thereby allow for evaluation criteria including inter alia the degree of pollution elimination. Pollution may lead to negative externalities in terms of deterioration of the environment, the cost of which is normally borne by the society as a whole.

If the criterion was to be construed less narrowly, a procuring entity, which is not liable to bear costs for externalities, might give a higher ranking to tenders that will produce less indirect negative effects on the environment in relation to other bids that are more harmful to environment as a whole. Similarly, public procurements might also give rise to positive externalities. Consider, for example, the building of a bridge. All tenders submitted by the qualified tenderers fulfil all the technical requirements. Awarding the contract to one of the tenderers may lead to a boost in the local economy where the bridge is built as a result of that one contractor is offering a bridge that for some reason will attract more tourists. The investment cost of the bridge itself is equal to the competitors, but it will generate higher maintenance cost. Under a wide interpretation of the criteria, positive externalities can be used as an award sub-criterion.

Accepting PPMs as permissible award criteria would allow the contracting entity not only to require that for example the food is organically grown (less pesticides and thereby, presumably, healthier) but also to give higher value to tenders covering products that it are harvested in a way that is protective of the environment, that the ships and trucks used for transport are environmental friendly etc, although this would not enhance the quality of for example the vegetables harvested.

The traditional approach, up to now proposed by the Commission, would, however, not allow for such a sub-criterion to be used at the award stage of the procurement as it would not give the procuring entity an economic advantage. In my view, the Commission's approach is correct as the alternative would indeed by a perilous route to follow, opening up for inclusion of any criteria related to various kinds of positive or negative externalities that can be very difficult to foresee and even more so to measure.

However, the *EVN*-case did in fact confirm that it was permissible to use a requirement of renewable energy sources, thus apparently affirming the admissibility of specifying PPM requirements. Kunzlik is of the opinion that it follows from the *EVN*-judgment that award criteria relating to other types of PPMs that do not affect the end characteristics of the service or products consequently are permitted to use by contracting authorities, at least as far as they are adequately

[69] P Kunzlik 'International Procurement Regimes and the Scope for the inclusion of Environmental Factors in Public Procurement' (2003 (3(4))) OECD Journal on Budgeting, p 107–51.

well-defined.[70] I my opinion, the permissibility of 'green electricity' in the *EVN*-case cannot be seen as generally accepting PPMs as award criteria. The product at hand in the case was electricity and should as such be compared with the product in the *Concordia Bus*-case. The product electricity is, however, subject to rather unique characteristics. It is consumed simultaneously as it is produced and it is practically impossible to trace the origin of the electricity provided as most power plants are interconnected in a large electricity grid. The balancing of input and output makes it however possible to see the amount of energy being produced from renewable resources. Today, therefore, some power companies offer 'green' electricity. Bearing in mind the unique characteristics of this product, the environmental friendliness cannot be attributed to the electricity itself, but from the configuration of the power plant that generates electric current, it must be viewed as the production of electricity—like operating buses—is not primarily a PPM but rather an integral part of the product itself. Therefore, it can be argued that the customer is in fact buying 'green' electricity, notwithstanding the fact that it remains a fiction. This is, one of few ways of establishing the 'quality' of the product electricity.

Following Kunzliks argument one might otherwise include aspects of how well the electricity company is performing of waste management from their offices, the number of low-emission service vehicles needed for maintenance and overhaul of power plants etc. Such aspects are without a doubt unrelated to the contract and should, in my opinion, be regarded as impermissible as award criteria. Slavicek underlines that any demand on a tenderer may not, according the fundamental principle of proportionality, regulate any activity of the undertaking that is not the subject matter of the contract.[71]

This question has not been properly addressed by the ECJ and there still remains some uncertainty in case law about using factors non-related to the contract at hand as award criteria. It would however, in my view, be unfortunate if the ECJ should decide include PPMs as permissible award criteria. The main problem is that the procuring entity thereby would go beyond what is required for the contract. Although preservation of the environment is commendable, procuring entities should not primarily use their buying power to create competition amongst tenderers on best achievement on public policy or political objectives which are not directly related to the contract. This is rather a matter to be dealt with by the legislator.

Another significant counter-argument to Kunzlik is that the requirement of linking award criteria to the subject-matter of the contract may indeed limit the scope of considering for example PPM as award criteria. Such considerations appear to be more related to contractual conditions, which are absolute require-

[70] P Kunzlik '"Green Procurement" Under the New Regime' in R Nielsen & S Treumer *The New EU Public Procurement Directive* (Copenhagen, Djøf Publishing, 2005).

[71] M Slavicek 'Mångfald och offentlig upphandling' 2001 *Report for Swedish Governmental Agency for Innovation Systems, Vinnova.*

ments and, to that effect, not award criteria. This will be developed further below.

5 THE TREATMENT NON-ECONOMICAL 'SOFT' CONSIDERATIONS AND THEIR RELATION TO THE AWARD CRITERIA

The new directives on public procurement do not explicitly state that social considerations can be use a basis for awarding the contract. However, it follows from the recitals of the directives that economic and qualitative criteria aimed at meeting environmental and social requirements may be used as award criteria. Contracting authorities may eg have decided or is under obligation to fulfil the needs of particularly disadvantaged groups of people, who are intended to receive or use the products, works or services that are covered by the contract. It is therefore natural that the contracting authority should be able to award highest amount of points to a tender that best satisfy these requirements.

Social requirements may, however, also relate other concerns that are not directly related to the contract at hand. If a contracting authority would decide to engage itself in a program that is designed to combat long-term unemployment, how could this be integrated in the procurement procedure and is it admissible to consider in the procurement procedure in general and as an award criterion in particular? These kinds of considerations can be denominated as external social requirements.

In *Beentjes*, the Dutch Arrondissementsrechtbank asked the ECJ for a preliminary ruling on inter alia whether community law precluded the rejection of a tender on grounds that the contractor was unable to employ long-term unemployed persons. The ECJ held that such a criterion had no relation neither to the contractors' economic and financial standing and their technical knowledge and skills, nor to the award criteria of contracts referred to in community law. The Court's statement in *Beentjes* appears to imply that such criteria are excluded from assessment both from the qualification stage and from the subsequent appraisal of the tenders submitted by the qualified tenderers (p 28). Also, Advocate General Darmon laid emphasis on that such a criterion had no relation to the intrinsic qualities of the work to carried out or to a service that were to be performed (p 38). The finding of the ECJ raises therefore questions if such additional criteria can be considered at all. If the answer is in the affirmative one must also determine whether these factors can be considered as an award criterion.

5.1 External social requirements and award criteria

In the *Nord-Pas-de-Calais*-case[72] the contracting authority had initiated a tendering procedure relating to the construction of a multipurpose secondary

[72] Case C-225/98 *Commission of the European Communities v French Republic* [2000] ECR I-7445.

school in France. The contract notice stated that tenders would be assessed by taking into account various award criteria; quality/price ratio, technical response, service, time limit for completion etc. There was also an *additional criterion* related to employment. The Commission claimed that the French authority had infringed the relevant procurement directive by setting forth an *award* criterion relating to employment linked to a local project to combat unemployment. Following the ruling in *Beentjes*, the Commission did, however, acknowledge that employment related projects could be regarded as a *condition* of performance, ie a mandatory additional condition known to the tenderer prior to submitting the tender and which is related to the performance of the contract in question. The French government contended, however, that the criterion in question did not constitute a primary criterion aimed at identifying the most advantageous tender, but a non-decisive secondary criterion.

The ECJ held that the rules on admissible criteria provided for in the old directives did not preclude all possibility to use as a criterion a condition linked to the campaign against unemployment, although this presupposed that it was consistent with fundamental principles of Community law and the procedural rules (para 50–1). The Court went on to say that the Commission criticised the reference to the unemployment criterion as an award criterion. The question was whether the ruling in *Beentjes* really was about a secondary additional condition related to the performance of the contract, or if the criterion had been used as an award criterion. In that respect, the ECJ stressed that as the criterion in *Beentjes* had been used as a basis for rejecting the tender, the usage of that criterion did in fact constitute an award criterion (see para 52–3).

In an interpretative communication on environmental issues and social considerations,[73] the Commission claims that the ruling in *Nord-Pas-de-Calais* should be construed as that these so called 'additional criteria' are to be considered when there are two or more economically equivalent bids. The Commission states that this kind of condition can be applied once the bid have been compared from a purely economic point of view.

The Commission's interpretation of the ruling in *Nord-Pas-de-Calais* is puzzling. To begin with, the judgment itself does not mention anything about a subsequent non-economic evaluation phase in the highly unlikely event that two or more bids are deemed to be on an equal footing from a pure economic point of view. This could perhaps be the result of an all too extensive interpretation of the French government's arguments in favour of the condition, but the Court did not confirm this standpoint and made no references to it. As such, the Commission's view is confusing. Furthermore, the interpretation presupposes that all factors are indeed of a pure economic nature. As have been demonstrated

[73] Commission interpretative communication on the Community law applicable to public procurement and the possibilities for integrating environmental considerations into public procurement COM(2001) 274 final of 4 July 2001, p 22. See also Interpretative communication of the Commission on the Community law applicable to public procurement and the possibilities for integrating social considerations into public procurement, COM (2001) 566 final of 15 October 2001.

above, the Court has ruled out that possibility, which would imply that the hypothetical situation the Commission is referring to will unquestionably never occur.

The question remains how the ruling in *Nord-Pas-de-Calais* shall be construed. Bovis interprets the ruling as if the Court has accepted employment considerations as an *award* criterion that is part of the most economically advantageous tender.[74] Nevertheless, it is suggested that this opinion is not correct, perhaps caused by a misconception. Krüger, on the other hand, offers four alternative interpretations of the ruling. First, it may be viewed as reconfirming *Beentjes*.[75] Secondly, it can be viewed, in line with the Commission's interpretation, as a subsequent criterion to be used after the economically most advantageous test has resulted in tenders of equal value. Thirdly, the criteria could also be regarded as an exclusion condition for contractors who are incapable of delivering according to the contract. Lastly, the ruling can be seen as extending the scope of the award criteria to encompass other 'soft' values. It follows, however, from the freedom of choice given to the authorities in formulating award criteria that it appears unreasonable if the contracting authority were to be unable to exclude tenderers that fail to comply with such conditions that in fact are consistent with the fundamental principles of Community law and the rules of procedure.[76] To this effect, Arnould submits that the restrictive effect of an additional condition must be 'proportionate to their expected contribution to their objective of general interest'.[77] This view is supported by Williams, who, in essence, contends that the ruling in *Nord-Pas-de-Calais*-judgment has not opened the flood gates for a wave of imaginative award criteria.[78] Arnould explains further that the background to the discussion about these aspects in literature and by the Commission is caused by a confusion related to different elements in the selection and award process.[79] A general principle from a selection point of view is that non-compliant bids must be rejected by the authority and in this Kunzlik agrees that the *Beentjes*-judgment was correct, while the *Nord-Pas-de-Calais*-judgment contributed to the overall confusion about standing of contract conditions.[80] In agreeing with Kunzlik it is submitted that such conditions have very little to do with the award procedure

[74] C Bovis 'Reforming the public sector in the EU: The new public procurement regime' (Jul/Aug 2005 (60)) *Amicus Curiae*, p 411; C Bovis 'The new public procurement regime of the European union: a critical analysis of policy, law and jurisprudence' above.

[75] K Krüger 'Non-economical "soft" and "green" considerations in public contract award procedures Critical comments on the ECJ C-226/98 "Nord-Pas-de-Calais" Judgement 26 September 2000', (2002 (1)) Europarättslig Tidskrift p 65–6.

[76] See *ibid* p 66.

[77] J Arnould 'Environmental criteria and the EC procurement directives: a note on the Concordia Bus Finland case' above.

[78] R Williams 'The proposed Commission draft communication on the environment and the impact of the Nord-Pas-de-Calais region case' (2001 (3)) *Public Procurement Law Review*, p 75–80.

[79] J Arnould 'Secondary Policies in public procurement: the innovation of the new directives' above.

[80] P Kunzlik ' "Green Procurement" Under the New Regime' above.

and that they as such should indeed be regarded as lawful, subject to compliance of fundamental principles of Community law and procedural rules. Thus, non-compliant tenders must be excluded prior to evaluating of the tenders according to the award criteria. Another reason to why these secondary policies or additional conditions not should be regarded as award criteria is that there is no requirement that they are related to the subject-matter of the contract.[81]

The contract documents may indicate mandatory requirements, from which the tenderers are not allowed to deviate. Such criteria can be referred to as *absolute criteria*. If the requirements in such a criterion are not met, the tender must be rejected. However, as such, they have little to do with either the selection of tenderer or process of establishing which tender offers the best value for money.

Consider a situation where the authority lists as a condition that the contractor must be able to employ a minimum of ten workers recruited amongst long-term unemployed persons in the area of execution of the contract. Suppose that the criterion is consistent with the principle of non-discrimination and has been duly communicated to all tenderers. How should one regard such a criterion? On the one hand it may be regarded as a simple condition linked to the execution of the contract. However, if the undertaking fails to fulfil the criterion it will, in accordance with *Nord-Pas-de-Calais*-judgment, be considered to be an award criterion; excluding tenderers that do not comply with the requirement. The criterion itself does not, however, leave any room for evaluation. Either an undertaking fulfils the requirement or not; it is binary in nature. According to the new directives, contracting entities nowadays have possibility to impose special conditions relating to the performance of a contract, provided that these are compatible with Community law and are indicated in the notice used as a means of calling for competition or in the specifications. The directives expressly indicate that conditions governing the *performance* of a contract, in particular, may concern social and environmental considerations.

It appears pointless to create another evaluation criterion that is assessed subsequent to the award process or to designate mandatory conditions of contract performance as award criteria as the execution of the contract has to be done in accordance with what was known prior to the award decision. These criteria could in fact be categorized as an *absolute* criteria and are, by their nature, an integral part of the procurement process, albeit separate from the selection and award process. It seems irrational and the wrong way round to first assess the tenders on grounds of what would give the contracting authority the best value for money and thereafter exclude those that do not fulfil absolute requirements. Krüger *et al* holds that these matters are actually subject to a transparent 'one shot' decision that takes place prior to the final award and should as such be distinguished from actual final award/assessment phase or in word of Krüger *et*

[81] J Arnould 'Environmental criteria and the EC procurement directives: a note on the Concordia Bus Finland case' above.

al 'the last and final lap of the race'.[82] For this reason it appears to be wrong to label absolute criteria as *award* criteria.

The ECJ said already in *Beentjes* that additional obligations must in all cases comply with the fundamental principles of community law, in particular the right of establishment, the freedom to provide services and prohibition of discrimination on grounds of nationality.[83] Whether an obligation to employ long-term unemployed persons in fact infringes the principle of non-discrimination remains a question of fact if the obligations would have such effects. Bearing in mind all the circumstances of the case it is, according to the ECJ, for national courts to determine whether additional obligations directly or indirectly could be deemed discriminatory. The ECJ pointed out that an additional obligation can be regarded as discriminatory if the clause only can be satisfied by national tenderers or that tenderers from other Member States only with difficulty could comply with it (p 29–30).

As the ECJ held in *Nord-Pas-de-Calais*, not even the old directives precluded the use of this kind of considerations. However, as has been developed in the discussion about non-economic criteria above, it must be held that these external social requirements lack the necessary link with the subject-matter of the contract and are better suited as performance conditions rather than award criteria. More generally, it must also be argued that they are ill-suited to determine was really is the economically most advantageous tender. Including these considerations in the award phase would in fact, as has been shown in this chapter, lead to that tenderers must be prepared not only to offer best value for money, but also best fulfilment of other public policy objectives not directly related to the contract at hand. This must be regarded as unlawful. Hence, a strict approach in formulating award criteria is still warranted.

All in all, using public procurement to pursue secondary policies can be viewed as a blunt instrument and perhaps better dealt with by the legislator in the respective Member States or at the Community level. Arrowsmith holds that the current directives appears to favour contract conditions as an instrument for policy implementation, when it would be more efficient to use secondary award criteria as 'one of the most appropriate policy mechanisms'.[84] Williams (2002) also expresses that it is unfortunate that more has not been done to clarify the distinction between the use primary objectives of the contracting and secondary purposes of eg social clauses.[85] As long as the directives do not prescribe that secondary policies should be pursued in addition to the current award criteria it is possible that the approach should remain restrictive on secondary policies. In support of this view and on a comment to this problem, Slavicek underlines that

[82] K Krüger, R Nielsen and N Bruun *European Public Contracts in a Labour Law Perspective* above.

[83] See also the joined cases 27 to 29/86 *CEI and Bellini* [1987] ECR 3347.

[84] S Arrowsmith *The Law of Public and Utilities Procurement* above. p 1272.

[85] R Williams 'Commission Communication on Social Considerations', (2002 (2)) *Public Procurement Law Review*, p 53–9.

embracing secondary policies will cause the entities to leave the contractual role and enter more into that of exercise of public authority, which would be harmful to transparency and the principle of proportionality.[86] The State should therefore not primarily use their buying power, but rather its legislative power, to pursue aims of public policy.

BIBLIOGRAPHY

Arnould, J, 'Environmental criteria and the EC procurement directives: a note on the Concordia Bus Finland case' (2003(1)) *Public Procurement Law Review*, p 3–8.

—— 'Secondary Policies in public procurement: the innovation of the new directives' (2004) *Public Procurement Law Review*, p 187–97.

Arrowsmith, S, 'The Application of the E.C. Treaty Rules to Public and Utilities Procurement' (1995) *Public Procurement Law Review*, p 225–80.

—— 'United Kingdom: Further Developments in the Luck Litigation Under the U.K. Public Services Contracts Regulations: The Decision of McDuff J in *Luck v London Borough of Tower Hamlets*', (2002 (5)) *Public Procurement Law Review*, p 105–13.

—— *The Law of Public and Utilities Procurement* (London, Sweet & Maxwell 2005, 2nd edn).

Bovis, C, 'Reforming the public sector in the EU: The new public procurement regime' (Jul/Aug 2005 (60)) *Amicus Curiae*, p 411.

—— 'The new public procurement regime of the European union: a critical analysis of policy, law and jurisprudence' (2005 (30(5))) *EL Rev*, 607–30.

Braun, P, 'The Use of Qualitative Award Criteria and the Difference between Award and Qualification Criteria: A Note on T-4/01, *Renco SpA v Council of the European Union*' (2003) *Public Procurement Law Review*, p 116–19.

Brown, A, 'Award Criteria under the E.C. Procurement Directives: A Note on the SIAC Construction Case' (2002) *Public Procurement Law Review*, p 25–9.

Dischendorfer, M, 'The Assessment of Variants under the EC Public Procurement rules: the Traunfellner Case' (2004 (3)) *Public Procurement Law Review*, p 67–73.

—— 'The Rules of Award Criteria under the EC Procurement Directives and the Effect of Using Unlawful Criteria: the EVN Case' (2004 (3)) *Public Procurement Law Review*, p 74–84.

Falk, J-E, 'Miljökrav vid upphandling' (2002(1)) *Europarättslig Tidskrift* p 45–56.

Krüger, K, Nielsen, R and Bruun, N, *European Public Contracts in a Labour Law Perspective* (Copenhagen, Djøf Publishing, 1998).

Krüger, K, 'Non-economical "soft" and "green" considerations in public contract award procedures Critical comments on the ECJ C-226/98 "Nord-Pas-de-Calais" Judgement 26 September 2000', (2002 (1)) Europarättslig Tidskrift p 57–67.

Kunzlik, P, ' "Green Procurement" Under the New Regime' in R Nielsen & S Treumer *The New EU Public Procurement Directive* (Copenhagen, Djøf Publishing, 2005).

—— 'International Procurement Regimes and the Scope for the inclusion of Environmental Factors in Public Procurement' (2003 (3(4))) OECD Journal on Budgeting, p 107–51.

[86] M Slavicek 'Upphandlingens olika ansikten' (2002 (1)) *Europarättslig Tidskrift*, p 15–34.

Slavicek, M, 'Mångfald och offentlig upphandling' 2001 *Report for Swedish Governmental Agency for Innovation Systems* Vinnova.
—— 'Upphandlingens olika ansikten' (2002 (1)) *Europarättslig Tidskrift*, p 15–34.
Treumer, S, *Ligebehandlingsprincippet i EU's utbudsregler* (Jurist- og Økonomforbundets Forlag, 2000).
Williams, R, 'The proposed Commission draft communication on the environment and the impact of the Nord-Pas-de-Calais region case' (2001 (3)) *Public Procurement Law Review*, p 75–80.
—— 'Commission Communication on Social Considerations', (2002 (2)) *Public Procurement Law Review*, p 53–9.

7

Citizenship Law—No Longer Exclusive National Competence Towards Individual European Union Membership Based on Domicile?

HEDVIG LOKRANTZ BERNITZ*

ABSTRACT

NATIONALITY LAW IN the EU Member States is regarded as part of the exclusive national competence. National citizenship is the basis for Union citizenship, and a person who is a national of a Member State is, according to the main principle, also a Union citizen. However, for historical and political reasons, the nationality laws of the Member States differ from each other in substantial ways and hence there is no common definition as to who is a Union citizen.

Citizenship is, in most countries, a matter carefully protected by the state, and forms an important part of the states' sovereignty. Union citizenship, however, should not be analysed with traditional legal concepts as applied to citizenship. It is not an actual citizenship in the traditional sense, as it lacks many of the characteristic features of a national citizenship. For example, it is no designation as to a people, the power does not stem from the citizens, etc. The starting point is instead that it is a complement to the national citizenship.

Union citizenship, however, creates a space for a dynamic development of citizenship within the Union, but the path it is to take still appears to be unclear. One alternative is to retain today's construction of Union citizenship and perhaps eventually harmonize and further strengthen the status of Union citizens.

* Hedvig Lokrantz Bernitz is a researcher and teacher at the Department of Law at Stockholm University. In 2004 she defended her doctor's treatise on Nationality and Citizenship in Sweden and the EU. The treatise examines national and Union citizenship, and the role of European citizenship within the legal concept of citizenship in general. The main purpose of the study was to analyse the legal effects and importance of citizenship for the individual in international law, European law and Swedish law.

Another alternative would be to introduce a new basis for Union citizenship. The new basis proposed here is domicile in a Member State. The concept 'domicile in a Member State' could be commonly defined on an EU level, which would have both rational and democratic advantages. It would increase fairness and equal treatment for *all* inhabitants of the Union, as individual EC rights would no longer be dependant on the Member States' divergent nationality laws. This would be especially important for third country nationals living and working within the Union, who are now excluded from many EC rights.

Apart from the individual advantages, a domicile based Union citizenship may also be used without troublesome harmonization attempts of the Member States nationality laws. To distinguish national citizenship from Union citizenship could be a possible solution to the influence of EC law on the nationality legislation of the Member States. Today the principles and limitations laid down in EC law sometimes collide with the Member States' sovereignty in this legal area. Both international law on nationality and free movement of persons are examples of EU principles that should be taken into account when the Member States legislate, in a manner that may influence the national citizenship. International law on nationality should be regarded as part of the human rights that are protected in the Union, as granting and withdrawal of citizenship immediately affects the individual's possibility to exercise his or her EC rights. As to free movement of Union citizens, this right has gradually been developed by the Court and has, in combination with the principle of non-discrimination, been used as a source of new individual rights. The effect of EC law on nationality law makes it possible to maintain that not even citizenship today can be considered completely within the national competence.

If Union citizenship were given a new form that created a specific, more direct relationship between the individual and the Union, it also appears easier to further build upon the European cooperation and create a true European identity. It would also be consistent with previous practice in which important concepts have been given an autonomous EC definition.

Defining a new basis for Union citizenship should, however, also be discussed from a federative perspective. The integration of the EU has continuously increased, and the ideas of a new constitution show that this development is continuing. The consequences of the proposed independent basis for Union citizenship is, however, hard to survey if Union citizenship is further developed. There is also a risk that the Member States feel that they loose control over third country citizens residing in the country. This is an area of possible conflict.

1 THE DIVERSITY OF THE NATIONALITY LAWS OF THE EU MEMBER STATES

The idea behind a common Union citizenship as a basis for individual rights within the Union is not difficult to understand if one considers the diversity of the national citizenship in the EU Member States. A review of the legislation concerning citizenship demonstrates significant differences, but also similarities and interesting trends.

The citizenship legislation in all Member States is based on *ius sanguinis* or *ius soli*, but some form of combination exists in all countries. The principle perceived as the main principle, however, varies. Germany, for example, applies a strong principle of *ius sanguinis*, while Great Britain applies *ius soli*. Sweden has historically had a strong *ius sanguinis* tradition, but through its new Citizenship Act of 2001, *ius soli*, as well as the principle of domicile, has gained much importance.

With respect to citizenship acquisition, the attitudes among the Member States vary. There is a trend in several EU countries towards stricter naturalisation policies. In Denmark, for example, citizenship is an important issue on the political agenda and the naturalisation policy has become more restrictive. Great Britain is another example of a country that is now sharpening its requirements. There are, however, also several EU countries that are heading in the opposite direction. Germany, for example, has traditionally had very strict regulations, but has now facilitated naturalisation. In Sweden citizenship is not a big political issue and naturalisation is regarded as an important part of the integration process. Sweden has therefore rather generous provisions on citizenship acquisition, and long-term residents can normally become citizens after a certain period of residency. The generous Swedish attitude towards the individual and the equalizing of citizens' and foreigners' rights is likely to continue.

As an example of differences regarding naturalisation requirements one could mention language requirements. In contrast to Sweden, language requirements for naturalisation exist in several EU countries, such as Finland, Denmark, France, Germany, Great Britain, Portugal and the Netherlands. Several EU countries also have examinations on knowledge about the country. In Sweden, the issue of language skills has been discussed upon several occasions, and the main arguments against language requirements has been integration and justice concerns as well as difficulties in determining and documenting levels of knowledge.

The view as to dual citizenship also varies between the Member States. Sweden, as well as Finland, take a very liberal view and allow dual and multiple nationalities in every situation. France, Great Britain, Ireland and Portugal are other examples of countries that allow dual citizenship, while Denmark, Germany and the Netherlands as a rule do not. In the famous *Micheletti case* (see below in 2.2) the ECJ, however, concluded that a dual national, who possesses the nationality of a Member State as well as the nationality of a third country, shall always be treated as a Union citizen.[1]

[1] C-369/90 *Mario Vincente Micheletti et al v Delegación del Gobierno en Cantabria,* (1992) ECR p I–4239.

As to loss of citizenship, a clear development in the nationality law of European countries is that more and more countries introduce the possibility of denaturalisation if the citizenship was acquired through fraudulent conduct, etc. This possibility, for example, has been enacted in Finland in 2003, in Denmark in 2002 and in the Netherlands in 2000. Similar regulations also exist, for example, in Great Britain and Ireland. No correspondence to these regulations exists in Sweden. There is even a prohibition against involuntary loss of citizenship in the Constitution (Instrument of Government, Chapter 2, Article 7). The issue has, however, been discussed upon several occasions and future amendments are, at present, being investigated.

Another example of differences between the nationality laws of the Member States concerns the relationship to their colonies and former colonies, which becomes particularly interesting when taking into consideration Union citizenship. If nothing to the contrary has been decided, one ought to consider *all* the country's citizens as Union citizens, even if they have their origin in colonies. This has the consequence that residents, for example, of Aruba and Netherlands Antilles are Union citizens,[2] while persons from British colonies often are not. This is a result of the EU Member States' right to self-determination in the area of citizenship, which is also applicable within the EU. If Union citizenship were based on a commonly defined concept of domicile, as proposed here, only those who actually reside within the Union would be Union citizens, irrespective of their nationality. A close tie between the Union and its residents would then be created, and non-European residents would be excluded. For citizens of former colonies and other third country nationals residing in the Union, becoming a Union citizen cannot be viewed as giving the individual dual citizenship. The reason is that Union citizenship is not to be considered a true citizenship in the traditional sense. National citizenship and Union citizenship are not comparable, and have different goals and different purposes.

To conclude: no consensus in the area of citizenship exists among the EU Member States today, and any common constitutional traditions are hard to find as concerns acquisition and loss of citizenship. Historical reasons and different attitudes towards immigration, integration and expatriates are important reasons for the diversity of citizenship provisions.

The European Convention on Nationality,[3] agreed upon by the member states of the Council of Europe in 1997, provides some minima-standards for nationality legislation that could be the basis for convergence. The convention certainly contains a considerably strengthened protection for the individual. The nationality laws of the European countries are, however, not heading towards similarity. On the contrary, the diversity is, as mentioned, in some aspects increasing.

[2] G-R de Groot 'The Relationship between the Nationality Legislation of the Member States of the European Union and European Citizenship' in M La Torre (ed) *European Citizenship, An Institutional Challenge* (The Hague, Kluwer Law, 1998), pp 130.

[3] European Treaty Series (ETS) 166.

The diversity of the nationality laws of the EU countries has several consequences on the EU level. One consequence is, for example, that a person, who fulfills the requirements for citizenship acquisition in one Member State, would perhaps not qualify in another. Equal treatment and fairness become an issue, as the persons who qualify for Union citizen's rights are not defined according to any common guidelines. Union citizens who exercise their right to free movement may also have difficulties in acquiring citizenship in another Member State if they move frequently between the EU countries and as a consequence do not fulfill the period of residency required for naturalisation. For third country nationals the problem is of course even bigger.

The differences between the nationality laws and the fact that citizenship is so closely connected to the sovereignty of every state will make any attempt to harmonize the nationality laws of the Member States very difficult. There is, however, no doubt that some kind of common basis would strengthen the Union citizenship.

2 THE CORE OF UNION CITIZENSHIP

2.1 International law on nationality

Citizenship in a Member State provides the citizen with supranational rights within the Union. Even though the nationality laws differ between the Member States in many ways, the national citizenship of the countries has therefore received a new dimension through the EU and ought to be viewed in a more international perspective than previously. In order to analyse the core of Union citizenship, as well as the core of national citizenship, a good starting point is therefore international law on nationality.

That national citizenship is a human right is emphasized in international law, and was first laid down in the UN Universal Declaration of Human Rights (1948). In Europe, this human right was not, however, provided in any binding convention until the European Convention on Nationality was enacted in 1997. This Council of Europe convention, intends to mirror the development and new attitude towards nationality among the European countries.

Even if legal protection for the individual's citizenship is slowly changing and being strengthened, it is, however, still the legal principles recognized in the Convention on Certain Questions Relating to the Conflict of Nationality from 1930 (the Hague Convention on Nationality), repeated in the European Convention on Nationality, that each state has the exclusive right to determine who is a national, which prevail. The state's interests therefore are still a central basis for the international conventions, and are often placed above the individual's interests. Aspects of sovereignty, for example, receive considerable attention. Even the special conventions for protection against statelessness are characterized by the desire to effectuate the interests of the states.[4] The states'

[4] See, for example, the UN Convention on Reduction of Statelessness (1961).

criteria for considering a person to be a national citizen are thus decisive for the entire discussion concerning nationality as a human right.

The state's exclusive right was also emphasized in the famous *Nottebohm case*, where the International Court of Justice (ICJ) stated that 'international law leaves it to each State to lay down the rules governing the grant of its own nationality'.[5] The ICJ also stated that every sovereign state, in this case Liechtenstein, has the right to 'settle by its own legislation the rules relating to the acquisition of its nationality, and to confer that nationality by naturalization granted by its own organs in accordance with that legislation'.[6]

Other states or international courts can never question the national citizenship's validity in national law, and no party can compel a state to give a certain person citizenship. That the international regulations do not prescribe which state in a specific case is to give a person citizenship results, however, in that the human right to citizenship could be seen instead as an expression of a value rather than as a guideline for the national legislation, and it can be questioned as to what extent the human right to citizenship in reality is an actual right for the individual, in any case in Europe. It is however accepted that the states must take the interests of the individual into account when legislating on nationality matters.

International law, however, gives a certain space for ignoring citizenship in the relation between states. In the above-mentioned *Nottebohm* case, the ICJ ruled that citizenship must be based on a genuine link between the state and the individual. If such a link is missing, other states don't have to recognise the citizenship. According to the Hague Convention on Nationality, nationality law shall be recognised by other states only in so far as it is consistent with international conventions, international custom, and the principles of law generally recognised with regard to nationality.[7] According to the Permanent Court of International Justice, every state must thus fulfil its international obligations in this area, and the jurisdiction, which, in principle, belongs solely to the state, is thus limited by rules of international law.[8] Temporary citizenship, citizenship granted for unlawful purposes or citizenship based on discrimination, are examples of citizenship that may be ignored by other states. The limitations of international law are not static, but change over time. The jurisdiction of every state in the area of nationality law is therefore dependant on the development of international law.

[5] *Nottebohm (Liechtenstein v Guatemala)*, ICJ Reports 1955 p 23.

[6] *Ibid*, p 20.

[7] The Hague Convention on Nationality, Art 1. See also the European Convention on Nationality, Art 3.2.

[8] Nationality Decrees Issued in Tunis and Morocco, (1923) PCIJ Publications Series B, No 4.

2.2 The right of the EU Member States to define those who are Union citizens

Despite the fact that the actual word Union citizenship indicates the opposite, the EU itself has no competence to determine those who are Union citizens. In Article 17 EC it is laid down that Union citizenship is based entirely on the national citizenship of the EU Member States and on the national concepts of citizenship.

The Member States' competence to decide their own citizenship was also recognized by the ECJ in the above-mentioned *Micheletti* case.[9] Micheletti, who was a dual citizen (in Argentina and Italy), was refused the right to establish himself in Spain as a dentist. The reason was that he, according to Spanish law, was considered holding only Argentinean citizenship as he had been residing in Argentina. Spain thus denied that Micheletti's Italian citizenship had any effects in Community law. The ECJ did not agree, and stated that it is under international law for each Member State to lay down the conditions for the acquisition and loss of nationality.

This statement by the ECJ is completely natural, considering the importance of national citizenship for preserving a country's independence and identity as an independent state. This can be particularly important within a larger international organization such as the EU. The Member States have carefully guarded their exclusive right. In a specific declaration on nationality in connection with the creation of the EU (Declaration on Nationality of a Member State[10]) the Member States emphasized their competence. This jurisdiction was also emphasized in the Declaration of the Edinburgh Summit[11] and in Denmark's unilateral amendment to this agreement. Article 17 EC is addressed to the Member States, and the individual cannot maintain any right to be a Union citizen in the same manner as a person has a human right to be a national citizen in a country.

The ECJ, however, in *Micheletti*, emphasized that it is not permissible for the legislation of a Member State to restrict the effects of the grant of the nationality of another Member State by imposing an additional condition for recognition of that nationality with a view to the exercise of the fundamental freedoms provided for in the Treaty.[12] This statement has recently been repeated in the *Garcia Avello* case[13] and the *Zhu and Chen* case.[14]

It appears herewith that the Member States have forfeited the possibility permitted under international law to question the citizenship of other Member

[9] C-369/90 *Mario Vincente Micheletti et al v Delegación del Gobierno en Cantabria,* (1992) ECR p I–4239.

[10] Attachment to the final act of the Treaty on EU.

[11] OJ 1992 C 348/2.

[12] C-369/90 *Mario Vincente Micheletti et al v Delegación del Gobierno en Cantabria,* (1992) ECR p I–4239, para 10.

[13] C-148/02 *Carlos Garcia Avello v Belgium,* (2003) ECR p I–11613, para 28.

[14] C-200/02, *Kunqian Catherine Zhu and Man Lavette Chen v Secretary of State for the Home Department*, (2004) ECR p I–9925, para 39.

States. For example, one Member State cannot choose to ignore another Member State's citizenship in accordance with Article 5 in the Hague Convention on Nationality (the principle of effective nationality), which article gives a third country the right to take into consideration only one of a double citizen's citizenships. Nor can a Member State demand a genuine link in accordance with the *Nottebohm* case, between another Member State and a citizen of that country. A Member State with strict rules for citizenship acquisition consequently cannot prevent a citizen from a country with more generous provisions from exercising his or her EC rights. Even though the Member States give important and far-reaching rights to foreign Union citizens, they lack any influence on the definition of who is included.

The exclusive power of the Member States to decide who is a Union Citizen is also emphasized by the Member States' possibility of making a specific declaration as to those who are nationals for Community purposes, which right the United Kingdom and Germany have exercised. The United Kingdom, through its definition, has narrowed its regulations concerning citizenship so that in principle only British nationals who have the right to abode in the United Kingdom are encompassed by Community law. In accordance to the German declaration, on the other hand, the circle was expanded to include all those who in Article 116 *Grundgezetz* are defined as Germans (in other words, all those who have their origin in the former German empire). The ECJ in *Kaur* has recognized that the British declaration is binding for the interpretation of those who are nationals of the United Kingdom.[15]

Because of its complementary nature, its goal and its purpose, Union citizenship cannot be analysed with traditional legal concepts as applied to citizenship. In contrast to a national citizenship, for example, in Sweden, in which the legal relationship is a basis of the definition, it is, however, still rather the rights and not the obligations that are the most characteristic in Union citizenship. Union citizenship lies, no doubt, in the core of EU politics. It has important federative aspects and the concept has pushed EU in a federative direction. The goal of Union citizenship is to create rights reflecting the economic, social and political developments within the EU, but there is also a dimension of giving the Union a more state-like and open character. Creating a European identity has become increasingly important.

As will be discussed below, the ECJ has strengthened the rights of the Union citizens, and the new Directive 2004/38/EC intends to give Union citizens migration rights that resembles the national citizens right to move freely within his or her own country. Where this development will finally end is yet unknown, but it is not likely that the Union will go as far as in the United States and actually create true citizenships on different levels, in any case not yet. The main focus of the US federation differs from that of the EU as foreign and security policy

[15] C-192/99 *The Queen v The Secretary of State for the Home Department, ex parte Manjit Kaur*, (2001) ECR p I–1237.

are treated on a federal level as well as important powers of taxation. The EU is not likely to head in that direction. The question of citizenship in the Union perhaps therefore still primarily has a significant political symbolic value.

The conclusion regarding the Treaty regulations, the declarations concerning citizenship and the case law is, however, that international customary law in the area of citizenship, with respect to the state's right to determine its rules on citizenship itself, also remains within the EU. The Member States in all likelihood will wish to retain the competence to define their own citizens indefinitely, and therefore one must search for other ways to strengthen and deepen Union citizenship.

2.3 The affect of EC law on the nationality law of the Member States

Union citizen's rights are considerably more extensive than the previously well-known rights in the European Community's internal market. Several rights, for example, the right to vote and be a candidate (Article 19 EC) and the right to protection by diplomatic or consular authorities of any Member State (Article 20 EC), go further than what is necessary in order for the market to function effectively. This perhaps can be seen as the beginning of a new community, a community to which each citizen in the Union belongs, and in which every person in the future can come to receive specific rights and obligations independent of national citizenship. Perhaps Union citizenship will be given a more operative effect, where all Member States are responsible for protecting direct individual rights, and the individual acts according to this. While national citizenship is an entirely internal concept in each EU Member State, another relationship is slowly being created between the individual and the EU in which the individual through participation in the European Parliament, through rights in relation to the Union itself, and through the direct effect of EC laws, receives a specific, more direct, relationship to the Union that creates a type of European identity. Thereby, one hopes to create a feeling of belonging to the Union in addition to the association to one's own Member State.

Even if the EU Member States have complete competence in the area of citizenship, it appears that EC law can still affect the national regulations concerning citizenship. This often has its basis in the desire to secure the efficacy of EC law, and the ECJ has applied the Treaty regulations so that they increasingly have received a true content for the individual. Despite its independence, citizenship of the Union and its rights therefore become a challenge for national citizenship and the national rights of citizenship in the Member States.

The fact that EU is not an ordinary international organization, and that the Member States have transferred some of their sovereignty, must be taken into account when analysing whether EC law affects nationality law in the Member States when the national citizenship has consequences within the Union. As mentioned, no express transfer of competence has, however, been made from the Member States to the Community in the citizenship area, and the influence of EC law must therefore be sought elsewhere.

In legal doctrine many opinions *pro et contra* the influence of EC law on nationality law have been expressed since the introduction of Union citizenship through the Treaty of Maastricht, signed in 1992.[16] Through the development in the case law of the ECJ, it now, however, seems clear that the provisions and goals of EC law can affect areas that fall within the competence of the Member States. In the *Garcia Avello* case, for example, the ECJ ruled on a matter concerning surnames, an area that falls outside the competence of the Community.[17] This case extended the principle of non-discrimination to embrace two children with dual citizenship (in Belgium and Spain), who had been denied registration in Belgium under a surname chosen in accordance with the tradition in Spain. The ECJ concluded that Article 17 EC on Union citizenship, in combination with the principle of non-discrimination in Article 12 EC, prevented a Member State from rejecting such an application.

A starting-point for the analysis of whether EC law and Union citizenship affect nationality law in the Member States is therefore the assumption that the Member States are not completely free to decide, in their own nationality laws, who has Union citizen's rights. Their exclusive competence in this area may be limited by their undertakings towards the Community as laid down in the treaties and in the case law of the ECJ.

In the early *Airola* case from 1975, the Court dealt with citizenship.[18] A Belgian woman had acquired Italian citizenship automatically through marriage to an Italian man. Such automatic acquisition was possible only for women, and not for men. The ECJ found that this was discriminating, but accepted the woman's citizenship, and thus admitted the exclusive competence of the Member States to decide their own citizenship. The Court, however, stated that the citizenship in this particular case had no legal effects in EC law, and that it was necessary to define the concept of present and previous nationality 'as excluding nationality imposed by law on a female official upon her marriage with a national of another State, when she has no possibility to renounce it'.[19] The concept of citizenship must, according to the Court, be interpreted so that men and women are treated equally. The Court thus concluded that the Community does not have to accept citizenship that conflicts with a general principle of law protected by the Court, in this case the prohibition against sex

[16] See, for example, HUJ D'Oliveira 'Nationality and the European Union after Amsterdam' in D O'Keeffe & P Twomey (eds) Legal Issues of the Amsterdam Treaty (Oxford, Hart, 1999), p 397; G-R de Groot 'The Relationship between the Nationality Legislation of the Member States of the European Union and European Citizenship' above, pp 115; A Evans 'Nationality law and European Integration' (1991) (16) *European Law Review*, p 194.

[17] C-148/02 *Carlos Garcia Avello v Belgium*, (2003) ECR p I–11613. See also C-385/00 *FWL de Groot v Staatssecreatris van Financiën*, (2002) ECR p I–11819, para 75; *C-209/01 Theodor Schilling and Angelika Fleck-Schilling v Finanzamt Nürnberg-Süd*, (2003) ECR p I–13389, para 22.

[18] 21/74 *Jeanne Airola v Commission*, (1975) ECR p 221.

[19] *Ibid*, para 12.

discrimination. It is likely that the Court's opinion is valid for all general principles within Community law, and that citizenship in conflict with a general principle will not be applied.[20]

The ECJ continued this development in the above-mentioned *Micheletti* case from 1992.[21] In *Micheletti*, the Court expressly stated that the Member States, when deciding their own citizenship, must have 'due regard to Community law'.[22] The Court, however, did not comment on the consequences in national legislation.

Stating that the Member States must take Community law into consideration, while the Union at the same time maintains the principle that the Member States have exclusive competence in matters regarding nationality law, could seem a bit ambiguous. It is, however, well in line with the case law of the Court, that the EC law shall not differ between the Member States.

With starting points in *Airola* and *Micheletti*, one can conclude that nationality law of the Member States may be in conflict with EC law, and that the Member States, when legislating in this area, are bound by the principles of EC law. It then seems likely that nationality law of the Member States, that is in conflict with EC law, shall not be applied. It shall, however, be noted that the conclusion of the Court in the *Micheletti* case was not repeated in either the Edinburgh Summit, or in later Treaty amendments.

It has been argued that the influence on national legislation concerning citizenship occurs primarily through international law as part of EC law and through the protection of free movement.[23] Theoretically, even the duty of solidarity could be cited, but in practice it appears that the EU Member States have been reluctant to invoke this principle. The influence of EC law as to the decisions regarding national citizenship, results in it being possible to argue that it is not altogether correct to maintain that the Member States have exclusive competence in the area of citizenship. In any case, the countries' legislation is affected by their general obligations with respect to the EU.

2.3.1 The influence of international law

As to international law, the Member States must fulfill their international commitments when granting or withdrawing citizenship. No right to a certain

[20] S Hall 'Loss of Union Citizenship in Breach of Fundamental Rights' (1996) (21) *European Law Review* p 133.

[21] C-369/90 *Mario Vincente Micheletti et al v Delegación del Gobierno en Cantabria*, (1992) ECR p I–4239.

[22] *Ibid*, para 10.

[23] G-R de Groot 'The Relationship between the Nationality Legislation of the Member States of the European Union and European Citizenship' op. cit, p 123; G-R de Groot *Towards a European Nationality Law* Inaugural lecture, 13 November 2003 (Maastricht, University of Maastricht), pp 18; H Lokrantz Bernitz *Medborgarskapet i Sverige och Europa, Räckvidd och Rättigheter* (Nationality and Citizenship in Sweden and the European Union) (Uppsala, Iustus Förlag, 2004), pp 234.

citizenship, however, exists within EC law, and the weakness which characterizes the individual's right to citizenship in national and international law therefore is given effect also within the EU.

As already mentioned, citizenship that has been granted by a Member State has to be accepted within the EU, and cannot be questioned. It seems, however, to be an unreasonable consequence if the Member States would not be able to disregard citizenship that has been granted or withdrawn in a manner that is incorrect according to international law.

International treaties on human rights concerning citizenship 'can supply guidelines which should be followed within the framework of Community law'.[24] The ECJ has, however, been reluctant to comment on whether 'an area which falls within the jurisdiction of the national legislator' corresponds to the ECHR.[25] An interesting question is therefore whether nationality is an area where rights according to the ECHR should be recognized also in EC law.

A starting point for this discussion is the fact that even though the Member States have exclusive competence to determine their own citizenship legislation, their decisions to grant or withdraw citizenship have great consequences for the individual's rights in EC law. Union citizenship uses national citizenship in the Member States as a connecting bond. Thus, a person who looses his or her citizenship of a Member State, also looses his or her Union citizenship. As the whole system of individual rights within the Community is built on national citizenship, such citizenship ought to be treated as part of the human rights that should be protected within EU.[26] This is particularly important for minorities that have difficulties in acquiring national citizenship.

Apart from the ECHR, other conventions that are signed by all Member States or in which the Member States have collaborated, may also be used as guiding principles within EC law.[27] Among such conventions there is, for example, the European Convention on Nationality. The provisions of the European Convention on Nationality could therefore, in the future, become of great importance within EC law, as the Convention guarantees the right to citizenship for some people (for example naturalisation of legal residents), and expressly establishes when loss of nationality *ex lege* or at the initiative of the state is acceptable.

As citizenship should thus be treated as part of the human rights that shall be protected within the Union, Community law ought to be able to ignore incorrectly derived citizenship (for example if citizenship, hypothetically, has been

[24] 4/73 *J Nold, Kohlen- und Baustoffgroßhandlung v Commission*, (1974) ECR p 491, para 13.

[25] 60/84, 61/84 *Cinéthèque v Féderation nationale des cinémas français*, (1985) ECR p 2605, para 26. This particular matter concerned a French law on audio-visual communication and the question of whether it was in breach with Art 10 ECHR on freedom of expression.

[26] S Hall *Nationality, Migration Rights and Citizenship of the Union* (Dordrecht, Martinus Nijhoff Publishers, 1995) p 84, Lokrantz Bernitz, Hedvig (2004), *Medborgarskapet i Sverige och Europa, Räckvidd och Rättigheter* (Nationality and Citizenship in Sweden and the European Union), Uppsala, Iustus Förlag, p 242.

[27] 4/73 *J Nold, Kohlen- und Baustoffgroßhandlung v Commission*, (1974) ECR p 491, para 13.

granted on religious grounds). Even if such citizenship can never be questioned in the national legislation of the Member State in question, such a person ought not to be considered a Union citizen.

Likewise, if a deprivation of citizenship is incorrect according to international law (for example based on discrimination), neither the Union nor the other Member States ought to be forced to accept the deprivation. A person who looses his or her national citizenship in a Member State indeed looses the Union citizenship as well, but if neither the Community nor the other Member States have to accept the deprivation because it is contrary to international law, there ought to be a certain space for such a person to keep his or her Union citizenship.[28] The person would then be considered a Union citizen, without being a national citizen of his Member State according to the national legislation of that state. He or she would then have the same rights as other foreign Union citizens have in that country.

Consequently, citizenship granted or withdrawn in conflict with international law could possibly imply that a person, contrary to the actual wording of Article 17 EC, can be a Union citizen without being a national citizen in an EU Member State and vice-versa. Another solution, however, would be to regard the decision within national law as invalid as conflicting with EC law.

2.3.2 The influence of the principle of solidarity

As to the principle of solidarity, Article 10 EC could, theoretically, imply restrictions in the exclusive competence of the Member States in the area of nationality law, and prevent Member States from legislating contrary to EC law. According to Article 10 the Member States shall take all appropriate measures to ensure fulfillment of the obligations arising out of the EC Treaty or resulting from action taken by the institutions of the Community. The Member States and the Community shall thus cooperate, and the Member States must ensure that their legislation corresponds with EC law.

The principle of solidarity has, however, not yet been invoked in any matter concerning nationality law, even though it is not unlikely that situations have occurred where it might have been possible. There are examples of Member States that have, unilaterally, decided on national citizenship issues affecting large groups of people, and thus included or excluded people from the Union citizens' rights. Germany, for example, unilaterally included all citizens of the former German Democratic Republic (GDR) in the Union without any amendments to the Treaties or any formal decision by the Union (in this particular case Germany could, however, refer to considerations taken earlier). The other Member States accepted the incorporation. Unilateral decisions on nationality issues have also been made regarding former colonies, for example, Hong-Kong and Macao. The fact that the principle of solidarity has not been invoked in this

[28] S Hall, *Nationality, Migration Rights and Citizenship of the Union*, above pp 83.

legal area shows that the Member States, in practice, respect each other's exclusive competence. Questioning each other's citizenship would mean that they also question each other's sovereignty. It does not seem likely that the principle of solidarity in the near future will be invoked in matters concerning nationality law.

2.3.3 The influence of free movement of persons

Free movement of persons was, initially, an economic concept, and the right encompassed only those who migrated for economic purposes. Through its case law the ECJ, however, widened the concept to encompass also economically non-active persons who were involved in economic activity. People seeking employment,[29] recipients of services,[30] etc thus received migration rights. In the 1990s three important directives widened the scope further, and students,[31] retired persons[32] and the residual group[33] received a right of residence. This right was, however, conditioned and only those who were covered by a sick-insurance and had sufficient recourses to avoid becoming a burden on the host state could benefit from it. Through the Treaty of Maastricht, Article 17 and 18 were introduced in the EC Treaty. Article 18 provides a general right to free movement that encompasses both economically active and non-active Union citizens. The article can therefore be said to constitute a basis for individual rights that Union citizens have in the EC treaty. Article 18, however, permits significant limitations and conditions in the right to free movement in accordance with the Treaty and secondary law. Limitations in accordance with the Treaty can be justified on grounds of public policy, public security and public health, and allow Member States to expel or refuse entry to foreign Union citizens. As regards limitations in secondary legislation, the conditions on sick-insurance and sufficient resources still apply. The limitations allowed with respect to foreign Union citizens in EC law are those that a state cannot take against its own citizens as they would be unlawful in accordance to international law. The goal of reaching freedom of movement in the EU and the national citizens' right to liberty of movement therefore appears still distant.

A new Residence Directive 2004/38/EC 'on the right of citizens of the Union and their family members to move and reside freely within the territory of the Member States', will replace the above-mentioned directives from the 1990s, as well as most other directives and regulations in this legal area. The Directive shall take effect by 30 April 2006. Even though the Directive contains only few novelties, there are some interesting news. For example, a right of permanent

[29] C-292/89 *The Queen v Immigration Appeal Tribunal, ex parte Antonissen*, (1991) ECR p I–745.

[30] 286/82, 26/83 *Graziana Luisi & Guiseppe Carbone v Ministero del Tesoro*, (1984) ECR p 377.

[31] Dir 93/96.

[32] Dir 90/365.

[33] Dir 90/364.

residence is introduced, the definition of family members is extended and the family members right to work is clarified.

When Union citizenship was first introduced in 1993, the ECJ was hesitant to refer to the concept in its decisions. Since then there has, however, been clear a change of attitude and the ECJ has in significant ways developed Union citizen's rights, emphasizing that Union citizenship is a concrete and dynamic legal concept.

The close interrelationship between free movement of persons and citizenship is, according to Reich, one of the fundamentals of the EU.[34] In several cases the Court has based its decisions on a combination of Article 18 EC on the general free movement of Union citizens and Article 12 EC on non-discrimination. It seems clear that the ECJ has detached Article 12 EC from its previous connection to economic activity. Union citizenship, and the exercising of the right to free movement, provides a link with Community law through which Union citizens gain the protection of Article 12. This gives access to benefits and rights on a non-discriminatory basis, and Union citizens can count on equal treatment as regards a number of social benefits that facilitate the exercise of the right to free movement.

The first time the ECJ combined Article 12 and Union citizenship was in *Sala*,[35] followed by *Grzelczyk*.[36] The Court used Article 12 EC independently of the other articles in the EC Treaty, and it was made clear that Union citizenship could be extended to bring new rights. In the *ratione personae*, it is sufficient that Union citizens are lawfully residing in another Member State. The development therefore goes towards a right to equal treatment resembling the citizens' rights in a state. In the *ratione materiae* the protection against discrimination is restricted, however, to such situations that fall within the EC law's area of competence. *Sala* concerned a Spanish woman living in Germany who was refused a child-raising allowance on the ground that she did not have a residence permit. The treatment of Ms Sala constituted, according to the Court, a discrimination that could not be justified under Community law. The Court concluded that equal treatment within the scope of the EC Treaty is a right that, according to Article 17.2 EC, is connected to a person's status as a Union citizen.

In the *Grzelczyk* case the Court continued this development. The Court ruled on the right to social benefits, and accepted that there is a certain degree of solidarity between the Member States also within this area. The case concerned a student who had been denied a minimum substance allowance in the host state, which students from the host state were entitled to. The Court declared that this was discrimination on grounds of nationality, and that the student could count on equal treatment. The Court also expressed that:

[34] N Reich 'The Constitutional Relevance of Citizenship and Free Movement in an Enlarged Union' (2005) (11(6)) *European Law Journal* p 676.

[35] C-85/96 *Martinez Sala v Freistaat Bayern*, (1998) ECR p I-2691.

[36] C-184/99 *Rudy Grzelczyk v Centre public d'aide sociale d'Ottignies-Louvain-la-Neuve*, (2001) ECR p I-6193.

> Union citizenship is destined to be the fundamental status of nationals of the Member States, enabling those who find themselves in the same situation to enjoy the same treatment in law irrespective of their nationality, subject to such exceptions as are expressly provided for.[37]

It seems clear from *Sala* and *Grzelczyk* that a Union citizen, who is lawfully residing in another Member State, can claim a right not to be discriminated on grounds of nationality with respect to non contributory benefits covered by Regulation 1612/68 or 1408/71.[38] This applies even if the Union citizen does not fall within the scope of application of these regulations.

In *D'Hoop* the Court extended the scope of Union citizens' rights *ratione personae*, and a student who had exercised her right to free movement could count on Union citizen's rights even in her own country.[39] In this particular case Belgium had refused a Belgian girl an unemployment benefit on the sole ground that she had completed her secondary education in France. As she was not a worker according to Article 39 EC, the case was decided according to Article 17 and 18 EC. The ECJ stressed that a Union citizen shall not be punished for using his or her right to free movement, and that freedom of movement cannot be given full effect if Union citizens are deterred from using it. Therefore it would be incompatible with the right of freedom of movement if a citizen, in the state of which she is a national, receives a less favourable treatment than she would have enjoyed if she had not used her EC right to migrate.

The final recognition that Article 18 EC has direct effect came in *Baumbast*.[40] It is now no longer only the economically active persons who can base a right to residence in the Union directly upon the EC Treaty, but rather *all* Union citizens can do so with the support of this article.[41] This is a considerable strengthening of the legal protection for the individual and a significant development as to the extent of Union citizenship, even if it is only valid within the area in which the EC has competence.

The Court recognised the direct effect of Article 18 despite the fact that it can be limited in secondary law. The article therefore receives somewhat the character of a complement to secondary law, which is used to fill out the gaps in legislation. The limitations, however, must occur within the boundaries of Community law, and in accordance with its general principles. In addition, they

[37] *Ibid*, para 31. That Union citizenship is the fundamental status of nationals of the Member States has later been repeted in, for example, C-413/99 *Baumbast and R v Secretary of State for the Home Department,* (2002) ECR p I–7091, para 82; C-148/02 *Carlos Garcia Avello v Belgium*, (2003) ECR p I–11613, para 22; C-200/02, *Kunqian Catherine Zhu and Man Lavette Chen v Secretary of State for the Home Department*, (2004) ECR p I–9925, para 25; C-209/03 *Dany Bidar v London Borough of Earling, Secretary of State for Education and Skills*, (2005) ECR p I-2119, para 31.

[38] K Lenaerts 'Union Citizenship and the Principle of non-discrimination on Grounds of Nationality' *Festskrift til Claus Gulman* (København, Forlaget Thomson, 2006), p 301.

[39] C-224/98 *Marie-Nathalie D'Hoop v Office national de l'emploi*, (2002) ECR p I–6191.

[40] C-413/99 *Baumbast and R v Secretary of State for the Home Department,* (2002) ECR p I–7091.

[41] *Ibid*, para 83. See also C-200/02, *Kunqian Catherine Zhu and Man Lavette Chen v Secretary of State for the Home Department*, (2004) ECR p I–9925, para 26.

can be placed under judicial review. Every Union citizen's right to residence is thus subordinated to legitimate interests of the Member States, but only as long as they are necessary and appropriate to attain the objective pursued.[42] Direct effect therefore has been viewed as still being possible.

Recognising the direct effect of Article 18 is a recognition of the free movement as a right for the individual. It is clear that the Court is developing Union citizenship into a source of rights, and what is primarily protected is an individual right that is no longer as strongly economically characterized as before. The free movement of economically non-active persons, previously mostly a right in principle that could be exercised only with difficulty in reality, has thus been strengthened.

The interrelationship between non-discrimination and Union citizenship has consistently been confirmed by the ECJ. In *Trojani*, the Court, again ruled on social benefits, and further developed the relationship between Article 12 and Union citizenship.[43] A French man, who lacked any financial resources, lived in a hostel in Brussels. He applied for the so called minimex (a minimum substance allowance), which he was denied. The ECJ concluded that Mr Trojani did not meet the conditions laid down in secondary law regarding sufficient resources, and therefore he could not base any right to residence in Belgium on Article 18 EC. If Mr Trojani was legally resident in Belgium under national law, the EC law principle of non-discrimination, however, was applicable as to his possibilities to receive the minimex. The Court held that a citizen 'who is not economically active may rely on Article 12 EC where he has been lawfully resident in the host Member State for a certain time or possesses a residence permit'.[44]

It appears that the ECJ has made the right to social benefits for non-economically active Union citizens dependant on lawful residence. But how is lawful residence defined? We learn from *Trojani* that legal residence under national law can give entitlement to equal treatment under EC law. Defining legal residence according to the divergent practices and laws of the Member States, however, opens up for potential restrictions in the rights of the Union citizen. In another recent case, *Bidar*, the Court stated that assistance provided to students lawfully resident in the host Member State to cover their maintenance costs, falls within the scope of the principle of non-discrimination in Article 12 EC.[45] Recalling its ruling in *Trojani*, the Court held, however, that a Member State may demand a certain degree of integration into society for granting assistance covering maintenance costs. The existence of a certain degree of integration may, according to the Court, be regarded as established by a finding

[42] C-413/99 *Baumbast and R v Secretary of State for the Home Department*, (2002) ECR p I–7091, para 90, 91.

[43] C-456/02 *Michel Trojani v Openbaar centrum voor maatschappelijk welzijn van Brussel*, (2004) ECR, p I–7573.

[44] *Ibid*, para 43.

[45] C-209/03 *Dany Bidar v London Borough of Earling, Secretary of State for Education and Skills*, (2005) ECR p I–2119.

that the student in question has resided in the host Member State for a certain length of time.

A similar reasoning can be found in *Collins*,[46] where the Court held it as legitimate for a Member State to grant job-seeker's allowance only after it has been possible to establish a genuine link between the person seeking work and the employment market of that state. Such a link may be determined by establishing that the person has genuinely sought work in the Member State in question.

The right of the Member States to demand a genuine connection between the foreign Union citizen and the host state, together with the requirements on sick-insurance and sufficient resources, prevent social tourism within the Union. The Court has, however, emphasized that the Member States have a certain economic responsibility for foreign Union citizens, if the Union citizen can demonstrate a link to the host state. This link seems to be established by simply residing or studying in the host state. The Court's willingness to extend the Union citizens rights to encompass social benefits, and to accept conditions laid down by the Member States for this access, however, seems to depend on the nature of the benefit in question. Lenaerts therefore concludes that the notion of lawful residence, as laid down in *Sala* and *Grzelczyk*, shall not be seen as a condition that has to be fulfilled in order for the Union citizen to rely on Article 12.[47] Instead it indicates that a Union citizen, who is lawfully residing in the territory of another Member State, normally demonstrates a sufficient link with that state and therefore shall not be subject to additional discriminatory conditions. White expresses the opinion that recent case law might make it possible to argue that a foreign Union citizen's right to reside in another Member State arises under Article 18 unless there is some evidence to the contrary.[48] Alternatively, it would be possible to argue that there is a presumption that admission of a Union citizen to another Member State gives rise to lawful residence under national law in the absence of evidence to the contrary. White concludes that the 'entitlement to equality of treatment with nationals is surprisingly powerful'.[49]

In the *Zhu and Chen case* the ECJ further developed the Union citizen's right to residence.[50] A Chinese couple went to Ireland to give birth to a child, and according to Irish nationality law (which has since then been changed) the baby became an Irish citizen. The baby and its mother then moved to the United Kingdom, where the mother was refused a permanent residence permit. The ECJ ruled that the baby had a right to reside in another Member State, as it was a Union citizen. The right of residence is thus not subject to any age limitation. As it was clear, however, that the young child could not exercise her right to res-

[46] C-138/02 *Brian Francis Collins v Secretary of State for Work and Pensions*, (2004) ECR I-2703.

[47] K Lenaerts op. cit, pp 304.

[48] R White 'Free Movement, Equal Treatment, and Citizenship of the Union' (2005) (54:4) *International & Comparative Law Quarterly*, p 892.

[49] *Ibid*, p 900.

[50] C-200/02 *Kunqian Catherine Zhu and Man Lavette Chen v Secretary of State for the Home Department*, (2004) ECR p I–9925.

idence unless her guardian accompanied her, the mother should, according to the Court, be allowed to reside with her child in the host Member State. The requirement that a Union citizen must bring sufficient resources was fulfilled, as the parents had enough money to support the baby. Consequently, there is no requirement as to the origin of the money. Zhu and Chen thus succeeded to find the back door to enter the United Kingdom.

It follows from case law that Union citizenship is not intended to extend the material scope of the Treaty to internal situations, which have no link to Community law.[51] In the recent *Schempp* case, the Court interpreted the meaning of internal situations, in a matter concerning maintenance.[52] Despite its earlier, very generous, interpretation of Union citizenship, the Court here clarified that there are limits. A German national resident in Germany paid maintenance to his former wife who lived in Austria. He was refused permission to deduct the maintenance payments in his tax declarations, something that would have been possible if his wife had been residing in Germany. Since the exercise by his former wife of her right to free movement had an effect on his right to deduct in his Member State of residence, such a situation could not, according to the Court, be regarded as an internal situation with no connection with Community law. The Court, however, interpreted Article 12 EC and Article 18 EC as not precluding a taxpayer living in a Member State from being unable under national legislation to deduct from his taxable income maintenance paid to a former spouse residing in another Member State. It was a question of differences in tax legislation, not discrimination.

The current development of Union citizenship is significant and very dynamic. Union citizenship, especially in combination with non-discrimination, can thus come to be the means used in order to create a true general free movement for all in the capacity as Union citizens. The intent with the new Residence Directive 2004/38/EC is that Union citizens shall be able to move freely upon terms and conditions that resemble those of a Member State's own citizens. As the Directive only gives economically active persons a right to residency that is not limited in time, this ambition, however, is rather crippled. For economic non-active Union citizens, sick-insurance and sufficient resources are still required. A time limited right to residency in a country can never, according to international law, be applied to citizens in their own country, for example Swedish citizens in Sweden. This demonstrates that Union citizenship still has important economic ties. No doubt the social and political ambitions are, however, gaining importance.

Free movement of persons is not only a fundamental principle within Community law, but also a fundamental right for the individual. The Member

[51] C-64/96, C-65/96 *Land Nordrhein-Westfalen v Kari Uecker*; *Vera Jacquet v Land Nordrhein-Westfalen*, (1997) ECR p I–3171 para 23; C-148/02 *Carlos Garcia Avello v Belgium*, (2003) ECR p I–11613, para 26.

[52] C-403/03 *Egon Schempp v Finanzamt München V*, judgment 12 July 2005.

States are therefore obliged to refrain from measures that limit the exercise of free movement within the Union. As regards nationality concerns, the Member States do not just have to abstain from imposing additional conditions for recognition of the nationality of other Member States with a view to the exercise of the fundamental freedoms provided for in the Treaty. Situations may also arise where a Member State's national legislation on acquisition or withdrawal of citizenship is in conflict with the right to free movement.

As an example, provisions on loss of citizenship may refrain Union citizens from migrating. One could think of a situation where a national provision states that a person, who settles abroad for a certain period of time, looses his or her citizenship.[53] Such a provision would imply that a person exercising his right to live and work in another Member State risks loosing his citizenship, and therewith also his Union citizenship. This consequence does not seem altogether consistent with the intentions of the right to free movement. To solve this problem, the Member States might have to abolish this kind of provisions, at least in relation to other Member States. In Sweden there is a provision on loss of citizenship after statutory limitation has expired (Citizenship Act, section 14). The Swedish provision, however, only concerns people born abroad, who have lost every contact with Sweden. People who risk losing his or her citizenship according to this provision may also apply for permission to retain it. The Swedish provision should therefore not be considered contrary to the EC provisions on free movement.

Another example of a provision that could be in conflict with the right to free movement is if a Member State, that applies *ius soli*, has provisions stating that a child born abroad could not become a citizen (and thus not a Union citizen). Every Member State today, however, applies a combination of *ius soli* and *ius sanguinis*, and for children born abroad there are possibilities to acquire citizenship through an act of registration with public authorities. The situation is therefore not likely to occur.

Also requirements for naturalisation may be affected by the right to free movement.[54] The Member States, today, have very divergent requirements, and a Union citizen, who migrates frequently within the Union, might find it difficult to fulfill the requirements, especially the requested period of domicile. A solution could be that the Member States accept residency in another Member State as equivalent to residency in their own country. However, that would probably be regarded as a too radical solution.

The development of the right to free movement of Union citizens has accelerated in case law, and the more it is developed and used in practice, the more the Member States will have to take EC law into consideration when deciding their own nationality law. This may result in important limitations that affect the

[53] G-R de Groot 'The Relationship between the Nationality Legislation of the Member States of the European Union and European Citizenship' above, pp 136.

[54] H Lokrantz Bernitz op. cit, pp 240.

Member States' competence in this legal area. This involves, no doubt, great challenges for the Member States.

2.4 Domicile as a new basis for the union citizenship

Even if it is clear that Union citizenship is a dynamic concept and a source of rights, it is still not an independent concept. For the future it is, however, an interesting question whether it is appropriate to usher Union citizenship in under traditional citizenship regulations, or if it would be possible instead to create a new basis of selection and distinguish Union citizenship from national citizenship. Until today Union citizenship has normally been a selection criterion to decide which individuals who are embraced by the rights in EC law. Such a selection criterion could, however, be defined in any manner whatsoever, and to tie it simply to citizenship in the Member States does not appear to be necessary.

Seen from a global perspective, citizenship is decreasing as a basis for rights in favour of the principle of domicile. This principle is considered having several practical advantages, both for the individual and for the state. Also in EC law, domicile within the Union may seem to be a more appropriate and more modern basis of selection for the rights of Union citizens, and it is already used in EC law as a complement to citizenship.[55] As Union citizenship is not a true citizenship in the traditional sense, a common concept of domicile would make it possible to distinguish Union citizenship from national citizenship, without affecting the Member States' carefully guarded sovereignty and without the troublesome harmonization of national legislation regarding citizenship.

The most significant advantage of choosing domicile as a basis would be that the EU would be able to give the concept 'domicile' a specific EC legal content and therewith create a uniform basis for Community legal rights. This would be consistent with previous practice in which important concepts have received a specific Community definition. For the Member States, a common principle of selection would give a better predictability as to who is encompassed by Union citizen's rights. A national decision on citizenship would then not have such far-reaching consequences for the actions of the other Member States as it has today.

For individuals, a common basis for the definition of Union citizens is rather a question of fairness and objectivity. The conditions for acquisition and loss of nationality are today imbalanced, which gives rise to large 'class differences' within the Union. From a perspective of democracy and equal treatment is seems, however, reasonable that all inhabitants of the Union shall have the same

[55] N Reich *Union citizenship—Yesterday, Today and Tomorrow* RSGL Working Paper No 3 (Riga, Riga Graduate School of law, 2001), pp 24; N Reich & S Harbacevič̌a 'The Stony Road to Brussels: The Many Ways of EA Nationals and Residents into Union Citizenship—and the Many Attempts to Keep Them Out' (2002) (3) *Europarättslig Tidskrift*, pp 414.

right to take part in the economical, political and cultural life of the Union. The imbalance is particularly evident as against third country nationals residing in the EU, and who, because of national provisions, have problems in becoming citizens and get access to Union citizen's rights. This is, for example, an obvious problem for the Russian minority living in the Baltic States. They have had great difficulties in acquiring citizenship in Latvia and Estonia, and many of them have been given the status of 'non-citizens'.[56] As Union citizenship only refers to national citizenship, they are treated as third country nationals within the Union, and are excluded from Union citizen's rights. Unlike guest workers, a concept known in some Member States, the Russians in the Baltic States have not chosen to go there voluntarily, but were transferred there to make the area more Soviet, and their problem therefore also has an important human rights perspective. The proposed concept of domicile would offer a solution in EU law especially for such groups of people.

The position of third country nationals is being focused on in the new Directive 2003/109/EC on long-term residents. A third country national who has permanently resided in an EU state for five years may, on application, be granted the status of long-term resident in that country. Under this status the person is to be guaranteed certain rights in that country. He or she is also entitled to free movement in the EU, and may settle in another Member State in order to work, for example. According to the new Family Reunification Directive (2003/86/EC) a third country national who is more permanently residing in a Member State is also entitled to be reunited with members or his or her nuclear family.

Third country nationals will, however, still face problems, for example, as regards the requirements for naturalisation. A third country national who exercises his or her right to work in another Member State, might have problems fulfilling the required period of residency for citizenship acquisition. Enabling them to become Union citizens would therefore facilitate integration, but also recognize their economic contribution in the Union.

Today, there is no common definition of the concept of domicile in the EU Member States, rather the concept is defined in each country's own internal legal system.[57] The expression 'reside in a Member State', however, is used in EC law, for example regarding the Union citizen's right to vote (Article 19 EC). The concept is, according to the ECJ, widely defined and is based on family ties, the duration of residence as well as the intentions of the person.[58] This concept could be used as the basis for an EC legal concept of domicile, perhaps with the

[56] N Reich, Norbert 'The Constitutional Relevance of Citizenship and Free Movement in an Enlarged Union' above, pp 691.

[57] M-J Garot 'A New Basis for European Citizenship: Residence?' in M La Torre (ed) *European Citizenship, An Institutional Challenge* (The Hague, Kluwer Law, 1998), p 238.

[58] 13/73 *Anciens Etablissements D. Angenieux fils aîné et Caisse primaire centrale d'assurance maladie de la région parisienne v Willy Hakenberg*, (1973) ECR p 935; 76/76 *Silvana di Paolo v Office national de l'emploi*, (1977) ECR p 315; 284/87 *Oskar Schäflein v Commission*, (1988) ECR p 4475.

amendment that, according to the decisions in for example *Sala*[59] and *Kaur*,[60] it has to be a lawful domicile.

The proposed concept of a domicile based Union citizenship is, of course, very radical. It also has an important federal perspective. If 'federative' is defined as areas where the Member States do not have any right of veto and where legislation has direct effect, the number of areas is steadily increasing. If Union citizenship was redefined and third country nationals residing in the Member States were included, the Member states might feel that they loose control, especially if third pillar matters are in the future treated according to the Community method. Perhaps the federal perspective, however, has much to do with the terminology used. One ought therefore in this context to discuss whether the term 'Union citizenship' is well chosen for the relationship one wishes to designate. It certainly creates a sense that there is a specific relationship between the individual and the Union. At the same time, however, it fosters ideas of a true citizenship with aspects of sovereignty, etc. Union citizenship perhaps is therefore a term one ought to avoid in this context. It has been suggested that one could call the phenomenon 'Union membership' instead,[61] and thereby indicate that it is not a citizenship in the traditional sense. Perhaps then Union citizenship would no longer be perceived as a serious threat against the sovereignty of the Member States. Union membership would also, perhaps, make it easier to include citizens of third countries.

3 CONCLUSIONS

The EU lacks both its own nationality and a true citizenship. Union citizenship is not, and does not appear in the future to be able to be, a true citizenship. This would require large sacrifices by the Member States and significant changes in the allocation of powers between the Member States and the Union. Neither does it appear likely that the ECJ will give the concept 'Union citizen' any particular, common EU definition as long as it is based on national citizenship. That there are already two specific legal Union concepts of citizenship, namely the definitions that Great Britain and Germany have adopted as to those persons considered citizens in relation to EC law is an important step on the way towards a common definition. Considerable changes, however, are required in the attitude and the desire from the European peoples.

The Union citizenship may be designated as a *sui generis* creation that gives particular rights to citizens in the Member States in certain specific areas. The intent is to strengthen former rights, introduce new rights and in the future even to introduce obligations. An expression perhaps can be borrowed from the idea

[59] C-85/96 *Martinez Sala v Freistaat Bayern*, (1998) ECR p I–2691.

[60] C-192/99 *The Queen v The Secretary of State for the Home Department, ex parte Manjit Kaur*, (2001) ECR p I–1237.

[61] R Davies 'Citizenship of the Union . . . rights for all?' (2002) (27) *European Law Review*, p 135.

as to a common Nordic citizenship during the 1940s, a 'natural association' between the European peoples can be the basis for some type of common belonging. The idea of a common Nordic citizenship was, however, never realized. The national identity and national legal traditions were seen as obstacles. Instead facilitated citizenship acquisition was introduced for other Nordic citizens. Such cooperation has not been politically possible within the Union.

The Member States have, however, a responsibility for the consequences of their nationality laws within the EU. Union citizenship provides a new and important dimension to the concept of citizenship and the more it is developed, the weaker national citizenships risk becoming. The effect of EC law on national citizenship is a consequence of using national citizenship as the basis for Union citizenship and for the individual rights within the Union. As Union citizenship is being developed in case law, creating a European identity, there is a possibility that the status of national citizenship will be weakened in the future, and the role of citizenship in general will be questioned. The immediate importance of national citizenship for the state's sovereignty can then begin to be questioned, particularly in countries such as Sweden where the status of citizenship is already weak. If the rights of citizenship become too international or governed by Community law, this can also finally affect the status of the state. That is a development that the Member States wish to avoid.

National citizenship and Union citizenship are two entirely different concepts. The rights of a Union citizen resemble in some ways the rights of a national citizen, but neither the relationship nor the rights are comparable to a national citizenship. It is therefore completely reasonable that each EU Member State continues to define those persons who are its citizens. In the same manner, it would be reasonable that the EU defines those who are Union citizens. One ought to be protective with respect to national citizenship and give it a clear content and value. The idea of creating a citizenship within the EU which resembles a national citizenship is, however, somewhat misdirected, as the EU does not intend to be a state and neither does it intend to take over the state's responsibility for its residents. A domicile-based process therefore seems better suited for the relationship between the Union and its inhabitants. A commonly defined Union membership would be an important means for creating the European association which the EU is striving for, and facilitating the fulfilment of the objective of the EU as to creating a European identity and a European people, a people, however, held together on grounds other than a state. Tying the Union citizens' rights to legal domicile would also be particularly important for long-term residents originating from third countries, a group which already in many contexts is exposed to discrimination.

The conclusion with respect to Union citizenship therefore is that it ought to be developed into something other than what it is today. It would be more natural to tie it to a permanent domicile in the EU. This would give the concept more substance, something that will not be easy as long as the strange ties to national citizenship existing today remain. To make clear that it is not a relationship comparable to a true citizenship, the term 'Union membership' might be a better expression than 'Union citizenship'. The EU's objectives and goals with Union citizenship are to give rights to those who live in Europe and to tie the peoples closer together. To base this on national citizenship belongs to antiquated ideas. The decisive question naturally, however, is, do we want to?

BIBLIOGRAPHY

Davies, R, 'Citizenship of the Union . . . rights for all?' (2002) (27) *European Law Review* pp 121.

D'Oliveira, HUJ, 'Nationality and the European Union after Amsterdam' in D O'Keeffe and P Twomey (eds) *Legal Issues of the Amsterdam Treaty* (Oxford, Hart, 1999), pp 395.

de Groot, G-R, 'The Relationship between the Nationality Legislation of the Member States of the European Union and European Citizenship' in M La Torre (ed) *European Citizenship, An Institutional Challenge* (The Hague, Kluwer Law, 1998), pp 115.

—— *Towards a European Nationality Law* Inaugural lecture, 13 November 2003 (Maastricht, University of Maastricht).

Evans, A, 'Nationality law and European Integration' (1991) (16) *European Law Review* pp 190.

Garot, M-J, 'A New Basis for European Citizenship: Residence?' in M La Torre (ed) *European Citizenship, An Institutional Challenge* (The Hague, Kluwer Law, 1998) pp 229.

Hall, S, *Nationality, Migration Rights and Citizenship of the Union* (Dordrecht, Martinus Nijhoff Publishers, 1995).

—— 'Loss of Union Citizenship in Breach of Fundamental Rights' (1996) (21) *European Law Review*, pp 129.

Lenaerts, K, 'Union Citizenship and the Principle of non-discrimination on Grounds of Nationality' *Festskrift til Claus Gulman* (København, Forlaget Thomson, 2006), pp 290.

Lokrantz Bernitz, H, '*Medborgarskapet i Sverige och Europa, Räckvidd och Rättigheter*, (Nationality and Citizenship in Sweden and the European Union) (Uppsala, Iustus Förlag, 2004).

Reich, N, '*Union citizenship—Yesterday, Today and Tomorrow*, RSGL Working Paper Nr.3 (Riga, Riga Graduate School of law, 2001).

—— 'The Constitutional Relevance of Citizenship and Free Movement in an Enlarged Union' (2005) (11(6)) *European Law Journal* pp 675.

——and Harbacevič̌a, S, 'The Stony Road to Brussels: The Many Ways of EA Nationals and Residents into Union Citizenship—and the Many Attempts to Keep Them Out' (2002) (3) *Europarättslig Tidskrift*, pp 411.

White, R, 'Free Movement, Equal Treatment, and Citizenship of the Union' (2005) (54:4) *International & Comparative Law Quarterly* pp 885.

8

Constructing Comparability: The Reasoning of the ECJ on Equality in Taxation

ROBERT PÅHLSSON*

ABSTRACT

THE ECJ HAS in several cases applied Article 39EC on the free movement for workers to national income tax provisions. In relation to direct taxes, the court has found that the situations of residents and of non-residents are not, as a rule, comparable. However, in a number of cases the court has held that certain circumstances overrule this principle. The article analyses the reasoning of the court when it deems the situations of residents and non-residents comparable, thus providing for equal treatment of the two categories of tax subjects. The criteria used by the court are examined with a method that distinguishes between arguments based on empirical observations and arguments that result from presumptions. The general purpose of the analysis is to provide for an opinion on the transparency and legitimacy of the legal reasoning in question.

1 INTRODUCTION

Equal treatment of comparable cases is the principal consequence of the demand for non-discrimination as stipulated in the EC treaty. The purpose of this

* Robert Påhlsson graduated at Lund university in 1989 and received his doctorate at Uppsala university in 1995. In 2000 he was appointed professor of tax law at Göteborg School of Business, Economics and Law. Påhlsson has written several text books and monographs relating mainly to income tax law. His dissertation examined the legal status of the publications of the Swedish tax administration. He has also published studies of the deductibility of marketing costs and of personal expenditure. In the English language Påhlsson has examined fields of international interest, such as the impact of electronic commerce on income tax law (European Business Organization Law Review, 3:1, 2002), the concept of personal income, restructuring of corporate groups, and taxation of maritime transport (International Tax Review, January 1999, December 1999 and December 2003).

article is to analyse the reasoning of the ECJ when subjects and situations are deemed comparable or not comparable.[1] Such analyses are of fundamental importance when the court applies the EC Treaty to national income tax law.

As a point of departure I will argue that the principle of equal treatment applies to comparable cases and not to identical cases. In principle, identical situations do not exist. There are always differences, at least in time and space, which call for an assessment of the juridical comparability between cases. As will be shown it follows clearly from the motivations in a number of cases decided by the ECJ, that such comparability in fact is the general prerequisite for equal treatment.

The disposition of the chapter is as follows. To begin, I will specify the purpose of my analyses. This includes a presentation of a model for investigating the motivations of the ECJ. In addition, I account for the EC Treaty provisions demanding equal treatment. This part is kept short, as many other authors have treated the subject of non-discrimination in great detail. The following section constitutes the main part of my study. The model of analysis is applied to a number of ECJ cases where the court has interpreted Article 39 EC on the free movement for workers and applied it to the national tax laws of member states.

Conclusions will be accounted for as with analyses. A summarizing commentary has also been added. Cases investigated will be referred to in some detail. However descriptions of the circumstances of the relatively well known cases are kept short, as the cases are easily accessible on the Internet and have indeed been treated in a number of books let alone in numerous articles.

2 BACKGROUND AND PURPOSE

This chapter has in fact two purposes. First, it aims at analysing the construction of comparability in cases where national income tax provisions are tried against the treaty regulation on free movement for workers. Secondly, in the course of this case study a qualitative model for critical analysis of the motivations of the ECJ is offered.

The appliance of critical analytical models to the reasoning of courts is of general importance to juridical scholarly work. Indeed, this line of research is of significant relevance to the motivations of the ECJ. This is for several reasons. The EC Treaty Articles on free movement are formulated in a general but also very vague manner. Initially, they were not at all considered applicable to income tax measures. It was not until the C-270/83 *Avoir Fiscal* case was decided in 1986, that the tax law community realized that the court's appraisal of the scope of the treaty included national income tax laws. Indeed, it is clearly

[1] The article is part of the research project Equality in Tax Law (Sw. Likhet inför skattelag), financed by The Bank of Sweden Tercentenary Foundation.

the ECJ's position that the realization of the internal market demands that the prohibitions of discrimination and restrictions provided for in the treaty are sustained throughout the field of tax law.

Interestingly, this position has forced the court to take on an extensive responsibility which normally would have, and perhaps should have, rested on the shoulders of the legislature. It is however common knowledge that the demand in the treaty for council decisions on tax matters to be unanimous, in combination with very diverse opinions among the member states, has led to very little progress indeed, when it comes to harmonizing direct taxation in Europe.[2] It could, perhaps somewhat exaggerated but not all untrue, be concluded that the vagueness of the treaty wordings and the legislature's de facto abdication from power over the field of direct taxation, has resulted in a transfer of power from the legislature to the ECJ. In my opinion this development has implications for the legitimacy of EC law. Consequently, it is part of my motivation for investigating the reasoning of the court.

The ECJ's exercise of power in the field of direct taxation is to large extent based on the principle of equal treatment (non-discrimination). Therefore, it is of importance for the legitimacy of EC tax law that the criteria and the arguments that lead to the court's construction of comparability are consequent, transparent and in general credible.[3] Consequently, investigating the justifications regarding comparability provided by the court in its motivations must be considered a matter of scholarly interest.

Only the visible justifications, the explicit motivations, by the court will be considered here. Evidently, like anyone else working within the field of law the judges of the ECJ may be influenced by other factors than those that are considered relevant to the case in question. Such influence may be conscious or

[2] Until quite recently there were only three important acts of legislation, the Parent/Subsidiary Directive (90/435/EEC), the Merger Directive (90/434/EEC) and the Arbitration Convention (90/436/EEC). The so called Tax Package includes the Savings Directive (2003/48/EC), the Directive on Cross-Border Payments of Interest and Royalties (2003/49/EC) and the Code of Conduct. The latter forms an annex to the conclusions of the Ecofin meeting of 1 December 1997 on tax policy. It is indeed a symptom of conflicting political interests in Europe that the Code is not a legally binding document.

[3] In contemporary legal theory a distinction is often made between empirical and normative legitimacy. In short, empirical legitimacy can be described as a measure of social acceptance. The expression normative legitimacy however, is used in order to analyse to what extent the legal system has the ability to solve conflicts, within the ethical framework on which it rests. This rather abstract legitimacy criterion may for example lead to the question of whether the rules subjected to investigation in fact result in equal treatment or not.

There are other expressions related to the notion of legitimacy and it seems true to say that the various legitimacy concepts are linked to each other. Additionally, there is an interesting tension between legitimacy and legality. However, these issues on jurisprudence fall well outside the scope of this study and I refer the reader to for example K Tuori *Discourse Ethics and the Legitimacy of Law* (No 2 July 1989) (2) *Ratio Juris* pp 125–43, and S Stendahl *Communicating Justice Providing Legitimacy* (Uppsala, Iustus Förlag, 2003), pp 65–76. These works also include numerous references on the subject.

unconscious.[4] As an example, it does not seem unrealistic that a judge has a preconception of legal problems, evolving from his education and practical experience. There are also significant differences in the constitutional traditions of the member states, for instance the extent to which courts may try the constitutional compatibility of statutory law. Thus, a judge who has been trained within the continental legal tradition may in some cases react differently than a colleague whose background lies in a common law-system. In short, the legal intuition of the ECJ judges may vary.

However, we cannot be sure of any of this. Therefore, it is reasonable to assess the quality and legitimacy of case law on the written motivations only. All other considerations tend to be speculations, or at the best sociological reflections. Consequently, scholarly analyses within the field of law should perhaps be based on the visible justification only.

Furthermore, it should be stressed that this qualitative study of the arguments provided by the ECJ is different from many of the previous analyses presented, the difference being that a majority of these analyses have aimed at concluding what is law at a given moment. Naturally, such prognosticating discussions may be valuable to both scholars and practioners. However, due to the vagueness of the EC Treaty regulations on free movement it is indeed difficult to base the prognoses on the written motivations only. Their reliability may in fact be dependant on factors related to for example legal culture, such as those mentioned earlier.

3 A QUALITATIVE METHOD FOR CASE ANALYSIS

The objective is to identify and discuss the criteria used by the ECJ to determine whether two situations are similar enough to be considered legally comparable, thus rendering it necessary to treat them equally, and prohibiting less favourable treatment of any one of them (discrimination). It should be noted that the following inventory also comprises criteria that are used by the court in order to *exclude* comparability. However, the actual identification of criteria is neither time- nor space-consuming. The criteria have indeed been pointed out by the court in a number of cases. Additionally, several authors have used them as means of determining what is or is not law in the field of European income taxation.

The second phase of investigation will prove to be more demanding, in that it aims not only to analyse the argumentation of the ECJ, but also to evaluate its

[4] The concepts of discovery and justification in legal decision-making have been subjected to much discussion over the years. See for example B Anderson *Discovery in Legal Decision-Making* (Dordrecht, Kluwer Academic, 1996), p 1 and J Bengoetxea *The Legal Reasoning of the European Court of Justice* (Oxford, Oxford University Press, 1992), p 119. This interesting discussion however falls outside the scope of traditional legal research, see K Popper *The Logic of Scientific Discovery* (London 1959) p 31. Since this article exclusively discusses explicit legal motivations no further references will be made here.

quality from a legitimacy perspective. When pursuing this purpose I will distinguish between the following two types of comparability criteria.

The first category of criteria indicating that two situations are comparable in the eyes of the ECJ is those that clearly result from observations. Here they will be called *empirical criteria*. An obvious example of an empirical criterion is the taxpayer's family situation, the number of children supported by him etc. Another example would be taxpayer's financial situation or place of residence.

The second category of comparability criteria is those that manifest *presumptions*. Assume for example, that the court finds that the taxpayer's personal or family situation ought to be considered. But for some reason the court abstains from considering actual observations of personal factors. Instead, the ECJ assumes that the personal situation of the tax subject show certain characteristics and bases its decision on those. In this line of reasoning the legal conceptual framework can also be used to construct *presumption criteria*. This is the case when law is used to describe reality. An example would be the conclusion that all taxpayers in certain situations are treated in a particular way, just because the law provides for such treatment. It is a well known fact that reality does not adjust itself to statutory law. For this reason, such a conclusion can be described as a presumption rather than an observation.

An important delimitation must be made before moving on to account for any findings. Due to the space and time at my disposal concentration is forced on analysis of the court's construction of comparability to a specific question: *Under what circumstances is the situation of a natural person who does not reside in a certain member state comparable to the situation of someone who actually resides there* (thus implying that they must receive equal treatment)?

It must be stressed however, that this question is merely a tool used for pursuing the primary objective of this study, which is the qualitative assessment of legitimacy in the ECJ's legal reasoning. It is for this purpose that I have applied the categorization described above to the different arguments presented by the court. Generally, an empirical criterion would seem more reliable and controllable than a presumption. It would thus render more legitimacy to the argumentation. On the other hand, a presumption could perhaps be a more practical solution, since it can be applied by the court without time or effort spent on observing the real circumstances. This qualitative discussion ought to be more comprehensive. Consequently, it belongs to the conclusions presented in the last section.

4 EQUAL TREATMENT IN EC LAW

In principle, discrimination will be the result when comparable situations are treated differently. For this reason it appears to be evident that the ECJ's construction of comparability is based on the treaty provisions prohibiting discrimination, and the case law that this legislation has given rise to. Indeed, equal treatment follows from the application of the non-discrimination principle, and non-discrimination is a consequence of adherence to the principle of equal treatment of comparable cases.

Article 12 EC holds the general prohibition of discrimination. Within the scope of the treaty any discrimination on grounds of nationality shall be prohibited. The provisions on free movement for workers in Article 39 also prohibits discrimination. However, the articles providing for freedom of establishment and free movement for services and capital are formulated differently. Despite the fact that the wordings of these provisions focus upon restrictions it is obvious that the ECJ considers them to prohibit discrimination as well.[5] As indicated above, I have used ECJ cases on discrimination for my analysis.

In the following sections the aim is to show that there are no objectively identical cases, and that equal treatment therefore must be based on subjective assessments of comparability. Such assessments may rest on presumptions or empirical observations.

5 COMPARABILITY CRITERIA IN ECJ CASE LAW

5.1 General

Article 39 EC holds the prohibition of discrimination on grounds of nationality regarding workers. In preliminary rulings the court has applied this provision to national income tax legislation on a number of occasions. Generally, it has been put to question whether the national legislation results in indirect discrimination against citizens of other member states than the one in which the national provision applies.[6] There are no cases on discrimination between different nationals who are citizens of the same member state.[7]

[5] This became clear already with the C-270/83 *Avoir Fiscal* case. During the last decade the ECJ has to considerable extent come to base its decisions on restriction, or 'barrier' analyses. One possible explanation could be the courts' own restrictive definition of the rule of reason doctrine which according to the C-55/94 *Gebhard* case applies only to restrictions which are not discriminatory. See M Dahlberg *Direct Taxation in Relation to the Freedom of Establishment and the Free Movement of Capital* (The Hague, Kluwer Law International, 2005), pp 114–24.

[6] Normally, there are no rules that are directly discriminatory in tax law ie that explicitly points out certain nationalities that are to be treated in specific ways.

[7] According to the prevailing opinion the EC treaty allows a member state to discriminate against its own citizens as long as the national measures are not liable to hinder or make less attractive the exercise of the fundamental freedoms, see for example C-55/94 *Gebhard*, C-385/00 *de Groot* and C-9/02 *Lasteyrie du Saillant*. Since the majority of member states hold more than one nationality on their territory there is a potential conflict between this principle and the wording of Art 39. Interestingly, the principle of equal treatment provided for in the Swedish constitution must be adhered to by the administration but *e contrario* not by the legislature.

5.2 The residence criterion as a point of departure

The residence criterion is indeed one of the most important conceptual tools used for distinguishing between different categories of tax subjects. The general principle of residence, implicating that a person who is resident within a specific tax jurisdiction is subject to unlimited tax liability there is fundamental to international tax law, as is the source principle whereby limited tax liability is justified. However, it is well known that there is a potential conflict between the demarcation between residents and non-residents and the demand for equal treatment/non-discrimination laid down in the EC Treaty. Consequently, a large number of the national tax rules that have been tried by the ECJ against the EC Treaty have been based on the distinction between residents and non-residents. Generally, one important question that has arisen is whether tax law provisions stipulating a more generous treatment for residents than for non-residents constitute indirect discrimination.[8]

In cases where this question has been asked the court has on several occasions held that, in cases concerning direct taxation, persons who are resident and persons who are not resident in a specific member state are *not generally in comparable situations*. The court has used different wordings to formulate this principal position, but the differences do not appear to be significant.[9]

Thus, it is clear that the ECJ uses the residence criterion to rule out comparability. This position may imply that the court would have regarded the situations of all EU citizens to be comparable, had the different places of residence not been considered. Indeed, such a view would seem to follow from the

[8] When discrimination has been established the ECJ has considered if the rule of reason doctrine can be applied to the case. The general implication of the rule of reason doctrine as laid down in C-55/94 *Gebhard* is that a rule which is in conflict with the treaty can be justified if it represents a strong general interest, and if it is suitable for obtaining its objective but does not go beyond what is necessary to obtain it. According to the 'Gebhard test' another condition for justification is that the tested provision is applied in a non-discriminatory manner. It would seem that this demand rules out the justification of indirectly discriminatory legislation in tax law. It is however not clear if this is the case, since the most important tax law case where the rule of reason was in fact applied concerned indirect discrimination (C-204/90 *Bachmann*). Issues relating to the rule of reason doctrine are indeed of great interest but since they fall outside the scope of this article shall not discuss them further.

[9] It seems plausible that such differences are the result of the work of the translators. For instance, according to C-279/93 *Schumacker,* para 31 the situations of residents and non-residents are 'as a rule' not comparable. In C-80/94 *Wielockx,* para 18 and C-107/94 *Asscher,* para 41 the situations are 'not generally' comparable. In all three French versions the formulation 'en règle générale' is used.

In some Swedish versions of judgments residents and non-residents are 'generally' not in comparable situations (Sw. 'generellt sett'). But in some cases the court has expressed the distinction by stating that the situations of the subjects in question seldom is comparable (Sw. 'sällan'), se for example C-169/03 *Wallentin,* para 15 and C-391/97 *Gschwind,* para 22, C-87/99 *Zurstrassen,* para 21 respectively. It should be underlined that only the *Wallentin* trial was originally held in Swedish. There may be an implied difference in frequency between the two ways of expression, indicating that 'seldom' is more often than 'generally'. However, no conclusions should be drawn from these observations. I do not think that a different nuance was intended. Instead, the analysis should be based on the complete argumentation presented by the court.

wordings of Article 12 and 39 EC. The point of departure would then be the principal equality of all EU citizens.

However, as a result of the enlargement of the union that took place in 2004 a number of restrictive measures were introduced in a majority of the 'old' member states, aiming at reducing the migration of workers and others from the new member states to the old member states. These temporary attempts to protect the national labour markets show that equal treatment and non-discrimination are subjected to pragmatic tests against other interests, at least on the European legislative level. It is however difficult to identify any such pragmatism in the reasoning of the court. On the contrary, the court seems determined to pursue the principle of non-discrimination without weighing it against other interests. The obvious unwillingness to apply the rule of reason doctrine to cases of direct taxation also speaks for this conclusion.

Moreover, it should be noted that the ECJ's choice of the residence criterion as a means of omitting comparability is indeed a choice. Obviously, it would have been possible for the court to see things differently, and to regard the wordings of Article 12 and 39 as imperatives requiring equal treatment in taxation for all EU citizens regardless of their state of residence. Even if the court can *objectively* identify where a person resides, the use of the residence criterion represents a choice and is thus *subjective*. The well-informed reader is aware of the fact that the court in several cases nevertheless has held that less favourable treatment of non-residents is incompatible with the treaty. However, as will be shown the motivation for this position has not been based on the residence criterion.

To conclude, the importance attached by the ECJ to the actual place of residence of a person indicates that the court begins its analysis with the *empirical* residence criterion. Comparability is initially excluded with the help of this observation of reality but as mentioned above, the use of this objectively applied empirical criterion represents a (subjective) choice. The next section will analyse the grounds on which the court makes that choice. In other words, how does the court motivate the use of the residence criterion for omitting comparability?

5.3 Justification of the residence criterion

In a large number of the cases where national income tax provisions have been tried against the freedoms of the EC Treaty the ECJ has explicitly used the residence criterion to define comparability. As mentioned above this case law is extensively referred to and commented upon in academic literature. This permits short descriptions. However, some of the expressions used by the court call for reflections based on the objective of this article.

To begin, it may be noted that there are a number of variations in the way in which the ECJ motivates the use of the residence criterion when it deems residents and non-residents of a member state not comparable. The main message stands clear however. According to the court there are in principle *objective differences* between these two categories of persons. In recent cases the court uses this expression regularly, while referring to C-279/93 *Schumacker* paragraph 34. However, there is in this paragraph nothing to be found about objective differences. Instead, this expression showed up for the first time (in an income tax matter) in C-80/94 *Wielockx* paragraph 18. The erroneous reference may of course be the result of one single mistake which have been repeatedly copied.

Naturally, it falls within the scope of this article to analyse the expression *objective differences*. Which are indeed these differences? In all of the cases but one that have been studied the court lays down two reasons for why the situations of residents and non-residents should not be considered comparable.[10] There is definitely a connection between the two reasons. The Court has held that the situations of residents and of non-residents are not generally comparable as far as direct taxes are concerned, since:

(i) income received in the territory of a state by a non-resident is in most cases only a part of his total income, which is concentrated at his place of residence
(ii) a non-resident's personal ability to pay tax, determined by reference to his aggregate income and his personal and family circumstances, is more easy to assess at the place where his personal and financial interests are centred, which in general is the place where he has his usual abode.[11]

The first reason is of course an assumption. Consequently, it may be confirmed in one case but proven false in another. In any event, it does not express an observation of the circumstances of the case in question. Therefore, if it does not correspond with reality it may lead to incorrect conclusions. With the terminology used in this study it must be defined as a *presumption criterion*. In my opinion, such an argument may be unreliable and thus provide little legitimacy to the decision.

However, in the light of how the presumption has been applied by the ECJ I still have the impression that it is integrated in an empirical argumentation. When the court holds that the taxpayer's income from the source state normally constitutes only a minor part of his total income, the court certainly makes an

[10] The case C-107/94 *Asscher* seems to represent a slightly different point of view. Here the court makes its general reflection on the incomparability of residents and non-residents in the following way. Comparability is not at hand, since (i) the income of the two persons derives from different sources. The court also refers to (ii) their tax capacity and (iii) the possibility to take into account their personal and family circumstances. Therefore, there are objective differences. The discrepancy between these wordings and the motivations in the other cases that I have investigated should however not be exaggerated, since the *Asscher* case contains references to both *Wielockx* and *Schumacker*. For further discussions regarding *Asscher* see below at s 5.4 and for instance N Winther-Sörensen *Beskatning av international erhvervsindkomst* (Köbenhavn, Thomson/Gadjura, 2000), p 696 and JF Avery Jones 'Further Thoughts on Non-discrimination in Europe Following Asscher' (1997) (75) *British Tax Review*.

[11] See for example C-279/93 *Schumacker*, para 32, C-80/94 *Wielockx*, para 18, C-107/94 *Asscher*, para 41, C-391/97 *Gschwind*, para 22, C-87/99 *Zurstrassen*, para 21, and C-169/03 *Wallentin*, para 16.

assumption about reality without observing the actual circumstances. The presumption is not applied unless it is not established (as a fact) that the taxpayer in question receives the majority of his income from the source state.[12] Consequently, the potentially negative effects of the presumption are disarmed by an empirical observation.

The second reason for why the ECJ claims that there are objective differences between residents and non-residents refers to actual circumstances. According to the court it is easier to take into account a person's overall tax capacity as well as personal and family circumstances in his state of residence. However, despite the reference to the taxpayer's individual situation this criterion too must be regarded as a presumption and not an observation of the circumstances of the case.[13]

This presumption may also be put to question. Throughout Europe the filing of tax returns is probably the most frequent administrative routine for establishing the tax capacity of a person. In principle, the information provided by the taxpayer in his tax return can be used by the tax administration in his state of residence as well as by its equivalent in another state from which he receives income. Consequently, it may be wrong to assume that it is simpler to make the assessment in the taxpayer's state of residence. It is perhaps more convenient to perform control measures in the residence state. However, arguments referring to control convenience aspects have generally been rejected by the court within the rule of reason test. In addition, the interest of control efficiency must be weighed against the demand for equal treatment. It may therefore be argued that the control aspect should not be considered here. It must thus be concluded that the second (ii) justification argument too, must be regarded as a presumption criterion. In my view, it does not provide the same legitimacy as an empirical observation, since it is lacking in reliability.

To sum up, the ECJ's initial use of the residence criterion in order to exclude comparability is based on an observation of the actual location of the residence of the taxpayer. Up to that point the argumentation is founded on facts. However, the motivation for choosing this empirical criterion is entirely based on presumptions, ie on assuming that certain circumstances are at hand. Moreover, the analysis shows that the credibility of these presumptions can be put to question. Even if the entire argumentation built by the ECJ around the expression 'objective differences' can be neutralized, or overruled, the conclusion may definitely be drawn that the residence criterion is only *seemingly* empirical.

[12] I will discuss this principle, which was laid down by the court in Schumacker, in s 5.4 below.

[13] The ECJ clearly uses the term tax capacity to express a concept of income where relevant costs for acquiring revenue as well as certain personal expenditure should be considered. A reason is probably that deductions for specific personal expenditure, for example costs for maintaining a family, are rather frequent at least in continental Europe. From a Scandinavian perspective this may seem surprising however, since Nordic tax regimes allow very few deductions of this kind.

5.4 Neutralization of the residence criterion

It has been shown that according to the ECJ the situations of residents of a member state are not generally comparable to the situations of persons who are not resident there, since there are objective differences between them, both from their ability to pay tax and the possibility of taking into account their personal and family circumstances. I have put to question whether the court's analysis really is founded on objective criteria. This section will treat the issue of neutralization of the residence criterion. Which arguments or criteria will remove the objective differences and thus reconstruct comparability?

According to the well-known principle established in C-279/93 *Schumacker* the effects of the two presumptions (i and ii above) are neutralized under two conditions. The two conditions are that:

(iii) the non-resident receives no significant income in the state of his residence and obtains the major part of his taxable income from an activity performed in the state of employment, with the result

(iv) that the state of his residence is not in a position to grant him the benefits resulting from the taking into account of his personal and family circumstances.[14]

From these wordings it seems clear that the court considers the actual circumstances of the particular case to be decisive. In the cases where the criteria (iii) and (iv) have been applied the court has had the facts about the taxpayer's revenue investigated. Furthermore, information about the applicable tax legislation in the source state has been collected. Therefore, this line of reasoning must be characterized as *empirically* founded.

In the cases mentioned above (footnote 14) the court formulates the neutralization criteria almost identically. Not surprisingly, those cases all dealt with deductions related to the personal or family situation of the taxpayer. However, as mentioned earlier the argumentation in C-107/94 *Asscher* shows somewhat different characteristics. The question in this case was not about a non-resident's access to the deductions that the source state only allowed its residents, but about the applicable tax rate.

Mr Asscher was an entrepreneur active in the Netherlands but resided in Belgium. The Netherlands applied a higher tax rate to his income than to income earned by persons resident in the Netherlands. The reason given was that non-residents did not have to pay social security fees in the Netherlands. Therefore, a higher tax rate had to be applied to the income of non-residents in order to achieve equal progression in taxation of residents and non-residents.

To begin, the ECJ referred to its own case law regarding the objective differences between residents and non-residents and the principal justification for this

[14] C-169/03 *Wallentin*, para 17, C-279/93 *Schumacker*, para 36, and C-385/00 *de Groot*, para 89. See also C-391/97 *Gschwind* and C-87/99 *Zurstrassen*.

point of view.[15] The neutralization criterion (iii) appears to have played the same role as in earlier cases. However, the court did not use or in any way relate to the second neutralization criterion mentioned above. This is hardly surprising, since the *Asscher* case was not about deductions but about progression. Consequently, the ECJ focused upon the latter. The court found that the method article in the double taxation treaty between Belgium and the Netherlands provided for exemption with progression.[16] This led to the conclusion that the same progression would apply to Mr Asscher's income irrespective of the special Dutch rule that was now on trial. For this reason, the residence criterion was neutralized, and the non-resident Asscher was deemed to be in a situation fully comparable to persons resident in the Netherlands.

For the purpose of this article it is interesting to discuss whether the court's line of reasoning in the *Asscher* case represents presumptions or empirical observations. The implication of the treaty article in question provided for Belgium to take into account Mr Asscher's income from the Netherlands when applying the tax rates of Belgium to his Belgian income. Thus any progressivity provided for under Belgian law would be applied. However, the ECJ does not seem to have investigated internal international Belgian tax law.[17] The judgment holds no conclusions regarding applicable tax rates or the position of Asscher's income in relation to tax brackets. The court's statement, indicating that Mr Asscher could not have escaped progressivity must therefore under the circumstances be characterized as a presumption.

To summarize, it can be concluded that the ECJ uses empirical criteria in order to neutralize the residence criterion in all of the investigated cases save for one (C-107/94 *Asscher*). Indeed, it will seem that references to observations are more likely to render legitimacy to the court's reasoning. This question will however be addressed in greater detail below.

6 CONCLUSION

This section begins with a summary of my conclusions on the ECJ's use of comparability criteria. In addition, I will pursue the second purpose of this article. This means that I aim to discuss further the implications on the legitimacy of the ECJ's reasoning. My discussion is of course based on the model applied above with which I have distinguished between presumption criteria and empirical criteria.

To summarize the analysis, the state of residence of the taxpayer constitutes an *empirical criterion*. This is used by the ECJ to omit comparability.

[15] See at s 5.2 and 5.3 above. It should be noted however that the court used somewhat different wordings when it referred to its own conclusions in earlier cases, see C107/94 *Asscher*, para 44.

[16] See C-107/94 *Asscher*, para 47 which refers to 24(2) of treaty and to Arts 23A(1) and 23A(3) of the OECD Model Convention on Income and on Capital.

[17] In any event there is no such indication in the judgment.

Interestingly, this criterion is only seemingly empirical, since it is based on two *presumption criteria*, namely that:

(i) income received by a non-resident is in most cases only a part of his total income, which is concentrated at his place of residence
(ii) a non-resident's personal ability to pay tax, determined by reference to his aggregate income and his personal and family circumstances, is more easy to assess at the place where his personal and financial interests are centred, which in general is the place where he has his usual abode.

However, these two assumptions can be neutralized with the help of two additional *empirical criteria* (iii and iv). Owing to the fact that the taxpayer in the particular case has no significant income in his state of residence, and for this reason cannot make the same deductions there that he would have been able to had he had such significant income, the taxpayer will be deemed to be in a situation comparable to the situation of a person resident in the state where he in fact has earned the majority of his income.

Indeed, it may seem that the court makes a long 'argumentation journey'. Moreover, the analysis shows that the reasoning by means of its complexity is lacking in transparency, irrespective of whether or not the result is considered reasonable. On the other hand, the fact that the reasoning is extensive, elaborate and to some extent complex does not necessarily mean that it deserves criticism.[18] In my opinion the comprehensiveness of the court's construction of comparability is not sufficient support for a conclusion regarding the legitimacy (as defined above) of the reasoning. Such criticism requires further analysis.

Naturally, it is important to establish that the construction of comparability is based on a mixture of presumptions and observations of circumstances in the particular case in question. However, it could be argued that most, or at least much, juridical argumentation is built in the same way. But if this is true, transparency becomes an even more important demand. From a transparency perspective, the most interesting observation is perhaps that the court's conclusions are formulated in way which makes them appear *objective*. However, the analysis shows that they result from choices that are altogether *subjective*.

It has already been shown that the court's choices of questions and criteria are subjective. But this can in fact be said about its decisions on concrete legal consequences too. As an example the significance with which the ECJ regards the internal tax law of the residence state can be mentioned. Indeed, the answer to the question of whether there is discrimination in the source state becomes dependant on the legislation of the state where the taxpayer resides.[19]

[18] Such a categorical point of view could certainly be used against the author of this chapter.

[19] The ECJ reasons in a similar way when applying Art. 43 on the freedom of establishment to subsidiaries and branches. Comparability between these two forms of establishment is made partially dependant on the tax regimes of the host state, see for example C-311/97 *Royal Bank of Scotland*, para 30.

The taxpayer who has no significant income in his state of residence and for this reason cannot make the deductions provided for under the laws of that state, does in fact gain access to the deductions of the source state. It could certainly have been argued that he should have been given the right to make deductions in accordance with tax provisions in his state of residence. In any event, the court's conclusions and solution is not an evident result of the analysis. In fact, the ECJ chooses to construct comparability, but only for those who practically work only in the source state and who do not have access to deductions anywhere else.

Thus, it can be concluded that the construction of comparability is based on the choices made by the court. The observation that some of the conclusions appear to be objective cannot hide the fact that this activity is clearly subjective and based on the personal values of the judges. There is however nothing strange with this. For how else could the reasoning have been performed? It is not possible to construct comparability in taxation, or in other fields of law, without the help of values.

In principle, all legal concepts are social constructions. They are human products although they sometimes can be perceived as something else. Some are consciously designed and form statutory law whereas some may fall under the influence of psychological processes such as the interpretation of laws. As an obvious example, a company only exist as a mental phenomenon, although it is manifested in variety of paperwork and perhaps in a factory or a shop.

But even if the ECJ's construction of comparability is a social construction among others the analysis in this article has led to the identification of a major transparency problem. This is caused by the misleading references to objectivity and by the fact that seemingly empirical arguments show to be just the result of assumptions. In addition, it appears to be a practical problem of some importance that the legislation in the residence state is decisive for determining if there is a case of discrimination in the source state. For the future it is essential that the ECJ interprets the EC Treaty in a straightforward and understandable way instead of producing extremely complex and partially inconsequent motivations.

BIBLIOGRAPHY

Anderson, B, *Discovery in Legal Decision-Making* (Dordrecht, Kluwer Academic, 1996).

Avery Jones, JF, 'Further Thoughts on Non-discrimination in Europe Following Asscher' (1997) (75) *British Tax Review*.

Bengoetxea, J, *The Legal Reasoning of the European Court of Justice* (Oxford, Oxford University Press, 1992).

Dahlberg, M, *Direct Taxation in Relation to the Freedom of Establishment and the Free Movement of Capital* (The Hague, Kluwer Law International, 2005).

Popper, KR, *The Logic of Scientific Discovery* (London 1959) p 31.

Stendahl, S, *Communicating Justice Providing Legitimacy* (Uppsala, Iustus Förlag, 2003).
Tuori, K, *Discourse Ethics and the Legitimacy of Law* (no 2 July 1989) (2) *Ratio Juris*.
Winther-Sörensen, N, *Beskatning av international erhvervsindkomst* (Köbenhavn, Thomson/Gadjura, 2000).

9

On the Emerging Obligation for Member State Authorities to Supervise and Enforce EC State Aid Law, and the Resulting Need to Consider Decentralisation

INGEBORG SIMONSSON*

ABSTRACT

ANALYSING THE RULINGS in *CIF*, *Pearle*, *Delena Wells* and *Kühne & Heitz*, this article concerns the emerging obligation for national administrative authorities and organs of EU Member States to supervise and enforce the state aid provisions of Articles 87(1) and 88(3) EC. It can be expected that many national authorities are unaware of and unprepared for this challenge.

Given that the Court of Justice has in effect made every Member State authority a state aid supervision and enforcement agency, there is reason to consider the content and extent of these obligations. Must an authority go outside of its mandate? Must issues of state aid be raised by an authority on its own motion (*ex officio*) or only in response to a complaint? What is the position of complainants? Will all natural and legal persons have standing to challenge actions or omissions by national authorities, and is standing determined by EC law or by national law? Must fundamental rights be protected? What about parallel proceedings? Does the obligation for national authorities to ensure state aid compliance affect the possibilities of access to court?

* Ingeborg Simonsson, born in 1969, LL.M. Stockholm University 1993, LL.M European Business law, University of Nijmegen, 1996. Ingeborg Simonsson served for three years in Swedish courts and was appointed assistant judge by the Court of Appeal in 1997. She then joined private practice and worked extensively with competition law and other EC law related matters for six years; the last three years at Mannheimer Swartling's practice group for EU and competition law. As from September 2003, Ingeborg Simonsson is a full time doctoral candidate and competition law lecturer at Stockholm University, focusing on supervision and enforcement of EC competition law.

An examination of the obligations of national authorities shows the complexity of the tasks allocated to them by the Court of Justice and leads to some considerations of an institutional nature. It is argued that Member States must establish separate state aid authorities in order to improve chances of compliance. Moreover, it is argued that the Commission's monopoly to assess compatibility of state aid measures is questionable, and that the option of distributing this power to Member State courts and authorities should be seriously considered. Any future state aid modernisation must however be coupled with establishment of an adequate institutional framework, as well as guarantees for the necessary know-how transfer to national authorities and courts.

1 STATE AID, THE COMMISSION'S CENTRAL ROLE AND SOME OF THE PROBLEMS RESULTING FROM THE CURRENT SYSTEM

1.1 The developing notion of state aid

Put in simplified terms, state aid occurs where one or several undertakings, unlike other undertakings, enjoy the benefit of having the State as a sponsor of their activities. There is a basic prohibition against state aid in Article 87(1) EC. The Court of Justice held already in 1961 that the concept of aid is wider than that of a subsidy because it embraces not only positive benefits but also measures which, in various forms, mitigate the normal burdens on the budget of an undertaking.[1]

The conditions in Article 87(1) EC are as follows: conferral of an advantage to one or several undertakings, intervention by the State or through State resources, distortion of competition and effect on intra-Community trade. The thresholds for distortion of competition and effect on trade, as interpreted by the Court of Justice, are relatively low. Competition is deemed to be distorted when state aid strengthens the position of an undertaking compared with other undertakings competing in intra-community trade.[2] In *Altmark*, the Court suggested an effect on trade for a public subsidy granted to an undertaking which provided only local or regional transport.[3] The notions of State imputability and transfer of State resources have been broadly interpreted in *Stardust Marine*.[4] Financing methods that form an integral part of an aid scheme are also unlawful and must be reimbursed in cases of unnotified aid.[5] The most valid defence against allegations that a measure constitutes state aid will thus

[1] Case 30/59 *Steenkolenmijnen* [1961] ECR 1.

[2] Case 730/79 *Philip Morris v Commission* [1980] ECR 2671.

[3] Case C-280/00 *Altmark Trans* [2003] ECR I-7747, p 77.

[4] Case C-482/99 *French Republic v Commission (Stardust Marine)* [2002] ECR I-4397, pp 53–6, on this, see B Vesterdorf. 'A Further Comment on the New State Aid Concept as this Concept Continues to be Reshaped'. (2005) (3) *European State Aid Law Quarterly*, 396.

[5] Joined cases C-261/01 and C-262/01 *Van Calster* [2003] ECR I-12249, p 54.

normally be found in the notion of advantage to one or several undertakings. The four criteria developed by the Court in *Altmark* can be of particular importance here,[6] as well as the case-law on the market economy investor principle.[7]

1.2 Compatibility

If a measure constitutes state aid, it can still be deemed compatible with the objectives of the EC Treaty pursuant to Article 87(3) EC. The Court has reminded that the basic prohibition of State aid is neither absolute nor unconditional, since Article 87(3) EC confers on the Commission a wide discretion to declare certain aid compatible with the common market.[8] Save for the Council's competence under Article 88(2) EC, the Commission has exclusive competence under Article 88 EC to declare state aid measures compatible with the common market.

Pursuant to Article 88(3) EC, State aid measures must be notified in advance to the Commission, already at the planning stage, and must not be implemented before the Commission has produced a favourable decision (the prohibition against implementation will be referred to as the stand-still obligation). The notification requirement and stand-still obligation have been interpreted strictly. With reference inter alia to *FNCE*, the Court held in *van Calster* that the Commission's final decision does not have the effect of regularising *ex post facto* implementing measures which were invalid because they had been taken in breach of the prohibition laid down by the last sentence of Article 88(3) EC. The Court held that:

> otherwise the direct effect of that prohibition would be impaired and the interests of individuals, whom are to be protected by national courts, would be disregarded. Any other interpretation would have the effect of according a favourable outcome to the non-observance of that provision by the Member State concerned and would deprive it of its effectiveness.[9]

Given the broad interpretation of Article 87(1) EC developed by the Community Courts, compatibility assessments under Article 87(3) EC are central in the application of state aid law. One may however search in vain in case-law for clarifying statements on the analytical framework for compatibility assessments. On the contrary, the Community Courts have emphasised on several occasions the wide discretion enjoyed by the Commission. In *Philip Morris*, the Court held that the Commission has a discretion the exercise of which involves economic and social assessments which must be made in a Community

[6] Case C-280/00 *Altmark Trans*, above, pp 89–93.

[7] For reasoning on this principle see joined cases T-228/99 and 233/99 *Westdeutsche Landesbank v Commission* [2003] ECR II-435, pp 207–10.

[8] Case C-143/99 *Adria-Wien Pipeline* [2001] ECR I-8365, p 30.

[9] Joined cases C-261/01 and C-262/01 *Van Calster*, above, p 63.

context.[10] There, the Court accepted assessments made by the Commission on the standard of living and serious under-employment in the Dutch Bergen-op-zoom area, in relation to the Community level, factors which in the Commission's view were not sufficient to justify investments aimed at creating jobs locally. In *Deufil*, the Court held that the Commission did not exceeded the limits of its discretion when it considered as contrary to the common interest the granting of aid for an investment, which increased production capacity in a sector where there was already considerable overproduction.[11] In *Vineyards*,[12] as well as in *Adria-Wien Pipeline*,[13] the discretion enjoyed by the Commission was described as wide. The CFI held in *Ladbroke* that in cases where Article 87(3) falls to be applied and where, accordingly, the Commission must rely on complex economic, social, regional and sectoral assessments, there is a broad discretion conferred on the Commission.[14] A somewhat more elaborate statement on regional aid was made in *AIUFASS and AKT*.[15] The CFI held that 'in exercising its discretion, the Commission has to ensure that the aims of free competition and Community solidarity are reconciled, whilst complying with the principle of proportionality'. In *SIDE v Commission*, the CFI annulled a decision where the Commission had authorised an aid scheme for French books. The CFI found that the information on which the decision was based was inadequate.[16] The Commission had failed to carry out an economic analysis of the sector concerned that would enable it to conclude that the grant of the disputed aids did not affect conditions of competition and trade to an extent contrary to the public interest.

The Commission's discretion is by no means exercised in a vacuum. On the contrary, the Commission has issued block exemptions and extensive soft-law in the forms of notices, communications and guidelines. Moreover, the Commission's discretion is balanced by procedural guarantees developed by the Community Courts.[17]

Nevertheless, EC state aid control has been subject to criticism, in particular as regards the limited role of competition analysis.[18] There is a somewhat incoherent approach to different types of aids and different sectors in the economy,

[10] Case 730/79 *Philip Morris v Commission*, above, p 24.

[11] Case 310/85 *Deufil v Commission* [1987] ECR 901, p 18.

[12] Case C-456/00 *French Republic v Commission* [2002] ECR I-11949, p 41.

[13] Case C-143/99 *Adria-Wien Pipeline*, above, p 30.

[14] Case T-67/94 *Ladbroke v Commission* [1998] ECR II-1, p 52.

[15] Case T-380/94 *AIUFASS and AKT v Commission* [1996] ECR II-2169. On this case see A Biondi and L Rubini 'Aims, Effects and Justifications: EC State Aid Law and Its Impact on National Social Policies' in E Spaventa and M Dougan (eds) *Social Welfare and EU Law*. (Oxford and Portland, Oregon, Hart, 2005) 102.

[16] Case T-49/93 *SIDE v Commission* [1995] ECR II-02501.

[17] On this aspect, see H P Nehl *Principles of Administrative Procedure in EC Law* (Oxford, Hart, 1999) 149 *ff*.

[18] C Ahlborn and C Berg 'Can State Aid Control Learn from Antitrust? The Need for a Greater Role for Competition Analysis under the State Aid Rules' in A Biondi, P Eeckhout and J Flynn (eds) *The Law of State Aid in the European Union* (Oxford, OUP, 2004).

and in the words of Commissioner Neelie Kroes, 'an unnecessarily complicated set of rules, exemptions, and guidelines has evolved'.[19] In June 2005, the Commission outlined a comprehensive reform of its state aid policy, recognising a need to focus attention on the most distortive types of aid and make state aid control more predictable and user friendly.[20] The Commission has also pleaded to strengthen its economic approach to state aid analysis.[21]

1.3 Services of general economic interest

The state aid provisions in Article 87 EC are modified by the provision in Article 86(2) EC on services of general economic interest. Undertakings entrusted with the operation of services of general economic interest are subject to the state aid rules insofar as they do not obstruct the performance of the particular tasks assigned to them, provided that development of trade is not adversely affected. This means that undertakings that operate such services, and the States that finance them, have some additional leeway in relation to Article 87 EC. More particularly, Article 86(2) EC leaves scope for cross-subsidies between profitable and unprofitable activities,[22] and possibly for accepting arrangements that fall outside the four Altmark-criteria. A practical example of the latter situation would be when the State finds it impossible to clearly define in advance the tasks of the undertaking performing services of general economic interests, deeming it necessary to delegate some discretion in this respect.

As demonstrated inter alia by the recent ruling in *Heiser*, the application of Article 86(2) EC is in the exclusive domain of the Commission.[23] Member States must notify aid pursuant to Article 88(3) EC even if they consider the aid measure a way of financing services of general economic interest. As is clear from *Altmark*, not all State financing of services is aid, but only those that confer a financial advantage on the recipient undertakings.[24] The typical example of an advantage would be overcompensation.

1.4 The *ex ante* control system

The obligation to notify and the stand-still obligation in Article 88(3) EC have direct effect.[25] Observance of Article 88(3) EC necessarily presupposes an

[19] Speech by Commissioner Neelie Kroes, London 14th July 2005, SPEECH/05/440.

[20] *State Aid Action Plan*. p 17, Consultation document published on http://europa.eu.int/comm/competition/state_aid/others/action_plan/.

[21] *Ibid*, p 21.

[22] *Commission Green Paper on Services of General Economic Interest*, COM (2003) 270 final, p 26.

[23] Case C-172/03 *Heiser* [2005] ECR I-1627, p 51, joined cases C-261/01 and C-262/01, *Van Calster*, above, p 61.

[24] Case C-280/00 *Altmark Trans*, above, p 87.

[25] Case 120/73 *Lorenz* [1973] ECR 1471, p 8.

assessment of whether a measure constitutes aid in the first place, and it follows that Article 87(1) EC is directly effective insofar as there may be cause to interpret the provision to determine whether there has been an infringement.[26]

The Court of Justice has underlined the Commission's central role and its exclusive competence to make compatibility assessments on several occasions. In *FNCE*, the Court made reference to the principal and exclusive role conferred on the Commission to hold aid to be incompatible with the common market where this is appropriate.[27] This role was held to be fundamentally different from the role of national courts, which in the wording of the Court do no more than preserve, until the final decision of the Commission, the rights of individuals. The Court specifically observed that national courts do not decide on the compatibility of the aid with the common market, the final determination on that matter being the exclusive responsibility of the Commission, subject to the supervision of the Court of Justice. In *Portuguese Pig Farmers*, which concerned the relation between the Council's and the Commission's respective competences under Article 88 EC, the Court once again made reference to 'central role for the Commission in determining whether aid is incompatible'.[28]

Supervision and enforcement of Articles 86, 87 and 88 EC thus suffers from the same problem as did Article 81 EC before the modernisation; a broad interpretation of the basic notion of prohibited aid and an *ex ante* control system of notification where the Commission has exclusive competence to declare state aid measures compatible or incompatible with the Treaty. There is no uniform system of supervision and enforcement of EC state aid law on the national level, leaving scope for each Member State to decide whether it wants to establish its own state aid authorities, and if so, what powers to vest those authorities with. Parties with claims based on the Treaty's state aid provisions have only one central enforcement authority to turn to—the Commission. In the absence of specialised Member State authorities for the supervision and enforcement of EC state aid matters, national authorities or other organs of Member States seeking guidance on state aid will have to carry out their own legal research, or ask the Commission.

While there are presently no indications of any forthcoming state aid modernisation similar to that of Articles 81 and 82 EC, it will be demonstrated that national authorities are already under a positive obligation to supervise and enforce EC state aid law, within the sphere of their competence. Since this obligation is far-reaching and complex, it will be argued that the only practical way for Member States to avoid repeated infringements of Articles 86 to 88 EC, is to establish their own national supervision and enforcement authorities, or, at least, agencies empowered to act as a national information and competence centre in state aid matters. Recent developments in the case-law of the

[26] Case C-345/02 *Pearle* [2004] ECR 2004 I-7139, p 31.
[27] Case C-354/90 *FNCE*, [1991] ECR I-5505, p 14.
[28] Case C-110/02 *Portuguese Pig Farmers* [2004] ECR I-6333, p 29.

Community Courts will thus force the Commission and the Member States towards modernisation of EC state aid enforcement. As will be explained, the question whether it would be appropriate to allow Member State courts and authorities to apply Articles 86(2) and 87(3) EC, giving them the power to decide whether state aid is compatible with the Treaty, is more complicated than was the distribution of the power to apply Article 81(3) EC. That is not only because the court or authority empowered to carry out compatibility assessments must possess a high level of independence and integrity in relation to the Member State that is seeking to introduce or maintain state aid measures. A more valid objection is that compatibility assessments are on the border between law and politics, and that the objectives for compatibility may change over time in a dynamic society. Finally, there are the issues of competence and consistency, in other words whether national authorities and courts will have the ability to balance different Community interests in a consistent manner.

2 SUBSTANTIVE CONSEQUENCES OF *CIF*, *PEARLE*, *DELENA WELLS* AND *KÜHNE & HEITZ*—A DUTY TO CHECK THE LAWS AND PRACTICES OF THE MEMBER STATE AGAINST EC LAW, AND TO TAKE ACTION AGAINST INFRINGEMENTS

Imagine any of the following situations:

(1) The parliament in a Member State has adopted tax legislation whereby certain categories of corporate taxpayers are exempted from energy tax. The legislation is supervised and enforced by the State tax authorities. The State collection authority collects unpaid taxes. There is reason to believe that the tax exemption scheme amounts to state aid. Is the tax authority under a Community law duty to check the legislation in relation to the Treaty, and possibly disapply it? Must the collection authority act to recover the benefits conferred on the taxpayers, even contrary to the intent of the government?

(2) The State-owned enterprise responsible for the operation and management of airports has contracted with a building and construction firm on the construction of new airport facilities. The contract was awarded without any public procurement procedure. With reference to business confidentiality, the parties refuse to provide the public with any details on the contract. It is reported in media that the price seems excessive. Must the civil aviation authority, or the national competition authority, investigate the existence of overcompensation amounting to state aid?

(3) A local municipality has granted a concession to a local company for the construction and operation of a car park. The opposition party in the local government claims that the terms confer state aid on the company. The local authorities must adopt a number of decisions before the car park can be built, including regulatory planning decisions and registration of land. Should they refuse to adopt such decisions until the state aid issue has been solved?

2.1 The 'classic' state aid enforcement approach

When considering the examples above, it becomes apparent that there are two different lines of case-law of relevance. The more classic state aid enforcement approach of the Court of Justice demonstrates an obligation for national courts, in the event of a possible breach by the national authorities of the notification requirement and stand-still obligation in Article 88(3) EC, to uphold the rights of the persons concerned.[29] National courts must take all the consequential measures under national law as regards both the validity of decisions giving effect to the aid measures concerned, the recovery of aid from the recipients[30] and possible interim measures.[31] It would thus seem that national courts can confine themselves to declaring invalid unnotified state aid measures, take interim measures and admit claims for recovery of unlawful aid. The reference to national law clearly seems to make the obligations of national courts subject to national procedural autonomy. With the risk of stating the obvious, it is appropriate to recall that courts will never act on their own motion to initiate proceedings, but can only open a case in response to actions initiated by plaintiffs. Furthermore, plaintiffs that take action must have standing to bring proceedings. Actions initiated in national courts by citizens or undertakings that cannot show any clear individual connection to an alleged state aid measure, will run the risk of being dismissed. Enforcement of Articles 87(1) and 88(3) EC in national courts thus depends on the presence of one or more parties, with standing to bring proceedings, who have the necessary incentive and resources to challenge a state aid measure. The recipients of state aid cannot be expected to act, and neither can the State that has granted the aid, this leaving competitors or concerned taxpayers as the only possible plaintiffs. It has been observed that the incentive for competitors and others to initiate proceedings in national courts are low, given the lengthy procedures, the costs and the obvious risk for parallel proceedings.[32] As will be seen however, the second line of case-law in effect broadens the group of possible plaintiffs, since it confers an obligation on Member State authorities to act.

2.2 The *CIF*-line of cases

The second line of case-law has been developed in contexts other than state aid, but has general application. All authorities are bound to abstain from any

[29] Case C-345/02 *Pearle* above, p 31.

[30] Case C-354/90 *FNCE*, above, p 30, joined Cases C-34/01 to C-38/01, *Enirisorse* [2003] ECR I-14243, p 42, joined cases C-261/01 and C-262/01 *Van Calster* above, p 64.

[31] Case C-143/99 *Adria-Wien Pipeline*, above, p 27.

[32] A Sinnaeve 'What to Expect from National Courts in the Fight against Unlawful State Aid?' (2005) (1) *European State Aid Law Quarterly*, p 2.

measure which could jeopardise the attainment of the objectives of the Treaty.[33] More recently, it has transpired that this includes an obligation for all organs of Member States to take all appropriate measures to enable Community law to be fully applied, including a duty to disapply any provision of national law which contravenes a Community rule.[34] It is for all the authorities of the Member States to ensure observance of the rules of Community law within the sphere of their competence.[35] Thus, it is for the competent authorities of a Member State, within the sphere of their competence, to take all the general or particular measures necessary to nullity the unlawful consequences of breaches of Community law.[36]

The second line of case-law may on first sight appear difficult to reconcile with the 'classic' approach in *FNCE* and other cases. How do we reconcile on the one hand an obligation for national courts to nullify unlawful state aid measures, admit recovery of such aid and take possible interim measures, subject to national procedural autonomy, and on the other hand an obligation for all organs of Member States to take all appropriate measures to enable Community law to be fully applied? In spite of the reference to national procedural autonomy in *Delena Wells*,[37] the second line of cases appears to go further than the 'classic' state aid enforcement approach. On second thought however, the distinction lies in the different tasks of courts and authorities respectively. The CFI pointed out in *Automec* that, unlike the civil courts, whose task is to safeguard the individual rights of private persons in their relations *inter se*, an administrative authority must act in the public interest.[38] The significance of the two lines of case-law is that Member State authorities can have a more far-reaching duty to act in order to enforce Community law, than national courts. It should also be recalled that the duties of national courts can be wider than that expressed in *FNCE* and the other cases referred to above, given the solid case-law on supremacy and full effect of EC law.[39]

2.2.1 National authorities must take action to ensure the full effect of Community law

In *CIF*, the Italian competition authority was considered to have a duty to disapply national law that contravened the combined provisions of Articles 10 and 81 EC.[40]

[33] This would follow from decades of case-law, see J Temple Lang 'Privatisation of Social Welfare: European Union Competition Law Rules' in E Spaventa and M Dougan (eds) above n 15, p 48, for a practical illustration see Case C-344/98 *Masterfoods* [2000] ECR I-11369, p 49.

[34] Case C-198/01 *CIF* [2003] ECR I-8055, pp 48–50.

[35] Case C-453/00 *Kühne & Heitz* [2004] ECR I-837, p 20.

[36] Case C-201/02 *Delena Wells* [2004] ECR I-723, pp 64–5.

[37] *Ibid*, p 65.

[38] Case T-24/90 *Automec v Commission* [1992] ECR II-2223, p 85.

[39] On this aspect, see J Engström 'Effektivt rättsskydd i förvirring—Nationell process och sanktionsrätt i ljuset av C-253/00 Munoz' (2003) (1) *Europarättslig Tidskrift*, p 167.

[40] Case C-198/01 *CIF* above, p 50.

In *Delena Wells*, the national court had referred a question on the obligation to remedy a failure to carry out an environmental impact assessment. With reference to the principle of cooperation in good faith in Article 10 EC, the Court underlined the duty for the competent authorities of a Member State to take, within the sphere of their competence, all the general or particular measures necessary to ensure that projects are examined in order to determine whether they are likely to have significant effects on the environment. This included in particular such measures as, subject to the limits laid down by the principle of procedural autonomy of the Member States, the revocation or suspension of a consent already granted, in order to carry out an assessment of the environmental effects.[41]

In *Kühne & Heitz*, the question referred was whether an administrative body is required to reopen a decision which has become final in order to ensure the full operation of Community law. The background was a national court judgment of final instance, which was based on an interpretation of Community law that proved to be contrary to a judgment given subsequently by the Court of Justice. The Court balanced the interest of the effect of EC law against the principle of legal certainty and concluded that Community law does not require that administrative bodies be placed under an obligation, in principle, to reopen administrative decisions.[42] However, since there was a possibility under the law of the Netherlands for the administrative authority to reopen its case, and given that the national court judgment of final instance was adopted without a question being referred to the Court for a preliminary ruling, *and* that the person concerned complained to the administrative body immediately after becoming aware of that judgment of the Court, there was still an obligation for the national authority to review its decision.[43]

On state aid in particular, the Court observed in *Pearle* the duties of national courts 'in the event of a possible breach by the national authorities of the obligations imposed on the Member States by Article [88(3)] of the Treaty'.[44] The Court held in *Streekgewest* that national authorities are required in principle to repay charges levied in breach of Community law in cases where a method of tax financing forms an integral part of the aid measure.[45] In *Spain v Commission*, two undertakings were held to have received state aid as a result of the failure by the competent authorities to initiate separate forced collection procedures to prevent the undertakings from continuing to operate without fulfilling their tax and social security obligations.[46]

It appears that the national authority must make full use of its domestic legal system to ensure the full effect of EC law, and it must in addition disapply

[41] Case C-201/02 *Delena Wells* above, p 65.
[42] Case C-453/00 *Kühne & Heitz* above, p 24.
[43] *Ibid*, p 28.
[44] Case C-345/02 *Pearle* above, p 31.
[45] Case C-174/02 *Streekgewest* [2005] ECR I-85, p 16.
[46] Case C-276/02 *Spain v Commission* [2004] ECR I-8091, p 26.

national law that contravenes EC law. From the case-law referred to, it follows that a third party can file a complaint to the relevant national authority, reminding the authority of its obligations under EC law, urging it to put an end to the infringement. This type of action is indeed envisaged by the Court of Justice in *Jégo-Quéré*.[47] There, the Court highlighted the possibility for national law to permit an individual directly concerned by a general legislative measure of national law, which cannot be directly contested before the courts, to seek from the national authorities under that legislation a measure which may itself be contested before the national courts, so that the individual may challenge the legislation indirectly.

This reasoning brings us back to the absence in several Member States of independent national state aid enforcement authorities. In such absence, is there any other authority to turn to for a complainant who seeks nullification of an unlawful state aid measure? The answer is clearly in the affirmative. As set out above, each Member State authority must ensure observance of Community law within the sphere of its competence.[48] It seems unlikely that state aid would be granted or effected without the assistance of at least one Member State authority. At any rate, there might be a Member State authority with the task of supervising the law-abidingness of other organs of the State. A complainant who knows his national legal system well enough should be able to pinpoint a relevant authority and file a complaint, thereby setting the wheels in motion. The authority can act on the complaint, or reject it. An action by the authority can put an end to the state aid measure, whereas a rejection of the complaint can be appealed (subject to national rules on standing, limitation periods etc). Whatever the outcome, the complainant will have achieved something, either action by the authority or improved chances of access to court.

Supposing that no complainant comes forward, the *CIF*-line of cases nevertheless obliges national authorities (once again within the sphere of their competence) to scrutinize national laws and practices to check their compatibility with Community law, and to take action if necessary.[49] This might be the most striking effect of this recent development in case-law—national authorities are made supervisors and enforcers of Community law. Given the experience with Member States that do not comply with the notification requirement and the stand-still obligation,[50] an obligation for national authorities to take action can be of particular importance for state aid supervision and enforcement.

[47] Case C-263/02 P *Commission v Jégo-Quéré* [2004] ECR I–3425, p 35.

[48] Case C-198/01 *CIF* above, p 50, Case C-201/02 *Delena Wells* above, p 64, Case C-453/00 *Kühne & Heitz* above, p 20.

[49] J Temple Lang 'National Measures Restricting Competition and National Authorities under Article 10 EC'. (2004) (29) *European Law Review*, p 403.

[50] Sinnaeve, *ibid*, p 1.

2.3 Procedural effects

The Community state aid procedure has some very specific features. There is a preliminary investigation phase carried out by the Commission, which in turn can lead to a formal investigation procedure.[51] On the other hand, actions by national authorities, whether initiated by the authority on its own motion or in response to a complaint, will be governed by national administrative procedures. Even so, the case-law developed by the Community Courts on standing and other remedies will have an impact on national procedure.

2.3.1 The ex officio *issue*

Is a national authority obliged to raise issues of state aid law on its own motion (*ex officio*)? In *Lorentz*, the Court held that a national court is required of its own motion to take account of the invalidity of a law which grants aid in contravention of Article 88(3) EC.[52] This obligation applied without any possibility of it being excluded by rules of national law of any kind whatsoever. Still, it was for the internal legal system of every Member State to determine the legal procedure leading to this result.

There seems to be no indication that the obligations of national authorities to apply state aid rules on their own motion would be less far-reaching than that of national courts. On the contrary, the *CIF*-line of cases imposes substantive duties on Member State authorities to check national laws in relation to Community law. The question of an authority's discretion is discussed below.

2.3.2 Will all complainants have standing in national authorities and courts?

Given that those whose interests might be affected by the granting of aid, in particular competing undertakings and trade associations, already have standing to challenge a Commission decision not to initiate a formal investigation procedure,[53] it could be argued that the interests of third parties are already met and that national rules on standing in state aid matters need not be very generous. However, the opposite argument appears just as valid; the full enforcement of EC state aid law requires Member States to grant concerned parties extensive access to justice. Furthermore, standing to challenge a Commission decision is insufficient if a party is seeking other remedies such as monetary compensation. Dougan has suggested that 'state aid has been identified by the Court as a distinct sector ripe for a distinct solution to the problems posed by Community reliance upon national remedies procedures for the decentralised enforcement

[51] Arts 4–6 Council Reg 659/1999, see Nehl, *ibid*, pp 149 *ff*.
[52] Case 120/73 *Lorenz* above, pp 7–9.
[53] Case C-198/91 *William Cook v Commission* [1993] ECR I-2487, pp 22–4.

of Treaty norms'.[54] Eilmansberger has taken the general position that the essence of individual rights should be determined by Community law, and not indirectly by national law and national remedies.[55]

On the subject of standing in state aid cases, the Court of Justice is balancing national procedural autonomy against the objective of effectiveness of Article 88(3) EC. In *Van Calster*, the Court underlined again the duty for national courts to uphold the *rights of the persons concerned* where a breach of Article 88(3) EC is invoked by individuals entitled to rely on it.[56] This does not clarify whether the determination of the group of concerned persons entitled to rely on Article 88(3) EC is a question for national law or Community law.[57] In *Streekgewest*, the Court held that the objective of ensuring the effectiveness of Article 88(3) EC justified the granting of standing in national courts to taxpayers that are seeking repayment of taxes used for financing aid measures.[58] It was held irrelevant whether the individual had been affected by a distortion of competition arising from the aid measure, the only fact to be taken into consideration being whether the individual was subject to a tax which is an integral part of an unlawful aid measure. The Court's reasoning in *Streekgewest* shows that standing in national courts in state aid matters must be determined with reference to Community law.

The conclusions of the Community Courts on standing to bring national proceedings in state aid matters can be expected to have some impact on the duties of national authorities. Still, there is a fundamental difference insofar as national courts can be expected to be obliged to deal with cases that are brought, provided that the parties have standing and that national procedural rules on admissibility etc are fulfilled, while, on the other hand, authorities can be expected to have some discretionary power in the exercise of their duties. An authority might for example have a discretion to set priorities on the use of its limited resources. This may lead to a policy to take action in cases which either involve clear infringements or are otherwise important from a policy perspective.[59] It is doubtful whether under EC law a complainant would have a right to require action from an authority.[60] As set out above, Member State authorities can have a more far-reaching duty to act in order to enforce Community law than national courts. A possible effect is to make less relevant the question whether a complainant has a right to require action from the authority—if the complainant does not have such a right, the authority can nevertheless be under

[54] M Dougan *National Remedies before the Court of Justice* (Oxford and Portland Oregon, Hart, 2004) p 356.

[55] T Eilmansberger 'The Relationship between Rights and Remedies in EC Law: In Search of the Missing Link'. (2004) (41) *Common Market Law Review*, 1199–246, p 1237.

[56] Joined cases C-261/01 and C-262/01 *Van Calster* above, p 64.

[57] Eilmansberger, above, p 1234.

[58] Case C-174/02 *Streekgewest* above, pp 18–21.

[59] On the issue of discretion left to authorities, see Case C-216/02 *Österreichischer Zuchtverband* [2004] ECR I-10683, p 36.

[60] Eilmansberger, above, p 1229.

a public policy duty to initiate proceedings of its own accord when faced with facts and arguments clearly indicating an infringement of EC state aid law. My suggestion is that the matter should not be dealt with in absolute terms, but rather as a matter of finding the relative degree of facts and arguments, put forward by the complainant or collected by the authority itself, that raises serious concerns.

2.3.3 Duty to protect fundamental rights

Where national legislation falls within the field of application of Community law, the national court must assess the compatibility of that legislation with fundamental rights.[61] The requirements of protection of fundamental rights are binding on Member States, which means that Member States must, as far as possible, apply those rules in accordance with those requirements.[62] If the cause of action in a national procedure falls within the field of EC law, fundamental rights will automatically be applicable and must be observed. This requirement ought to apply to the procedure of a national authority when it is looking into a possible infringement of the state aid rules. In *Textile and clothing sector*, the Court held that observance of the right to be heard is, in all proceedings initiated against a person which are liable to culminate in a measure adversely affecting that person, a fundamental principle of community law which must be guaranteed even in the absence of any rules governing the procedure in question.[63] The application of that principle in that particular case was to impose an adversarial principle to the Commission's investigation under Article 88(2) EC. A different outcome can be observed in *Commission v Sytraval*, where the Commission was held to be under no obligation to conduct an exchange of views and arguments with a complainant in the context of a preliminary examination under Article 88(3) EC.[64] This is not the place for an attempt to outline all possible implications of fundamental rights in national procedures on state aid.[65] In the context of this chapter, it suffices to observe that national authorities and courts must not only assess their national laws and practices against EC state aid law. Having commenced such an examination, they must in addition check their national procedural rules and practices against fundamental principles of EC law. This exercise is not entirely trivial since it requires a thorough understanding of both general principles of EC law and national procedure. Establishment of national state aid authorities would be a step towards pooling competence for this type of assessment.

[61] Case C-159/90 *The Society for the Protection of Unborn Children Ireland* [1991] ECR I-4685, p 31; case C-299/95 *Kremzow* [1997] ECR I-2629, p 15.

[62] Case 5/88 *Wachauf* [1989] ECR 2609, pp 17–19.

[63] Case 259/85 *French Republic v Commission* [1987] ECR 4393, p 12.

[64] Case C-367/95 P *Commission v Sytraval* [1998] ECR I-01719, p 58.

[65] On the principle of care, see Nehl, H.P. *ibid*, p 107 *ff*.

3 INSTITUTIONAL ASPECTS

The Commission has suggested in its State Aid Action Plan the establishment of independent authorities in Member States for facilitating the tasks of the Commission in terms of state aid enforcement.[66] Drawing from the experience with operationally independent monitoring authorities in the new Member States in the context of enlargement, the Commission envisages assistance by national authorities in the detection and provisional recovery of illegal aid and execution of recovery decisions. A suggestion made by the Commission is the establishment of a network of state aid authorities, or contact points, in order to facilitate the flow of information and exchange of best practices.[67]

3.1 The principle of institutional autonomy

At the present state of Community law, there seems to be no legal basis for forcing Member States to establish separate authorities for the supervision and enforcement of state aid. The Court held, as early as in 1971, that Member States enjoy institutional autonomy. In the wording of the Court:

> When provisions of the Treaty or of regulations confer power or impose obligations upon the States for the purposes of the implementation of Community law the question of how the exercise of such powers and the fulfilment of such obligations may be entrusted by Member States to specific national bodies is solely a matter for the constitutional system of each state.[68]

Advocate General Jacobs expressed recently in *DEI*[69] that:

> [a]ccording to the system of the division of powers established by the EC Treaty, in the absence of applicable Community rules, the responsibility for the implementation, application and enforcement of Community rules falls upon the Member States in accordance with their national legal systems, subject, of course, to the constraints of the principle of effectiveness as developed by the Court.

The establishment of independent state aid supervision and enforcement authorities in the Member States would in consequence depend on either introduction of new legislation or consensus between Member States.

[66] State Aid Action Plan above, p 51.
[67] State Aid Action Plan *ibid*, p 53.
[68] Joined cases 51 to 54/71 *International Fruit Company* [1971] ECR 1107, pp 3–4.
[69] Opinion of Advocate General Jacobs delivered on 24 February 2005 in case C-394/02 *Commission v Greece*, p 27.

3.2 The need to establish national state aid supervision and enforcement authorities

For practical purposes, and in order to avoid repeated infringements of Article 87 EC, Member States should establish their own state aid authorities. As set out, national authorities are already obliged to supervise and enforce the Treaty rules on state aid, within the sphere of their competence. Given the complexity of the state aid legislative system as such, in combination with the duty to protect fundamental rights, it will be impossible for each and every national authority and organ of the state to possess the necessary knowledge. Conversely, a national state aid authority could pool competence and ensure the effective enforcement of the Member State's obligations.

In addition, there will always be cases where state aid is conferred without the clear involvement of any national authority, for example when national legislation as such confers state aid on one or more undertakings. At present, those infringements could be addressed by complainants in two ways—direct court action and a complaint to the Commission. It would be helpful if there was, in every Member State, a central national state aid supervision and enforcement agency which could take action. A national authority might be better placed to act given its advantageous position in understanding the legislative framework and market situation on the local level. There is also an advantage for a complainant to address an authority in the complainant's own language, using familiar national procedural rules. Not to mention the advantage of pooling state aid law competence in a single national authority.

3.3 The risk that the Commission will be innundated with notifications

The broad interpretation of Article 87(1) EC, the fact that Member States cannot rely on Article 86(2) EC on services of general economic interest to avoid stand-still and notification, the emerging obligation for national authorities to supervise and enforce the Treaty's state aid rules, as well as recent interpretations on standing, will put pressure on Member States to notify state aid measures to the Commission. The unfortunate logic of the present system is that strengthened enforcement of state aid rules on the national level makes the Commission's handling of notifications a bottleneck sector. This, and the enlargement of the Union, can be expected to contribute to an increased workload for the Commission. If the Commission succeeds (as suggested in the State Aid Action Plan) in making Member States establish independent state aid authorities for assisting the Commission, intensified supervision and enforcement activities are likely to produce even more notifications. Given the experiences with Article 81(3) notifications, it seems unrealistic to preserve an *ex ante* control system, unless some very substantive resources are allocated to this area.

It should of course be kept in mind that all national procedures on EC state aid will not result in notifications. Faced with action by a national authority, a Member State may chose to abandon an alleged aid measure rather than filing a notification. However, that type of decision-making presupposes the existence of clear guidelines for self-assessment of compatibility. It could be questioned whether the present state aid soft-law is sufficient in this respect. The possibilities of modernisation of state aid control are discussed below.

4 MODERNISATION—IS THERE A CASE FOR DISTRIBUTION OF THE POWER TO DECLARE STATE AID MEASURES COMPATIBLE WITH THE TREATY

In its State Aid Action Plan, the Commission considers delegating to national judges the control of whether measures fall under a block exemption or under the *de minimis* thresholds. The Commission envisages a need to review its Notice on cooperation between national courts and the Commission, in particular to expand its scope to other national bodies.[70] The Commission's approach appears to draw inspiration from the suggestions on partial decentralisation made by Nicolaides.[71] As will be explained, the obstacles raised by the present system are probably too high to be remedied by such measures.

While the Commission's exclusive competence to take compatibility decisions in the state aid context follows explicitly from the Treaty, the ratio for this has not been discussed much in case-law. The statements made by the Court in early cases such as *Commission v United Kingdom* (Article 88(3) EC being explained as 'the means of safeguarding the machinery for review laid down by that article which, in turn, is essential for protecting the proper functioning of the common market'),[72] are not very helpful since they refer not to the Commission's exclusive competence as such, but to the stand-still obligation and notification requirement.

In his opinion in *Portuguese Pig Farmers*, Advocate General Jacobs explains the Commission's primary responsibility for assessing the compatibility of an aid as a way of securing the effective and impartial control of State aid.[73] Although the statement is made in the context of the relation between the Council's and the Commission's competences under Article 88 EC, the objectives of effectiveness and impartiality seem highly relevant and will be discussed below.

[70] State Aid Action Plan above, p 57.

[71] P Nicolaides 'Decentralised State Aid Control in an Enlarged European Union: Feasible, Necessary or both?' (2003) (26(2)) *World Competition*, pp 263–76.

[72] Joined cases 31/77 R and 53/77 R *Commission v United Kingdom* [1977] ECR 921, p 20.

[73] Opinion of Advocate General Jacobs delivered on 11 December 2003 in case C-110/02 *Portuguese Pig Farmers* above, p 22.

4.1 Impartiality

The impartiality issue has been raised by Ross.[74] In my view, the perceived impartiality problem appears largely exaggerated. Conflicts between individuals and the state are tried on an everyday basis by courts and authorities in Member States, and such conflicts recurrently involve the application of EC law, where the State can have interests contrary to the objectives of the Common market. We cannot work from any other assumption than that national courts are independent in relation to their governments. Whether a national authority is independent enough is a different matter, this depending on the constitutional system in each Member State. A national authority can be ultimately responsible in relation to a Ministry, or otherwise controlled or supervised by the government. Still, national authorities are entrusted with supervision and enforcement of Articles 87(1) and 88(3) EC as set out above. It seems just as likely that the Treaty state aid provisions would be compromised by incorrect application of Article 87(1) as by application of Article 87(3) EC. My conclusion is that impartiality concerns are unconvincing as reason for reserving compatibility decisions to the Commission.

4.2 Effectiveness

The modernisation of Articles 81 and 82 EC were dictated by arguments on efficiency and the need to focus on hardcore infringements.[75] In decentralising, a policy choice was made in favour of *ex post* control of possible anti-competitive measures. The advantages and disadvantages of *ex ante* versus *ex post* control are analysed extensively by Wils, who concludes that there are four decisive factors for determining whether to chose an *ex ante* or *ex post* system:

(i) credibility of deterrence
(ii) relative knowledge and predictability of substantive rules
(iii) enforcement costs
(iv) specific problems with voluntary pre-screening.[76]

While the fourth factor is of no significance in EC state aid control which includes mandatory notification, the first three factors would seem equally valid for state aid control as for Article 81 EC. On the first factor; credibility of

[74] M Ross 'Decentralization, Effectiveness, and Modernisation: Contradiction in Terms?' in A Biondi, P Eeckhout and J Flynn (eds) *The Law of State Aid in the European Union* (Oxford University Press, 2004), p 86.

[75] JS Venit 'Brave New World: The Modernization and Decentralisation of Enforcement under Arts 81 and 82 of the EC Treaty' (2003) (40) *Common Market Law Review*, p 546.

[76] WPJ Wils *The Optimal Enforcement of EC Antitrust Law, Essays in Law and Economics* European Monographs 33 (The Hague/London/New York, Kluwer Law International, 2002), chs 5 and 6.

enforcement, Wils takes as a starting point that *ex post* enforcement will only work if the expected sanction for violation exceeds the expected benefits.[77] On the second factor; relative knowledge and predictability of substantive rules, Wils prefers *ex post* enforcement. This is because undertakings, with the help of their legal advisors, can be expected to make fewer errors in the advance assessment than a pre-screening authority, provided that the law is a real rule of law.[78] In addition, there is the informational disadvantage suffered by the pre-screening authority. On enforcement costs, Wils, conclusion is that the overall social cost of *ex post* control is likely to be lower than *ex ante* control, partly because *ex post* control can be limited to cases of violations of legal rules, partly because the parties do not need to convince an authority, who will have to cross-check facts before clearance.[79] Another possible argument is that of imperfect *ex ante* control, in other words whether all state aid measures, and in particular the most serious of them, are actually notified.

Wils' conclusion on Articles 81 and 82 EC is that *ex ante* enforcement is generally unsuited. The same conclusion could be made on state aid control. However, the argument on deterrence weighs heavier in state aid control than in the enforcement of Articles 81 and 82 EC, because there are no penalties (fines) for infringements of the Treaty's state aid provisions.[80] The question is whether the risk beneficiaries of state aid run of repaying the aid plus interest, in combination with the risk for liability in damages for Member States, is sufficient deterrence. To these risks shall be added the risk of costs for litigation in state aid matters. If one is to move from *ex ante* to *ex post* control, either the risk of detection or the deterrence must necessarily be increased in order to compensate for the deterrence offered by *ex ante* control. This objective could be achieved either by introduction of fines (increased deterrence), or by the establishment of a network of national state aid enforcement authorities (increased detection). The Commission is apparently considering these options in the State Aid Action Plan.[81] One of the tools that could be employed by the Commission is action under Articles 88(2), 226 and 228 EC. It should be observed that, given this possibility, the Commission would actually be better empowered following a decentralisation of state aid control than after the modernisation of Articles 81 and 82 EC. States can be brought to the Court under the said Articles, while undertakings cannot.

[77] *Ibid*, p 114.
[78] *Ibid*, p 120.
[79] *Ibid*, p 125.
[80] On this problem, see P Nicolaides 'Control of State Aid in the European Union—Compliance, Sanctions and Rational Behaviour' (2002) (25(3)) *World Competition*, pp 249–62.
[81] State Aid Action Plan above, p 51, 53 and 58.

4.3 Are compatibility assessments political as opposed to legal?

The Commission explains its exclusive competence to apply Article 87(3) EC as follows:

> Member States have different traditions of state intervention and different levels of financial resources. The European Commission, as an independent body, is best able to represent the common interest of all European citizens and to control the way national governments use state aid to serve the common interest. Member States have to notify a proposed state aid to the Commission, before it can be implemented. The Commission may authorise the aid, if on balance the presumed benefits for the common interest outweigh the distortions to competition and trade.[82]

When considering decentralisation, the primary question seems to be whether compatibility decisions under Article 87(3) EC are political as opposed to legal decisions. If they are indeed political, it will be impossible to decentralise.[83] It should be recalled from *Philip Morris*, that in deciding whether an aid measure is compatible with the Treaty, the Commission has a discretion the exercise of which involves economic and social assessments which must be made in a Community context.[84]

In my view, the proposition that compatibility decisions are of a political nature must be rejected, for the following reasons. As explained, the Commission has made use of its wide discretion by issuing extensive soft-law. The soft-law giving rise to legitimate expectations,[85] many of the appeals to the Community Courts circle around questions of whether the Commission applied its own guidelines correctly.[86] It seems clear that these are legal assessments. A comparison can also be made with the application of the exemption rule in Article 81(3) EC. As illustrated by the Commission Guidelines on Article 81(3) EC,[87] exemption of agreements that restrict competition is possible if the economic benefits outweigh the negative effects. The intrinsic nature of such economic assessments did not prevent decentralisation. It could however be argued that, in addition to economic assessments, there is a further political element in state aid compatibility assessments, in terms of social assessments and the overriding Community context. Now, if it is possible to explain the analytical framework for economic assessments, as with Article 81(3) EC, it should be possible to explain a similar framework for social assessments. A clear attempt to explain both economic and social objectives in a Community context is made in the Commission's State Aid Action Plan, where a key element is the analysis of

[82] MEMO/05/195 of 7/06/2005.

[83] See Wils above, pp 118–19; P Nicolaides 'Decentralised State Aid Control in an Enlarged European Union: Feasible, Necessary of both?' above p 271.

[84] Case 730/79 *Philip Morris v Commission*, above p 24.

[85] Case C-351/98 *Spain v Commission* [2002] ECR I-8031, p 53.

[86] See for example case T-171/02 *Regione autonoma della Sardegna v Commission* [2005] ECR II-0000, pp 126, 137, 142 and 149.

[87] *Guidelines on the application of Article 81(3) of the Treaty*, OJ C 101/97, 27 April 2004.

market failures, that is the justification of state aid when the markets fail to produce the desired objectives of common interest.[88] Key priorities, such as innovation and research and development, are described with reference to the Lisbon strategy for growth and jobs. The importance of services of general economic interest is recognised as a key component of the European welfare state. This, and the soft-law available, could be seen as a way of converting any remaining political elements into law.

If compatibility decisions are legal assessments, decentralisation should be possible, subject to introduction of necessary institutional framework and know-how transfer. The Commission will then be forced to go even further in articulating its policy, as it evolves over time. This has been done with Article 81 EC following modernisation. An important observation is that following modernisation of Articles 81 and 82 EC, the Commission has produced guidelines explaining their policy. In particular, commentators have observed that the Commission has abandoned the position that the granting of an exemption under Article 81(3) EC requires a considerable degree of discretion. Instead, the Commission has produced detailed guidelines on criteria for exemption. The guidelines seem to deviate from the Commission's previous decision making practice in a number of respects.[89] The example shows how decentralisation has resulted not only in an attempt to codify existing practices, but also in a need to develop and express a body of legal rules that can be applied by all courts and competition authorities. Decentralisation has thus increased transparency and availability of competition law policy in the context of Article 81 EC. The same type of development can be envisaged if application of Article 87(3) EC were to be decentralised.

4.4 Competence and consistency

Given the Commission's present decision-making monopoly, it is natural that national courts have no experience of deciding whether state aid is compatible with the Treaty. Against the background of the complex and extensive case-law and soft-law on state aid, can it really be expected that national judges will be able to handle this challenge? It may seem that fears of inconsistent application is the most valid objection against decentralisation.[90] However, lack of knowledge can be cured, given sufficient resources. In addition, it is hazardous to base an argument on the presumption that the present body of state aid law (as developed by the Commission) will continue to exist. It is possible, or even likely, that decentralisation will call for further attempts to increase transparency and

[88] State Aid Action Plan above, p 23.

[89] See R Whish *Competition Law* (5th edn, LexisNexis, 2003), p 152 *ff*.

[90] On this challenge in the context of modernisation of Arts 81 and 82 EC, see HM Gilliams 'Modernisation: From Policy to Practice' (2003) (28(4)) *European Law Review*, 451–74, p 457; Venit, above, pp 559–64.

workability of state aid law. This development has already begun and will continue as the State Aid Action Plan is put into effect.

4.5 Balancing the pros and cons of decentralisation of State aid control

When seen in isolation, none of the arguments against decentralisation of state aid are entirely convincing. The most solid arguments are found in the uncertainty produced by the combined aspects; a possible political element in compatibility decisions, concerns of competence and effectiveness—in other words, what will happen if the careful balancing of economic and social assessments in a Community context, presently done *ex ante* by the Commission, is done *ex post* by national judges who are entirely unfamiliar with this type of exercise? Will not decentralisation, at least in the short- or medium-term, produce inconsistent assessments with adverse effects on the Community?

I take the position that the costs of further developing workable legal rules and distributing competence among national judges must be weighed against the drawbacks of the present system. The incentive for injured parties to bring proceedings in national courts, or file complaints to national authorities, is presently low given that national authorities and courts are unable to carry out a full legal assessment. In the absence of empowerment for national courts to evaluate whether an aid measure is compatible with the common market under Article 87(3) EC, complainants will face a high likelihood of parallel proceedings. *If* they are successful in demonstrating to the national authority or court that a measure is state aid under Article 87(1) EC, the Member State will be under a positive obligation to notify the measure to the Commission (provided of course that the legal analysis made by the national court or authority is correct). National proceedings will then run in parallel with the proceedings initiated by the Member State's notification to the Commission. The notification to the Commission can result in an appeal to the Community Courts. Meanwhile, the national proceedings are likely to be stayed. Referrals to the Court of Justice are no way to obtain answers to the application of Article 87(3) EC, since this procedure must be set in motion by a notification to the Commission. However, there may be referrals on the interpretation of the notion of state aid in Article 87(1) EC, which means that there can be at least three parallel proceedings in a single state aid case.

The high likelihood of parallel proceedings, with the resulting complexity and substantive costs incurred, will effectively discourage many injured parties from relying on national authorities and courts. The first choice for those parties will be to file a complaint to the Commission. That, precisely, was the state of affairs with Article 81 EC prior to modernisation. In spite of attempts from the Commission to encourage competition law enforcement in national courts, the number of cases brought remained low. As explained, the obligation for national authorities to take action can, at least partly, remedy the present failures of private enforcement. Still, if this route proves successful, the Commission's resources for handling notifications will be strained, possibly to the point of exhaustion.

My proposition is that in spite of the cost of convergence and any (temporary) problems with consistency, the poor procedural economy resulting from the present system can only be remedied by way of decentralisation. Lenaerts and Gerard have observed that, since Community law is rooted in a decentralised enforcement scheme, decentralisation of Articles 81 and 82 EC was 'nothing more than a "return to normal" for an area of law which was subject for an important part [ ] to exclusive enforcement by the Commission through the *ex ante* notification requirement'.[91] There are indeed costs and inconveniences connected with a transition from a centralised to a decentralised system. Hopefully, the present article will have demonstrated that we are already working under a semi-decentralised system of state aid control where it is becoming increasingly difficult to justify the notification requirement and the Commission's exclusive competence to take compatibility decisions.

BIBLIOGRAPHY

Ahlborn, C and Berg, C, 'Can State Aid Control Learn from Antitrust? The Need for a Greater Role for Competition Analysis under the State Aid Rules' in A Biondi, P Eeckhout and J Flynn (eds) *The Law of State Aid in the European Union* (Oxford, OUP, 2004).

Biondi, A and Rubini, L, 'Aims, Effects and Justifications: EC State Aid Law and Its Impact on National Social Policies' in E Spaventa and M Dougan (eds) *Social Welfare and EU Law*. (Oxford and Portland, Oregon, Hart, 2005).

Dougan, M, *National Remedies before the Court of Justice* (Oxford and Portland Oregon, Hart, 2004).

Engström, J, 'Effektivt rättsskydd i förvirring—Nationell process och sanktionsrätt i ljuset av C-253/00 Munoz' (2003) (1) *Europarättslig Tidskrift*, p 167.

Eilmansberger, T, 'The Relationship between Rights and Remedies in EC Law: In Search of the Missing Link' (2004) (41) *Common Market Law Review*, pp 1199–246.

Gilliams, HM, 'Modernisation: From Policy to Practice' (2003) (28(4)) *European Law Review*, pp 451–74.

Lenaerts, K and Gerard, D, 'Decentralisation of EC Competition Law Enforcement: Judges in the Frontline' (2004) (27(3)) *World Competition*, pp 313–49.

Nehl, HP, *Administrative Procedure in EC Law* (Oxford, Hart, 1999).

Nicolaides, P, 'Control of State Aid in the European Union—Compliance, Sanctions and Rational Behaviour' (2002) (25(3)) *World Competition*, pp 249–62.

—— 'Decentralised State Aid Control in an Enlarged European Union: Feasible, Necessary or both?' (2003) (26(2)) *World Competition*, pp 263–76.

[91] K Lenaerts and D Gerard 'Decentralisation of EC Competition Law Enforcement: Judges in the Frontline' (2004) (27(3)) *World Competition*, p 318.

Ross, M, 'Decentralization, Effectiveness, and Modernisation: Contradiction in Terms?' in A Biondi, P Eeckhout and J Flynn (eds) *The Law of State Aid in the European Union* (Oxford University Press, 2004).

Sinnaeve, A, 'What to Expect from National Courts in the Fight against Unlawful State Aid?' (2005) (1) *European State Aid Law Quarterly*, pp 1–2.

Temple Lang, J, 'National Measures Restricting Competition and National Authorities under Article 10 EC' (2004) (29(3)) *European Law Review*, pp 397–406.

—— 'Privatisation of Social Welfare: European Union Competition Law Rules' in E Spaventa and M Dougan (eds) *Social Welfare and EU Law* (Oxford and Portland, Oregon, Hart, 2005).

Venit, JS, 'Brave New World: The Modernization and Decentralisation of Enforcement under Articles 81 and 82 of the EC Treaty' (2003) (40) *Common Market Law Review*, pp 545–80.

Vesterdorf, B, 'A Further Comment on the New State Aid Concept as this Concept Continues to be Reshaped' (2005) (3) *European State Aid Law Quarterly*, pp 393–9.

Whish, R, *Competition Law* (5th ed, LexisNexis, 2003).

Wils, WPJ, *The Optimal Enforcement of EC Antitrust Law, Essays in Law and Economics* European Monographs 33 (The Hague/London/New York, Kluwer Law International, 2002).

10

Access to Justice in the EU—Knocking on Heaven's Door?

OLA ZETTERQUIST*

ABSTRACT

THIS ARTICLE IS concerned with the issues of access to justice for individuals and the rule of law in the context of the European Community (EC). These issues are classical both in constitutional theory and have featured prominently in the case law of the Court of Justice of the European Communities (ECJ) as constituting one of the normative foundations of the Community legal order. However, recent case law on the issue of individual access to the ECJ seems to be moving in a direction with less, rather than more, such access. This is the case both regarding the preliminary ruling (Article 234) and the action for annulment (Article 230.4). The article will first deal with the issue of access to justice and the rule of law in normative constitutional theory in general. Secondly, attention will be given to the role of these concepts within the Community legal order and to some of the recent case law, some of it with Swedish connections, from the ECJ that is of concern. Thirdly the article aims to problematise this development from a normative point of view and assess whether it is compromising the constitutional legitimacy of the EC.

* Ola Zetterquist is Assistant Professor of Constitutional and European law at the Department of Law at the School of Business of Göteborg University. He holds an LL.M. in European Community Law from Universidad Autónoma de Madrid and a LL.D in jurisprudence from Lund University. He has previously served two years at the district court in Eslöv Sweden and as an assistant professor at the Faculty of Law of Lund University, Sweden. He is currently engaged in the multi-disciplinary research project *Democracy Unbound*, headed by the department of philosophy of Stockholm University, concerning above statal democracy.

1 CONSTITUTIONAL THEORY, RULE OF LAW AND ACCESS TO JUSTICE

1.1 Divine justice . . .

The idea that law and government is concerned with (and, most would say, limited to) human conduct in this world may seem trivial today. However, this secular notion of law and government is a comparatively recent phenomenon. It was not until the enlightenment that the umbilical cord between law and religion was finally severed, but the idea of a linkage between law and justice in the sense of *moral authority* was maintained and serious effort was being made to put this linkage on a rational foundation that was not dependent on clerical authority. Although God was no longer the sole explanation, the divine did not completely vanish from the scene. The argumentation sometimes went as far as to liken, with the words of Thomas Hobbes, the political and legal order of the State to a '*Mortall God*'.[1] John Locke for his part held that an absence of access to justice, concerning rights and duties of the individual, triggered a right to *appeal to heaven* (ie the right to revolution), thus making access to justice and rule of law one of the most essential requirements for the legitimacy of any political government.

Law has often been held to constitute the fundamental moral bond between different individuals starting with Cicero's famous statement that '. . . a [re]public is . . . a numerous gathering brought together by legal consent and community of interest'.[2] The legal order thus makes up the common good, the *res publica*, of individuals which binds them together in political community and which confers moral legitimacy on this community. This idea is particularly prominent in Lockean political thought:

> . . . 'tis in their *Legislative*, that the Members of a Commonwealth are united, and combined together into one coherent living Body. This *is the Soul that gives Form, Life and Unity* to the Commonwealth: From hence the several Members have their mutual Influence, Sympathy and Connexion.[3]

Law thus seems to have a transcendental moral dimension that is connected to the very foundations of political and legal legitimacy. Accordingly, the rule of law is one of the most important constitutional ideals in the present day world, sometimes characterized as 'a universal human good'.[4] The point here is not to

[1] T Hobbes *Leviathan* (Cambridge, Cambridge University Press, [1651] 1991) p 120.

[2] Cicero 'The Republic' in *The Republic, The Laws* (Oxford, Oxford University Press, 1998) p 19, I–39.

[3] J Locke *Two Treatsies of Government* (Cambridge, Cambridge University Press, [1651] 1988) p 407, s 212.

[4] *Cf* BZ Tamanaha *On the Rule of Law—History, Politics, Theory* (Cambridge, Cambridge University Press, 2004) p 137–41.

describe all of these theories in detail but simply to draw attention to the fact that when we are speaking about the law and the importance of access to justice in general we are not only referring to legal technicalities but also to the deepest moral foundations of society (its transcendental dimension); we are, so to speak, knocking on heaven's door.

1.2 Rule of law as a constitutional ideal

1.2.1 An ancient ideal with modern roots

Rule of law as a constitutional ideal has a long history dating back to antiquity when Aristotle famously stated that 'The law ought to be supreme over all . . .'.[5] Aristotle's idea that law could indeed rule over mighty men has ever since then had a lasting appeal to moral philosophers and lawyers alike.

The enlightenment, however, signified an important turn in the view of the law when Hobbes, under the influence of the scientific revolution taking place in the fields of natural science and mathematics, flatly rejected both the notion that law was divinely ordained and that it was the law that actually ruled a society; '. . . it is Men and Arms, not Words, and Promises, that make the Force and Power of the Laws'.[6] In this sense Hobbes advocated an unashamedly frank theory of 'the rule of men', based on human will, rather than the rule of some sort of eternal law, as a constitutional ideal.[7] The essence of his point was that the law in itself is a powerless nothing and that the law can only be given force and meaning when it is employed by some (artificial or natural) person or body that, by his will and actions, effectuates the law.[8]

1.2.2 The thin notion of rule of law

Hobbes took an entirely new approach to the importance of the law defining it as the commands of a sovereign backed up with the threat of coercive enforcement.[9] Any norm not enjoying the sanction of the sovereign would thus not qualify as a legal norm at all. If a norm did emanate from another, apparently, independent source, such as customary law or an international treaty, it was by virtue of the sovereigns sanction rather than any other metaphysical reason that

[5] Aristotle 'The Politics' in *The Politics and The Constitution of Athens* (Cambridge, Cambridge University Press, 1996) p 99, IV:4.

[6] Hobbes above, p 471.

[7] *Cf* J Hampton 'Democracy and the Rule of Law' in I Shapiro (ed) *The Rule of Law—Nomos XXXVI* (New York, New York University Press, 1994) pp 13–44 p 14 *ff*.

[8] The point was succinctly reformulated by the somewhat later James Harrington with a colorful comparison: 'the magistrate upon his bench is that unto the law, which a gunner upon his platform is unto his cannon'. J Harrington 'The Commonwealth of Oceana' in *The Commonwealth of Oceana and A System of Politics* (Cambridge, Cambridge University Press, [1656] 1992) p 9.

[9] Hobbes above, p 183 *ff*.

it was to be considered as law.[10] All legal theories that hold the sanction to be the binding element of the law thus fall back on Hobbes' realist principles. Hobbes made further lasting contributions to modern legal theory in the shape of the principle of legality by holding that 'The Greatest Liberty of Subjects dependeth on the Silence of the Law'[11] and that punishment without legal basis amounts to 'hostility' rather than legal enforcement[12] and by holding that laws should be public, general (prospective) and equally administered to all subjects.[13]

In spite of these important principles, Hobbes' is not the theory generally associated with the ideal of the rule of law in the sense of limited government (constrained by law) since he recognised no substantial limits to the sovereign's lawmaking powers. On the contrary, any command that emanates from the sovereign qualifies as law.[14] His principles are more concerned with the effectiveness of the legal system rather than its moral objectives. Hobbes therefore constitutes the important starting point for legal theories that emphasise the institutional origin of legal norms, at the very heart of the theories of legal positivism, rather than the substantial content of these.[15] This can be said to be rule of law understood in a rather thin sense; namely that what has been properly enacted by the sovereign (democratic or not) power should count as law regardless of its moral qualities and that there should be a clear separation between law and morals. A Hobbesian interpretation of the rule of law thus rejects the importation (particularly by the courts) of values into the legal system if these values have not been incorporated into and expressed in positive law.[16] Hobbes emphasised that there is a close connection between the (political) will of the sovereign and the law. In modern democracy a contemporary Hobbesian would hold that the people rules by enacting laws that are implemented by enforcement agencies and courts, ie the people rules through the laws of the society.[17]

1.2.3 The substantial notion of the rule of law

The thin definition of the rule of law is often held to be too narrow since it holds that any command, however bizarre or arbitrary, of the sovereign is to be treated as law if it is enacted in the proper way. The problem with a thin account

[10] This idea was later developed by Jeremy Bentham who explained these seemingly independent sources (in reality 'subordinate powerholders') with the notions of 'adoption' and 'pre-adoption' by the sovereign. See further J Bentham *Of Laws in General* (Athlone Press, 1970) p 18 *ff*.

[11] Hobbes above, p 152.

[12] *Ibid*, p 216.

[13] *Ibid*, p 231 and p 237.

[14] *Ibid*, p 183.

[15] *Cf* TRS Allan *Constitutional Justice—A Liberal Theory of the Rule of Law* (Oxford, Oxford University Press, 2001) p 11, see also H Kelsen *Introduction to the Problems of Legal Theory* (Oxford, Oxford University Press, 1992) p 7 and 63 *ff*.

[16] MP Zuckert 'Hobbes Locke, and the Problem of the Rule of Law' in I Shapiro (ed) *The Rule of Law—Nomos XXXVI* (New York, New York University Press, 1994) p 69.

[17] See Hampton above, p 14 *ff*.

of the rule of law is that it collapses into a confusion of rule of law with rule of the government (or rule *by* law) since any government may qualify under these formal conditions.[18] To the extent that we wish to identify rule of law with limited government and the protection of the moral rights of individuals, two ingredients that are often held to be indispensable components of the rule of law, we have to embrace a more substantial notion of the rule of law. It is clear that such a view of the rule of law can only be sustained by reference to some ideal external to the political process, ie the political bodies are not entirely free to shape the ideals of society at will.

A substantial view of the rule of law accordingly implies the creation of a sphere of individual autonomy and self-determination that is immune from (political) state interference.[19] The individual sphere is commonly associated with principle of human dignity, and serves as the 'touchstone' or external ideal for this rights-based perspective of the rule of law and is thus to be considered as the 'mother right' of all other rights that the individual may have.[20] The protection of the individual sphere is defined in law and constitutes the moral objective (the *telos*) of the legal and political order.

A substantial notion of the rule of law also means that the procedural questions and interpretation of the law are to be understood in connection with the question of the purpose (ie the morality) of the law.[21] It may be recalled that according to Locke it is the access to an impartial judge to decide over controversies that is the very essence of a (civil) government.[22] In this sense there is a strong link between the material rights of the individual and the rights of access to justice. If a right cannot be asserted before a court of law, it is not properly a (legal) right at all. Law is on this view instrumental for securing the moral rights of the individual. Such an interpretation of the notion of the rule of law also squares well with the third recital of the preamble to the Universal Declaration of Human Rights of the General Assembly of the United Nations, 10 December, 1948:

> Whereas it is essential, if man is not to be compelled to have recourse, as a last resort, to rebellion against tyranny and oppression, that human rights should be protected by the rule of law.

Just as Locke held that the denial of justice meant that the oppressed were entitled to 'appeal to heaven', the Declaration holds that, in the last resort, rebellion may be justified where the law does not adequately protect human rights. It thus seems that the different views on the rule of law correlate to the different views on the origin and character of the moral rights of the individual

[18] Tamanaha above, p 92; Allan above, p 35 *f*.

[19] RS Kay 'American Constitutionalism' in L Alexander (ed) *Constitutionalism—Philosophical Foundations* (Cambridge, Cambridge University Press, 1998) pp 22–4.

[20] Allan above, p 61 *ff*.

[21] Allan *ibid*, p 61 and Zuckert above, p 77, for a contrary view see HLA Hart *Essays in Jurisprudence and Philosophy* (Oxford, Oxford University Press, 1983) p 350.

[22] Locke above, s 89.

and the role of the legal order for securing these. The main idea of the substantial interpretations of the rule of law is that the procedural canons of the legal order must be interpreted in the light of the further principles that explain the relationship between law and justice. Just as in individual relations, failing to stay faithful to the foundational principles of the relation may result in irreparable damage to the authority of the legal order.[23]

1.2.4 The rule of law and the principle of equality

A starting point for the substantial notion of the rule of law is often taken in the principle of *equality* of the individuals making up the legal order. By equality is not meant so much that people actually are the same (since they are obviously not), nor that everyone should be made the same, but rather that no one is born into a certain political relationship[24] and that the legal order must to recognize this. The law must thus treat all of its addressees as equal and rational beings and cannot single out a few for preferential or detrimental treatment without such a distinction being objectively justified by reference to the common good.[25] The principle of equality can be formulated as stipulating that legislative and administrative action must be able to meet the criteria of *universalisability*, often associated with the philosophy of Richard Hare.[26] His thesis on universalisability seeks to build a bridge between *is* and *ought*, in terms of universalising value judgments. If A considers that it is wrong (or right) to punish B for a certain action, A is for logical reasons bound to consider it wrong (or right) to punish all those in the same situation as B.[27] Hare's argument is thus in the first instance not a moral prescription but logical, since we know nothing of the values for judging B's presumptive guilt. Hare's argument prescribes that the person who states a given value judgment is obliged, as a logical consequence, to apply that judgment to all similar cases even if (or especially when) it would affect himself.

By transferring the principle of universalisability to the legal domain, the aim is to ensure that legislative and administrative action conforms to the principle of universalisability in order to be consistent with the common good. Universalisability is particularly important in the fields of freedom of expression and public debate in order for the members of the political community to be engaged in continuous and open debate over the more precise content of the common good. In order to secure this open and ongoing debate, the courts are required to play an active role in striking down action that impairs this debate

[23] Allan above, p 58 *f*.

[24] Locke above, s 4.

[25] Allan above, p 121 *ff*.

[26] R Hare, *Freedom and reason* (Oxford, Oxford University Press, 1963). For a more nuanced presentation of the various principles related to the universalisability principle see W Rabinowicz *Universalizability—A study in Morals and Metaphysics* (Reidel Publishing Company, 1979) pp 11–19.

[27] Hare above, p 30 *ff*.

among political equals.[28] The political and legal machinery cannot be used as a vehicle for offsetting this fundamental equality among the individual members. All legislative action infringing the autonomy of the individual must therefore be justifiable with regard to the overriding interest of the common good.[29] This imposes a requirement on the legislator or executive to present coherent and convincing reasons for the action in question, reasons that, in the end, aspire to the assent of rational and autonomous individuals[30] and that the legislation applies equally to all affected. The courts are charged with the duty of ascertaining whether the other branches of government have actually complied with these requirements and this is what underpins the moral authority of judicial review. It is thus not primarily a question of the judges imposing 'their view' of the morally good on the other branches of government. This ideal of equal protection and rational argumentation amounts to the concept of *integrity* in the law, meaning that the courts should enforce the law as a coherent and principled whole rather than as isolated *ad hoc* pieces.[31]

1.2.5 Access to justice and the democratic process

A basic question concerning the legitimacy of law is that of the moral authority of the political community that, ultimately, stands as the author of legal norms. In modern democracy this role belongs to the elected representatives of the people (or the people directly). The scope for legislative action, however, is limited by the principles of individual autonomy and the principle of equality in the sense mentioned above, ie that such action must be rationally founded and argued.

Ideally this rational argumentation should, in accordance with the Lockean principle, take place in the legislative assembly which, according to him, is the indispensable institution for rational political dialogue. The rule of law also requires, however, that the officials should be able to justify their actions before an impartial arbiter, the court. Due process between (procedurally) equal parties is therefore an essential part of the rational legitimacy of the legal order.[32] In legal proceedings before ordinary courts the state normally has no privileged standing. On the contrary, the legal procedure takes place between two equal parties that both expose their reasons in order to convince a third party of the merits of their case. The court in turn must be able to resolve the dispute on reasons that in principle, if not in the actual outcome, both parties hold to be morally legitimate.[33]

[28] *Cf* JH Ely *Democracy and Distrust—A Theory of Judicial Review* (Harvard University Press, 1980) p 105ff and Allan above, p 123 *f.*

[29] *Cf* Locke above, s 131: '. . . the power of the Society . . . *can never be suppos'd to extend farther than the common good*'.

[30] Allan above, p 65.

[31] R Dworkin *Law's Empire* (Harvard University Press, 1986).

[32] Allan above, p 172.

[33] Allan *ibid*, p 187 *f.*

As de Toqueville famously remarked on the American constitution, the judicial process offers the politically weak an opportunity to have their voice heard and obliges the judge (and thereby the state) to answer their arguments rationally.[34] The importance of this right is proportional to the political weakness of the individual. Rationality and access to justice, just like the democratic process, therefore have a fundamental importance for the moral authority of the political order. It is true that the courts do not possess a monopoly on rational argumentation, but neither do the political bodies.[35]

2 RULE OF LAW AND ACCESS TO JUSTICE IN THE EUROPEAN UNION—THE CHARACTERISTICS OF THE EUROPEAN CONSTITUTION

2.1 The rule of law as a foundational ideal of the EEC

The EEC was originally founded on the idea of constructing a supra-national community of binding rules of law with a designated court, the ECJ, to be the arbiter on the interpretation of the treaty. The system was furthermore explicitly built on a system of checks and balances where the different institutions were charged with different duties according to the Treaty. The very foundation of the EEC was thus to a very large degree based on a general notion of the rule of law, at least in the thin Hobbesian sense mentioned above (section 1.2.2). From this uncontroversial starting point, however, it is a far cry to characterize, as the ECJ has done, the system set up as constitutional in the sense that the system is *independent* of the constitutional law of the Member States. This claim is (obviously) not based on the idea that a European people have actually ordained that the EU is a constitutional and independent entity. Nor has, at any later point, the European Parliament (EP) emerged as a democratic sovereign (state style) Parliament of Europe, thus conferring constitutional authority on the EU. Instead the claim for constitutional status of the EC may rather stem from the claim of moral authority laid down in the legal order of the community, or to be more general, from the authority of the rule of law.

An argument against the rule of law based constitutional theory of the EC may be that the moral authority of its legal order derives from the Member States and more specifically in the assent given by their Parliaments when ratifying the Treaties and their continuous acceptance (by not revoking its original assent) of the Community legal order. This view, however, cannot account for the constitutional principles of the ECJ (notably not the principle of supremacy of EC law in relation to national constitutional law) and would mean, if taken seriously, that each such Parliament would be free to revoke the treaties, ie the

[34] A de Tocqueville *Democracy in America* (Fontana Press, [1850] 1969) p 698.
[35] *Cf* Allan above, p 163.

constitution of the EU. There would not, in such a case, be any point to refer to the Treaty as a constitution other than in the same sense as one refers to constitutions of subordinate power holders such as local councils or corporations.[36]

2.2 The development of the idea of rule of law in the EC

The ECJ has elaborated significantly on the idea of the rule of law that is implicit in the structure of the EC. The idea that the treaties (no doubt entered into in legal form) conferred rights on European individuals was held to justify that the treaties had, so to speak, mutated from public international law to constitutional law.[37] This *exodus* from public international law started in the landmark cases in the 1960s and 1970s when the ECJ established the constitutional principles of direct effect,[38] supremacy[39] and pre-emption.[40] Furthermore, in the case *Costa v ENEL*, the Court, laying out the reasons for the (constitutional) supremacy of EC-law, stated that it was impossible to accord preference to national law without giving rise to such discrimination between European individuals that was prohibited according to the principle of equality laid down in Article 7, now Article 12 (section 594 in the judgment). The very operating system of the EEC was thus transformed from public international law to constitutional law with the idea of the rule of law, the principle of equality and the rights of the individual serving as the base for this transformation.

Even though the legal principles invoked by the ECJ may be of some weight, one might still be unconvinced, from a democratic point of view, that the EC could claim constitutional status alongside the Member States. One former judge, Federico Mancini, of the ECJ however, connected the rule of law (understood as the direct effect and justiciability of EC law) with the democratic principle holding that the effect of the introduction of direct effect was '. . . to take Community law out of the hands of politicians and bureaucrats and to give it to the people. Of all the Court's democratizing achievements none can rank so highly in practical terms'.[41] Another former judge on the Court, Pierre Pescatore, also connected the idea that the European Community conferred rights on individuals with 'the democratic ideal' in the sense of excluding arbitrary power, holding that this 'highly political ideal' entailed that the norms of EC-law should be directly effective.[42] Both judges evidently seem to hold that

[36] *Cf* AV Dicey *Introduction to the Study of the Law of the Constitution* (Liberty Fund, 1982) p 39 *f*.

[37] F Mancini & D Keeling 'Democracy and the European Court of Justice' (1994) *The Modern Law Review* p 181 *ff*.

[38] Case 26/62 *van Gend en Loos v Nederlandse Administratie der Belastingen* [1963] ECR 1.

[39] Case 6/64, *Costa v ENEL* [1964] ECR 585.

[40] Case 106/77, *Amministrazione delle Finanze dello Stato v Simmenthal SpA* [1978] ECR 629.

[41] Mancini & Keeling above p 183.

[42] P Pescatore 'The Doctrine of "Direct Effect": An Infant Disease of Community Law' (1983) *European Law Review* p 158.

the substantial notion of the rule of law is an integral part of modern democracy, Mancini, stating explicitly that:

> . . . under the rule of law, democracy is not just a matter of ensuring that the people's elected representatives play a full role in the process of law-making; democracy is also about protecting the rights of the individual. No society can be considered truly democratic if its citizens are denied the possibility of vindicating their rights in judicial proceedings.[43]

Pescatore and Mancini explain the constitutional character of the EC by connecting it to the substantial notion of the rule of law (and the Courts own crucial function in this regard) as being an essential part of modern democracy. They both connect the classical constitutional ideal of the substantial rule of law with a system of checks and balances as the principal way of securing limited government and individual autonomy as moral fundamental values.[44] This position is further supported by the reasoning of the Advocate General Stix-Hackl in the case C-36/02 *Omega*[45] where she held that the principle of human dignity is one of the fundamental principles of the EU (section 90). The reasoning of the Advocate General (in sections 76–80 of the opinion) is quite informative as regards the moral foundations of the Community legal order:

> Human dignity . . . forms the underlying basis and starting point for all human rights . . . The right to respect for human rights runs counter in this respect to the idea that human regard is negotiable by the State, the people and the majority . . . All in all, human dignity has its roots deep in the origins of a conception of mankind in European culture that regards man as an entity capable of spontaneity and self-determination . . . Furthermore, the concept of the legal equality of all is also inherent in the idea of human rights in general and human dignity in particular . . ..

The principle of human dignity is, just as in the case of the substantial rule of law, to be understood as the source of all other fundamental rights enjoyed by the individual in EC-law and establishes their status as equals under this legal order. The question of right of access to justice in EC-law should be seen in this broader picture.

Along these lines, the principle of the rule of law was indeed held by the ECJ to be something akin to a supra-constitutional principle in the sense that it prevails even over what (at least apparently) seemed to be 'black letter law' of the Treaty. In the case 294/83, *Les Verts*,[46] the Court was faced with the question of whether the EP could be sued in spite of the fact that it was not mentioned among the institutions in Article 230 (then Article 173).The court held (in section 23) that:

[43] Mancini & Keeling above p 181.

[44] *Cf* Mancini & Keeling *ibid* p 181.

[45] Case C-36/02 *Omega Spielhallen- und Automatenaufstellungs-GmbH v Oberbürgermeisterin der Bundesstadt Bonn* [2004] ECR I-9609.

[46] Case 294/83 *Parti écologiste 'Les Verts' v European Parliament* [1986] ECR 1339.

> . . . the [EEC] is a Community based on the rule of law, inasmuch as neither its Member States nor its institutions can avoid a review of the question whether the measures adopted by them are in conformity with the basic constitutional charter, the Treaty.

The reasoning of the court is interesting on several accounts. Firstly it explicitly refers to the Treaty as the constitutional charter, ie as the constitution, of the Community and, secondly, holds that where there is such a constitutional charter, the rule of law requires that there must be a legal remedy against either state- or community action within its field of application. The ECJ thus in the *Les Verts* drew the conclusion that the ideal of the rule of law (as the touchstone of the EC legal order) also required that the rights protected in EC-law be *justiciable*, ie subject to judicial review, ultimately by the ECJ itself. In the case before the Court, the principle of the rule of law required that an action for annulment against acts of the EP had to be available regardless of the wording of the Treaty. The argument was even more directly stated by the Advocate General Mancini who went as far as to state that the principle of the rule of law would empower the ECJ to disregard treaty provisions that would impede its powers of review.

> Whenever required in the interest of judicial protection, the Court is prepared to correct or complete rules which limits its powers in the name of the principle which defines its mission.

From the reasoning, particularly of the Advocate General, in the *Les Verts* case it is clear that the principle of the rule of law holds a very fundamental position in the Community legal order precisely because of the paramount interest of judicial protection of individuals.

2.3 The preliminary ruling

The procedural mechanism of the preliminary ruling (Article 234), whereby a court in the Member States may request the ECJ to interpret a provision of Community law or to assess its validity, has been one of the most important instruments for upholding the rule of law within the EC. It should be remembered that all of the three most significant constitutionalising cases mentioned before, as well as numerous more, started in the national courts. By enlisting the national courts the ECJ has significantly boosted the impact and effectiveness of EC-law.[47] Had it not been for their (mostly) loyal cooperation, it seems reasonable to assume that EC-law would never have grown out of the domains of traditional international law.

[47] F Mancini 'The Making of a Constitution for Europe' (1989) *Common Market Law Review* p 597 and pp 604–6.

The ECJ stated in the *Les Verts* case that for the purpose of securing the rule of law within the EC, the Treaty had set up 'a complete system of remedies' by the mechanisms laid down in Articles 230 (the action for annulment) and 241 (the plea of illegality), on the one hand, and Article 234 (the request for a preliminary ruling) on the other. The system under Article 234 is thus one of the essential safeguards for the rule of law within the EC, whereby individuals may obtain redress for infringements of their rights under EC law. The preliminary ruling ultimately gives the individual an access to the only competent court to rule on the legality and final interpretation of Community law.[48]

The preliminary ruling is, with few exceptions, the channel whereby the individual can exercise the right to judicial review of Member state or Community action having effect on the rights conferred by EC-law. The preliminary ruling is also the mechanism that allows the ECJ to ascertain to what extent such action can be justified with reference to the common good understood as the protection of the rights of all parties concerned. The evaluation of whether such action can be justified can, in principle, only be undertaken by the ECJ since only the ECJ has the overview and composition as to take into account the European common good.[49] For this objective to be attained, it is necessary that the national court takes its constitutional role as Community court of general jurisdiction seriously and that they thus refer to the ECJ whenever 'a question of Community law' arises before it.[50]

To a considerable extent the mechanism of the preliminary ruling illustrates the *exodus* of EC-law from its *genesis* in public international law to a constitutional legal order. The judicial architecture was originally geared towards a horizontal relationship between national courts and the ECJ where the task of applying (and, ultimately, refusing to apply) EC law rested with the national courts. The subsequent constitutionalisation (by the doctrines of direct effect, supremacy and pre-emption) of the treaties and, by the ECJ and, by virtue of the doctrines of precedent[51] and *acte claire*[52] the creation of a more vertical relationship between the ECJ and the national courts, the question of individual access to justice has become more problematic. The distinction between interpretation and application has become blurred.

It has long been accepted that a national court *may* refer to the ECJ. The more complicated question has been which national courts that *should* refer (Article 234.3) to the ECJ for a preliminary ruling. From the point of view of the substantial rule of law this is no trivial question. A denial of access to the ECJ is

[48] As the Court held in ss 11–20 of the Case 314/85 *Foto-Frost v Hauptzollamt Lübeck-Ost* [1987] ECR 4199.

[49] *Cf* s 18 of the case 314/85, *Foto Frost ibid.*

[50] J Temple Lang 'The Duties of National Courts under Community Constitutional Law' (1997) *European Law Review* p 5 and pp 16–18.

[51] Case 28-30/62 *Da Costa en Schaake NV and others v Administratie der Belastingen* [1963] ECR 61.

[52] Case 283/81 *CILFIT v Ministero della Sanità* [1982] ECR 3415.

tantamount to a denial of access to justice (enshrined both in the ECHR[53] Articles 6 and 13 and in the general principles of EC-law) since only the ECJ may grant relief against Community action. A court that cannot grant relief is by definition not an effective legal remedy (as held by the ECtHR in the case *Klass and others*).[54]

Two possible answers exist as to which court that is obliged to refer: the court that is formally the final court, ie the supreme court, or the court that is for practical purposes the final court, eg when leave to appeal is required in order to gain access to the supreme court. The early case law of the ECJ seemed to indicate that it was the court that was in fact and practice the final court to deal with the case (ie not necessarily the Supreme Court). The court stated, in a dictum in the *Costa v ENEL* case (where the case was pending in a national court of first instance):

> . . . by the terms of [Article 234], however, national courts against whose decision, *as in the present case*, there is no judicial remedy, must refer the matter to the Court of Justice.[55]

Such an interpretation accords well with the protection of the rights of the individual as the primary concern. From this point of view, it is secondary that the preliminary ruling also secures a uniform interpretation when the supreme courts are concerned. That argument is primarily practical or utilitarian in nature and therefore unsatisfactory from the normative point of view.

2.4 The turning point in Lyckeskog . . .[56]

In the *Lyckeskog* case however, the Court was faced with the explicit question of which court was obliged to refer to the ECJ. In this case the ECJ departs from its position in the *Costa v ENEL* case and states unambiguously that only the supreme courts are covered by the obligation to refer.

> That objective [to prevent a body of national case-law that is not in accordance with the rules of Community law from coming into existence in any Member State] is secured when . . . supreme courts are bound by this obligation to refer.[57]

It may be tempting to conclude that the ECJ in *Lyckeskog* has moved away from its earlier position of connecting the procedure under Article 234 to the protection of individual rights under EC-law. Before reaching this conclusion however one should observe that the ECJ includes a caveat: the supreme courts ought to grant leave to appeal when a question of EC-law is central to the case,

[53] European Convention on Human Rights.

[54] *Case of Klass and others v Germany* judgment of 6 September 1978, ser A, No 28, s 64.

[55] Case 6/64 at s 592, author's italics.

[56] Case 99/00 *Lyckeskog* [2002[ECR I-4839.

[57] *Ibid* s 15.

thus securing that the case might, in the end, reach the ECJ This opinion was also expressed in the seminal case C-224/01, *Köbler* (establishing the principle that state liability might occur even in cases where the national courts were responsible for the breach of Community law and the breach is 'sufficiently serious') where the Court held:

> . . . it is, in particular, in order to prevent rights conferred on individuals by Community law from being infringed that under the third paragraph of Article 234 EC a court against whose decisions there is no judicial remedy under national law is required to make reference to the Court of Justice. (Köbler, section 35).[58]

From the perspective of the individual, however, the obligation that the *Lyckeskog* and *Köbler* judgments placed on the last instances may be of little comfort. This interpretation of the obligation still means that the individual litigant will have to await the final instance (plus the time required for the preliminary ruling) before they can have their claim settled and possibly need to initiate another action, with the costs and risk such an action entails, for damages subsequent to the failure of the court of last instance to observe the duty to refer to the ECJ.[59]

The argumentation of the Court (as well as the Advocate General) in the *Lyckeskog* case turned entirely on the purpose of the preliminary ruling as being to prevent the emergence of a case law in the Member States at odds with that of the ECJ. The argument concerning judicial protection of the individual, which seemed to be central both in the *Les Verts* and *Costa v ENEL* cases, is absent from the argumentation in the *Lyckeskog* case. The main impression of the judgment in the *Lyckeskog* case is that the ECJ holds that the national courts should decide on their own as many of the cases involving interpretation of EC-law as possible. The fact that this means a considerable reduction of individual access to the ECJ cannot have been lost on the Court.

The *Lyckeskog* judgment also resulted, indirectly, in a hitherto unprecedented action by the Commission. On 13 October 2004 the Commission held, in a reasoned opinion[60] according to Article 226 of the Treaty, that Sweden was in breach of its obligations under the Treaty since the Swedish supreme courts do not refer questions to the ECJ in sufficient numbers and that they decline to give

[58] The decision handed down in the *Köbler* case was without precedent and probably marked a new turn in the relationship between the ECJ and the national courts. The ECJ had in earlier days held the relationship with the national courts to be of vital importance for the achievement of the objectives of the Treaties and therefore strived hard to win the goodwill and loyal co-operation of the national courts (*cf* Mancini p 605). With the *Köbler* judgment, however, the ECJ acknowledges that breaches of EC-law are not the prerogative of the political or administrative bodies of the Member States and that there is a need for remedies in those cases. One might therefore reasonably expect the relation between the ECJ and the national courts to become somewhat cooler in the future.

[59] Case 99/00 *Lyckeskog* s 18.

[60] C (2004) 3899 07/10/2004 *AM-2003-2161 SUEDE:* No *Infraction/État Membre—Manquement de la cour suprêm Suédoise: Refus de presenter question prejudicielle devant la CJCE (Cour de justice des Communautés européennes).*

reasons for refusing to hear cases involving EC-law. Neither the Commission nor the private party can thus be sure whether Sweden has in fact observed the obligation under Article 234 of the Treaty. It is clear from the reasoned opinion of the Commission that the preliminary ruling is, at best, a precarious way of safeguarding the rule of law within the EC. In this regard it could be argued that the *Köbler* judgment finally laid down a remedy for this problem in the shape of a right to compensation for damages resulting from the last instances having refrained from their duties under Article 234. Any such fault must however be 'sufficiently serious' and it is still rather unclear what sort of fault that may be. The 'complete system of remedies' thus seems to be somewhat incomplete in practice.

2.5 . . . and the Union de Pequeños Agricultores

The legacy of the origin in public international law seems to haunt the judicial architecture in another important aspect of access to justice—the possibility (*locus standi*) of an individual to bring an action for annulment (according to Article 230.4) directly before the ECJ in those cases where the individual is 'directly and individually' concerned.

The action for annulment was designed to ensure that the Community institutions complied with the principle of conferred powers laid down in the treaty (now Articles 5.1 and 7), thus securing the rule of law in the Treaty. In the 1950s it was assumed that this was primarily a concern for the Member States but it was also recognized that when, occasionally, an individual was addressed directly by the Community institutions, access to the Court had to be granted. At the time it was not believed that the Community legal order would be 'a new legal order' of constitutional character and the judicial architecture reflected this assumption. The ECJ held early on in the case, 25/62 *Plaumann*[61] that an individual had in fact to be the addressee of a *decision* in order to have standing before the Court in order to challenge acts by the Community institutions. In all other cases the proper procedure would be to either await subsequent Community action, which could be challenged by virtue of the plea of illegality laid down in Article 241, or to challenge national acts (based on the Community act) before the national courts.

As the Community has evolved, however, this architecture has become ever more problematic as the impact, from the individual's perspective, of Community law today can reasonably be said to equal that of the State while the possibilities to bring an action against these measures have remained as slim as they were in the 1950s.[62] It is thus not surprising that the existing rules on individual access to the Court have been criticized as being, ultimately, incompatible

[61] Case 25/62 *Plaumann v Commission EEC* [1963] ECR 199.

[62] *Cf* Mancini & Keeling above p 182.

with the rule of law. Mancini, among others, held the results of the Court's *Plaumann* doctrine to be '. . . bizarre and paradoxical, if not downright perverse'.[63]

The question of individual *locus standi* was again raised before the ECJ in the case C-50/00,[64] *Union de Pequeños Agricultores* (UPA), where the appellant claimed that the current system of remedies violated their rights to an effective legal remedy. The Advocate General of the case (Jacobs) seemed to take a position close to Mancini's holding (section 78 of the opinion) that:

> . . . although the European Communities originate in a set of Treaties concluded by the Member States in the context of public international law, the Community legal order has developed in such a way that it would no longer be accurate to describe it as a system of intergovernmental cooperation, nor would it be appropriate to describe the Court of Justice as an international tribunal.

The thrust of Jacob's argument was that in order to keep pace with the constitutional development of the Community legal order, the rules on access to justice must evolve from its origin in public international law and accommodate individual claims where these are directly concerned and no other adequate remedy can be found (section 36–48). It was stressed in the opinion that such an interpretation was not at odds with the provisions of the Treaty but merely a re-interpretation of Article 230.4 in order to secure an effective legal remedy and avoiding possible situations of *dení de justice*. According to Jacobs these objectives could not satisfactorily be secured by the procedure of the preliminary ruling (especially not, one could assume, after the interpretation handed down in the *Lyckeskog* case).

The arguments of Advocate General Jacobs were also employed by the CFI in the case T-177/01, *Jégo-Quéré*,[65] citing not only the general principles of community law concerning the rule of law (notably similar to Articles 6 and 13 of the ECHR) but also the rights laid down in the European Charter of Fundamental Rights that are intended to secure the rule of law (section 47 of the judgment). With these two moves many thought that the ECJ would follow suit and change its longstanding position from the *Plaumann* case.

The ECJ did agree with the Advocate General that the Community is based on the rule of law and that it, against this background, is essential to secure effective legal remedies in the Community legal order (section 38). The principle of an effective legal remedy contained in, for example, the ECHR Articles 6 and 13 forms part of the general principles of law that the Court upholds (section 39). It further stated that the right to bring an action according to Article 230.4 should be interpreted '. . . in the light of the principle of effective judicial protection' (section 44).

[63] Mancini & Keeling *ibid* p 188.

[64] Case C-50/00 *Unión de Pequeños Agricultores v Council of the European Union* [2002] ECR I-6677.

[65] Case T-177/01 *Jégo-Quéré et Cie SA v Commission of the European Communities* [2002] ECR II-2365.

The ECJ, however, held that it would go beyond its jurisdiction were it to examine in each particular case whether there were adequate remedies in the legal order of the Member States (section 43). Neither, held the Court, could it, as proposed by the Advocate General, re-interpret the condition of 'individual concern' of Article 230.4 without going beyond the jurisdiction conferred on it by the Treaty (section 44). Instead the Court stated that it was for the Member States to ensure that adequate remedies should be available for individuals in their domestic legal order (section 41). The Court seemed to recognize that there might be a problem in the present structure but leaves it to the Member States to correct it:

> While it is, admittedly, possible to envisage a system of judicial review of the legality of Community measures of general application different from that established by the founding Treaty and never amended as to its principles, it is for the Member States, if necessary, in accordance with Article 48 EU, to reform the system currently in force'. (section 45)

The argumentation of Advocate General Jacobs, that the Court thus rejected, is very much in line with those of his predecessor Mancini in the *Les Verts* case, where, it should be recalled, the principle of the rule of law was important enough to displace the provisions of the Treaty itself. It is arguably a bolder step to include, as the Court did in *Les Verts*, an institution that is, conspicuously, not mentioned in the Treaty than to re-interpret the meaning of 'individual concern' as the Court declined to do in the *UPA*. The ECJ did, by abstaining from re-interpreting the *Plaumann* doctrine, not follow its reasoning from the *Les Verts* case, namely that 'the principle which defines its mission', ie the securing of the rule of law and judicial protection of individuals would prevail even over the provisions of the Treaty. The ECJ would even seem to hold itself to a rather lower standard than what it requires of national courts when these are faced with problems of judicial protection of claims of individuals based on the Treaty. As an example the ECJ held both in the *Simmenthal II* and C-213/89, *Factortame*[66] cases that:

> . . . any provision . . . which might impair the effectiveness of Community law by withholding from the national court . . . the power to do everything necessary at the moment of its application to set aside national legislative provisions which might prevent, even temporarily, Community rules from having full force and effect are incompatible with those requirements, which are the very essence of Community law.

It seems reasonable to assume that the same reasoning concerning 'the very essence of Community law' could be applied to a case where the individual is trying to assert a right against the Community institutions. Threats to the effectiveness of the rights of individuals may originate from the Community institutions as well as from the Member States. Contrary to this assumption

[66] Case C-213/89 *The Queen v Secretary of State for Transport, ex parte: Factortame Ltd and others* [1990] ECR I-2433.

however, the Court in the *UPA* case seems to take the same position as in the *Lyckeskog* case: claims of individuals should, as far as possible, be dealt with by the national courts, leaving the Court herself pretty much in the position of an international court (although of a peculiar kind) judging over issues referred by organs of the Member States rather than being a constitutional court protecting the rights of individuals.

3 A COMMUNITY (STILL) BASED ON THE RULE OF LAW?

The constitutional character of the Community legal order has been largely explained and justified by reference to the substantial notion of the rule of law. The protection of the rights of the individual has had a central role in the argumentation of the ECJ in this regard. The procedural mechanism for this development has mainly been that of the preliminary ruling but major steps in the constitutionalisation of the Treaties have also been taken within the framework of the action for annulment. The emerging picture can reasonably be said to be one of a supra-national (or more properly supra-statal) constitution built around the empowerment of the European citizens and the rule of law. The procedural canons of Community law cannot be separated from the broader issue of the purposes of the EC which seem to be, from the case law of the ECJ (and from the articles by Pescatore and Mancini), a strengthening of the European individual and the rule of law.

From this, essentially constitutionalist perspective, the safeguarding of the rights of the individual seems to be the most essential function of the preliminary ruling. If EC-law is to be considered as constitutional (and as such having supremacy over Member State law), it is necessary to secure an effective legal remedy against both Member state and Community action. To hold otherwise would either mean that one accepts a power unrestrained by law (and thereby arbitrary) or, as a necessary corollary, that one accords the power of judicial review of the acts of the Community institutions to the courts of the Member States.

The question of access to justice can also be said to be more pressing in the EU than in the (ordinary) state context. The EU does not, as Advocate General Jacobs pointed out in his opinion in the *UPA* case (section 86 of the opinion), have the same democratic mechanisms as do the member states. The moral dialogue between equal citizens that the legislative process should ideally safeguard and express[67] is to a significant degree absent or, at best, imperfect in the EU. It is precisely because of this absence of a genuine European democracy that the ECJ has been not only entitled to but also obliged to take a leading role in developing a constitution for Europe.[68] Admittedly, the position of the EP has been

[67] *Cf* J Waldron *The Dignity of Legislation* (Cambridge, Cambridge University Press, 1999) pp 88–91.

[68] Mancini above, p 612 *f*.

strengthened in several aspects since the days when the ECJ constitutionalised the Treaty, but its powers remain (at its most) those of reaction and veto. Actually, no European institution can take blame or glory for the policy and performance of the EU. There is no way a disenchanted electorate can 'kick the scoundrels out' at elections and this state of affairs constitutes a serious problem of legitimacy for the EU.[69] The fact is that the only available mechanism the European citizens have in order to directly affect the EC presently goes through the ECJ.

A conclusion from the democratic deficit might be that the EC (and the ECJ along with it) is hopelessly left behind the Member States in terms of democratic legitimacy. One can, however, in the spirit of Pescatore, make a case for the EC as a democratic entity with its own legitimacy (not necessarily indirectly mediated through the Member States). The Treaties are, after all, the only body of EC-law that has been adopted by democratic assemblies in their entirety. In several cases they were also adopted after referendums in the Member States and in all cases preceded by lengthy and thorough (and unforced) debate. This is as democratic an origin as one could ever ask for in constitutional law and in this regard at least as good as that of the Member States themselves.

It is beyond dispute that the Treaties gave rise to an institutional system and to legal norms, adopted by these institutions that could not have been generated by the Member States operating on their own. Through the development of the case law of the ECJ, this legal order has further bestowed an important set of rights on the European individuals, strengthening and expanding their possibilities for self-determination. In this sense Community rights have been held to be a species of 'higher law' than the statutes enacted by national Parliaments.[70] It is no exaggeration to hold that these rights have at the same time strengthened the rule of law by requiring both the Member States and the Community institutions to justify their actions within the sphere of EC-law with reference to objective criteria of the common good. These criteria must also, when called for, be explained and defended in legal proceedings. In this sense, the ECJ is, like any constitutional court, the sword and shield of the politically weak, ie those who do not have the ear of the Member State governments or the Commission. The Treaties can thus reasonably be said to be endowed with a moral authority comparable to that of any constitution aspiring to be in conformity with the principles of constitutionalism.

If one combines the democratic origin of the Treaties and the arguments from the substantial rule of law, it is clear that the ECJ, to the extent that it enforces the Treaties both as against the Community institutions and the Member States, is enforcing *both* democracy and the rule of law. Only the ECJ is, in the end, competent to rule on the legality and final interpretation of EC-law precisely because it is the only court specifically created to be the guardian of the Treaty.

[69] *Cf* T Hartley *Constitutional Problems of the European Union* (Hart Publishing, 1999) p 18 *f*.
[70] Mancini & Keeling above p 185.

It alone, among the thousands of European courts, has the composition and resources to conduct reasoning on what actually constitutes the 'common good' within the Community. The ECJ therefore offers the European citizen a possibility of moral dialogue that cannot be achieved in the Member State courts by themselves. This is, in my view, the most compelling argument for the constitutional supremacy of Community law over Member State law.

To cut back on individual access to the ECJ is a dangerous path since, as long as there is no fully fledged European democracy through the EP, it potentially endangers this moral dialogue. The position taken by the ECJ in the *Lyckeskog* and *UPA* cases seem actually to reflect more of a thin or formal notion of the rule of law, more akin to Hobbes' version of the concept than to Locke's moral understanding of the rule of law. The new tendencies that can be detected in the case law of the ECJ are thus not only about procedural matters and technicalities. They call into question the deepest moral foundations of the EC as an autonomous legal order.

The repatriation of the rule of law to the Member States also necessarily means that claims by European individuals based on the same provisions of Community law will, in fact, be governed differently in different Member States thus giving rise to unequal treatment among individuals. It is hard to reconcile the principle of equality, invoked by the court in the *Costa v ENEL* case as being a core characteristic of the constitutional authority of Community law, with its markedly cooler attitude in regard to individual access to the ECJ.

4 CONCLUSION

The ECJ seems to be throwing the ball back to the national courts thus drawing the constitutional circle back to its end—the legal protection of the rights of the individual and, as a consequence, the rule of law are seen primarily as a national concern. It is an inescapable consequence of the position taken by the Court in the *UPA* and *Lyckeskog* cases that considerably fewer cases will actually reach the ECJ. The other cases will be decided, wrongly or correctly, by national courts having neither the resources nor the explicit constitutional mission to secure the objectives of the Treaty. The ECJ can therefore be said to jeopardize the integrity of the Community legal order by abstaining from its fundamental duty according to the rule of law of securing rights and upholding the equality of the European individuals by making sure that any infringement is properly justified according to the common good. Even if no actual harm comes out of the narrow interpretation on individual access to the ECJ, the position of the court risks doing serious damage to the constitutional legitimacy of the EC.

Put in Lockean terms, by refusing to give the European individual an 'appeal on Earth' to the common judge, the ECJ is exposing him to the risk of a power without right and thus opening the gates to the 'appeal to heaven', ie the right to civil disobedience that any person under arbitrary rule is entitled to. By undermining its own fundamental rule of constitutional morality, the ECJ may be said to risk losing its soul, or to sing with the famous lyrics of the rock-group R.E.M., losing its religion.

BIBLIOGRAPHY

Allan, TRS, *Constitutional Justice—A Liberal Theory of the Rule of Law* (Oxford, Oxford University Press, 2001).

Aristotle, 'The Politics' in *The Politics and The Constitution of Athens* (Cambridge, Cambridge University Press, 1996).

Bentham, J, *Of Laws in General* (Athlone Press, 1970).

Cicero, 'The Republic' in *The Republic, The Laws* (Oxford, Oxford University Press, 1998).

Dicey, AV, *Introduction to the Study of the Law of the Constitution* (Liberty Fund, 1982).

Dworkin, R, *Law's Empire* (Harvard University Press, 1986).

Ely, JH, *Democracy and Distrust—A Theory of Judicial Review* (Harvard University Press, 1980).

Hartley, T, *Constitutional Problems of the European Union* (Hart Publishing, 1999).

Hare, R, *Freedom and Reason* (Oxford, Oxford University Press, 1963).

Hampton, J, 'Democracy and the Rule of Law' in I Shapiro (ed) *The Rule of Law—Nomos XXXVI* (New York, New York University Press, 1994) pp 13–44.

Harrington, J, 'The Commonwealth of Oceana' in *The Commonwealth of Oceana and A System of Politics* (Cambridge, Cambridge University Press, [1656] 1992).

Hart, HLA, *Essays in Jurisprudence and Philosophy* (Oxford, Oxford University Press, 1983).

Hobbes, T, *Leviathan* (Cambridge, Cambridge University Press, [1651] 1991).

Kay, RS, 'American Constitutionalism' in L Alexander (ed) *Constitutionalism—Philosophical Foundations* (Cambridge, Cambridge University Press, 1998).

Kelsen, H, *Introduction to the Problems of Legal Theory* (Oxford, Oxford University Press, 1992).

Locke, J, *Two Treatsies of Government* (Cambridge, Cambridge University Press, [1651] 1988).

Mancini, F, 'The Making of a Constitution for Europe' (1989) *Common Market Law Review* pp 595–614.

——and Keeling, D, 'Democracy and the European Court of Justice' (1994) *The Modern Law Review* pp 175–90.

Pescatore, P, 'The Doctrine of "Direct Effect": An Infant Disease of Community Law' (1983) *Eureopan Law Review* pp 155–77.

Rabinowicz, W, *Universalizability—A study in Morals and Metaphysics* (Reidel Publishing Company, 1979).

Tamanaha, BZ, *On the Rule of Law—History, Politics, Theory* (Cambridge, Cambridge University Press, 2004).

Temple Lang, J, 'The Duties of National Courts under Community Constitutional Law' (1997) *European Law Review* pp 3–18.

de Tocqueville, A, *Democracy in America* (Fontana Press, [1850] 1969).
Waldron, J, *The Dignity of Legislation* (Cambridge, Cambridge University Press, 1999).
Zuckert, MP, 'Hobbes Locke, and the Problem of the Rule of Law' in I Shapiro (ed) *The Rule of Law—Nomos XXXVI* (New York, New York University Press, 1994).

11

Who Wags Who? The EU and the Use of Military Force in a Global Context

INGER ÖSTERDAHL[1]

ABSTRACT

The developing security and defence policy of the EU raises numerous issues of international law as well as issues of EU law and domestic law of the Member States. This article looks at the evolving relationship between the EU as a regional organisation with military ambitions and the UN as the global organisation with the exclusive right to decide on the international use of force.

The strengthening and clarifying EU policy and capability in the field of security and defence may be seen as a challenge to the weakening global grip on international peace and security of the UN. Ultimately, an active and capable EU may come to be regarded as an alternative to the UN both in a factual and then in a normative sense, which would alter the hierarchical relationship hitherto reigning between the organisations.

A militarily strengthened EU, however, not only constitutes a challenge to the UN. If the two organisations manage to cooperate in the field of international security, the EU may contribute to strengthening the UN as well. Under any circumstances a normative shift seems to be under way in the global-regional relationship due to changing relations of political and military force on the ground.

1. INTRODUCTION

The growth in strength of regional organisations may weaken the centralised monopoly on the use of international military force of the UN Security Council.

[1] Inger Österdahl is Professor of Public International Law at the University of Uppsala. She is currently pursuing a research project entitled 'Collective or Individual Security? The Transformation of the UN Collective Security System'. Recent publications include 'The Exception as the Rule. Lawmaking on Force and Human Rights by the UN Security Council', (2005) *Journal of Conflict and Security Law* and 'Preach What You Practice. The Security Council and the Legalisation ex post facto of the Unilateral Use of Force', (2005) *Nordic Journal of International Law*.

In this chapter, the EU is regarded as an increasingly significant regional military actor whose far-reaching ambitions may potentially challenge the current system of collective security under the UN Charter. The chapter will look at the security and defence policy from the inside, from the European perspective—and from the outside, from the perspective of the global international legal system.

The emphasis of the article will be on the normative question of who may legitimately decide on the use of international military force. This question will be considered from the point of view of the EU and from the UN. The answer to the question may be the same or may differ depending on whose perspective is applied. The EU is not entirely clear as to its relationship to the UN Security Council and the position of the UN is not entirely unambiguous either. In recent efforts at reforming the UN, there are signs that regional organisations have been given a more important and perhaps more independent role in the global collective security system.

The central question is whether the EU will take advantage of the apparent shift in the power relationship between itself and the UN in order to act without Security Council authorisation when necessary and what effect such a policy on the part of the EU will have on the legal monopoly, until now, on decision-making by the Security Council. A number of relevant issues will have to be left out of the discussion. The role of NATO and other important regional organisations closely related to the EU will not be dealt with. The same limitation applies to the transatlantic link and the role of Russia in relation to the EU. The overall political or military setting, regionally or globally, of the European Security and Defence Policy (ESDP) will not be analysed, nor will the actual development of the EU Rapid Reaction Force on the ground or the operations already undertaken under the ESDP. Suffice it to say that since 2003 the EU has undertaken military, police, rule of law, monitoring and other kinds of missions to the former Yugoslav Republic of Macedonia, the Democratic Republic of Congo, Bosnia and Herzegovina, Georgia, Iraq, Sudan and Aceh.[2]

With respect to the relationship between the EU and the UN Security Council there will be no detailed examination of the contents of Chapter VIII on regional arrangements in the UN Charter, and the issue whether or not the EU should be

[2] For an overview see http://ue.eu.int/cms3_fo/showPage.asp?lang=en&id=268&mode=g&name= (last visited 21.11.05). For further background information on the ESDP, see for instance TC Salmon and AJK Shepherd (eds), *Toward a European Army. A Military Power in the Making?* (Lynne Rienner Publishers, Boulder and London, 2003); M Holland (ed), *Common Foreign and Security Policy,* 2nd edn (London and New York, Continuum, 2004); P Bonnén, *Towards a Common European Security and Defence Policy. The Ways and Means of Making It a Reality* (Münster, Hamburg and London, Lit Verlag, 2003); N Gnesotto (ed), *EU Security and Defence Policy. The First Five Years (1999–2004)* (Institute for Security Studies, European Union, Paris, 2004); M Kerttunen, T Koivula & T Jeppsson, *EU Battlegroups. Theory and Development in the Light of Finnish-Swedish Co-operation* Series 2, Research Reports No 30 (National Defence College, Department of Strategic and Defence Studies, Helsinki, 2005); K von Wogau (ed), *The Path to European Defence* (Antwerpen and Apeldoorn, Maklu Publishers, 2004); J Howorth & JTS Keeler, *Defending Europe. The EU, NATO and the Quest for European Autonomy* (New York and Houndmills, Basingstoke, Palgrave MacMillan, 2003).

considered a regional arrangement will be left aside. There will be no discussion on the substantive international law on the use of force nor on the right to self-defence. Thus, there will be no analysis of the right to unilateral use of force on the part of organisations or of individual states and the possible development of the law in that respect.

There will be no investigation of the opinions of the individual Member States on the issue of the legality or legitimacy of the unilateral use of force, on the part of the EU or on the part of the Member States themselves. Such opinions are, of course, important for the future development of the ESDP, but this article focuses on the policy of the EU as such. Also, and along the same lines there will be no analysis of the national defence policies of the members of the EU.

Thus the focus of this article is normative and institutional.

The layout of the article will be as follows. First, the mandate of the EU under the ESDP will be examined. Questions such as for what purposes, how and where the EU may act militarily will be posed. The so called solidarity clause in the draft Treaty on a Constitution for Europe (draft TCE) will be included in the discussion as an indication of possible future developments of the security and defence cooperation in relation to new security threats.[3] The EU Security Strategy of 2003 will be studied in order to find complementary information relating to the mandate of the EU in defence matters and to the purposes of the ESDP.[4]

Secondly, the official line of the EU as concerns the relationship between the EU and the UN Security Council as decision-maker on the use of international force will be extracted, to the extent possible, from the treaties and the EU Security Strategy.

Thirdly, the perspective of the UN will be applied to the use of international force by the EU. Without going into details, the schematic relationship of authority between the UN Security Council and regional security organisations under the UN Charter will be presented. This presentation will be supplemented and to a certain extent made more relative by the introduction of the recent reform discussions in the UN and the reports and other official documents that these discussions have generated. The greater emphasis on regional organisations and the emerging doctrine on the 'responsibility to protect' may affect the absolute concept hitherto of the role of the Security Council inherent in the UN Charter.

[3] Draft Treaty Establishing a Constitution for Europe (draft TCE), Official Journal of the European Union C 310/01, 16 Dec 2004; europa.eu.int/eur-lex/lex/JOHtml.do?uri=OJ:C:2004:310:SOM:EN:HTML (last visited 21.11.05).

[4] *A Secure Europe in a Better World*, European Security Strategy, Brussels, 12 Dec 2003; ue.eu.int/uedocs/cmsUpload/78367.pdf (last visited 21.11.05). On the European Security Strategy, see for instance S Biscop, *The European Security Strategy. A Global Agenda for Positive Power* (Ashgate, Aldershot and Burlington, VT, 2005); JY Haine, 'The Union Inaugural Address' in J Pilegaard (ed), *The Politics of European Security, Danish Institute for International Studies* (Copenhagen, 2004) 39–53; F Heisbourg, 'The 'European Security Strategy' is not a security strategy' in S Everts *et al*, *A European Way of War* (London, Centre for European Reform, 2004) 27–39.

Fourthly, there will be a summary of the main findings of the article together with a conclusion on the degree of normative consolidation of the EU as a global military actor.

2. THE DEFENCE MANDATE OF THE EU

2.1 The Goals

Among the stated objectives of the Common Foreign and Security Policy in the Treaty on European Union (TEU), those that are most relevant for a future defence policy are the following.[5]

Firstly, the objective to safeguard the common values, fundamental interests, independence and integrity of the EU in conformity with the principles of the UN Charter.[6] Secondly, the objective to strengthen the security of the EU in every way.[7] Thirdly, to preserve peace and strengthen international security, in accordance with the principles of the UN Charter, as well as the principles of the Helsinki Final Act and the objectives of the Paris Charter, including those on external borders.[8] And fourthly, to develop and consolidate democracy and the rule of law, and respect for human rights and fundamental freedoms.[9] As to the contents of the foreign and security policy, it is stated in the TEU that this policy shall include all questions relating to the security of the Union, including the progressive framing of a common defence policy, which might lead to a common defence, should the European Council so decide.[10]

It should be noted that the important objective to consolidate and support democracy was given a more prominent position in the list of objectives of the external action of the EU in the TCE than in the corresponding list in the TEU. In the draft TCE the objective of supporting democracy was listed second among the objectives—after safeguarding the values, fundamental interests, security, independence and integrity of the EU, but before preserving peace, preventing conflicts and strengthening international security.

In the TEU the objective of supporting democracy is listed fourth and last of the objectives of the Common Foreign and Security Policy. The upgrading of democracy as an objective of the foreign policy of the EU in the draft TCE may be due more to drafting technicalities and to the fact that the listed objectives

[5] Consolidated version of the Treaty on European Union (TEU) (Official Journal C 325/5 of 24 Dec 2002; europa.eu.int/eur-lex/lex/en/treaties/dat/12002M/pdf/12002M_EN.pdf (last visited 21.11.05).

[6] TEU Art 11(1).

[7] TEU Art 11(1).

[8] TEU Art 11(1). Conference on Security and Co-operation in Europe Final Act, 1 Aug 1975 (www.osce.org/documents/mcs/1975/08/4044/_en.pdf (last visited 21.11.05)); Charter of Paris for a New Europe, 19–21 Nov 1990 (www.osce.org/documents/mcs/1990/11/4045/_en.pdf (last visited 21.11.05)).

[9] TEU Art 11(1).

[10] TEU Art 17(1).

cover all of the external actions of the EU and not only the foreign, security and defence policy, than to a conscious wish to emphasise the importance of spreading democracy. In either case, however, the draft TCE probably mirrors the real priorities better than the TEU as far as the real relevance is concerned of democracy, rule of law and respect for human rights in the security and defence policy of the EU.[11]

The draft TCE is a sign of where the development is going, and this development will continue irrespective of whether there is a formal revision of the TEU or not. From a legal point of view many developments can still take place within the current framework of the text of the TEU before the limits of the treaty are reached.

An important objective of the Common (sic!) Security and Defence Policy in the draft TCE, which is only indirectly added, is the objective of fighting terrorism.[12] When the Common Security and Defence Policy is operationalised, the draft TCE states that the tasks involved may contribute to the fight against terrorism, including supporting third countries in combating terrorism in their territories.[13] Again, this probably reflects what is already taking place, an assumption supported by the European Security Strategy of 2003 in which terrorism is singled out as one of five key threats to European security.[14] There is no legal obstacle in the TEU to fighting terrorism within the framework of the current Common Foreign and Security Policy. The fact that terrorism is taken up among the common security and defence issues, even if indirectly, illustrates that the new security threats are decidedly making their way into the very definition of what security and defence policy is all about.[15]

One entirely new and interesting feature in the draft TCE which may or may not be a reflection of current realities was the proposed collective defence clause which would add to the already existing objectives the objective of being an organisation for the mutual defence of the members. The draft TCE stated that if a Member State is a victim of armed aggression on its territory, the other Member States shall have towards it an obligation of aid and assistance by all the means in their power, in accordance with Article 51 of the UN Charter.[16] Due to protests from, among others, Sweden, the addition was made that this shall not prejudice the specific character of the security and defence policy of

[11] This assumption is supported by the following statement, among others, in *A Secure Europe in a Better World*, above n 4, s II. Strategic Objectives: 'The quality of international society depends on the quality of the governments that are its foundation. The best protection for our security is a world of well-governed democratic states. Spreading good governance, supporting social and political reform, dealing with corruption and abuse of power, establishing the rule of law and protecting human rights are the best means of strengthening the international order.'

[12] Pt III, Title V, Ch II, s 2, Art III-309(1) draft TCE.

[13] Art III-309(1) draft TCE.

[14] *A Secure Europe in a Better World*, above n 4, s I. The Security Environment: Global Challenges and Key Threats.

[15] *Cf* A Missiroli (ed), *Disasters, Diseases, Disruptions: a new D-drive for the EU*, Chaillot Paper No 83 (Institute for Security Studies, European Union, Paris, Sep 2005).

[16] Art I-41(7) draft TCE.

certain Member States, namely the neutral ones.[17] Many members are already tied together by mutual defence obligations either through the NATO treaty or through the WEU treaty so in that sense the new clause in the draft TCE was a reflection of the reality.[18] Also, the actual obligation was to provide aid and assistance by all the means in one's power, which would soften the actual defence obligations of the Member States. Whether this clause is also an indication of where the development is going is more uncertain, but it is not impossible that a situation of a de facto union of collective defence will arise without the implicit political or moral obligations being legalised in Treaty form.

2.2 The Actions

Having looked at the objectives of the EU in the fields of foreign security and defence, we will now turn to what action the EU plans to take in order to realise its objectives.

The EU is supposed to be able to undertake a broad range of military operations of different kinds and intensity under its foreign and security policy, including its security and defence policy. The so called Petersberg tasks, which include all kinds of military action that the EU is supposed to take, are listed in the TEU under the general title of Provisions on a Common Foreign and Security Policy.[19]

The Petersberg tasks thus range from humanitarian and rescue tasks to peace-keeping tasks and tasks of combat forces in crisis management, including peace-making.[20] Most interesting to note, for the purposes of this article, is that the tasks include active military fighting on the part of the troops commanded by the EU.

Typically, it is the last form of forcible military action—peace-making—which would require authorisation from the UN Security Council. The term peace-*making* implies an active forcible military effort to make peace, not merely to observe a peaceful situation already achieved by others.

In contrast, operations of a peace-*keeping* nature build on the consent of the representatives of the state where the peace-keeping operation is supposed to be carried out and is thus, by definition, built on a voluntary agreement which makes prior authorisation by the UN Security Council superfluous, at least from a strictly legal point of view.

The boundary between forcible and non-forcible action, however, is not crystal clear either, in theory or in practice. Peace-keeping operations today often

[17] Art I-41(7) draft TCE.

[18] North Atlantic Treaty, 4 Apr 1949 (http://www.nato.int/docu/basictxt/treaty.htm (last visited 21.11.05)); the Brussels Treaty, 17 Mar 1948, modified by the Paris Agreements, 23 Oct 1954 (www.weu.int (last visited 21.11.05)).

[19] Art 17(2) TEU. Western European Council of Ministers, Petersberg Declaration, Bonn 19 June 1992 (www.weu.int/documents/920619peten.pdf (last visited 21.11.05)).

[20] Art 17(2) TEU.

consist of a mixture of forcible measures and measures agreed to by the parties concerned. (They also consist of a mixture of civil and military action.) Moreover, what was originally intended as a pure peace-keeping operation may in time partly develop into a peace-making operation. For political as well as legal reasons it may thus be an advantage to secure Security Council backing of a peace-keeping operation under all circumstances.

Looked upon strictly from the point of view of legal principle, the EU is free to undertake whatever external military action it wishes (although restricted by the law of war) as long as the action is based on the consent of the representatives of the state receiving the troops. On the other hand, if the military action is forcible, it will always need authorisation from the Security Council, for whatever purpose the operation is undertaken.

Looking at the military actions undertaken so far under the ESDP they have all been part of peace-keeping operations and moreover they have all been authorised by the UN Security Council. These are most likely typical examples of the kind of military action to be expected from the EU, situated at the less intense end of the Petersberg tasks.

As far as the objective of developing democracy and human rights is concerned within the framework of the Common Foreign and Security Policy, one may wonder what means the EU might consider possible in order to reach that goal. As stated by the EU in the European Security Strategy, 'the integration of acceding states increases our security but also brings the EU closer to troubled areas'.[21]

The task of the EU, according to the Security Strategy, is to promote a ring of well- governed countries to the East of the European Union and on the borders of the Mediterranean.[22] The question is whether the EU would ever consider taking forcible military action in order to contribute to the development and consolidation of democracy and human rights protection in this ring of countries, ie humanitarian intervention or even regime change intervention. The EU military action in the Balkans and some Member States' humanitarian intervention in Kosovo via NATO—strongly supported by those Member States who did not participate—seems to indicate that at least the EU would be prepared to consider humanitarian intervention even if perhaps not outright regime change intervention, but that remains to be seen.[23]

[21] *A Secure Europe in a Better World*, above n 4, s II.

[22] *A Secure Europe in a Better World*, above n 4, s II. *Cf* R Dannreuther (ed), *European Union Foreign and Security Policy. Towards a Neighbourhood Strategy* (London, New York, Routledge, 2004).

[23] It also remains to be seen whether the EU will wish to intervene militarily in a third state in order to combat terrorist activities in the territory of the third state either before or after the terrorist activities have made themselves felt in the EU, perhaps invoking the right of self-defence (on the topical issue of prevention *cf A Secure Europe in a Better World*, above n 4, s II. Strategic Objectives: 'Our traditional concept of self-defence—up to and including the Cold War—was based on the threat of invasion. With the new threats, the first line of defence will often be abroad. The new threats are dynamic. The risks of proliferation grow over time; left alone, terrorist networks will become ever more dangerous . . . This implies that we should be ready to act before a crisis occurs. Conflict prevention and threat prevention cannot start too early').

In the draft TCE the kinds of tasks enumerated under the rubric of the Common Security and Defence Policy are more numerous than in the TEU, but the difference of legal principle between peace-keeping and peace-making or between non-forcible and forcible action in public international law remains.

The draft TCE states that the Common Security and Defence Policy is intended to provide the EU with an operational capacity.[24] Of the tasks enumerated in the draft TCE, we recognise some whereas several are new. It should be noted that, as in the case of the TEU, the draft Treaty states that the tasks 'shall include' the following actions. This formulation does not exclude other kinds of action—it rather exemplifies what actions may be taken. On the other hand, the formulation stipulates what action may be taken as a miminum.

Thus under the draft TCE, the military operations shall include joint disarmament operations, humanitarian and rescue tasks, military advice and assistance tasks, conflict prevention and peace-keeping tasks, tasks of combat forces in crisis management, including peace-making and post-conflict stabilisation.[25]

We can see that security and defence policy is considerably developed and refined under the draft TCE. The situations in which the EU will most likely risk becoming involved in active military fighting are in tasks of combat forces in crisis management, including peace-making and post-conflict stabilisation. Also, in joint disarmament operations there would seem to be a risk of active military engagement, depending on how much coercion must be applied in order to achieve the disarmament. In peace-keeping as well, as noted earlier, there is a risk that the situation on the ground may change so that the troops find themselves becoming involved in more active fighting than was originally intended. Also, large peace operations often include both forcible and non-forcible elements from the outset.

Judging by the draft TCE, the EU envisages an expanding military repertory and will take the risk of becoming more involved in military combat, whether it had intended to or not. The interesting question, from the point of view of the relation of the EU to the UN collective security system, is how the EU will act if it wishes to take forcible military action (or for that matter is compelled to take forcible action irrespective of its own original intention), but the UN Security Council has not or obviously will not be able to agree on a resolution authorising such action.

As in the case of the solidarity clause proposed in the draft TCE, with respect to the new tasks added to the existing list in the TEU in the field of the security and defence policy, it would in principle be possible to undertake them all within the framework of the broad and general text of the current TEU.[26]

Considering the politically sensitive nature of the Common Security and Defence Policy and considering also the real possibility of loss of life in active

[24] Art I-41 draft TCE.
[25] Art III-309(1) draft TCE.
[26] Art 17(2) TEU.

combat and the resulting issues such as the need for a democratic anchorage of the EU security and defence policy, there are likely to be limits to how far the EU is prepared to go in the direction of the draft TCE without a formal Treaty amendment.[27]

2.3 The Reach

The operations already undertaken by the EU under the ESDP show that the EU does not consider itself limited to taking action in its immediate geographical neighbourhood.[28] It is no concidence that the most important operations so far have been carried out in the Balkans. It is natural that the closest area geographically speaking is the most immediate concern to the EU in particular where, as in the Balkans, bloody wars and persecution of civilians are raging or have recently been raging. Even in an era of globalisation, as the European Security Strategy states, geography is still important and it is in the European interest that countries on its borders are well-governed.[29]

As a sign of the importance that the EU attaches to its neighbourhood, it is stated in the European Security Strategy, referring to the Balkans, that the credibility of the EU foreign policy depends on the consolidation of the EU's achievements there.[30] The EU itself places high stakes on its capability to manage the situation in the Balkans.

In contrast to the view that it is reasonable to expect the EU to be particularly concerned with security issues on its borders, however, some argue that the EU engages primarily in matters relevant to global security not related to selfish domestic motives.[31]

Neither in the TEU nor in the draft TCE is there any hint of any geographical limits to the freedom of action of the EU. Perhaps the most telling positive statement of the global concerns of the EU is the one in the European Security Strategy that 'Europe should be ready to share in the responsibility for global security and in building a better world.'[32]

The only geographical limitation is the one mentioned in the draft TCE that the EU may undertake action under the Common Security and Defence Policy *outside* the EU, which probably excludes such action within the EU.[33]

[27] *Cf* W Wagner, *The Democratic Legitimacy of European Security and Defence Policy* Occasional Paper No 57 (Institute for Security Studies, European Union, Paris, Apr 2005). See also I Ioannides, *The European Rapid Reaction Force: Implications for Democratic Accountability* Paper 24 (Bonn International Center for Conversion, Bonn, 2002); and G Aybet, *A European Security Architecture after the Cold War. Questions of Legitimacy* (Houndmills, Basingstoke, MacMillan Press, 2000).

[28] *Cf* above n 2.

[29] *A Secure Europe in a Better World*, above n 4, s II.

[30] *Ibid*.

[31] *Cf* M Ortega, *Military Intervention and the European Union* Chaillot Paper No 45 (Institute for Security Studies, Western European Union, Paris, March 2001).

[32] *A Secure Europe in a Better World*, above n 4, Introduction.

[33] Art I-41(1) draft TCE.

The European Security Strategy states that in an era of globalisation, distant threats may be as much of a concern as those that are near at hand.[34] Nuclear activities in North Korea, nuclear risks in South Asia, and proliferation in the Middle East are all of concern to Europe.[35] Terrorists and criminals are now able to operate worldwide, the European Security Strategy continues: their activities in central or south-east Asia may be a threat to European countries or their citizens.[36] One may note that the European Security Strategy makes a distinction, significant or not, between terrorists on the one hand and criminals on the other.

Finally, on the geographic reach of the concerns of the EU, the European Security Strategy states that global communication increases awareness in Europe of regional conflicts or humanitarian tragedies anywhere in the world.[37] Such awareness on the part of people in general may create political pressure within the EU in such a way as to cause the EU to intervene far away.

It is obviously not only by military means that the EU may intervene abroad under its Common Foreign and Security Policy or its European/Common Security and Defence Policy. We have already seen that the EU has set itself a broad range of tasks including both civilian, non-forcible military action and forcible military action.[38] Different forms of military intervention, however, pose the most difficult legal problems and probably also the strongest political concerns.

2.4 The Solidarity Clause

An invention in the draft TCE that will be considered here is the introduction of a so- called 'solidarity clause' which was not intended for defence purposes in a narrow sense.[39] The solidarity clause is included in the discussion here because it illustrates the new kinds of security threats that the EU has to respond to.

The solidarity clause is also included because it is related to the defence policy in a broader sense and in that context the solidarity clause is interesting because it does not concern the defence of the EU against external threats or against threats originating from states, but it concerns mutual defence or mutual assistance against internal threats originating from non-state actors, ie terrorists.[40] The solidarity clause also ties together the security and defence policy,

[34] *A Secure Europe in a Better World*, above n 4, s II.
[35] *Ibid.*
[36] *Ibid.*
[37] *Ibid.*
[38] *Cf* above n 20.
[39] Arts I-43 and III-329 draft TCE.
[40] *Cf* the Declaration by the European Council on the Contribution of the CFSP, including the ESDP, to the Fight Against Terrorism, adopted at the Seville European Council 21 and 22 June 2002 and included in the Presidency Conclusions as Annex V (ue.eu.int/ueDocs/newsWord/en/ec/72638.doc) (last visited 18.11.05).

external and internal, with the Justice and Home Affairs policy.[41] If it is ever put into action, the solidarity clause implies that the Union and its Member States shall act jointly in a spirit of solidarity if a Member State is the object of a terrorist attack or the victim of a natural or man-made disaster.[42]

Under the solidarity clause the Union shall mobilise all the instruments at its disposal, including the military resources made available by the Member States.[43] This illustrates the connection of the solidarity clause to the defence policy. The Union and the Member States shall act in order to prevent the terrorist threat in the Member States, protect democratic institutions and the civilian population from attacks, and assist a Member State in its territory, at the request of its political authorities, in the event of a terrorist attack.[44] Also, with respect to disasters, the Union and the Member States shall assist a Member State in its territory, at the request of its political authorities, in the event of a natural or man-made disaster.[45]

It is important to note that in the context of the 'domestic' solidarity clause, involving, ultimately, different forms of outside interference (even if benevolent) in the countries struck by terrorist attacks or disasters, it was emphasised in the draft TCE that there must be a request from the political authorities in the country concerned before the EU and the other Member States may assist the affected state in its territory. This would seem to rule out forceful humanitarian interventions within the EU. Looking at the Petersberg tasks on the other hand, which include humanitarian and rescue tasks intended to be carried out outside the EU territory, there is no mention of request or consent of the political authorities in the states concerned. It can be noted that on the subject of the Common Security and Defence Policy it was specified in the draft TCE that the civil and military assets placed at the disposal of the EU under the Common Security and Defence Policy may be used on missions *outside* the EU.[46] This does not rule out the use of Common Security and Defence Policy assets inside the EU, but seems to constitute a strong indication that external security and defence is one thing and internal security and defence is another.

It seems possible that the kind of rescue action envisaged by the solidarity clause could be taken today, although according to the TEU this kind of action is currently only intended for use outside the EU territory. Provided the Member States consent to being helped in their territories there would seem to be no bar to the them acting jointly with the EU to assist each other in case of disasters or

[41] It is noted that in the European Security Strategy there is a crucial need for better co-ordination of external action and Justice and Home Affairs policies in the fight both against terrorism and organised crime (*A Secure Europe in a Better World*, above n 4, s III).

[42] Art I-43(1) draft TCE. One may wonder whether disturbances such as those in the French suburbs in Oct/Nov 2005 would count as a man-made disaster which would trigger the solidarity clause, or if they would perhaps be regarded as terrorist attacks.

[43] Art I-43(1) draft TCE.

[44] Art I-43(1)(a) draft TCE.

[45] Art I-43(1)(b) draft TCE.

[46] Art I-41(1) draft TCE.

terrorist attacks. If questions arise concerning the competence of the EU in the field of 'domestic' rescue action the Member States may always cooperate on their own outside the EU framework.

The handling of purely domestic terrorism, however, may be a more sensitive political issue than that of international terrorism. This may make the EU Member States more reluctant to accept help from other states, even if the other states are also EU Member States, and help in particular from the EU tends to imply that it is entitled to interfere in this potentially sensitive area.

3. DOES THE EU NEED UN SECURITY COUNCIL AUTHORISATION?

As has been pointed out several times, for the purposes of this article the crucial moment arrives when the EU wishes to undertake forcible military action but does not receive authorization from the UN Security Council for such an operation. It might be a humanitarian intervention for instance, like the NATO intervention in Kosovo in 1999, or an intervention to combat terrorism or organised crime originating from the territory of a foreign state, a kind of forcible support to such third countries that are neither able nor willing to combat terrorism or organised crime themselves.

What do the official documents show as to the attitude of the EU toward the use of military force in cases where authorisation by the UN Security Council would be a prerequisite under the UN Charter? They all show a certain ambiguity as to the exact relation of authority between the EU and the UN Security Council.

In the TEU the loyalty of the EU toward the principles of the UN Charter is emphasised twice in the context where the objectives of the Common Foreign and Security Policy are enumerated.[47] It is the objective of the Common Foreign and Security Policy to safeguard the common values etc of the EU 'in conformity with the principles of the United Nations Charter' and to preserve peace and strengthen international security 'in accordance with the principles of the United Nations Charter'.[48]

It must be made clear that the EU is not bound by the UN Charter since it is not a party to the Treaty (nor is the EC).[49] The EU is bound, however, by the substantive contents of the UN Charter in so far as the latter has developed into customary international law, as in the case of the prohibition on the threat or

[47] Art 11(1) TEU. *Cf* above n 6 and 8.

[48] Art 11(1) TEU.

[49] *Cf mutatis mutandis*, *Ahmed Ali Yusuf et al v Council of the European Union and Commission of the European Communities*, Case T-306/01, Judgment of the Court of First Instance, 21 Sep 2005, para 242. HG Schermers & N Blokker, *International Institutional Law. Unity Within Diversity* 4th rev edn, (The Hague, London, Boston, Martinus Nijhoff Publishers, 2003), p 1003 § 1580, however, argue that since decisions of the UN Security Council can bind all UN member states they will be binding on all organisations formed by UN Member States.

use of military force.[50] The EU is also bound by the contents of the UN Charter in so far as the EU has taken over the competence of its Member States in the area concerned—like the EC in the field of foreign trade[51]—but such a transference of powers to the EU in the field of security and defence policy has not taken place.

The decision-making rules in Chapter VII of the UN Charter as to military enforcement measures indirectly conferring a monopoly on the use of international force on the Security Council, do not make up part of customary international law and nor does the rule in Chapter V that the Security Council holds the primary responsibility for the maintenance of international peace and security.[52] Nevertheless, the other aspect of this monopoly on the use of international force on the part of the UN Security Council is the prohibition on the use of force in Article 2(4) of the UN Charter in Chapter I entitled 'purposes and principles', directed it is true to 'All Members [of the UN]' but generally considered to have developed into customary international law (and even *jus cogens*) binding on all including the EU.

Irrespective of the question of whether the EU is formally bound by the UN Charter or not, or for that matter the question whether all or parts of the UN Charter on the use of force have developed into customary law, the discussion in this section concerns the views of the EU as to whether it will unconditionally follow the UN Charter or whether under special circumstances it will allow itself to deviate from the Charter as concerns the correct locus of decision-making on the use of international force.

In a particular case the EU may choose to subordinate itself or not to the UN in the field of international peace and security. This is partly a legal issue, but also, and perhaps mostly, a political issue which in time may effect the development of international law.

The formulations used in the TEU where the EU pledges allegiance to the principles of the UN Charter on the one hand, are witness to a strong loyalty to the UN Charter on the part of the EU which would be natural considering the UN-friendly climate still reigning in Europe at large. According to the TEU, the objectives of the Common Foreign and Security Policy shall be to safeguard the common values, fundamental interests etc of the Union *in conformity with* the principles of the UN Charter.[53] Furthermore, one objective of the Common Foreign and Security Policy shall be to preserve peace and strengthen

[50] On the application of international law to international organisations, *cf* Schermers & Blokker, above n 49, pp 994–1004 §§1572–1581. On the legal effect of international law in EU law in particular, *cf*, for instance, P Eeckhout, *External Relations of the European Union. Legal and Constitutional Foundation* (Oxford, New York, Oxford University Press, 2004), ch 9.

[51] *Cf Ahmed Ali Yusuf et al v Council of the European Union and Commission of the European Communities*, Case T-306/01, Judgment of the Court of First Instance, 21 Sep 2005, paras 252, 253; *International Fruit Company v Produktschap voor Groenten en Fruit*, Cases 21–24/72, Judgment of 12 Dec 1972, [1972] European Court Reports 1219.

[52] *Cf mutatis mutandis* DW Greig, 'Self-Defence and the Security Council: What Does Article 51 Require?' (1991) (40) *International and Comparative Law Quarterly* 366–402.

[53] Art 11(1) TEU.

international security *in accordance with* the principles of the UN Charter.[54] This sounds as if the EU intends to follow the UN Charter.

On the other hand, the term 'principle' (of the UN Charter) hints that it may not be the actual rules contained in the UN Charter which the EU will necessarily follow (either it is legally bound to or not: see above) but the principles which may be extracted from the Charter and which may be equivalent or not to the rules given in the actual articles of the Charter. In all circumstances, the principles of the UN Charter seem to be something other than and separate from the UN Charter itself.

It may be that the drafters of the TEU (and of the draft TCE) used the term 'principles of the UN Charter' when they described what the EU would follow because, in line with what was said earlier, since the EU cannot be bound by the Charter the EU can only commit itself to follow the principles inherent in the Charter. If so, it could be that the statements in the TEU that the EU will act in conformity with the principles of the UN Charter is the strongest way the EU can express its intention to abide by the Charter. In this chapter, however, it is presumed instead that the choice of terms does not depend on a desire on the part of the EU to commit itself as strongly as possible, but rather to maintain some freedom of action.

If the EU wished to commit itself strongly to the UN Charter it could, theoretically, have included in the TEU a passage implicitly or explicitly confirming Chapter VIII in the UN Charter on regional arrangements. The TEU could then have stated something to the effect that 'no military enforcement action shall be taken without the authorisation of the Security Council'.[55] Regardless of whether it might be desirable, it is unrealistic to think that the EU would ever circumscribe its own freedom of action in this way.

Again, it could be that the choice of the formulation 'principles of the UN Charter' hints at Chapter I of the UN Charter, mentioned earlier, entitled 'Purposes and principles'. The principles of the organisation are contained in Article 2 includings some general substantive rules of behaviour for all member states, among others, the prohibition on the threat or use of force in paragraph 4.

It is unlikely, however, that the term 'principles of the UN Charter' in the TEU would implicitly refer to one specific Article in the UN Charter. It is more likely that the term 'principle' is used in a more general and unspecific sense.

In any case it must be presumed that it is the substantive content of the UN Charter which is alluded to by 'principles of the UN Charter', particularly if one interprets this formulation as a way of maintaining scope for manoeuvre for the EU as to what means it might use to realise the objectives of the Common Foreign and Security Policy or the ESDP. Otherwise, the EU would also subscribe to the procedural rules contained in the UN Charter for instance on the decision-making in the field of international security, which would mean the EU

[55] Art 53(1) of the UN Charter.
[54] Art 11(1) TEU.

accepting that the Security Council keeps an absolute monopoly on the use of international force, at least in principle.

The normative answers or the result that the application of the vague and general and to a certain extent self-contradictory principles of the UN Charter would generate—whatever content is intended—is often far from obvious when applied to a particular situation. Thus the degree of predictability inherent in the principles of the UN Charter is rather small. From the point of view of the UN Member States or other relevant actors like the EU, the prescriptive content of the principles of the UN Charter (as well as of the Charter text itself) is consequently also low.

From this it follows that the EU, or any other comparable organisation or state, still retains a large measure of freedom of action even if it subscribes to the principles of the UN Charter. Paradoxically in this context, the prohibition of the international use of force, however, is relatively clear even as a principle of the UN Charter.

Finally, on the subject of the principles of the UN Charter referred to in the TEU, it could be asked whether they say anything as to the means that may be used in order to achieve the goals of the UN or whether the principles only contain substantive higher norms or values to be striven for, leaving aside the question of ways and means. This is not clear, of course, from the text of the TEU and it could be argued that the prohibition on the use of international force is both a substantive norm and a statement about the means that may or may not be used in order to achieve the ultimate purposes of the UN.

In the European Security Strategy there is no lack of references to the UN and to the cooperation between the EU and the UN. As to the hierarchical relationship between the two organisations in the field of international peace and security, if the worst comes to the worst, the European Security Strategy is as enigmatic as the TEU.

According to the European Security Strategy, the EU strives to strengthen the UN and to equip it to fulfil its responsibilities and to act effectively.[56] Also, on policy implications, the European Security Strategy states that the EU should support the UN as it responds to threats to international peace and security.[57] The EU would seem to be an attractive and reliable partner to the UN as the EU is both willing and able to contribute resources to peace-keeping operations, and two EU states are actually represented on the Security Council.

In the context of dealing with effective multilateralism and the international rule of law, the European Security Strategy states that the fundamental framework for international relations is the UN Charter.[58] The UN Security Council,

[56] *A Secure Europe in a Better World*, above n 4, s II.

[57] *Ibid*, s III.

[58] *A Secure Europe in a Better World*, above n 4, s II. See further M Ortega (ed), *The European Union and the United Nations. Partners in Effective Multilateralism*, Chaillot Paper No 78 (Institute for Security Studies, European Union, Paris, June 2005); EB Eide (ed), *'Effective Multilateralism': Europe, Regional Security and a Revitalised UN* (London, The Foreign Policy Centre, 2004); A Novosseloff, *EU-UN Partnership in Crisis Management: Developments and Prospects* (International Peace Academy, New York, June 2004).

states that the European Security Strategy has the primary responsibility for the maintenance of international peace and security.[59] Strengthening the UN, furthermore, as we saw earlier, and equipping it to fulfil its responsibilities and to act effectively, according to the European Security Strategy, is a European priority.[60] As has been stated many times before, the fact that one cites the primary responsibility of the Security Council for international peace and security does not necessarily mean that one considers this responsibility to be exclusive, but the European Security Strategy of course leaves this open.

In another section of the European Security Strategy it is stated that the EU should support the UN as it responds to threats to international peace and security.[61] This leaves open whether the EU should also 'support' the UN when the latter chooses not to respond to threats to international peace and security. Further, the EU is committed to reinforcing its cooperation with the UN to assist countries emerging from conflicts, and to enhancing its support for the UN in short-term crisis management situations.[62]

As to the support of the UN, it could be argued, and has been in the context of unilateral military interventions, that states and organisations are justified in intervening in support of the purposes of the UN even though the organ charged with the primary responsibility for international peace and security has abstained from action (due for the most part to disagreement among the members of the Security Council) or has not acted forcefully enough.[63]

In the context of the implementation of the resolutions of the Security Council, it has been argued that unilateral intervention is justified in order to achieve such implementation or to punish non-implementation. The UN and the UN Security Council in particular would then be strengthened *malgré soi*, which would seem paradoxical, but not entirely far-fetched, assuming that the Security Council was indeed designed to constitute a credible military threat to wrong-doers, ie designed to actually take military action sometimes, and assuming also that the veto was not intended to be used for arbitrary reasons or purposes not related to the circumstances of the case at hand.

In the case where there are one or several Security Council resolutions on the matter but no authorisation of the use of force, it has been argued that the resolution or resolutions nevertheless constitute a form of authorisation for anyone who is willing and able to enforce their content if the UN Security Council is itself unable to do so. Then, so the argument goes, Member States and/or other organisations would help the UN Security Council to implement its resolution or resolutions (and presume that the Security Council wishes the

[59] *A Secure Europe in a Better World*, above n 4, s II.

[60] *Ibid*. *Cf* also the Joint Declaration on EU-UN Co-operation in Crisis Management, 24 Sep 2003.

[61] *A Secure Europe in a Better World*, above n 4, s III.

[62] *Ibid*.

[63] *Cf*, among others, S Spiliopoulou Åkermark, 'Storms, Foxes, and Nebulous Legal Arguments: Twelve Years of Force Against Iraq, 1991–2003' (2005) (54) *International and Comparative Law Quarterly* 221–235.

resolutions to be enforced in spite of the fact that the Security Council has not been able to agree on a decision on enforcement measures).

As to the enforcement of Security Council resolutions when the Security Council is not prepared to authorise such enforcement, the following statement in the European Security Strategy may be interpreted as an indication, even if weak, that the EU would be prepared to use force even unilaterally in case of non-implementation or breach of such resolutions: 'We want international organizations, regimes and treaties to be effective in confronting threats to international peace and security, and must therefore be ready to act when their rules are broken.'[64] The statement is rather non-committal, but at least it does not exclude unilateral action by force.

It could be that if the UN Security Council were to rely on the EU as a capable partner in matters of international peace and security, which the EU would seem to have the potential to be or become, then the Security Council would or could become more prone to act in different situations and in particular to decide on military enforcement measures. If the Security Council knew that it could count on the EU to help enforce its decisions, to become the military branch of the UN so to speak, then it might be easier for the Security Council to act, to make decisions, because it would know that none of the usual insecurities surrounding the setting up of peace-keeping or peace-making operations would prevail. True, the EU could not possibly, even in theory, run all UN mandated peace operations around the world, but still it has the potential to play a significant role as an effictive partner of the Security Council. Then, of course, for its part the EU would really show its commitment to the principles of the UN Charter.

Looked upon from this perspective, the relationship between the EU and the UN is complementary or mutually-reinforcing and not (potentially) competitive. The strengthening of the EU's military capability which is currently taking place would not be a potential source of tension between the EU and the UN but in fact would strengthen both organisations, if they cooperate. The EU would become stronger and if the UN can use the EU as an active partner in matters of international peace and security the UN would also become stronger because its decisions would be efficiently implemented—a global spill-over effect. The partnership, or balance of power, could become mutually beneficial. Practice and norms could be affected in other ways as well by the changing relations of force between the UN Security Council and the EU, as well as other organisations and states, but all possible variations of this interplay will not be inquired into here.[65]

Even today, judging by both the TEU and the European Security Strategy, the predominant tendency is one of cooperation and support of the UN. There are no signs, at least no explicit ones, that the EU would strive for a position as an

[64] *A Secure Europe in a Better World*, above n 4, s II.

[65] *Cf* 'Procedure and Content of the Rules on the Use of Force', work in progress by the current author.

independent semi-aggressive military actor with global ambitions. There seems to be no wish on the part of the EU to challenge the UN. Rather, there is reason to believe that the EU is sincere when it pledges allegiance to the UN Charter and accepts the position of the UN Security Council as primarily responsible for the maintenance of international peace and security. There seems to be reason to believe, furthermore, that the permanent structured cooperation outlined in the draft TCE is not intended to be used for selfish EU purposes, but is intended rather to strengthen the EU's capability to act as the loyal partner to the UN as it is here presumed to be.

In sum as to the use of military force on the part of the EU, the impression one gets from studying the official documentation of the EU is that the EU thinks that it is best, probably for all kinds of reasons, if the EU receives authorisation of the Security Council before it acts militarily, but that such authorisation if the worst comes to the worst is not regarded as a *sine qua non* of a forcible military intervention by the EU.

One has the impression that the EU is of the opinion that the last word lies not with the UN Security Council but with the EU itself. The EU does not seem to consider itself absolutely bound by the will or lack thereof of the Security Council, but only relatively as a weighty argument. It seems unlikely that the EU would make its own decision completely dependent on the decision of the UN Security Council.

With the expansion and development of the tasks that the EU wishes to undertake in the field of the Common Security and Defence Policy and with the gradual concretisation of the EU Rapid Reaction Force, ie with the growing capability and strength with which the EU security and defence policy can be carried out, much would speak in favour of the EU eventually seeking a doctrine for unilateral action in case of need, ie a doctrine according to which the EU may take forcible military action without a UN Security Council mandate, probably as a last resort in certain defined situations.[66]

Whether and how the EU will use the freedom of action it is allowed under the TEU to undertake forcible military operations without the blessing of the UN Security Council will depend on the attitude of its Member states. If the view grows among the Member States that the EU should act unilaterally when the Security Council will not, there is room for such a development under the TEU.

4. THE UN SECURITY COUNCIL VIEW

We will start by the obvious rule in the UN Charter that 'no enforcement action shall be taken under regional arrangements or by regional agencies without the

[66] *Cf* Ortega 2001, above n 31, who advocates such a development.

authorization of the Security Council'.[67] The view then of the Security Council is absolute, there is no room for manoeuvre at all for regional organisations (or for any other) to undertake military action under the UN Charter, except for self-defence.

In recent years, however, there has been a development, even though still in its infancy, in the direction of according the regional organisations a larger measure of freedom of action. Thus, the development within the EU of strengthening the EU's military capability and thus of potentially strengthening the EU as an international military actor, parallels by coincidence or not, a development within the UN of granting the regional organisations a more significant and potentially independent role in the global collective security system.

The signs of such a development will briefly be discussed and evaluated here.

The first and most evident signs which have later been softened, appeared in the report of the International Commission on Intervention and State Sovereignty (ICISS) entitled *The Responsibility to Protect*.[68] The Commission was not part of the UN, formally speaking, but was set up by the Government of Canada in 2000 in response to the challenge issued by the UN Secretary-General to the international community in 1999 (after Kosovo) to forge a new consensus on how to approach gross and systematic violations of human rights.[69] The Commission and its Report is closely connected to the UN and to the recent UN reform process, however, and the report was the first in a row of reports, concluding, in modified form, as the Final Document of the World Summit in 2005.[70]

In *The Responsibility to Protect* the ICISS proposes that when the Security Council fails to act because it is unable or unwilling, one alternative option would be for a regional or sub-regional organisation to intervene within its defining boundaries.[71]

The EU as we have seen would not be able, under the TEU, or the draft TCE, to intervene militarily within its borders, but the defence policy is entirely directed outward.[72] The ICISS notes the NATO intervention in Kosovo and finds that it was outside the NATO area, but that it was a matter of direct concern to the NATO because of the risk of spill-over into NATO territory.[73] The ICISS also notes, without specifying any examples, that other regional and sub-regional organisations have acted strictly within their geographical boundaries against Member States.[74] If the EU acts militarily within its neighbourhood then

[67] Art 53(1) UN Charter. See further Gustaf Lind, *The Revival of Chapter VIII of the UN Charter. Regional Organisations and Collective Security*, dissertation, Department of Law, Stockholm University, 2004, in particular pp 48–50 on the EU.

[68] Published by The International Development Research Centre, Ottawa, Canada, 2001.

[69] *Ibid*, Foreword.

[70] UN General Assembly, Doc. No. A/60/L.1, 20 Sep 2005.

[71] *The Responsibility to Protect*, above n 68, Foreword.

[72] *Cf* above n 45.

[73] *The Responsibility to Protect*, above n 68, p 54.

[74] *Ibid*.

it could also argue that there is an imminent risk that the conflict will spill over into the EU and that action by the EU is therefore justified although the action is undertaken abroad. If the EU takes unilateral military action further from its own territory, this line of argument would be more difficult to pursue.

Nevertheless, the ICISS raises and seems to support the idea that regional organisations may take unilateral action, where the Security Council fails to act. A further condition, in addition to the condition that the action is taken against a member or within the area of membership of the regional organisation, is that the regional organisation seeks subsequent authorisation from the Security Council.[75]

The next important step in the discussion of the role of the regional organisations in the UN collective security system was taken by the High-level Panel on Threats, Challenges and Change this time convened by the UN Secretary-General.[76] The High-level Panel, a bit surprisingly perhaps, pursues the idea of the ICISS that regional organisations may be entitled to act unilaterally in exceptional cases. The High-level Panel encourages the Security Council to make fuller and more effective use of the Chapter VIII provisions of the UN Charter (on Regional arrangements) than has hitherto been the case.[77] The High-level Panel continues:

> Recent experience has demonstrated that regional organizations can be a vital part of the multilateral system. Their efforts need not contradict United Nations efforts, nor do they absolve the United Nations of its primary responsibilities for peace and security. The key is to organize regional action within the framework of the Charter and the purposes of the United Nations, and to ensure that the United Nations and any regional organization with which it works do so in a more integrated fashion than has up to now occurred.[78]

One of the ways to ensure that regional action is kept within the framework of the Charter and the purposes of the UN, according to the High-level Panel, is to require that authorisation from the Security Council is sought in all cases of regional peace operations' recognizing that in some urgent situations that authorization may be sought after such operations have commenced'.[79] Thus, the High-level panel subscribes to the idea that regional organisations may be justified in taking military measures unilaterally, but in order to be acceptable the regional action must be sealed by a decision of the Security Council even if after the fact.

[75] *The Responsibility to Protect*, above n 68, p 54, and Synopsis p XIII. See further by this author 'Preach What You Practice. The Security Council and the Legalization *ex post facto* of the Unilateral Use of Force', 2005 (74) *Nordic Journal of International Law* 231–260.

[76] *A More Secure World: Our Shared Responsibility*, UN General Assembly Doc. No. A/59/565, 2 Dec 2004.

[77] *Ibid* at para 270, p 70.

[78] *Ibid* at para 272, p 71.

[79] *Ibid* at para 272(a), p 71.

All in all, the High-level Panel suggests openings for regional organisations which are interesting and bold and even more interesting is the fact that the content of this report is a kind of global minimum and thus that there may still be strong tendencies among several participants to go even further, both with respect to the position of regional organisations and with respect to the unilateral use of international force more generally.[80]

The prospect of a larger freedom of action for regional organizations, however, along the lines of the High-level Panel Report is not followed up in the report of the UN Secretary-General Kofi Annan which followed shortly after.[81] The section on regional organisations in the Secretary-General's report is brief and void of substantive content.[82] A closer association between the UN and regional organisations is dealt with indirectly when the Secretary-General suggests that the rules of the UN peace-keeping budget should be amended to give the UN the option, in very exceptional circumstances, to use assessed contributions to finance regional operations authorised by the Security Council, or the participation of regional organisations in multi-pillar peace operations under the overall UN umbrella.[83] Nothing is said about whether the authorisation must take place prior to the operation of the regional organisation or not, but it is unlikely that the Secretary-General would endorse the idea of Security Council authorisation after the operation has commenced as suggested in the High-level Panel Report.[84] The Secretary-General does, however, think in terms of closer relations between the UN and regional organisations.

In the Final Document of the World Summit 2005, the bold proposals of the ICISS and the High-level Panel have not left many traces.[85] In the Final Document the leaders of the world clearly state that they support a stronger relationship between the UN and regional and sub-regional organisations.[86] The action agreed upon to achieve this stronger relationship is rather feeble and expressed in such general terms that it is difficult to judge what its effects will be. The most important action mentioned, relatively speaking, is to expand consultation and cooperation between the UN and regional and sub-regional organisations through formalised agreements between the respective secretariats and, as appropriate, involvement of regional organisations in the work of the Security Council.[87] Next, the World Summit Document resolves to ensure that regional organisations which have the capacity for the prevention of armed

[80] *Cf* for instance the section on the 'responsibility to protect', *ibid* at paras' 199–203, pp 56–57.

[81] *In Larger Freedom: Towards Development, Security and Human Rights for All*, UN General Assembly Doc. No. A/59/2005, 21 Mar 2005.

[82] *Ibid* at paras 213–15, p 52.

[83] *Ibid* at para 215, p 52.

[84] *Cf* above n 79.

[85] 2005 World Summit Outcome, UN General Assembly Doc. No. A/60/L.1, 20 Sep 2005.

[86] *Ibid* at para 170, p 39.

[87] *Ibid* at para 170(a), p 39. *Cf* also Security Council Res. 1631 of 17 Oct 2005.

conflict or peace-keeping, consider the option of placing such capacity in the framework of the UN Standby Arrangements System.[88]

In another and potentially more dynamic context in the World Summit Document, regional organisations are mentioned as partners of the UN in military action.[89] In the section of the Summit Document dealing with the responsibility to protect, it is stated that the sponsors of the document, ie the heads of state and government of the world, are prepared to take collective action including under Chapter VII of the UN Charter *in cooperation with relevant regional organisations as appropriate*, should peaceful means be inadequate (and national authorities are manifestly failing to protect their populations).[90] Here, the regional organisations are built into the very process of undertaking humanitarian interventions through the UN Security Council. It is an indication of the importance of regional organisations in the military field.

Even if their resolutions are rather vague, it seems as if the idea of a stronger relationship between the UN and regional organisations has taken root in the international community. From the point of view of the EU this is an encouraging sign because it must necessarily mean that the EU among other possible regional organisations will grow in importance as a potential partner to the UN.

The idea of a stronger relationship between the UN and the regional organisations can also be interpreted as a sign of weakness and dependency on the part of the UN on the capability of the regional organisations which also serves to favour the EU among others. The resolve to strive for stronger global-regional relations arises from a position of weakness on the part of the UN and not from a position of strength. What the UN has to offer the EU is the legal and political legitimacy flowing from the support of the UN for the international military action of the EU. This may be a valuable asset. The capability of the EU combined with the presumed legitimacy of the UN may serve to strengthen both organisations.[91]

From the legal point of view, nothing in the World Summit Document suggests an intention to change the law on the use of international force either in substance or, and more important here, as concerns the procedures for decision-making. If a change in the law nevertheless comes about through practice, the development will most likely be driven by the regional organisations themselves. The growing strength of the security and defence capability of the EU, for instance, may make the EU more prone to take action and since there is a kind of vacuum as to military capability on the global level it may be that the EU will not meet that strong a resistence on the part of the UN should the EU decide to begin a more activist security and defence policy. The weakening of the global

[88] 2005 World Summit Outcome, UN General Assembly Doc. No. A/60/L.1, 20 Sep 2005 at para 170(b), p 39. (The UN Standby Arrangements System, see further www.un.org/ Depts/dpko/milad/ fgs2/unsas_files/sba.htm (last visited 22.11.05)).

[89] *Ibid* at para139, p 31.

[90] *Ibid.*

[91] *Cf* above p 295.

mechanism for dealing with international peace and security creates a scope for action on the part of the regional organisations which, if they use it, may result in a change in the law. Even if the military strength of the regional organisations is used for the mutual benefit of both the EU in our case and the UN, the dependency of the UN on the regional organisations may nevertheless come to have an effect on the law.

In sum, global law stays intact for the time being, but in the recent reform process the importance of the regional organisations in the field of international peace and security has been emphasised even in the official documentation. During the earlier stages of the reform process, when the discussions were not as official as they became at the World Summit 2005, it was obvious that there was a strong wish to go further than the documents suggest, both as to procedure and substance on the part of important segments of the international community.

5. CONCLUSION

The structural shell of the ESDP is gradually beginning to fill with policy goals and the means to fulfil the policies. The European Security Strategy adopted in 2003 is a sign of this. Developments seem to be progressing more rapidly on the ground than that mirrored in the Treaty text in force. Except for the projected institutional changes, it seems as if the co-operation in the field of security and defence in substance is developing according to any plan the EU might have had prior to the unsuccessful efforts to have the draft TCE ratified. Thus real developments seem to move forward although the Treaty text stays the same. From a legal point of view, there is nothing in the current Treaty text that would hinder a deeper and broader co-operation in the field of security and defence policy between the EU members.

On the international level the EU seems to have the ambition to be an active contributor to increased international peace and security, mostly in close cooperation with the UN, as well as other organisations and states. The Treaty on European Union, as well as the draft Treaty on a Constitution for Europe are both witness to a strong commitment to the UN on the part of the EU, and the intention of the EU seems to be to support and try to get the support of the UN Security Council to the furthest extent possible.

The text of the Treaty, however, if looked at closely, does not swear unconditional allegiance to the UN Charter including its decision-making rules on the use of international force, but is sufficiently ambiguous to leave room for unilateral EU action if this were considered inevitable due to a lack of UN Security Council authorisation. Judging from the official documentation, the EU strives to act in line with the UN Charter and in co-operation with the UN Security Council, but does not seem to rule out the possibility that it might act unilaterally.

Within the framework of the recent efforts at reform, the UN for its part seems to be developing in the direction of affording more room to regional organisations such as the EU within the global system of collective security. No exceptions are officially suggested to the monopoly on decision-making on the use of international force of the UN Security Council, but there is enough vagueness and uncertainty in the texts to give the impression that even the UN is hesitating over viability, in fact and in normative terms, of the monopoly on the use of force of the Security Council. A consolidated and capable EU in the field of security and defence may tip the normative balance in favour of the regional organisations.

Such a development would not necessarily be combined with the disappearance of the primary responsibility of the UN Security Council for international peace and security. The Security Council could maintain its primary responsibility under the collective security system, but if this responsibility is not seriously shouldered by the Security Council, then the EU might legitimately, and lawfully, intervene by military force if necessary.

Considering the current inability, largely on the part of the Security Council, to manage the conflicts of the world in a sufficiently powerful way, due among other things to the disagreement between its permanent members, it would seem likely that exceptions to the decision-making monopoly of the Security Council on the use of force will emerge in practice and ultimately in law. Faced with an inactive Security Council, a regional organisation like the EU with the capacity and will to act globally in the sphere of security and defence can hardly accept being held back by a theoretical normative construction under which it would be obliged to wait endlessly for an authorisation in cases where outside involvement is acutely needed and reasonably justifiable. Such unauthorised use of force, however, would probably be undertaken unwillingly by the EU due to the lack of any other responsible global actor taking the lead. It is not a situation that the EU should tend to actively desire.

The next step in the development, depending on the remaining relative strength of the Security Council, could be the erosion of the primary positition of the Security Council altogether. Then the regional organisations would be on a par with the UN as to their legal power to make decisions on the international use of force and would not have to wait for an authorisation. Not only the regional organisations but individual states and their possible ad hoc allies would be favoured by such a development, which is hardly desirable. The EU seems to realise that its own destiny as a significant global actor in the field of peace and security is closely tied to the one of the UN. The effective multilateralism for which the EU strives is equally dependent on both organisations and it is in the interest of the EU not to let the normative balance tip too far in its favour.

BIBLIOGRAPHY

G Aybet, *A European Security Architecture after the Cold War. Questions of Legitimacy* (Houndmills, Basingstoke, MacMillan Press, 2000)

P Bonnén, *Towards a Common European Security and Defence Policy. The Ways and Means of Making It a Reality* (Münster, Hamburg and London, Lit Verlag, 2003)

S Biscop, *The European Security Strategy. A Global Agenda for Positive Power*, (Ashgate, Aldershot and Burlington, VT, 2005)

R Dannreuther (ed), *European Union Foreign and Security Policy. Towards a Neighbourhood Strategy* (London, New York, Routledge, 2004)

P Eeckhout, *External Relations of the European Union's Legal and Constitutional Foundation* (Oxford, New York, Oxford University Press, 2004)

E B Eide (ed), *'Effective Multilateralism': Europe, Regional Security and a Revitalised UN* (London, The Foreign Policy Centre, 2004)

N Gnesotto (ed), *EU Security and Defence Policy. The First Five Years (1999–2004)* (Institute for Security Studies, European Union, Paris, 2004)

D W Greig, 'Self-Defence and the Security Council: What Does Article 51 Require? 1991 (40) *International and Comparative Law Quarterly* 366–402

J-Y Haine, 'The Union Inaugural Address' in J Pilegaard (ed,), *The Politics of European Security, Danish Institute for International Studies* (Copenhagen, 2004) 39–53

F Heisbourg, 'The "European Security Strategy" is not a Security Strategy' in S Everts *et al*, *A European Way of War* (London, Centre for European Reform, 2004) 27–39

M Holland (ed), *Common Foreign and Security Policy* 2nd edn, (London and New York, Continuum, 2004)

J Howorth & J T S Keeler, *Defending Europe. The EU, NATO and the Quest for European Autonomy* (New York and Houndmills, Basingstoke, Palgrave MacMillan, 2003)

I Ioannides, *The European Rapid Reaction Force: Implications for Democratic Accountability* Paper 24 (Bonn International Center for Conversion, Bonn, 2002)

M Kerttunen, T Koivula & T Jeppsson *EU Battlegroups. Theory and Development in the Light of Finnish-Swedish Co-operation* Series 2, Research Reports No 30 (National Defence College, Department of Strategic and Defence Studies, Helsinki, 2005)

A Missiroli (ed), *Disasters, Diseases, Disruptions: a new D-drive for the EU*, Chaillot Paper No 83 (Institute for Security Studies, European Union, Paris, September 2005)

A Novosseloff *EU-UN Partnership in Crisis Management: Developments and Prospects* (International Peace Academy, New York, June 2004)

M Ortega (ed), *The European Union and the United Nations. Partners in Effective Multilateralism* Chaillot Paper No 78 (Institute for Security Studies, European Union, Paris, June 2005)

M Ortega, *Military Intervention and the European Union* Chaillot Paper No 45 (Institute for Security Studies, Western European Union, Paris, March 2001)

The Responsibility to Protect Report of the International Commission on Intervention and State Sovereignty (ICISS) (Published by The International Development Research Centre, Ottawa, Canada, 2001)

TC Salmon and AJK Shepherd (eds), *Toward a European Army. A Military Power in the Making?* (Lynne Rienner Publishers, Boulder and London, 2003)

HG Schermers & N Blokker, *International Institutional Law. Unity Within Diversity* 4th rev edn, (The Hague, London, Boston, Martinus Nijhoff Publishers, 2003)

W Wagner, *The Democratic Legitimacy of European Security and Defence Policy* Occasional Paper No 57 (Institute for Security Studies, European Union, Paris, April 2005)

K von Wogau (ed), *The Path to European Defence* (Antwerpen and Apeldoorn, Maklu Publishers, 2004)

S Spiliopoulou Åkermark 'Storms, Foxes, and Nebulous Legal Arguments: Twelve Years of Force Against Iraq, 1991–2003' 2005 (54) *International and Comparative Law Quarterly* 221–235

EU DOCUMENTS

A Secure Europe in a Better World, European Security Strategy, Brussels, 12 December 2003

Declaration by the European Council on the Contribution of the CFSP, Including the ESDP, to the Fight Against Terrorism, adopted at the Seville European Council 21 and 22 June 2002 and included in the Presidency Conclusions as Annex V

Joint Declaration on EU-UN Co-operation in Crisis Management, 24 September 2003

UN DOCUMENTS

A More Secure World: Our Shared Responsibility, Report of the High-level Panel on Threats, Challenges and Change, UN General Assembly Doc. No. A/59/565, 2 Dec 2004

In Larger Freedom: Towards Development, Security and Human Rights for All, Report of the Secretary-General, UN General Assembly Doc. No. A/59/2005, 21 Mar 2005

2005 World Summit Outcome, UN General Assembly Doc. No. A/60/L.1, 20 Sep 2005

Security Council Res. 1631 of 17 Oct 2005

Index